STALINGRAD
LIVES

STALINGRAD LIVES

Stories of

Combat and Survival

IAN GARNER

MCGILL-QUEEN'S UNIVERSITY PRESS
Montreal & Kingston · London · Chicago

© McGill-Queen's University Press 2022

ISBN 978-0-2280-1418-8 (cloth)
ISBN 978-0-2280-1516-1 (ePDF)
ISBN 978-0-2280-1517-8 (ePUB)

Legal deposit fourth quarter 2022
Bibliothèque nationale du Québec

This book has been published with the help of a grant from the
Federation for the Humanities and Social Sciences, through the
Awards to Scholarly Publications Program, using funds provided by
the Social Sciences and Humanities Research Council of Canada.

Printed in Canada on acid-free paper that is 100% ancient forest
free (100% post-consumer recycled), processed chlorine free

We acknowledge the support of the Canada Council for the Arts.
Nous remercions le Conseil des arts du Canada de son soutien.

Library and Archives Canada Cataloguing in Publication

Title: Stalingrad lives : stories of combat and survival / Ian Garner.
Names: Garner, Ian, author.
Description: Includes bibliographical references and index.
Identifiers: Canadiana (print) 20220272433 | Canadiana (ebook)
    20220272573 | ISBN 9780228014188 (cloth) | ISBN 9780228015161
    (ePDF) | ISBN 9780228015178 (ePUB)
Subjects: LCSH: Stalingrad, Battle of, Volgograd, Russia, 1942-1943—
    Personal narratives, Soviet. | LCSH: Stalingrad, Battle of,
    Volgograd, Russia, 1942-1943—Propaganda. | LCSH: Stalingrad,
    Battle of, Volgograd, Russia, 1942-1943, in literature.
Classification: LCC D764.3.S7 G37 2022 | DDC 940.54/21747—dc23

In memory of Leonid Kabluchko

CONTENTS

FIGURES

PREFACE

As I write in March 2022, Russia is a month into its invasion of Ukraine. The language of the Second World War is ever-present in the flood of coverage deluging our screens. Vladimir Putin's speeches constantly allude to the Soviet Union's sacrifices and victories in the war. He is drawing on a deep well of symbolic and rhetorical material to justify a war of aggression, incite fear of purported fascism, and rally his people for the sacrifices they will have to make in the coming months and years. For Ukraine's leaders too, the Second World War is a rhetorical centre of gravity. President Volodymyr Zelensky has alluded to Ukraine's role in defeating fascism and compared his citizens' plight to the suffering of those trapped by the Nazis in Leningrad.

And at the very heart of this rhetorical battle is a contest for the memory of Stalingrad. The siege of Kyiv is endlessly compared to that of Stalingrad in the media. On 10 March 2022, Kyiv mayor Vitaly Klitschko promised that the city "has been turned into a fortress ... Every street and every house is being fortified ... The city stands, and it will continue to stand."[1] Any Russian-speaker would immediately identify this as the language of Stalingrad: a language born at the front in 1942 and honed over eight decades of reuse; a language of national sacrifice, unity, and rebirth. Perhaps no myth is more powerful for Russian-speakers today than that of Stalingrad. In *Stalingrad Lives*, I reveal why.

As the Soviet Union faced an overwhelming German military force in the fall of 1942, the cream of Soviet writing was sent to the Stalingrad Front. The pack was led by Vasily Grossman, a thirty-six-year-old former chemical engineer who had volunteered for the front as soon as war broke out in 1941, and Konstantin Simonov, a dashing figure already renowned for his work at Khalkin Gol in 1939. They were joined by a group of enthusiastic writers and ordinary soldiers – the young Stalingrader Vasily Koroteev, the affable screenwriter

Evgeny Kriger, the rank-and-file soldier Anatoly Nedzelsky, and many more –
who had the chance to make their names by writing alongside these literary
celebrities. Perhaps no other event in the history of war has seen such a con-
centration of literary talent living and working together in one place at one
time. Working shoulder-to-shoulder with the army in a battle of unprecedented scale and danger, these soldier-writers filled the pages of the Soviet
newspapers with literary fiction throughout the long months of fighting on
the river Volga. *Stalingrad Lives* gathers a sample of these writers' short stories,
translated into English for the first time, and delves into the historical and literary circumstances of their creation.

Should you choose to dive straight into the translated stories, you will de-
velop an idea of what it felt like to follow the unfolding Stalingrad story in
1942–43, a better understanding of the atmosphere during one of history's
deadliest battles, and an insight into the narrative of Stalingrad as a miraculous
resurrection that dominated the Soviet postwar imagination. You will encounter images of Stalingrad that have been endlessly reproduced in Russian
novels, films, diaries, memoirs, and even works of dissident literature like Vasily
Grossman's masterpiece *Life and Fate*. Familiar stories of houses defended to
the death, of Christ-like soldiers sacrificing themselves, of troops rowing into
the city across a flaming Volga, and of dawn breaking as victory finally comes
all have their origins here. Every invocation of Stalingrad in text or on screen
owes these stories a semantic and narrative debt.

By presenting a selection of these works in translation, I aim to conjure up
the lively literary atmosphere of the wartime newspapers, to mark out the
literary landmarks of the battle in their first invocations, and to revive a col-
laboratively produced narrative of Stalingrad that has never before been
reproduced in English. I include forgotten work by Vasily Grossman that has
not been published in either Russian or English since 1942, untranslated material by literary luminaries like Konstantin Simonov, Boris Polevoy, and Ilya
Ehrenburg, stories by those who found fame in the wartime newspapers, and,
in a coda, material by Viktor Nekrasov, the Stalingrad veteran and writer who
would eventually be exiled for his refusal to toe the line on memory of the war.
Aside from a handful of translated Grossman stories, very little Soviet frontline writing has appeared in English translation at all. No translations of the
original texts from the wartime Soviet papers – which are wildly different
from subsequent republications even in Russian – have ever graced English-

language collections.² Few readers are aware even of the difference between the newspaper stories and heavily edited versions that appeared in postwar Russian-language anthologies; fewer still have had the chance to read these materials in English.

While I consistently refer to my collection as representing "*the* Stalingrad story," the narrative I present was always subject to the government's whims. You might be surprised at the emotional and literary depth of Soviet writing produced in nightmarish conditions and at the extent of freedom accorded to writers to think and do as they pleased at the front. However, the Soviet government was always ready to assert control the minute victory looked certain. Limits always existed: references to the Soviets' bombing of their own population, to strategic errors, to the extent of the punitive regime, or to the real plight of the starving and homeless population eking out an existence within Stalingrad were always difficult to print. Moreover, mine is a story dominated by white, male Russians: female Soviets and people of colour are all but absent, in spite of official claims that victory in the Second World War was a truly national effort. Thus while this collection presents *a* narrative of Stalingrad – the narrative that was most widely disseminated and that has been widely embraced by Russians and Russian governments since the battle – it is neither exhaustive nor inclusive of all Soviets' experiences.

Stalingrad Lives includes detailed commentary alongside new translations. In an introductory chapter, I explore how the Soviet authorities came to send some of the nation's leading prose writers to the frontline to pen fiction as a "weapon." I trace the literary and rhetorical roots of their works in Russian and Soviet culture, showing how authors used existing materials to underpin frank accounts of what they witnessed in Stalingrad. Concurrently, I read letters, diaries, and memoirs to show how Soviet readers embraced these works. Borrowing phrases, motifs, and entire stories from published accounts, readers framed their own wartime experiences within and around the Stalingrad narrative, echoing how the Stalingrad writers themselves drew on historical and contemporary sources to make sense of horrors that seemed to defy human description. The government controlled the story; then ordinary Soviets embraced and contributed to it.

I urge you to read the translated stories for their literary content, for their humanity, and for their moments of temporal and poetic harmony. Read them knowing that individuals, the state, and the nation faced total obliteration at

Stalingrad – and then delighted in what seemed like a miraculous turnaround that led to victory. Read the stories, then, the way that Konstantin Simonov implored the budding authors who wrote to him for advice in the years after Stalingrad: "Don't read [the Stalingrad stories] at face value. They are made up of text and subtext, but above all of emotions hidden amongst the words."[3]

Some of the claims made about Stalingrad as a resurrection might seem outlandish, but the works are sprinkled with narratives and motifs that had a profound emotional resonance for many Soviet readers. However, as I show in the coda to this volume, the unity around Stalingrad forged between the state, its authors, and its people was fragile. It was as likely to collapse as it was to grow in the postwar years, when it became clearer that ordinary Soviets' sacrifices on the Volga in 1942–43 had been instrumentalized in the name of state power, not national resurrection. Nonetheless, Stalingrad, encoded in a group of images and motifs created at the front, has always been a site of self-creation for both people and rulers. No matter how interpretations have shifted, the stories gathered here deserve to be read as part of the Russian canon of great war literature, not as the mere propaganda of a totalitarian state.

NOTE ON TRANSLITERATION

In endnotes and citations, I have stuck to the Library of Congress transliteration system. For readability's sake, I have in the main text simplified the system by, for instance, removing apostrophes for the Russian soft sign and shortening words ending in "-ii" to "-y".

STALINGRAD
LIVES

INTRODUCTION
Stalingrad Lives

February 2018. The temperature hovers at freezing as a light fog envelops Volgograd's concrete skyline. President Vladimir Putin has arrived to mark the seventy-fifth anniversary of the end of the Second World War's bloodiest battle. Flanked by soldiers and veterans, Putin pauses to lay a wreath at the vast memorial complex on the Mamaev Kurgan, the hill where much of the heaviest fighting took place.[1] Later that evening, a crowd of veterans, functionaries, and locals listens reverentially as the president speaks. A sombre Putin describes the battle that unfolded on this spot: "Stalingrad was turned into an invincible, impregnable fortress to halt the progress of Nazism. Our Soviet soldiers and our wounded land were as one. Our soldiers turned every street, trench, house, and firing point into a fortress. The locals fought the enemy just as bravely."[2] Putin's speech could have been taken almost verbatim from one of the thousands of Russian memoirs, stories, and novels about Stalingrad written between 1943 and 2018.

Three quarters of a century earlier, a small group of famous Russian writers were huddled in a cold and cramped barrack on the desolate steppe just outside Stalingrad. Accompanied by constant explosions and machine gun fire, these men were writing – almost to the letter – the words that Putin would recite in 2018: "Every house [in Stalingrad] has become an impregnable fortress ... Stalingrad's defenders are fighting for every house, every barn, and every garden. Every house has become a firing position. Stalingrad's defenders are performing miracles of bravery, dedication, and loyalty to and for the motherland." As the future of the Soviet Union hung in the balance, the writers implored their readers to defend Stalingrad to the last: "Fight for every street, every house, every floor, and every room! Fight to the last bullet and the last drop of blood! Fight with every last ounce of hatred for the enemy!"[3]

Figure I.1   Troops carrying anti-tank weapons into Stalingrad, fall 1942.

A who's who of Soviet writing talent had been assembled to file stories for the nation's newspapers. Vasily Grossman (1905–1964), Konstantin Simonov (1915–1979), Ilya Ehrenburg (1891–1967), Boris Polevoy (1908–1981), and a group of lesser-known peers sent story after story back to Moscow throughout the war. Published in the Soviet central papers, *Pravda*, *Krasnaya Zvezda*, and *Izvestiya* (*Truth*, *Red Star*, and *The News*), their work had 150 million Soviet citizens holding their breath as they followed events at Stalingrad. The Stalingrad narrative they produced both documents life at the front in detail and tells the story of a city almost destroyed in an infernal onslaught but miraculously brought back from the dead through Soviet self-sacrifice. A resurrection story packed with Soviet, classical, and Orthodox religious symbolism, Stalingrad promised to bring order and life in the aftermath of a nightmare of destruction.

1942: THE DEATH OF STALINGRAD

In the year after the war began on the Eastern Front in June 1941, the German army had seized swathes of Soviet territory, murdered hundreds of thousands of civilians, and come dangerously close to taking Moscow. In the summer of 1942, Hitler launched a new offensive. An army comprising 70 percent of the German military forces would drive hard and fast from Ukraine toward the Soviet oilfields in the Caucasus. Cut off from its oil supply, the Red Army would crumble and the war in the east would be over.

By mid-August, only one bastion remained between the Wehrmacht and the Caucasus: Stalingrad, a city of 850,000 on the west bank of the Volga. The city's strategic significance was equalled by the symbolic significance of holding the city named after Joseph Stalin: the place where, according to Soviet legend, a young Stalin had led his Bolshevik troops to a miraculous victory in the Civil War twenty-five years earlier. How humiliating it would be for Stalin to lose a city so associated with his own glorious myth. How disastrous for the Russians to be routed from the great city on the Volga. How calamitous for the Red Army to capitulate.

The Germans began their assault on Stalingrad in late August 1942. In spite of the Red Army's disorganization and the overwhelming size of the German forces, the Soviet defenders held firm. By early fall, the Wehrmacht and the Red Army were locked in a quagmire in Stalingrad and on the flat steppe for hundreds of kilometres around. Thousands of troops were dying every day as the hand-to-hand fighting, tank battles, bombing raids, and artillery attacks went on without end. In the city, the few thousand civilians who had not fled or been killed were slowly starving. Exhaustion set in. The Soviets looked as if they would crumble. A sudden hope in the dark: a Soviet counterattack on 19 November. The German 6th Army was encircled and, just two and a half months later, offered unconditional surrender. The Axis powers would never again make real inroads into Soviet territory. The march to Berlin had begun. Victory had been seized from the jaws of defeat.

But winning at Stalingrad came at vast human cost. Nearly one million So-viet soldiers and civilians had been killed. Barely ten thousand residents were left to eke out an existence in bombed-out cellars and caves dug into the Volga's bank.[4] Haunting images of the battle's aftermath show urban landscapes flooded with concrete, rubble, and metal detritus, and mile after mile of scorched emptiness where wooden dwellings and modern housing had once stood. Stalingrad had for months on end been, as the frontline writers had told their readers, a hell on earth.

In the West's imagination, "Stalingrad" has become a byword for a vicious, inhuman battle, for death and destruction, for brutal fighting on industrial wastelands, for freezing cold and starvation, for Soviet commissars gunning down their own retreating men, and for the venal stupidity of totalitarian regimes that sent hundreds of thousands of soldiers to their deaths in battle. Stalingrad in Western eyes was, in short, the Somme of the Second World War: the apogee of apocalyptic modern warfare.[5]

The Russian story of Stalingrad is, on the contrary, full of utopian hope. Even as they struggled to recover from the human costs of victory, Soviets em-braced victory at Stalingrad as a turning point in national history, a moment of martyrdom and resurrection that had brought the country and its people back from the dead. "Stalingrad lives," ran the popular slogan, and conse-quently, so too did the Soviet Union. Mention the battle to a Russian today and you are likely to be regaled with tales of glorious sacrifice, resurrection, new life, and utopia – likely using the language and forms codified at the front in 1942. In spite of its association with Stalin's regime, the unthinkable death toll, and the unappealing monumentalism of late Soviet films, books, and war memorials, the Russians' Stalingrad story is not about the death of a million Soviets but about the birth of hope.

In the years after the battle, it was almost impossible to find a book that did not at least mention the battle as a turning point in the hero's and the nation's life.[6] Hundreds of books printed in vast quantities, dozens of films screened across the Soviet Union, and a seemingly endless supply of plays, poems, paint-ings, and songs were dedicated to the battle. An identikit of phrases, tropes, and motifs crops up in everything from Soviet novels – blockbusters like Yury Bondarev's 1968 smash-hit *Hot Snow*, which sold two and a half million copies in twenty-six printings in the Soviet period[7] – to record-shattering Putin-era war movies such as Fyodor Bondarchuk's 2013 *Stalingrad*. Even in the raucous chaos of the Russian 1990s and postmodern 2000s, nothing caused a stir like Stalingrad.[8] Western readers may be unfamiliar with much Stalingrad fiction beyond Vasily Grossman's two great novels, *Stalingrad* and *Life and Fate*, but Russians have for decades constantly returned to the textual sites of Stalingrad as a means to frame their inner lives in hopeful terms.

Putin's pilgrimages to Volgograd tap into a rich vein of emotion that courses with hope, religiosity, and the sense of a unifying national epic. By invoking the text of Stalingrad in his 2018 speech, Putin was encouraging listeners to reflect on the nature and interrelation of personal and national pasts, so as to prompt them to conclude that the new can emerge from even the most hopeless situations – even from death itself. That any literature at all was produced in the appalling conditions at Stalingrad is impressive. That writers gave birth to this wholesale myth of Stalingrad on the ground and under fire is astonishing. Yet in spite of the pedigree of its authors, its importance to Russian culture, and the harsh conditions in which it was produced, this body of wartime work has never before been interpreted as serious literature. To understand it, however, requires us to return to the beginning of the war on the Eastern Front.

1941: MOBILIZING THE PROPAGANDA MACHINE

On the first day of the war in the east in June 1941 – just as the Red Army's flimsy defences were collapsing in the face of the German Blitzkrieg – a flurry of telephone calls, telegrams, and couriered messages summoned the Soviet Union's leading literary figures to Moscow's newspaper offices. The frenzy of activity could not conceal slapdash preparation.[9] While the state had for several years been releasing anti-fascist propaganda to prepare the people for war, and despite a last-minute program to train college and university graduates as war correspondents, Soviet propagandists were just as unready as the country's military to face the German Blitzkrieg.[10] Nobody had thought – or been permitted – to prepare newspaper articles, radio broadcasts, or other propaganda for this portentous occasion. The logistics of running a frontline propaganda network had barely been considered.[11] On the radio, the only interruption to a day-long program of light music was a brief announcement at noon that hostilities had broken out: "Today at 4 a.m. ... without a declaration of war, Germany attacked our country ... Ours is a righteous cause. The enemy shall be defeated. Victory will be ours."[12] At this crucial moment, a massive propaganda apparatus that required "organizational strength [and] dogged attention to problems" to function well lacked men, materials, and focus.[13] A great mobilization of cultural power, however, was just beginning.

The results were astonishing. By 1942, almost 14 million copies of newspapers were being distributed every day across Soviet territory. The military alone was publishing 465 frontline papers, and thousands of editors, photographers, journalists, and support staff were at work across a vast front.[14] In spite of production shortages and delivery problems when military action disrupted supply channels, few things in the wartime Soviet Union would become as reliable or well-anticipated in the trenches or behind the lines as the arrival of *Pravda*, *Krasnaya Zvezda*, and *Izvestiya*. No wartime texts were more widely read than the daily newspapers, each of which comprised a scant couple of large sheets of gossamer-thin paper. Readers of all castes were gripped by the epic tales of military heroism within. Attaining this breadth of production, readership, and literary interest was no mean feat.

On the third day of the war, the government formed Sovinformbyuro (the Soviet Information Office), a new national news agency. The office was to lead information and propaganda efforts during what the Kremlin recognized would be a chaotic period.[15] Sovinformbyuro's mandate was both straightforward and hugely complex: its remit spanned "updates on international events, the country's internal life, and military proceedings."[16] Sovinformbyuro's purview was all information flowing around, between, and through the Kremlin, the military, the newspapers, and the Soviet radio network. It had the authority to make logistical, personnel, and artistic decisions and to guide and constrain the work of newspaper writers before, during, and after Stalingrad. Aleksandr Shcherbakov (1901–1945), a seasoned bureaucrat and Civil War veteran, was appointed head of Sovinformbyuro. He was to be Stalin's eyes and ears in the propaganda war.

Within days, Shcherbakov had named David Ortenberg (1904–1998) editor of the army newspaper *Krasnaya Zvezda*, which was second in distribution only to *Pravda*, the leading Soviet paper. For Ortenberg, a Civil War veteran and son of a railway clerk, who had barely finished elementary school but nevertheless risen through the journalistic ranks, this was a major promotion.[17] For the first two and a half years of the war, Ortenberg was to play the middleman between two groups: a Kremlin propaganda directorate whose instructions swung from opaque to transparent and from obstructive to permissive at the drop of a hat; and a sometimes temperamental group of writers scattered across a gargantuan front. The *Krasnaya Zvezda* editor spent much of his time placating the one while urging on the other, treading the line between official enforcer and artist's muse.

Shcherbakov quickly convened a series of internal groups whose work focused on different aspects of the war, culture, and daily life. Informally, Ortenberg was most attached to a group whose purview was literature and art.[18] Where his fellow editors, Petr Pospelov (*Pravda*) and Lev Rovinsky (*Izvestiya*), constantly wrote to their superiors asking for permission merely to publish or acquire material, Ortenberg's questions were almost always about literature: Who could he hire? Was a writer permitted to work up a piece on a given theme? Could he give his writers leave to work up longer pieces? The answers he received were often frustratingly restrictive, but Shcherbakov was a talented *apparatchik* who supported Ortenberg's approach – at least for as long as doing so was politically convenient. The relationship Shcherbakov and Ortenberg developed was for several years one of genuine curiosity that bears little resemblance to the popular image of Soviet propaganda cronies scurrying to do the Kremlin's work while fearing for their own lives.

The new editor of *Krasnaya Zvezda* was no stranger to this line of work. He had risked his own neck to protect his charges during the purges of the 1930s, arguing that the state needed quality writing more than it needed to execute or exile supposed wrongdoers. Only senior minister Lev Mekhlis's patronage had kept Ortenberg from harm at the time.[19] In 1941, Ortenberg repeated the argument. The Soviet Union needed the best writers, regardless of their past misdeeds, and they had to be able to go about their business unimpeded. Now all were agreed: the government was desperate for all the writers it could get its hands on. Ortenberg would strive to ensure that his staff were safe from the enemy and their own government alike – even if the editor was also the messenger passing on bad news and Shcherbakov's criticisms to his charges.[20] In collaboration with Sovinformbyuro, David Ortenberg and his fellow editors set to work from their shared offices in a pre-revolutionary mansion on Malaya Dmitrovka, an elegant boulevard just north of the Kremlin in Moscow. Firing off dozens of telegrams and racing around the streets of the capital on foot and in whatever cars had not been requisitioned for the front, the editorial team worked to recruit the nation's best writers for the war effort. In a

Figure I.2 David Ortenberg (L) and the photographer Viktor Temin near
Stalingrad, 1942.

Moscow of "crowds, darkness, and chaos," theirs was a tough task.[21] Working night and day through the "stupefying heat" of midsummer, Ortenberg hastily scribbled missives to well-known and junior writers all over the Soviet Union, taking advantage of the military's reliable communication channels to ensure quick responses. The request was simple: join the media campaign to save the nation from the fascist threat and, come what may, "send no less than two stories a week."[22]

The response was overwhelmingly positive. Writers were as enthusiastic as anyone to get to grips with the enemy. Vasily Grossman, then a relative unknown, was one of many who raced to enlist.[23] Ortenberg's efforts to recruit the best writers, including those who had fallen out of official favour, were bold. Men who had found it impossible to make it into print in the terror-filled 1930s were now welcomed back into the literary fold. Taking the great risk of appealing to the capricious and bloody-minded leader about such matters, Ortenberg lobbied Stalin on behalf of his favourite writers.[24] Stalin frequently telephoned personally to give Ortenberg permission to proceed.[25]

Though many recruits were military novices, some were experienced war correspondents. Konstantin Simonov, the author of poems, plays, and stories that were as widely publicized by the government as they were beloved by the public, had been at Khalkin Gol, the Soviet–Japanese conflict of the summer of 1939. He would soon become the Soviet Union's most important frontline writer, "beloved and respected by the readers of *Krasnaya Zvezda* and *Pravda*, the listeners of the All-Union Radio, and by admirers of poetry. Even the collective of frontline correspondents welcomed him with a great sense of warmth."[26] Simonov was usually the man entrusted by David Ortenberg with the most important reporting tasks. He alone was able to publish regularly in both *Pravda* and *Krasnaya Zvezda*, to request leave when he needed to work up longer pieces, and to print plays, stories, journalism, and even a whole novel – the first Stalingrad novel, *Days and Nights* – during the war.[27]

Ilya Ehrenburg, another famous veteran journalist who had covered the Russian and Spanish Civil Wars, shared his peers' enthusiasm for supporting the war. He later recalled that there was no question of dissidence while the Soviet Union was under attack: "War not only clothes everything in protective colouring but allows no room for spiritual diversity: age, individual traits of character – everything that goes to make up a distinctive personal life – gives way before its demands. During the war years I thought and felt like all my compatriots."[28] Whatever fear and turmoil might have plagued society and the army in the 1930s gave way to a wave of patriotic support for the war effort and for Stalin's leadership.[29]

The work of the newspapers was, however, never far from the Soviet leader's thoughts – and it was always subject to his control. A keen writer who had produced poetry as a youth in Georgia and penned large chunks of official textbooks in the 1930s, Stalin often personally oversaw the newspapers' output. He even frequently found time to mark up the day's editorials. "There's a war going on!," Ortenberg once exclaimed to Aleksandr Shcherbakov after Stalin had yet again made an insertion into the day's draft.[30] The leader, as stubborn and callous as he may have been, was pragmatic: he knew good writing when he saw it, and he was set on having writing of the highest calibre in the wartime papers. Ortenberg's hiring decisions caused minor scandals among some Party elites in Moscow, but the editor persisted and found a sympathetic ear in Aleksandr Shcherbakov.[31] Indeed, while censorship continued throughout the war, *Krasnaya Zvezda* succeeded in avoiding much of the censor's red pen. Few articles were rejected for publication, even if tight editing was necessary due to space constraints. On questions of content, though, the need for quality writing reduced any likelihood of the terrifying oppression of the 1930s being repeated on the literary front.

WRITING: THE SOVIETS' SPIRITUAL WEAPON

Ortenberg, Shcherbakov, and their colleagues brought an abundance of literary talent into the newspapers' fold. Within weeks of the war's outbreak, thirty *Krasnaya Zvezda* correspondents had been given military ranks, trained in the rudiments of fighting, and sent to the front as "special correspondents" with access to military communications and logistics apparatuses. For the next four years, they were to live shoulder-to-shoulder with the rank and file and send back literary fiction from the front. Where soldiers fought with bullets and bombs, the Soviet writers' weapons were pens and typewriters, their ammunition ink. "We have in our hands," Ilya Ehrenburg explained at the time, "a weapon made not for anthologies, but for war."[32] In the minds of Soviet readers, the war was being fought and would be won by writers as much as soldiers. Their "books served as spiritual weapons," and their works became an integral "part of the war."[33] Indeed, in the Soviet imagination – in correspondence, histories, and vernacular language – the writers of the Second World War are usually referred to as *frontoviki*: "frontliners."[34] Those who did not brave the front were scorned as writers of "total balderdash" who could never truly understand the war.[35]

The government considered war writing an essentially *military* task that would help readers find ways to make meaning out of a conflict in which upwards of 25 million Soviet citizens would be killed. Since the early 1900s, the Bolsheviks had placed a high value on literary propaganda.[36] In two and a half decades in power, the state had done much to improve literacy levels and build a functional newspaper industry. Literary works and newspaper texts propagandized the government's achievements, excused its errors, and encouraged readers to reimagine themselves as distinctly *Soviet* citizens. The new Soviet world had been built as much on paper as in the physical world; thus, fighting through writing was every bit as soldierly as wielding a rifle, driving a tank, or firing a mortar.

Wartime newspapers were structurally almost identical. News, propaganda, entertainment, and art were all crammed into four pages. On the front page, morale-building slogans were plastered above the masthead, the latest editorial written by David Ortenberg or his fellow editors (and always personally approved by the Kremlin) commented on the war's progress, and a handful of communiqués provided by Sovinformbyuro gave news updates. Unfurling the paper, the reader was regaled with photographs, poems, and stories and tales of the front, printed in tiny font and densely packed side by side. This was the literary heart of the paper, where creative imaginations blossomed. Each day's paper culminated in a review of foreign press coverage and laconic cartoons that lampooned the Wehrmacht and its leaders as snivelling cowards, shortsighted incompetents, and petit bourgeois fools.

Centring literary content in this collage of cultural material was a means for Soviet writers and readers to cling to some sort of order in a monstrous war.[37] Every military conflict invites disorder and chaos that overwhelm both time and the individual – what Freud referred to as a "whirlwind" – so that war resists comprehension by ordinary means.[38] In this war of unprecedented scale, speed, and ferocity, the epistemological challenge was all the greater. As thousands of civilians and troops perished across Soviet territory every day for months on end, news reports alone could not convey the scale of the

catastrophe, motivate the public to greater efforts, or help counter the funda-
mentally disorienting nature of the war.

Even the most compassionate Soviet reader could not have extended their
empathy to thousands of individuals at a time. Psychologists refer to the ten-
dency for empathy to decrease as numbers in a tragedy increase as "psychic
numbing":[39] had readers learned of thousands of deaths at a time on great lists
– that is, had they been exposed to the vast scale of the Eastern Front in composite form – they would have grown increasingly indifferent. But to extend
one's empathy to a small group of heroes in a narrative full of comfortingly
familiar tropes from Russian and Soviet literary history? Or to understand
one's own experience by reading a literary tale laden with human emotion? At
a time when Soviet soldiers were dying *en masse*, towns and villages lay in ruins,
and the nation teetered on the brink of collapse, a human-focused literature
was most suited to making sense of events.

Indeed, the Stalingrad stories we will read have more in common with Soviet
and Russian literature of the prewar period than with conventional journalism.
Sovinformbyuro's communiqués gave only snippets of information about what
was going on at the front (and, inevitably, they excluded much of the bad
news). Drawing that news into the realms of the familiar was the writer's task:
"In the newspapers," explained one critic, "first we read the communiqué, then
articles, sketches, and tales and stories. People are thus drawn into the reality
of war."[40] Narrative colour – themes from the classical and European past and
prerevolutionary Russian patriotic culture, and motifs from folk narratives –
mingled with interviews with frontline soldiers, observations on day-to-day
military action, and hopes for a life reborn after the war.

A patchwork of allusions and borrowed tropes was cobbled together according to the Socialist Realist method. Socialist Realism had been the Soviet
Union's official and only artistic genre since the mid-1930s. The genre is known
for its hyperbolic positive heroes – construction workers, soldiers, and farm
labourers who cheerily carry out unlikely missions and sacrifices in the name
of production, labour, and the Communist Party – and for its neglect of the
day at hand's suffering and tragedy. As unlikely as it may sound, while often
scorned as artistically and emotionally moribund, Socialist Realism found its
moment during the war.[41]

In its basic form, the genre was intended to show "a combination of the
most matter-of-fact, everyday reality, and the most heroic prospects."[42] In prac-

tice, that meant revealing progress in the most hopeless of situations and positivity in spite of all the odds – even if that meant a distinctly *un*realistic "varnishing" of daily life. Socialist Realism's temporal focus was never the present. Its concern was the epic: a time of heroes completing great nation-building or nation-saving deeds; or, in the literary critic Mikhail Bakhtin's terms, a site of "wholeness" and "organic fullness," an unironic place of "beginning" that stands in contrast to and must logically remain bounded off from the chaotic becoming of the present.[43]

Superficially, then, the product of Socialist Realism was a two-dimensional work that crudely layered the feel of the epic onto eyewitness material. However, scratching the surface of the method reveals a more complex literary-historical dynamic. The "realism" of Socialist Realism had, as Svetlana Boym notes, "virtually nothing to do with the everyday existence of Soviet citizens; it does not even attempt to mimic or imitate it. The point is to enact the mythical and utopian world and thus bring it into existence."[44] Soviet literary writing may have begun by documenting reality, but it strove to literally *create* – "enact" – reality. Theoretically, the artist's power to organize and create reality was limitless.[45] Soviet literature before the war may have appeared absurdly optimistic about the achievements of the present, but the great prewar Socialist Realist works – the production novels of Nikolay Ostrovsky and Fyodor Gladkov, and the military tales of Mikhail Sholokhov and Dmitry Furmanov – were meant to usher elements of utopia into the reader's present, providing a means for the reader to vicariously experience utopia in the here and now.

Socialist Realism, far from being purely documentary or mendacious, collapsed elements of the literary and epic past, the recorded present, and imagined futures into a single space. Here the heroically extraordinary epic nature of the reader's reality was both revealed *and actually made*: stasis, chaos, and suffering could be replaced by motion, order, and hope. Socialist Realism was a literary mode designed to guide the reader, both internally and externally, toward harmony and peace (even though its topics and language were frequently martial).[46] The genre was almost tailor-made to repudiate the destruction of war; its epic temporality could provide the setting for even a monstrously destructive war to become a time of new beginnings.[47] Writing was a weapon that sought to create victory and thus peace from the remnants of destruction.

But producing work that could create an epic victory was no easy task. The chasm between the disappointing present and the wondrous epic in Socialist

Realist works had often left readers adrift.[48] This temporal divide was meant to be bridged by referring to a series of turning points – Revolution, Civil War, and now the Great Patriotic War – when epic time coincided with the present, thus drawing mundane existence into the realms of the heroic. These turning points deliberately resembled the sacrificial turning point at the heart of Christian theology: Christ's sacrifice. Indeed, Soviet culture borrowed liberally from Russia's Orthodox heritage: "The mission of the proletariat, the end of prehistory thanks to the Revolution, the reign of liberty – it is easy to recognize the source of these ideas: the Messiah, the break with the past, the Kingdom of God."[49] Transposed elements of Orthodoxy were everywhere in and before the war: in a focus on the deification of man into "Homo Sovieticus," in the use of textual styles that imitated religious myths and centred on salvational heroes, and in the overriding belief that Russia's destiny, and that of all other Christian nations, was messianic.[50] The supposedly atheist Bolsheviks saw nothing wrong in using any available method to preach their gospel.[51]

During the war, the messianic elements of Soviet writing would become more and more prominent. At a time when the nation was being martyred at the hands of the German invaders, a great military turning point like Stalingrad offered a form of spiritual salvation. This new turning point promised to tease meaning and motion out of the deaths of 25 million Soviets in the war. If a literal miracle was needed to make utopia possible, then Stalingrad, the greatest turnaround of the war, was the perfect candidate to become the new *velikiy perelom* – "great turning point."

Indeed, an aura of the miraculous is woven throughout the space of the wartime papers, especially as regards Stalingrad, where the motif of the *podvig*, or miraculous feat, is dominant. *Podvig* has no perfect English translation, but it signifies some deed of great import: defending and dying for the nation, slaying an improbable number of enemies, or conquering or driving out demons. In Russian culture, the *podvig* has long been loaded with profound religious connotations.[52] Although its origins were in the medieval Orthodox saints' lives – texts offered to believers as models for imitation – the *podvig* has had a long life in national Russian culture. Many of the medieval Russian tales of Orthodox saints related *podvigi* as great deeds that ended in the death of the hero.

Similarly, Russian military-patriotic culture has always emphasized the importance of sacrifice over survival in battle.[53] For the Orthodox believer, to die in pursuit of a great *podvig* was not just acceptable, it was in some ways desirable. The tsars eagerly aligned themselves with military and spiritual leaders and martyrs of the past, blending church and state motifs into a mishmash of power-affirming rituals, processions, parades, and images. No tsarist coronation could be held, no great palace or church constructed, without reference to a canon of *podvig*-achieving figures from the Russian past. Even during the First World War, depictions of heroic action at the front were framed in terms of heroic sacrifice in the name of God.[54]

Soviet literature continued to elevate the *podvig* as a path to sainthood. In the works of the doyen of the Socialist Realist genre, Maxim Gorky, the progenitor of the "positive hero" whose path toward consciousness was to serve as a model "saint's life" for Soviet readers, the achievement of a *podvig* lent the hero's action the aura of "immortality."[55] The Soviet revolutionary hero – inspired by a tradition of radical, sacrificial martyrdom stretching back to the anti-tsarist Decembrist Revolt of 1825 – generally achieved such a *podvig* through enormous self-sacrifice.[56] The heroes of Socialist Realism were thus always messianic.[57] The real-life heroes of the Soviet Union, meanwhile, had since long before the Second World War been transformed into immortal, saintly heroes by the Soviet literary production line.[58] At times, the Soviet characterization of the *podvig*-achieving heroes of the 1930s imitated Orthodox models surprisingly closely:[59] the religious, the worldly, the fictional, and the real were bundled together in the image of the *podvig* and its hero.

While this world of messianic heroes may seem fantastic, Soviet readers and viewers strongly identified with such hagiographic narratives. Soviet Russian readers interpreted their lives in terms of a history that extended deep into the past, long before the birth of Soviet power, and were drawn particularly to readings of catastrophe and sacrifice.[60] These ordinary Soviets believed in a version of personal history centred on "sacrificial historicism": in individuals' imaginations, utopian futures were always linked to moments of religious martyrdom and sacrifice. The motifs, tropes, and meanings of the *podvigi* described at Stalingrad had a historical and religious appeal that vaulted them well beyond cartoonish or totalitarian propaganda.

In the Stalingrad stories in this volume, the word *podvig* – which I have for convenience's sake translated generally as *miraculous feat* – crops up again and again. We will see Soviet troops both individually and *en masse* apparently willingly go to their deaths, small groups of Red Army men throw themselves into

unwinnable conflicts, and improbable individual feats of derring-do. The religious connotations of this trope underpin the entire Stalingrad narrative.
Sacrifice was not just tolerable; it was *desirable* when attached to the messianic
goal of saving the nation. By reading about *podvigi*, readers could engage in a
form of Orthodox imitation when they too found themselves engaged in war
work behind the lines or facing down a German at the front. The wartime was
littered with tales of great deeds, and Stalingrad and its defenders were to
achieve the greatest *podvig* of all.

TO THE FRONT: DEALING WITH THE DISASTERS OF 1941

In the summer of 1941, David Ortenberg and his writer-soldiers were left
wondering how to weave the present, the epic, and the spiritual into a cohesive
artistic framework as they faced an unprecedented war that threatened not
just defeat but total obliteration. How could they produce Socialist Realist
works about an imminent utopian future or suggest that a great turning point
was about to arrive when the Germans occupied most of Ukraine and Belarus,
when Leningrad was besieged, when hundreds of thousands of civilians and
soldiers lay dead on lost territory, and when total collapse at Moscow had only
just been avoided in December 1941?

For a year, the writers attempted to address this difficulty while adjusting
to newfound personal and artistic freedoms. Despite David Ortenberg's best
efforts, Konstantin Simonov and Ilya Ehrenburg's wartime experience, and
the patriotic enthusiasm among the journalistic corps' ranks, the team was at
first logistically and creatively ill-equipped to tackle their challenges. Writers
lacked basic supplies and were constantly exposed to dangerous fire; their
stories were anyway often delayed en route to Moscow.[61] Occasionally, these
difficulties led to rancour among the journalistic corps. Ortenberg's induce-
ments and stern orders to write about heroism at the front seemed useless to
writers like Vasily Grossman when all around was chaos.[62] Writers found
gathering and writing stories such tough going that Konstantin Simonov called
the first months of the war a time of artistic and military "naivety."[63] Sovinformbyuro had failed to create an efficient propaganda machine running at
full steam.

Figure I.3 Konstantin Simonov (L) and Evgeny Kriger (second from right) at the front.

As a result, the early wartime papers were filled with dry, detail-heavy propaganda laid out in dense blocks of text. Editors and writers, driven by a desire to aid the war effort, turned in the first months of the war to make-believe to produce legends of *podvigi* like those of the twenty-eight Panfilovites and the Podolsk Cadets. These mostly imagined and hyperbolic stories of heroic defensive efforts against the German invaders may have been disseminated widely, but they were barely credible.[64] Sovinformbyuro's news updates often egregiously contradicted reality. For instance, when the war broke out, *Pravda* and *Krasnaya Zvezda* printed the text of Vyacheslav Molotov's radio speech, a series of soldiers' declarations of fealty to the motherland, and a range of articles about events on the Western Front. There were no works of fiction, no poems, no cartoons, and few photographs – all features that would make the Stalingrad story so engaging when it began to take shape a year later. Sovinformbyuro and Aleksandr Shcherbakov were irate, and in June 1941 they took the editors of *Izvestiya* and *Krasnaya Zvezda* to task for writing "academic" – that is, dry – material.[65] Yet Shcherbakov himself had few answers; he and his peers acknowledged behind closed doors that they "had not found a way to make the unfolding disaster [of summer 1941] comprehensible to the population." The frustrated anger of the writers and their masters was reflected in occasional public discord.[66]

Driven by their enthusiasm, Grossman, Simonov, and their peers nonetheless spent the second half of 1941 travelling to hotspots and attempting to hone a wartime literary method.[67] Such was their eagerness that Ortenberg struggled to keep his journalists from harm.[68] Senior writers, who were given offices in the editorial building on Malaya Dmitrovka and encouraged to stay put, were dismayed not to be in the thick of the action.[69] Ilya Ehrenburg, who was often stuck in Moscow, repeatedly pleaded with David Ortenberg to be sent to the front. His editor refused: Ehrenburg was too important to risk. Ortenberg himself was no hypocrite: the editor wrote later of his own "bitter disappointment" that he was rarely able to visit the front, even though he made regular forays to see the action up close.[70]

As chaos reigned in the Kremlin, and as the Germans made massive inroads into Soviet territory, both editors in Moscow and writers at the front struggled to stay abreast of events. They spent days and weeks living with the troops, traversing constantly shifting battlefields, enduring bombardments, and engaging in gun battles.[71] Tossed from position to position, writers often found themselves chasing the Red Army across rapidly shrinking Soviet territory.[72] These months of retreat left the corps of journalists mentally and physically fatigued: "Sometimes it feels," wrote Vasily Grossman in the spring of 1942, "as if I've spent my whole life in trucks and sleeping in barns."[73] Many newspaper personnel died. Eleven *Krasnaya Zvezda* staff – writers, editors, artists, photographers – were killed or went missing between May and August 1942 alone.[74] Simply surviving, let alone finding subjects to describe or connecting events on the ground with strategic developments or an epic vision of history, was desperately difficult.

Over time, the government's central propaganda apparatus began to offer clearer guidance about what to write at the front and how to write it, as well as providing better logistical support so that the journalists could complete their work efficiently. By the spring of 1942, the newspaper and propaganda industries were well prepared to write and distribute papers.[75] The literary historian Lazar Lazarev describes the war as a time of "spontaneous de-Stalinization," which gave writers new freedoms to report on what they saw at the front.[76] Ortenberg did not generally restrict or direct his writers beyond instructing them to "explore frontline life and write whatever struck [them]." Thereafter, they were mostly left to their own devices.[77] Ortenberg's orders – to seek out some interesting character or officer, to visit some or another town, and, always, to send one or two stories or poems a week – ran to a handful of lines at most.[78] Writers were able to travel as freely as was possible given the dangers at the front, to interview soldiers as they pleased, and to discuss work and the world with one another and even with Western journalists.[79] They operated safe in the knowledge that Ortenberg and his editorial staff would shield them from repercussions and that the government needed frontline writers more than it needed new Gulag prisoners.

Behind the scenes, Ortenberg's relationship with Sovinformbyuro and Aleksandr Shcherbakov was through early 1942 generally unconstrained. The central authorities gave broad direction, but they also accepted advice from their editors, and changes to the papers were not contentious. Shcherbakov, Ortenberg, and the editors of *Pravda* and *Izvestiya*, Petr Pospelov and Lev Rovinsky, engaged in vigorous debates, openly sharing their often contradictory views. Shcherbakov's censors rejected almost no material: in the second quarter of 1942, *Krasnaya Zvezda* saw just 5 of 815 articles outright refused; *Pravda* fared only slightly worse at 16 of 415 articles.[80] Almost all the censorship carried out involved removing the names and locations of units, deleting the details of new offensives, and expunging information about industrial installations.[81]

Limits, of course, existed. No article was permitted to describe, for instance, the shooting of German prisoners of war, mistakes that led to the deaths of Soviet civilians, or faults in industrial activity. Writers did not, however, fear submitting such materials; Ortenberg, Pospelov, or Rovinsky would simply ask for permission to publish from Aleksandr Shcherbakov. At worst, they could expect an ear-bashing. Even after Stalingrad, when controls began to tighten again, writers who had made a "mistake" that might have ended in death in the prewar years might have lost their jobs, but they kept their lives.[82]

Nobody feared mentioning bad news. The retreats, disasters, poor military decisions, and human tragedies of the first year of the war were all recorded in materials sent back to the editorial offices.[83] Writers might have attempted to cover the vagaries of war, but much of this material ended up on the cutting room floor (albeit the fact that it was produced at all was a new development for Soviet literature). Readers were well into 1942 forced to read between the lines to understand the Red Army's real strategic outlook. The lack of maps showing retreat meant that only allusions to towns where fighting had taken place revealed where the army actually was, and even those town names were often replaced by vague allusions to fighting "in the region of" some or another province. Material that eventually reached the reader was heavily edited; nevertheless, writers had found new freedoms to travel widely, explore new lexicons, and interview ordinary and elite Soviets as they pleased.

EXPERIMENTS IN TIME: FORMING THE EPIC

Writers were now encouraged to experiment too with a broad palette of historical and literary references; anything was fair game if it would prove to be effective propaganda. Overt references to Marx, Engels, and class consciousness all but disappeared from fiction in place of a more nuanced approach to Soviet life that drew on source materials from across literary traditions. When the survival of the Soviet Union was at stake, mobilizing the newspapers to find hints of victory was the only task that mattered. Socialist Realist atemporality enabled writers to function as arrangers of literary pasts, documentary presents, and utopian futures; they could source and re-form material however they liked. What looked like new literary freedom for writers was, of course, a face-saving ploy by Stalin – whose hitherto omnipresent image barely appeared in the newspapers after mid-1941 – to fill a void left by his absence.[84] Only when Stalingrad was won would Stalin emerge from his cultural hiding place to re-assert himself as the architect of history and the next in line of a lineage of great Russian generals.

The freedom to move beyond rote Bolshevik references was not unprecedented.[85] In the late 1930s, the government had encouraged writers to incorporate tropes from the Russian national past and even from European cultures and the classical period as a means to engage ordinary readers.[86] That "search for a usable past" was accelerated by the German invasion. The war was on its first day christened the "Great Patriotic War" in reference to Russia's victory over Napoleon (and, of course, to Lev Tolstoy's canonical patriotic history of that victory, *War and Peace*). In turn, Sovinformbyuro prompted frontline writers, through David Ortenberg's editorial team, to include specific themes

– the "miraculous and heroic feats of the Russian people in the patriotic war of 1812," for instance – in their work.[87]

Stalin himself underscored the importance of the Russian national past in a November 1941 speech by reeling off a list of tsarist-era heroes – those who had completed great national *podvigi* – for emulation: "May we take inspiration from the greatest of our forebears: Aleksandr Nevsky, Dmitry Donskoy, Kuzma Minin, Dmitry Pozharsky, Aleksandr Suvorov, and Mikhail Kutuzov!"[88] These kings and military leaders were lauded for defending medieval and nineteenth-century Russia against invaders. Each had been incorporated into tsarist official culture as an axis around which to construct visions of self- and national sacrifice.[89] Kuzma Minin, purportedly an ordinary butcher who had defeated the Poles in 1612, was just the sort of hero for the hour in 1941: a reference to Minin suggested that even a quite average man could be sanctified for defeating the European threat.

Authors were just as likely to propose historical comparisons themselves as they were to receive them from the government. They eagerly rummaged through the Soviet, Russian, and European canons and beyond for models. Konstantin Simonov revered both Tolstoy and Ernest Hemingway's war writing, and Vasily Grossman, who had never shown any particular interest in slavishly adhering to the Soviet literary method, devoured everything from Tolstoy to Pushkin, Gogol, Nikolay Nekrasov, and Sergey Aksakov at the front.[90] Conservative, liberal, nationalist, European, American, classical: the literary repertoire provided a boon for a desperate government, creative writers, and bored readers alike.

The writers at the front were asked to pack these references into what were effectively micro-fictions. Most pieces ran at a scant thousand words in the early months of the war. Very few authors were given space even for two or three thousand word pieces, and serialized pieces were rare. The frontline writers were no strangers to literary short forms, which in recent years had been just as important to Russian and Soviet writing as full-length novels.[91] In the twentieth century, writers like Vasily Rozanov, Daniil Kharms, Vladimir Mayakovsky, and Isaac Babel had modelled the short form as a site for literary creativity and for writing about war. The short story form may have been a necessity but it also suited the task of producing huge amounts of work in difficult conditions. A frantic Ortenberg often had to hurry his charges, and they responded by pumping out works by the dozen. Ilya Ehrenburg alone cranked out some two thousand articles – almost one and a half per day – during the war.[92]

The short form was quite capable of summoning the aura of the epic, which is usually associated with length, when individual stories were enhanced through collaboration and juxtaposition. A single story was always placed alongside other texts, poems, and images on the same theme, phrases and themes were repeated, and authors responded to their peers' work in new stories. The same heroes and the same *podvigi* were staged and restaged from every angle. Layered together day after day across the central and local newspapers, which were practically identical, individual texts added up to something with the scope and span of an epic. The Soviet epic did not need to come in a thousand-page novel. It could be produced over time as editors and writers heaped staccato textual utterances onto one another.

Quickfire reads matched the quickfire nature of wartime existence for fatigued readers who snatched minutes in between battles, marches, and watches to consume the latest paper – even if this hinted at tensions between military life in motion and the epic. The emergence of mediatized warfare in the nineteenth century had given rise to friction between "live" coverage of battle and the creation of bounded, epic forms. Models for "miniature" epics of reportage, however, did exist. Tolstoy, who had served in the Crimean War – the first major conflict to be widely covered by photographers and reports[93] – balanced "reportage, the eyewitness account, the diary, the notes of a war correspondent," and literary and epic elements in his *Sevastopol Stories* from the front.[94]

The nature of Soviet identity creation provided readers of the wartime newspapers with a means to resolve these tensions. Soviets were used to reading anaphoric texts – which closely resembled Orthodox saints' lives – in which shorthand and single words were understood as coded forms. For writers, this meant that mentioning "Borodino" or a "son of Tsaritsyn" would instantly identify a protagonist with the epic time and space of the victory over Napoleon in 1812 or Stalin's crusade against the Whites in Civil War–era Stalingrad. While a tension between present and epic temporalities inevitably remained, the Soviet reader was primed to grasp a *sense* of the wholeness of Mikhail Bakhtin's epic time and space through allusion. This context, and the layering of motifs and phrases over days and weeks in the newspapers, created counter-

Figure I.4 Konstantin Simonov (2nd left) and Evgeny Kriger (2nd right) on the roads of the front.

weights to the ambivalence of a war experienced as both potentially endless and, contrarily – terrifyingly – fast.

Given the exhaustion brought about by retreat and defeat, the first year of the war ought to have been as disastrous for writers as it was for the military leadership. Nonetheless, glimpses of an epic of the war began to emerge in the pages of the Soviet newspapers. A handful of literary landmarks that drew on Socialist Realist classics, popular stories, myths of the prerevolutionary military past, and documentary observation from the front appeared. The early successes were short: Konstantin Simonov's poem *Wait for Me* (July–August 1941) and Ilya Ehrenburg's angry invectives from late 1941 were hugely popular. However, the emergence of full-length prose pieces by the summer of 1942 suggests that writers were becoming more experienced with the demands of what was still a losing war. Simonov's *The Russian People* and Grossman's *The People Immortal*, both of which were serialized in the papers that summer, are miniature epics of human and national tragedy.[95] A refined rhetorical arsenal was ready for deployment at Stalingrad. It would transform the city and its defenders into the architects of the greatest *podvig* in history. In the following chapters,

I present in translations a selection of works that reveal this *podvig* in its creation and re-creation. The brief exploration of themes in the following pages will guide broad interpretation of those stories.

TO STALINGRAD: THE RESURRECTION OF THE NATION

Writers hurried to the Volga in the late summer of 1942 as the Germans rampaged toward Stalingrad. Billeted together in a dilapidated wooden house in the village of Srednyaya Akhtuba, just east of Stalingrad, which the authors often referred to simply as "Akhtuba," writers swapped, discussed, and developed one another's motifs, characters, and narrative ideas.[96] Each day, they would venture across the Volga into Stalingrad or out onto the vast steppe to visit the front. There, they interviewed everyone from ordinary soldiers to senior officers and observed action at close quarters. Within weeks of the battle's outbreak, writers were discussing the possibility of total obliteration at Stalingrad. The threat of destruction was paired with a new epic of national resurrection assembled from a hodgepodge of Christian, Soviet, and classical imagery. Drawing on all the mimetic creativity of the Socialist Realist method, writers painted Stalingrad and its defenders as martyrs slain so that the nation and the world itself might be saved from death.

Hints of the resurrection to come are discernable in even the first translations I include. References to Stalingrad as "hell" – a site of ever-present death and heroic self-creation engulfed by fire, flames, and smoke – are always present.[97] Beginning with Vasily Grossman's "On the Volga," the first Stalingrad story printed in *Krasnaya Zvezda* in 1942 and the first translation in this volume, the river Volga appears as a boundary between life and death, just as the Styx had separated the human and underworlds in classical myth. Grossman draws the brewing battle into a vast conceptual space – the "broad and mighty river of Russian freedom cascad[ing] onto the endless steppe" – before asserting the equally enormous significance of the *podvig* his heroes will presumably accomplish at Stalingrad: "The fate of the nation is in our hands," his characters insist. This strand of thinking would grow to monumental proportions within weeks. Konstantin Simonov's September work "A Soldier's Glory," translated in full here, introduces the motif of *birth*, which was almost as common as mentions of death in subsequent Stalingrad stories, to suggest that to cross the

Volga was to enter hell, to die, and to be symbolically reborn. At Stalingrad, Soviet troops could, like the heroes of classical myth or of the Orthodox *podvig*, rescue humanity from the brink of death through their own acts of epic heroism.[98] Readers, meanwhile, could do the same through reflection on and imitation of these saintly figures.

The action at Stalingrad was thus soon conceived of as part of an overarching *podvig* – the moment when the threat of total obliteration would be replaced by life anew. In the stories in this volume, we will see the deeds of individual soldiers projected onto and reflected in the image of a living, warrior Stalingrad that strikes down its tormentors. Death at Stalingrad is reframed as a *necessary* and *exemplary* national sacrifice. Individuals' deaths, paired with the city's own death, catalyze a turn away from war's assault on existence and toward meaning and order. Individual *podvigi* thus collide with epic visions of nation, history, and religious myth around the symbolic death and return to life of Stalingrad.

The screenwriter-turned-prose writer Evgeny Kriger produced the first comprehensive vision of this resurrection narrative in October 1942. Kriger's "This Is Stalingrad," translated in this volume for the first time, describes a city mutilated and symbolically murdered, as if the "death" of Stalingrad were a Christlike sacrifice. The city rises up to assail its German tormentors. As "This Is Stalingrad" thunders to a crescendo, an ordinary soldier asserts, "They can't kill me now. I've already been dead once." Death ceases to hinder the immortal spirit of the martyred city and its defenders. The Soviet faithful are assured that human tragedy is part of a linear historical path toward betterment that resists the disordering chaos of war. Kriger would capture the spirit of resurrection in the rallying cry "Stalingrad lives!," which would be recycled in dozens of cinematic and textual narratives in the postwar years.

When the news of 19 November's successful counterattack came, the fairy tale seemed to have become reality. Stalingrad's martyrdom really had brought about a historic victory. Hundreds of thousands may have died, but Stalingrad and the nation with it had survived. Stalingrad had become a new turning point in Soviet history, a moment to match 1917 and the Civil War as a new beginning – a great turning point: a *podvig* carried out by millions of Soviets. Earlier texts could be read in a new light so that any death at or beyond Stalingrad had been a necessary precursor to victory and therefore to resurrection. In the last works written from the battle – those I translate from January and

February 1943 – the authors linger on what this rebirth will mean for themselves and other soldiers.

Developing this narrative of resurrection – let alone making readers really believe it – was no mean feat. In the early weeks of the battle, writers struggled to deal with their own shock at the vicious fighting in Stalingrad, to comprehend their sense that death at the city seemed inevitable, yet also to understand how the Soviets still clung on. Writers found an ally in the Socialist Realist form, which helped them project temporal structure onto the personal and collective disordering of Stalingrad.

REALITY AND FAIRY TALE

The process of coming to terms began with first-hand observation. All of the translated stories in this volume brim over with details of life at the front. The Stalingrad stories reveal details of fighting on the steppe and the water and in the air, fields, houses, basements, trenches, and bunkers in and around Stalingrad, conveying the totality of a battle that traversed a huge swathe of territory. Every corner of this textual world is packed with the paraphernalia and phenomena of warfare: capes used as bunker doors, burning or breaking wooden beams, picture frames and photographs, oilcloth couches, bed frames, utensils; guns, bullets, and casings; cigarettes cadged and quietly enjoyed; the light of the sun, of rockets, of army-issue "bat lamps," or of makeshift torches; broken and battered bodies and helmets.

The sometimes humdrum relations of daily existence, or *byt* in the Russian, were as important to nineteenth-century writers like Pushkin and Goncharov as they were to prewar Soviet stylists like Mikhail Zoshchenko.[99] The accumulation of detail in the Stalingrad stories owes a particular debt to Isaac Babel's tales of the Civil War, which read almost as ethnographical catalogues of frontline life and were widely read during this war as well.[100] Indeed, documentary observation was at the heart of all Socialist Realism. The Stalingrad stories, even before they touch on mythical and epic elements, draw the reader in with their frank accounts of soldierly life at the front and their links to a familiar canon of war writing.

As in canonical Socialist Realist works by authors like Maksim Gorky and Nikolay Ostrovsky, authors attempted to trace the individual soldier's relationship both to this *byt* and to their comrades, offering models for readers to construct their own rapport with distant or unimaginable events and to the *podvigi* described. Almost every work included in this volume focuses on one or two ordinary soldiers (less often, officers), who were interviewed at the front and then fictionalized.[101] However, where pre-Stalingrad works might have been full of exaggeration and embellishment, creating Stakhanovite pastiches of real people or caricaturing the doers of cooked-up *podvigi*, the Stalingrad stories overflow with the language of reality. Verbatim quotations from interviews conducted at the front, and even whole stories related almost word-for-word by soldiers to writers, filled the newspapers for the months of the battle. The stories are packed with slang, humour, and forthright expressions of what it felt like to be at Stalingrad. Even at the bleakest moments of the battle, the writers found room for ordinary people's opinions and words.

This wealth of detail about people, places, and objects provides a fairly accurate record of life at the front. Many stories can be traced back to exact names, quotes, and events recorded in writers' notebooks. Now, when government, writers, and readers were all working toward the same end – defending Stalingrad – editors could more than ever, as David Ortenberg noted, "simply print the sketches as [authors] had written them."[102] Sovinformbyuro may often have presented exaggerated or downright false information in its daily news updates, but Ortenberg's team had little reason to lie or exaggerate by the time of Stalingrad. Sovinformbyuro, as I have noted, rejected little of what was submitted for publication. This vast battle was recorded for posterity not in soldiers' diaries – which were forbidden – or by cameras – which were hard to come by – but in the stories printed in the newspapers. The language and realia of war are all poured into these stories, making them a fulcrum between planes of reality, fantasy, documentary, and epic.

Some of the scenes presented in the newspaper stories lean on colloquialism so heavily as to seem artistically simplistic. For example, take how Vasily Grossman and Vasily Koroteev describe a celebration of the anniversary of the October Revolution in their co-written "In Stalin's City": "Men and women alike wore the same boots and cotton bodywarmers. Everybody had a revolver, and many even held submachine guns. Soldiers and commanders of the Red Army and workers and factory directors sat side by side." These observations might seem rather banal; the sentences short; the vocabulary colourless. However, the authors mark out this apparently ordinary gathering as *extra*ordinary by sheer dint of the objects and people they have collected in it. Listing acts as a counterpoint to the destructiveness of the autumn of 1942, elevating the ordinary to a place of significance. Fantasy ceding textual ground to reality began with first-hand observation and these descriptions of *byt*; the high-flown idea of Stalingrad as resurrection found its footing in reality, not in myth. Prewar literary "fairy tales" were making way for truly unimaginable events and real military heroes.[103]

The descriptions of the astonishing *podvigi* completed at Stalingrad may not be perfectly reliable evidential sources, but their basis in *byt* makes them indicative of the many examples of Soviet heroism that went "unrecorded for posterity" during this period.[104] Writers were keen that this should be the case. Konstantin Simonov spoke of his duty to relate events at Stalingrad "humbly" and "through another's eyes" without making up facts or stories.[105] He believed that to focus on *byt* was to reject the dehumanizing nature of a war that treated human life as an irrelevance. Writing fiction was thus a means of reconstituting, not repudiating, reality:

> Alongside death, glory and sacrifice, [I wrote] about the *byt* that exists in every war, the day-to-day of war, the little snippets of life, when people in the most unthinkable conditions somehow remain human. They chatter away, joke, sing, fill up a homemade lamp with oil, fix a stopped watch, or race around to show off a kitten that happened into their dugout.[106]

For Simonov, writing about *byt* was not just a way of cataloguing ordinary life at the front; it was also a way of preserving and perpetuating life itself. Fiction in this projective, demiurgic mode resisted the destructive onslaught of the German invasion, creating life where death reigned.

Describing quotidian reality at the front in turn, therefore, was a response to writers' *own* experiences of the front. The work of Simonov's colleague Vasily Koroteev (1911–1964), a native Stalingrader who had written for local newspapers before the war, encapsulates Stalingrad writing as resistance to trauma.[107] The tireless Koroteev served as a local guide for the visiting writers besides writing a number of the pieces translated here.[108] For him, Stalingrad was no far-off epic land; for him, its destruction was an intensely personal assault. *Byt* to Koroteev meant documenting his own life, his own memories, and his own town. By chronicling the city's destruction and resurrection in a series of articles from the front, he created a cohesive inner narrative, repudiating destruction through acts of literary construction.[109] The stories by Koroteev translated here, none of which have ever before appeared in English, suggest a writer trying to piece together his own experiences from odds and ends of literary models, eyewitness accounts, and documentary materials. Koroteev orchestrates motifs from elsewhere around the narrative of Stalingrad as an act of *self*-reinvention, using fiction as a means to make his own "fairy tale" come true.

SLOGANEERING AND THE SOVIET SELF

Understanding these acts of self- and national creation gives us a means to interpret the slew of epithets and slogans from official sources such as Sovinformbyuro and Stalin's speeches, which litter the Stalingrad stories. What was printed in Sovinformbyuro's communiqués marked the boundaries of the permissible; writers worked stock phrases into every one of their stories throughout the months of the battle. "Every house is a fortress!"; "There is no land for us behind the Volga!"; "We must defend Stalingrad at any price!"; "No step backward"'; "There'll be a holiday on our street!"; "There is nowhere to retreat": almost all of these now famous lines appeared in Sovinformbyuro communiqués or editorials before being used in work filed from the front.[110]

Yet these stock phrases were not included just to appease censors. Sloganeering was a means to quickly thrust narratives toward the epic. Theoretically, at least, the Kremlin's words were meant to accord a lofty sheen to documentary observations, and thus they appeared frequently throughout Soviet literature.[111] However, these epithets also reflect the creative impulses of the pre-Socialist Realist era, when staccato rallying cries filled the poetic outpourings of the avant-garde. Evgeny Kriger's slogan "Stalingrad lives!" alludes to Vladimir Mayakovsky's famous lines on Lenin's death: "Lenin lived, Lenin lives, Lenin will live!" For the Soviet reader, the allusion would have been instantly recognizable from all manner of posters, speeches, and placards. Kriger's phrase came to be used widely by ordinary Soviets, indicating that the use of slogans was not unidirectional. Writers voluntarily incorporated the government's slogans and created their *own* slogans as an expression of demiurgic creativity and as a means to find language that suited the task of writing about a battle that defied description; the government then adopted and disseminated these slogans; in turn, ordinary people began to use this language.

As private and public languages bled together, the newspapers were becoming a meeting place for the state's and individuals' *cris de coeur*. The collaborative and voluntary nature of authorial acts around Stalingrad suggests that incorporating slogans and other official materials was a means to help writers themselves come to terms with the mass deaths, atrocious conditions, and horrendous losses they were witnessing. Especially in the early stages of the battle, when defeat not just at Stalingrad but in the war as a whole seemed likely, writers working at breakneck speed and under immense psychological pressure could use these formulaic patterns to describe events that were almost beyond comprehension. We will see in Anatoly Nedzelsky's first story from Stalingrad, "Tales of Stalingrad's Defenders," a strikingly raw example of this patchwork approach to literary construction.

Staccato epithets and slogans were not the only means of negating disorder. Ilya Ehrenburg's stories, which were filed from Moscow, leaned on another Soviet mode: the language of *agitatsiya* – agitation. Agitation was intended to appeal to emotion: to enrage the reader or, as was Ehrenburg's wartime task, to "sustain the Soviet people's moral spirit."[112] Ehrenburg peppered his regular summative pieces – four of his stories are translated in this volume – with insults, sarcasm, and stories of pantomime German villainy. The writer mixes apocryphal quotes from German newspapers and diaries with familiar themes of sacrifice and hope, then suffuses that mix with bloody-minded rage. The more piquant passages might seem *de trop*, but this sort of writing was hugely popular. Ehrenburg gave voice in the newspapers to the emotions of ordinary Soviets, who were as angry as they were anxious.[113] Ehrenburg took great relish in his role as chief morale-raiser and German-mocker at *Krasnaya Zvezda*, working closely with David Ortenberg to polish his invective. Writing agitation was for Ehrenburg not just a means of enraging the reader on behalf of the Kremlin. Agitation was, especially in September and October 1942, a vessel for the writer's *own* anger.

BORROWING FROM THE SOVIET AND RUSSIAN PAST

Alongside narratives and expressions of individual heroism and suffering, writers packed their works with Soviet literary and historical content. Filling works with allusions to Soviet legends – particularly to Stalin's Civil War–era defence of Tsaritsyn, which was integral to the myth of the leader's transformation into a semi-deity[114] – did not just curry favour with the regime but gave temporal and narrative structure to action at the front. The keen reader will spot dozens of allusions to Soviet writing in the Stalingrad stories translated in this volume.

Drawing on Soviet accounts of the epic military past was a natural means to find form and structure when those things were tangibly under attack during the war. References to the Civil War dominate: Mikhail Bulgakov's *The White Guard* – whose stage version was beloved by Stalin – like many of the Stalingrad stories, constantly describes war in musical metaphors (here, Anatoly Nedzelsky and Vasily Grossman's stories are filled with sonority); the protagonists and setting of Mikhail Sholokhov's epic *And Quiet Flows the Don* clearly influenced the portrayal of Stalingrad characters such as Vasily Koroteev's Polyakov ("The Man from the Volga").

The most prevalent Soviet literary borrowings, though, are the generic character signifiers used for almost all the heroes in the stories. The briefest of allusions to a famous character was enough to shift Stalingrad's chaos into the stable world of Socialist Realism. The production novel had been one of the most important genres of the 1930s. At Stalingrad, Konstantin Simonov's Tkalenko, the hero of "Battle on the Outskirts," is "stoic," "calm," and "dry" – characteristics commonly attributed to heroes in production novels that signify the characters' status as the completers of great *podvigi*.[115] The Stalingrad stories' doughty protagonists, who persist in even the most hopeless battles, are every bit like the heroes of earlier Civil War and production novels. Frequently, the characters in the Stalingrad stories even approach war as if they were going to work: for instance, Vasily Koroteev's Polyakov, the hero of "The Man from the Volga," experiences the battlefield as a construction site. Elsewhere there are myriad examples of manual labour and of the building of emplacements and defensive lines, further emphasizing a continuity between the Soviet production novel and the wartime sketch.[116] Characters begin early –

even in October's stories – to imagine the act of rebuilding Stalingrad, which
would form the basis for postwar imaginings of the battle. Any hero of Stalingrad could be turned into a great martyr, any site of Stalingrad made into a
future monument, through the use of these markers, thus assuring the reader
that the torments and travails of the present belonged in a bounded and epic
temporal space.

The most significant yardstick for epic feats was allusion to the Soviet military tale. Writers drew on popular models of Soviet military heroes, in particular Vasily Chapaev, the real-life Civil War hero and protagonist of Dmitry
Furmanov's wildly popular eponymous novel and a 1934 film by the Vasilyev
brothers.[117] The allusion to Chapaev in particular could imbue the heroes of
Stalingrad with the aura of a figure who was "one of us [but] something out
of the ordinary": a mythical leader with the extraordinary capacity to complete
a *podvig*.[118] Konstantin Simonov, for example, describes Tkalenko as literally
resembling Chapaev. Conveyed even in such brief allusions, Chapaev's transformation from man to myth could be read into the characters and stories of
Stalingrad and thus into the reader's own experience. Dragging real human
models such as Tkalenko the other way – into the realms of the recognizably
epic – promised that the wartime was not, perhaps, a totally obliterative phenomenon after all. Yet these fictional references were not just mimetic projec-
tions. The Stalingrad authors' notes suggest that their characters really *did* act
like Socialist Realist heroes. Chapaev, and many other Socialist Realist heroes,
were real – and really outstanding soldiers – before they were fictionalized.
Emulating this phenomenon, the Stalingrad stories seem poised between reality and fiction; the one plane informs the other to create continuities between
the literary and real past and present, edging the experience of the present
closer to an epic continuum of national heroes.

Authors at the front, however, were not limited to referencing Socialist Realist classics. By the time of Stalingrad, they had become masters of the Socialist
Realist method, gathering and reordering material from any part of the "usable
past." Materials borrowed from prerevolutionary sources aligned the experience of Stalingrad with victorious moments from national and world history.
Stalingrad was compared to Verdun, Cannae, and Troy and to the renowned
Russian victories over the Golden Horde at Kulikovo and Napoleon at Borodino. Although these allusions are present throughout the texts, they were
particularly beloved by Evgeny Kriger and Konstantin Simonov. This is es-

pecially significant since the former was the progenitor of the Stalingrad-as-martyred-city motif.

And references did not end at the historical: the *literary* allusion was just as widespread. Nods to prerevolutionary Romantic takes on Russian folk motifs are particularly common. Mentions of folk heroes like the *bogatyr* – the chivalrous folk-hero knight of Russian fairy tale – continued the prewar trend of using terms with popular appeal to describe exceptional workers.[119] Another Romanticized folk model is that of the Volga, which appears in some form in almost every one of the stories in this volume. The image of the Volga as a life-giving force not just for individuals but for the whole nation harks back to Russian folk tales and to the work of, for example, the nineteenth-century poet Nikolay Nekrasov. Both these sources would have been instantly recognizable to wartime readers: Nekrasov was widely taught in the Soviet 1930s and even read by Vasily Grossman at the front, and songs and tales of the Volga were common in many households, including Grossman's own.[120]

Although hardly a novelty for Soviet literature, the constant invocation of the Volga's placid beauty pulls us in two directions. Stalingrad seems to stand in the way of a war tearing deep into the stability of a timeless, idyllic Russian existence represented by the river. Nonetheless, even as death looms closer as troops cross the Styx-like river into Stalingrad's hell, the Volga courses with life-giving potential. In the texts from after 19 November translated in this volume, the Volga is tightly linked to images of melting ice, of verdant springtime, and of mothers and children. Russian civilization seems to bubble up from the river's waters, offering a potential future even as death reigns over the banks and the ever dangerous crossing into the city.

Nor did writers limit themselves to popular materials; they also mined deep into the Russian literary-patriotic past for inspiration. The narrators' frequently omniscient visions of the battlefield and their stories' epic framing nod to eighteenth-century odes to tsarist victories like Mikhail Lomonosov's *Ode on the Capture of Khotin* (*Oda na vzyatie Khotina*, 1739), while the references to dead soldiers as sleeping and to the great cycles of nature conjure up the classical tonalities of Gavriil Derzhavin's *Waterfall* (*Vodopad*, 1791). The idea of a heroic martyrdom on the Russian steppe, meanwhile, brings to mind the medieval epic poems *The Lay of Igor's Campaign* and *Zadonshchina*, two Russian literary landmarks that centre on *podvigi*. Any work that suggested that Stalingrad belonged in a line of great national victories was plundered for material to further reinforce the sense that at Stalingrad an incredible, quasi-religious, time-defying feat was in the offing – even before it had actually happened.

The *ur*text for writers at the front was Tolstoy's *War and Peace*. Tolstoy's novel, which describes the "Great Patriotic War" that eventually repelled Napoleon from Russian territory, was everywhere in the Soviet Second World War.[121] The work was serialized for radio broadcast in 1941, printed in mammoth quantities, and eagerly read by soldiers at the front and workers behind the lines.[122] Indeed, Vasily Grossman had read the work twice in the months before Stalingrad and had even made a pilgrimage to Tolstoy's estate at Yasnaya Polyana while en route to the city in 1942. Konstantin Simonov was during and after the war "totally in thrall to the Tolstoyan tradition."[123] Tolstoy's philosophical and artistic fingerprints are all over the arc of improbable resistance followed by stunning victory presented at Stalingrad.

Tolstoy's emphasis on the Russian people's role in achieving victory over Napoleon, and on a form of mystic nationalism that interpreted victory in 1812 as a providential miracle, was especially appealing when defeat loomed in 1942.[124] For Tolstoy, national spirit and military miracles were every bit as important as battlefield *nous* or tactics for explaining how Napoleon was driven off Russian soil. When Grossman, Simonov, Koroteev, Ehrenburg, and their peers mention the Red Army soldier's indomitable spirit, whether the troops are grouped in close-quarters fighting or alone on the steppe – which functions in the texts as a blank canvas for exploration of soldiers' psychology – allusions to *War and Peace* are unmistakable.

The Stalingrad stories also draw on *War and Peace* to make sense of soldiers' battlefield motivations and experiences. Anatoly Nedzelsky's short story "Tales of Stalingrad's Defenders," for instance, explores how a new recruit experiences the turmoil of war by using an image from Tolstoy's battlefield. Nedzelsky's hero, Leontev, is trapped in a tank. Staring at a chink of sky, and contemplating death, Leontev realizes that he "doesn't really understand" battle. In one of the most important scenes in *War and Peace*, the protagonist Andrey Bolkonsky lies injured. The chaos of battle recedes as he gazes at the sky, reflecting on his individuality and the infinity of nature. Both Tolstoy's and Nedzelsky's characters have an epiphany: Bolkonsky sheds his obsession with individual battlefield glory; Leontev is seized by an instinctual rage that drives him back to the fight. In Nedzelsky's text, the Tolstoyan warrior and the Soviet agitative mode are drawn into a single textual space. Faithfulness to Tolstoy's artistic and historic visions was unimportant; the allusion to a patriotic tradition of Russian battlefield heroism was enough to drive Leontev to complete a *podvig* of sorts.

Vasily Grossman took the Tolstoyan line further than any other writer at Stalingrad. In *War and Peace*, Tolstoy explains the improbable victory over Napoleon in 1812 in terms of Russian spirit and *nous*.[125] In the five Grossman stories included in this volume, the author suggests that soldiers fight best when liberated from military-strategic calculations. Even in moments of peril and grief, Grossman's troops are full of camaraderie, wisecracking, and back-slapping cheer: soldierly intuition, Grossman suggests, was more important than tactical calculation on the battlefield. Suggesting that Red Army troops might not need their political leaders would have been impossible months or years before; only the wartime context allowed Grossman to pursue this literary avenue. Above all, then, the Tolstoyan literary heritage provided structuring models to counter the aporia of an unprecedented war and an extraordinary battle. What could not be explained through rational deduction could be explained by providential miracle and patriotic spirit.

Few readers can have consciously understood the significance of coded references to medieval epics, Derzhavin, Lomonosov, or even Tolstoy as anything more than vague nods to great individual *podvigi* or national battles of the past. However, by placing allusions to national history and folk stories alongside the experience of the present, writers appealed to Russian readers' patriotism, encouraging them to believe that action in the present could create an unparalleled national victory. Writers were deliberately summoning up pre-revolutionary imperial visions of Russia's messianic destiny: Russia, above all others, was fated to be the defender of civilization and the Christian world. The reader, they promised, could be at the heart of this national epic.

The Soviet literary establishment was frank about this approach. Tolstoy's work, wrote the Soviet novelist Alexey Tolstoy in 1943, was the progenitor of Stalingrad literature: nobody could better convey "the earth, the people, the inextinguishable moral strength of the people," than Tolstoy.[126] Imitation, the all-important approach to the relationship between believer and saint in Orthodox culture, was the goal. By emulating heroes and *podvigi* of the past, the defenders of Stalingrad – and readers themselves – could become folk heroes, *bogatyrs*, and defenders of the nation against European invaders. They could thereby rise to an epic, spiritual space. Little matter that the hodgepodge of

national, religious, Soviet, and documentary content was theologically and
often artistically contradictory. The heroes of Stalingrad were completing lit-
erarily and historically extraordinary deeds in an extraordinary place; readers
might too, therefore, find themselves in this world of *podvigi*.

CHARTING A PATH FROM PAST TO PRESENT

As the battle progressed, writers increasingly wove one another's ideas into
their works. Key phrases began to be repeated from one story to another, so
that, for example, the image of Stalingrad as a "dead" city – taken from a note
Vasily Grossman made when he first arrived on the Volga in August 1942 –
turned into the image of the wounded city and then the resurrected city. That
motif provided fodder for men like Vasily Koroteev to structure their own responses to the fighting (see "At Stalingrad," which borrows Grossman's motif).
Some stories were even written entirely in response to texts printed earlier in
the battle. Of the works in this volume, for example, Grossman's "Today in
Stalingrad" unmistakably mirrors Konstantin Simonov's "Days and Nights"
in style and structure: Simonov's text from September 1942 is mired in hope-
lessness; Grossman's, from early January 1943, is an introspective take on the
significance of victory, written when the "resurrection" had already taken place.
Ilya Ehrenburg's two stories titled "Stalingrad," meanwhile, have the author
engaged in a dialogue between his pre-victory and post-victory authorial
selves. These works all revolve around multilayered governmental, individual,
intertextual, and social interactions. They beg to be read collectively as sites of
exchange between the past and the present.

The great challenge on the ground, however, was still to find a way to in-
strumentalize that textual exchange so as to make a present defined by death
and suffering seem epic and utopian. For the first three months of fighting at
Stalingrad, this seemed almost impossible. Stalingrad was constantly written
into a sealed space – a city of outskirts, borders, and hellish river crossings –
that at first seemed physically inaccessible to outsiders. Death became so ubi-
quitous and the struggle so hopeless that the war felt endless.[127] The stories
from September and October 1942 in this volume are representative of this
unending nowness. In works like Konstantin Simonov's "Days and Nights"

there are no allusions to a peaceful future. Time itself seems to be on hold as night and day blend into one ceaseless wave of fighting. Stalingrad, cut off from the reader by thousands of kilometres of land and by the Volga itself, seems like a distinct temporal and experiential world. Peace seems distant, a utopian future altogether unthinkable.

The use of the "battlefield tour" narrative was the chief means to bridge the disjuncture between heroic past, nightmarish present, and utopian future. This form, in which a first-person narrator visits the "sites" of the battlefield, describing the sights and sounds he encounters along the way, was the most frequently used form in the newspaper stories and appears in most of this volume's translations. A simple way to introduce the reader to Stalingrad's heroic space, the form is yet another example of a borrowed device: it is almost impossible to read a story like Simonov's "Days and Nights," which itself became a model text for postwar Stalingrad stories, without thinking of Tolstoy's "Sevastopol in May," the first of the earlier author's Crimean War despatches. Throughout the Stalingrad stories, the author-narrator continually shares his own shock at a world of startling violence, deafening noise, graphic injury, and ever-present death. He introduces the reader to troops at the front, who in turn relate their own experiences. Following the narrator's physical and psychological encounter with Stalingrad and Stalingraders, the reader, as if digesting the story of an Orthodox saint, experiences their own journey of inner revelation.

Vasily Grossman's "Today in Stalingrad," found in chapter 4 of this volume, is an especially personal invocation of the battlefield tour. Grossman takes the reader on an introspective journey into the nature and meaning of victory at Stalingrad, weaving together myriad historical and literary references, allusions to his peers' recent work, and his impressions at the birth of what seems like an entirely new world as the dawn revives a "slain" city. Following the narrator's journey across the Volga and into the becalmed Stalingrad, the reader shares the narrator's awe and relief. The final story from the period of the battle translated here, Vasily Koroteev's "Goodbye, Stalingrad!," picks up Grossman's baton, responding in an even more intimate way to the relief of victory by exploring the emotions of a broad swathe of Soviets as people, narrator, and troops all turn their thoughts from past destruction to future creation.

Writers found other ways to bring epic modalities into human experience. Starting in September, Sovinformbyuro began to disseminate – alongside photographs of destroyed homes – the slogan "Every house at Stalingrad is a fortress!" The Stalingrad authors' response, which I term the "house defence story," provided the reader with a new means to project their own experience onto Stalingrad, and for Stalingrad to enter the life of the reader. In the house defence narrative, the author-narrator travels into Stalingrad and either witnesses or hears the story of how a small group of outgunned Soviets defended a single house – one of the city's four or five-storey apartment buildings – against an overwhelming German force. *Pravda* correspondent Boris Polevoy's mid-October tale "House 21a," translated in the second chapter here, was the first to introduce this setting to Stalingrad fiction, although Vasily Grossman has often been erroneously credited as the trope's inventor. By documenting the house as a home, and introducing memories or remnants of its inhabitants or prewar life into the text, Polevoy transposes the defence of Stalingrad and therefore the entire nation into a single, familiar site. To the reader whose home was under threat from invasion, loss, bombing, or evacuation, any house could stand in for the entire war.

The trope had particular resonance at Stalingrad, where a battle for every home really was happening and "the front [was often] a corridor between burnt-out rooms."[128] Leafing through the October newspapers, the reader might have mistakenly thought there was no war at all beyond the walls of Stalingrad's houses: every hope was condensed into and projected onto this domestic location. While the house defence story was not entirely new, it has become inextricably linked with Stalingrad. The battle for single houses at Stalingrad would survive in post-battle myths such as that of Pavlov's House, which still stands as a semi-preserved monument in Volgograd, as well as in the postwar Stalingrad novels of, among others, Konstantin Simonov and Vasily Grossman.[129]

Once victory at Stalingrad looked certain, the heady cocktail of individual sacrifice, epic battle, and doughty Russian military bravery – the "Stalingrad spirit," as it would become known – could be projected out of individual houses and onto action across the Eastern Front. Boris Gorbatov's "The Mountains and the People," translated in the December section of this book, is an example of how the "Stalingrad spirit" was applied across the front in late 1942.

In Gorbatov's text, the desire to fight their own Stalingrad drives troops in the Caucasus to complete their own improbable and explicitly "holy" *podvig*.

The writers at Stalingrad in this way completed a circuit from documentary observation into the lofty spaces of the epic and military history and back down toward the reader's own experience. Intertwining various temporal, literary, and spatial planes, journalists painted their protagonists as mythical heroes who travelled to the underworld to defy death and win victory for life, yet simultaneously suggested that Stalingrad was the pivot where human and sacred worlds and experiences met – and where Soviet soldiers and the Soviet nation underwent a symbolic death and resurrection.

THE READERS OF STALINGRAD:
INSTRUMENTALIZATION AND IDENTIFICATION

The Stalingrad works' documentary immediacy and wealth of literary allusions separate them from the bland propaganda of the 1930s and the early war months. Stalingrad's textual space was all-embracing, making way for state and individual, past, present, and future, and loss and triumphalism alike.[130] Authors, indeed, were not just "creating" that external narrative on behalf of the government; they were creating their own, inner worlds through writing, piecing together their own traumatic present even as they found ways to imagine a peaceful future. The frank, almost confessional material published from Stalingrad – especially the works here by Konstantin Simonov, Vasily Koroteev, and Evgeny Kriger – would have been almost unthinkable prior to Stalingrad. For the first time, Socialist Realist writers were showing that the present was salvational – that an epic, messianic turning point had occurred in the life of the Soviet nation – and that they, as authors, were already witnessing and experiencing Stalingrad as a moment of both trauma and salvation.

Indeed, for all the suffering of the battle, the state too showed moments of compassion at Stalingrad. In spite of popular myth about the battle, there was at Stalingrad no great spike in executions of Soviet troops, there was no deliberate abandonment of the population, and there were no roving NKVD battalions shooting their own men.[131] All the same, David Ortenberg and his colleagues were also creating a new justification for Stalin's rule. From November

1942 on, the leader was increasingly prominent as the supposed genius behind the resurrection at Stalingrad. I include among my translations an editorial from late November, "There'll Be a Celebration on Our Street Too," which reveals a sharp turning point in the Stalingrad narrative. This Sovinformbyuro-approved piece was published in every central paper and, almost out of the blue, accorded every ounce of credit for the *podvig* accomplished at Stalingrad not to the Russian people's fortitude and spirit but to Stalin alone.

During and after the war, the regime used the Stalingrad story – and the real sufferings of the citizens and soldiers of Stalingrad described within that story – to reinforce its hold on power. In spite of appearances of exploratory artistic freedom, the state "assumed the height of its massive mobilizing power" between 1941 and 1945.[132] It enforced rules, regulations, and military diktats across the Soviet Union in ways that were tighter than ever before. The creation and dissemination of the Stalingrad story in the newspapers was part of this great mobilization and therefore subject to strict limits that, while usually unwritten, manifested themselves in various ways.

The writer-soldiers rarely sought out civilians to interview at the front. Whether it was forbidden to do so or whether, as I suspect, they simply chose not to because they intuited Sovinformbyuro's and therefore their editors' expectations, is hard to tell. Whatever the case, civilians were, willingly or not, confined to a narrative of glorious self-sacrifice at Stalingrad. We will read stories of civilian suffering: of old men who are killed by Germans as they cross the lines; of children suffering from hunger and homelessness; of victims of rape; and of locals who lose their homes and work. But these figures are heroic only for the destruction wrought on their bodies. Their stories are left in outline form, and their narrative function is usually limited to enraging a soldier enough to complete a great *podvig*. Civilians' suffering is subjugated to a process of rewriting past missteps; their needless deaths are rewritten as essential sacrifices in order to achieve victory at Stalingrad. Aleksandr Shcherbakov's group was always eager to turn "ideals into facts":[133] just as in the tsarist era, reality and myth alike were always being reimagined to suit the ruler's needs and agendas. The Stalingrad story's great humanity, then, was only ever permitted when it served the government's needs. Through December 1942 and into January 1943, more and more invocations of Stalin's genius pulled the Stalingrad story ever closer into the leader's orbit and ever further away from the rank and file and the civilian population.

In spite of the realities of the state's instrumentalization of its citizens' sufferings and sacrifices both during and after Stalingrad, many Soviet readers strove to model themselves after the heroes of the battle. As the Stalingrad general Mikhail Shumilov would later recall, the Stalingrad stories left "an indelible mark in all of our lives."[134] That "indelible mark" was a narrative that Soviet writers and readers would use to shape and reshape their relationships to power, to their peers, and to their inner selves. Ilya Ehrenburg's work alone, boasted Minister of Foreign Affairs Vyacheslav Molotov to a visiting counterpart, was worth a division of troops.[135] The effect of the stories on morale was not transient. It penetrated the Soviet reader's psyche, creating structure, form, and connection out of the whirlwind of the war as tropes were eagerly absorbed and used to rewrite lives.

Shumilov's "indelible mark" had its roots in the voracious appetite for reading at the front and behind the lines. Viktor Nekrasov, the writer and Stalingrad veteran, remembered that "the signallers read more than anybody. I knew one who got through the whole of *War and Peace* in the battalion HQ right at the front, two hundred metres from the enemy. There he was, sat with a receiver pressed to his ear ... with his head buried in a book."[136] Nekrasov and his comrades pored over every newspaper "again and again until the pages were tattered." They read and reread every story by Ehrenburg, Grossman, and Simonov, whom they idolized.[137] Partisans on occupied territory reportedly exchanged guns and ammunition for copies of stories from Stalingrad, and soldiers bore clippings into battle like the Russians of old had wielded icons.[138] Vasily Grossman wrote to his father with some surprise that "*everyone* at the front reads" the newspaper: "Wherever I go," explained Grossman, "I see my work in foxholes and dugouts."[139] Behind the lines, the newspaper was a great comfort to families worried about their sons' and daughters' fates.[140] Good news, or the mention of a local town or a loved one, was especially well-received – and usually resulted in treasured cuttings being stashed away in tunic pockets and photo frames.[141] No wonder David Ortenberg was desperate to sate the public's appetite by filling his paper's pages with the latest works.[142]

Writers and readers of Soviet texts found reassurance in the miraculous reality of the victory at Stalingrad. Readers of the Stalingrad stories could become better Soviets in a better Soviet Union – and share vicariously in a nationally unifying event – by "experiencing" the process of becoming more ideal through fighting and achieving *podvigi* at Stalingrad. In recent years, scholars

Figure I.5 Soldiers reading at the front, June 1942.

like Jochen Hellbeck, Igal Halfin, and Stephen Kotkin have shown that many – if not most – Soviets willingly interrogated their private selves in the hopes of becoming better Soviet citizens.[143] Hellbeck's study of Soviet diaries in particular uncovered an inner world of ordinary citizens reading their lives against narratives of revolutionary turning points such as the 1917 Revolution and the Civil War, then conscientiously interrogating their own behaviours as they attempted to follow the examples of characters from Soviet stories.[144] Stalingrad was the latest event to be adopted in this way, and no event was more widely embraced than Stalingrad.

We can endlessly argue about the moral culpability of the Stalinist regime in failing to evacuate civilians from the battle in time, the extent of the NKVD's punitive frontline discipline, the military errors that sent thousands to their death, and the extent to which the Stalingrad narrative I present silences these tragedies and excludes women, people of colour, and other non-Russians.[145] However, Hellbeck's and Stephen Kotkin's work in particular suggests that throughout the Soviet period, coercion and fear alone do not sufficiently explain ordinary Soviets' engagement with the state's texts and textual forms – and therefore the power of Stalingrad as an enduring cultural symbol.

Rather, we must view the creation of and response to the Stalingrad narrative disseminated in 1942–43 as a means for authors and readers to engage in a process of self-(re)creation anchored in the language of the state. We cannot ignore the abundant evidence that many Soviets *did* willingly frame their own biographical experiences around those stories, drawing on both Soviet modes of reading and older traditions of Orthodox worship and Russian "sacrificial historicism" to do so. Indeed, as Stephen Kotkin notes, even in the troubled 1930s, the state and the ordinary people found that there was often more common ground than not.[146] The idea that Stalingrad was a great individual and national *podvig*, a transformational space for all, had great appeal for a traumatized nation.

For readers in the distant industrial factories of the Urals, on the Pacific line of defence at Kamchatka and Vladivostok, or at the front, the trove of stories printed in the newspapers functioned as a repository of collective experience and, therefore, a measure and model for selfhood. Making the vicarious textual journey across the Volga and into Stalingrad, readers could bring order to what was happening in the present, drawing on narratives to frame their own lives and engage in a shared conversation about the experience of the war – just as the writers at the front were doing, publicly, in the newspapers. As they went about this reading and writing process in the years following 1945, war survivors found that they had a "shared formative, myth-building experience [in] their collective identity."[147] The Soviet state was joined by peasant-soldiers, who saw the war as "an autobiographical point of reference and a point of departure" in widely propagating war myths.[148] The postwar creation and perpetuation of the Stalingrad narrative was a tool to rebuild selves and a society torn apart by fighting; readers and writers turned almost compulsively to the textual site of Stalingrad as a source for framing their own life narratives. Personal fates were linked to the history of the Battle of Stalingrad and to the act of writing Stalingrad so that the battle became a central event in many citizens' telling of their own biographies.

A slew of semi-private letters, diaries, and memoirs produced during and after Stalingrad show readers incorporating words, phrases, images, tropes, and plots into their own life narratives. While keeping a diary was officially forbidden at the front, the many Soviets who broke or bent the rules to keep journals often pictured their writings as the start of a future literary career.[149] Letters, in particular, often saw surprisingly frank exchanges between Soviet citizens and the state or its agents (for example, famous authors seen as close to power, such as Konstantin Simonov) as senders sought to navigate and establish discursive communities.[150] If the newspapers provide a means to trace how writers' and soldiers' stories became public, then letters and other personal writings reveal that public discourse was ushered back into the private sphere.

The process of narrative and semantic exchange between the public and private spheres began in the earliest days of the fighting at Stalingrad. Readers, just like writers, grasped for stock frames, forms, and frameworks to make sense of what seemed in the early fall like an impossible situation. Diaries were packed with material from the Stalingrad stories, and interviews with Stalingrad veterans at the time of the battle show them using quotations from the newspaper stories in everyday conversation. One soldier, for example, used language almost verbatim from the newspapers to describe the meeting of the Don and Stalingrad fronts after the November counterattack as "an unforgettable day," and described the German surrender on 2 February in terms that stressed its importance as a historical turning point: "You can consider 2:30pm a historical moment."[151]

Readers even reimagined language from newspapers to apply it to their own wartime situation. One Jewish soldier, from example, wrote from his station at Stalingrad to explain that "Hitler's bloody hands want to subjugate the Jews and, what is worse, to wipe them off the face of the earth ... I am fighting the enemy courageously and heroically as a member of the Jewish people."[152] Soviet readers were fully conversant with the newspaper narrative even as it was still being created. They followed its twists and turns vicariously, adopting and adapting them to order their own experiences. In the following chapters, I draw attention to the ways in which readers incorporated material from the newspapers into their own language in letters and biographical writing, focusing on texts by Leonid Kovalev, the fêted hero of a *podvig* at Stalingrad, Lidia Medvedeva, a tank lieutenant and eager reader, Pavel Mikhnov, a young Red Army private, Petr Borisov, an NKVD officer at Stalingrad, and Viktor Nekrasov.

This phenomenon did not dissipate when victory at Stalingrad was certain. Konstantin Simonov for years received floods of letters in which Soviet readers claimed that the author had in one story or another described the fate or heroic deed of a loved one. Simonov's stories seem to have given readers the language and form to express their innermost thoughts, allowing them to imagine their own experiences as the author had written his characters' stories. Some of Simonov's real-life protagonists even wrote to explain how his stories were "true" even though they could barely remember their own participation in the events described. Viktoriya Shchepetya, the real heroine of the story "Days and Nights," wrote to Simonov in the 1970s to praise the author for writing what was "true" and "close" to her own recollections.[153] Simonov, however, confessed to having imagined many of Shchepetya's words after losing a crucial notebook in the hustle and bustle of frontline work. Shchepetya, like many other Soviets, used war writing to literally create her own memories of the war.[154] Occasionally, Stalingrad veterans wrote to authors with complaints that they had not been personally acknowledged as the model for a particular character, even when a character had actually been imagined or formed from a composite of sources.[155] If Socialist Realism intended to create reality, then here it was successful: Soviet readers' real memories were being made and remade according to fictional stories.

The Stalingrad story had a powerful effect on readers, who suddenly "forgave Stalin everything." Ordinary men and women "became soldiers and believed the whole myth with a clear conscience."[156] The masses of Stalingrad semi-autobiographical novels and memoirs that arrived on the Soviet Union's bookshelves in the postwar decades are indebted to the wartime newspaper stories for the recurring image of Stalingrad as a new dawn, a new day, or a great turning point, and for the accompanying motifs of the slain city, the burning Volga, and the plucky and stoic everyman hero. Every one of the hundreds of postwar Stalingrad accounts I have read in the past decade of work on the topic relies on material drawn directly from the frontline work. Soviets used the Stalingrad stories to create memories, to imagine their own lives as heroic, and to align their biographical experiences with a shared, epic enterprise. Socialist Realism had leapt from the page and into quotidian reality; the epic of Stalingrad had found its way into the *byt* of postwar life.

In spite of this widespread enthusiasm, embrace of Stalingrad as the start of a new day was not universal. Stalin's capture of the Stalingrad story shattered the delicate literary equilibrium that had existed in 1942–43. In the last section of this volume, I include two translated works from the 1950s and 1960s by Vasily Koroteev and Viktor Nekrasov, a sapper at Stalingrad who would go on to pen a string of popular Stalingrad novellas and stories. These final works show how the two veterans attempted – Koroteev successfully, Nekrasov not – to use the textual memories of Stalingrad to parse their wartime and postwar experiences. In Nekrasov's story, "An Incident on the Mamaev Kurgan," the veteran adopts – or at least attempts to adopt – a Socialist Realist method, seeking evidence of heroic utopianism in the present. Yet where short pieces of quickfire writing had organized and structured the bleak chaos of 1942, Nekrasov's story collapses in on itself as the narrator is buried under successive and contradictory temporal and narrative layers. The imperfect present and the utopian epic remain at loggerheads. Nekrasov's narrator simply sinks ever deeper into psychological and temporal inconsistency.

Yet as Koroteev's story shows, such irresolvable psychological ruptures were exceedingly rare. His "Ten Years On" mirrors Nekrasov's story with its battle-field tour form but presents a more typical version of the Soviet Stalingrad story in which the city's resurrection has created a miraculous personal and national present. The work is emblematic of what seem like typical Soviet stories – tales of miners and builders at war, of improbable troops, of jolly comrades racing to meet death – that are actually deeply rooted in Soviet culture, a pre-Soviet national-religious culture, and personal experiences of the war. The vast majority of Soviets, like Koroteev, seem to have absorbed the Stalingrad story into their own biographical and lexical imaginations.

Western observers could not comprehend that writers and readers embraced the Stalingrad stories in this way.[157] Accusations that Soviet wartime writing was "doggerel," "mostly bad," or even "miserably laboured" were made by those with no understanding of the nature of psychic numbing, of the difficulties of negating the Wehrmacht's phenomenological and epistemological destruction, or of the extraordinary impact the Stalingrad story had on readers as the fate of the Soviet Union hung in the balance.[158] Likewise, historians' claims that the Soviet war effort was propped up by unwilling conscripts' fears of machine-gun-wielding secret police and political commissars have taken no account of the ways in which language, power, and the public existed in an albeit fragile symbiosis at and around Stalingrad.[159] While the "rules" of the language might have come from the centre of power, which always held the power of publication and censorship, Soviet people "appropriated [those rules] and conceptualized the world and their lives" in the language of official discourse.[160] The act of rereading or rewriting Stalingrad as miraculous resurrection is an act of becoming, an act that begins with external threat and internal discord and ends in a cadential moment of self-transformation.

A NOTE ON ORGANIZATION AND SELECTION

In the following chapters, you can follow how the story of sacrifice and resurrection was forged at the front as the nation held its breath and hoped for a miracle. I have aimed to create an immersive sense of what it felt like to read about Stalingrad day-by-day in 1942–43. The selection of texts, and the accompanying historical and literary commentaries, began with my reading every issue of every Soviet "central" paper from July 1942 to April 1943.[161] The approach is inspired particularly by the historian Wayne Dowler's work in *Russia in 1913*. Dowler read every issue of a selection of newspapers from his period of study in order to "see what history had piled up" over time, and to "experience ... the rhythms and dislocations of the daily news as Russians experienced them."[162] Then, he explains, he aimed to conjoin these two phenomena – the experience of history and the experience of the present through the newspaper medium – within a single work. While my compilation of historical commentary and translation, like Dowler's, conveys something of the contemporary feel of the papers, it presents only one version – in this case, a deeply monumental and state-approved version – of the Stalingrad story.[163]

In spite of that limitation, the method allowed me to make substantial discoveries: first, the closeness of every subsequent Stalingrad text to these frontline works is so striking that it is shocking it has never before been explored; second, the fact that even where texts were republished, they only ever reappeared with substantial editing; third, scholars of Vasily Grossman have incorrectly identified which of the author's stories were published during the battle and which were written afterwards – a fact that led me to the discovery of the apparently lost "On the Volga" and "In Stalin's City," both of which appear here.

Given the temporal significance of Stalingrad as a spiritual turning point, I have organized the five chapters chronologically. Each chapter includes a brief historical and literary commentary and then presents in translation a representative sample of stories key to the development of Stalingrad's main literary tropes. The commentaries account for how writers spent their time at Stalingrad and how they drew on historical and literary sources, eyewitness interviews, and their own fighting experiences to work up their stories. Simultaneously, I use letters and diaries to explore how readers at home and at the front absorbed the words, phrases, and ideas they were reading in the newspapers to frame and make sense of their own experiences in this most horrific of wars. I have endeavoured to reveal how writers drew on one another's material and responded to their own traumatic experiences at the front, how readers found themselves reflected in this widely disseminated material, and how a broad hierarchy of Soviet social classes wrote or spoke through the Stalingrad story.

My chronology is based around the timeline laid out during the battle in the newspapers. I home in on the development of key motifs and dates that were most closely associated with the notion of Stalingrad as a messianic turning point. Russian historians and cultural producers today broadly split the battle into two: a "defensive stage" leading up to 19 November, and an "offensive stage" that ended with the German surrender on 2 February 1943.[164] My timeline broadly follows this periodization, which had its inception in 1942, when

19 November was first marked out as the great "turning point": Chapter 1 (August–September) presents the first shadows of the approaching battle, a number of tales of individual *podvigi*, and the nascence of the idea of Stalingrad both as a dead city and as a blank canvas for creation of the self; Chapter 2 (October–November) is dominated by tales of resolute defence and a turn to sheer faith in the coming victory; Chapter 3 (November–December) shows how past suffering was rewritten into necessary sacrifice as part of Stalin's purportedly brilliant plan to trap the enemy at Stalingrad; Chapter 4 (January–February) shows the excitement of Stalingrad spilling over into visions of lives anew and naked revanchism across the front. In the final chapter, I show how writers and readers perpetually revisited Stalingrad in text and in person in the postwar years as they strove to use the narrative of the city produced at the front to imagine themselves as integrated Soviet subjects – even if that sometimes led to ruptures as the promise of Stalingrad turned to dust.

At times, my periodization differs from the timeline that is widespread today. For example, my introductory chapter's stories contain no details of the bombing raid of 23 August that is commonly acknowledged in Russia and abroad as the start of the battle, but which was not mentioned in the Soviet newspapers until October 1942 (one of many examples of undesirable news and civilian deaths being left out of official material I reproduce). Contrarily, the anniversary of the October Revolution in November was linked to Stalingrad in 1942, and therefore crops up in Grossman and Koroteev's "In Stalin's City" in my second chapter. The date has all but disappeared from Stalingrad memory today. Likewise, 1 January 1943, the "new day" Grossman describes in the story of that name in this volume and that Ehrenburg names as the "verge" of victory, was hailed as a moment of beginning during the battle but has now lost its lustre in comparison to 19 November, the date of the counterattack.

I have had to make tough decisions about which stories to include and exclude. Every Soviet newspaper was packed with almost nothing but Stalingrad from the beginning of September 1942 until the middle of February 1943. Each published at least one or two works of fiction almost every day for the six months of the battle, so a literary corpus of some eight hundred texts awaits exploration. My approach was to work backwards from the major tropes and motifs – those of Stalingrad as resurrection, of the Volga on fire, of the house defence – that survive today, tracing their origins to stories produced at the front. To those I added works that reproduce and recontextualize these morsels of narrative. As the volume continues, the selected stories uncover how the myth of Stalingrad grew from individual *podvigi* into a vast, all-national myth whose power spread into the past, the future, across the entire Eastern Front (here, see the stories by Vsevolod Ivanov and Boris Gorbatov), and into the future (the final stories, by Vasily Koroteev and Viktor Nekrasov).

I have weighted my selection toward Vasily Grossman and Konstantin Simonov, who were the most influential figures at Akhtuba and have achieved some international renown, and toward those who were famous in the Soviet Union but neglected abroad (Ilya Ehrenburg, Boris Polevoy, Vsevolod Ivanov). I have also elected to include an array of stories that reveal how ordinary soldiers like Anatoly Nedzelsky took part in the writing effort and how lesser-known and now forgotten men like Vasily Koroteev and Evgeny Kriger were synonymous with the battle at the time. The single anonymous editorial completes the picture of an effort involving every rung of Soviet society.

Many more Stalingrad stories deserve to be read in translation. A book could be filled with Grossman's twelve Stalingrad stories alone. A handful of these have been translated, but readers should be aware that nobody has translated any original texts as they appeared in the newspapers. Likewise, although Russian speakers will find it easy to source many supposedly authentic materials online, most websites feature stories that were substantially rewritten in the postwar years. I have not included any stories that have already been translated, instead selecting from Grossman's oeuvre the works that best show his interactions and collaborations with other writers at the front. By drawing on this work, I hope to correct the widespread but mistaken view that Grossman's approach to war writing at Stalingrad was unique, that Grossman alone wrote from the frontline, and that Grossman was a "lone wolf" desperate to cast off the shackles of Soviet officialdom during the war.

By placing these works side-by-side, I reveal the development of a semantic and literary structure for the depiction of Stalingrad in postwar art – in the late Stalinist era, the Thaw, and the Brezhnev-era stagnation, and beyond. The final pair of works show with particular clarity how the narrative of Stalingrad as resurrection, and the constellation of phrases and motifs developed in 1942–43, were sites of exchange between public and private, fact and fiction, present and epic, and hope and despair in the postwar years. They reveal, furthermore, a bifurcation in memory of Stalingrad as the promise of utopia and the memory of real *podvigi* gave way to the government's monumental narrative of the battle; in this sense, they stand in for wider divisions in war memory in the postwar years.

In sum, the reader of *Stalingrad Lives* will have a microcosmic sense of the patchwork epic that readers experienced as Stalingrad unfolded and the ways in which a *podvig* that seemed to make fairy tales come true emerged. The picture is inevitably incomplete, but it provides material for an understanding of the subjective experience of history that has been lacking in work on Stalingrad. Natalya Narochnitskaya describes her 2013 Russian-language compilation of English and American journalists' work about Stalingrad as resembling "impressionists' canvases: standing close, you see only separate daubs of paint, but further away you perceive the mass of paint turning into an actual image."[165] My approach is similarly impressionistic: each individual story's significance is comprehensible only in the collective; the mass of the gathered work creates a holistic meaning absent in isolation.

1

23 AUGUST–30 SEPTEMBER
Idyll and Annihilation

In late August 1942, Stalingrad's residents were trying to cope with a blisteringly hot and dry summer. They wandered the promenades and gardens of the city and bathed in the Volga's waters to keep cool. Many stayed put, unaware of the gathering storm, even as the Germans approached. On 23 August, the enemy struck with a gargantuan air raid. More than one thousand German bombers flew in for hours on end.[1] By nightfall, the Luftwaffe had destroyed most of Stalingrad's housing. Forty thousand Soviets had been killed by explosions, shrapnel, and fires that tore through the hot summer streets:[2]

> People were writhing around on the ground, bleeding heavily or already burned black. Others suffocated from smoke trying to escape the fire in sewers. Those who managed to get out – carrying children, throwing off smouldering clothes until they were half-naked – were running toward yet more fires on the Volga. Everything there was on fire too. The quays, steamers, warehouses, and barges were all in flames.[3]

The survivors of this bombardment took refuge in barns, huts, and tents, on the steppe outside the city and in caves and basements dotted along the banks of the Volga. Stalingrad, engulfed in an inferno, looked certain to fall.

The Soviet command had done little to prevent this civilian tragedy. Broad evacuation of Stalingrad's residents was not authorized until mid-August, and the official order to remove the entire population to safety was only issued the day after the 23 August bombing.[4] Military preparation relied on hope as much as planning. On 28 July, Stalin's Order No. 227 insisted that there could be "no step backward." Saving Stalingrad was to be a last-ditch effort to save

Figure 1.1 Smoke rises over a destroyed airfield in Stalingrad, 26 August 1942.

the nation. Stalin soon resorted to begging his allies for support;[5] the troops defending the city from the German advance found themselves in disarray in August.[6] Not a word of these civilian and military disasters was to be found in the Soviet newspapers of August 1942.

Nevertheless, David Ortenberg and his colleagues knew how to read the signs when, by early August, "not a single report from [their] special corre-spondents" failed to mention "the advance on Stalingrad and the Caucasus."[7] The speed of the German advance through August, though, left even the editor and his writers scrambling to respond. Ortenberg received urgent instructions to despatch writers to Stalingrad in the third week of August. He sent his top men to the Volga post-haste.

The dozen writers who streamed into Stalingrad would discover exactly how bad the situation was only after the catastrophe of 23 August had already struck. Vasily Grossman was first into the fray. The writer was one of many who had a sense of foreboding: four days before his departure for Stalingrad, he wrote to his father that he had an "unusual feeling" about events in Russia's south.[8] Before Grossman even arrived in Stalingrad, Ortenberg had charged his writer with producing a morale-boosting call to arms to defend Stalingrad and the Volga. Grossman's response was the short story "On the Volga," the first in this volume. Published on 21 August 1942, just two days before the German bom-bardment, "On the Volga" marked the start of the Battle of Stalingrad in the public consciousness.

On the way to the front, Grossman had stopped off at a handful of villages to make observations about life during the war. His notebook records visions of bucolic life and a languorous Indian summer. Grossman was struck by the war's intrusion into a timeless pastorale: "There are vehicles loaded with bombs on the barge. Planes crack out machine gun rounds overhead. But the Volga is unhurried, carefree. Little boys are casting rods off the fire-breathing barge."[9] His first Stalingrad story, "On the Volga," dovetails nineteenth-century depic-tions of Russian village life – a world of "maiden" rivers, verdant meadows, dense forests, and lush produce – with Sovinformbyuro's euphemistic refer-ences to "fierce fighting" and the author's own reaction to the destruction of wartime. War annihilates Grossman's bucolic scene: village houses have be-come "white skulls"; memories of lively village life are obliterated by the Ger-man enemy's presence. "On the Volga" builds toward a climactic call to arms in defence of idyll: "The fate of the nation is in our hands. We must resist. We must be victorious!" David Ortenberg was delighted to receive a call to arms that so seamlessly synthesized Russian, patriotic, and personal material. He rushed the text into the newspaper alongside photographs of and oaths made by the Red Army division featured in Grossman's story.

Grossman arrived in Stalingrad just after "On the Volga" appeared in *Krasnaya Zvezda*. First to greet Grossman was the young journalist Vasily Koroteev. Grossman was keen to get close to the action as quickly as possible, so he and Koroteev made the Volga crossing on a wooden raft. Grossman was so terrified by the prospect of the trip that he wrote to David Ortenberg asking that his family receive aid in the event of his death.[10] The author was only further shocked by what he saw: a "burned out, dead city" of destroyed schools, homes, educational institutes, and hospitals.[11] He could barely fathom the scale of the destruction, compulsively reiterating words in his notebook: "Stalingrad is burning. Stalingrad is burning." The city, Grossman wrote, had "died"; Stalingrad had "the face of a man dead from a serious illness and now at eternal rest. More and more bombing of a city that's already dead."[12] Even the morbid undertones of "On the Volga" could hardly anticipate this visceral reaction, which already lays out the idea of Stalingrad as a sacrificial body for the nation.

By early September, the frontline had swept into the city of Stalingrad. Fighting raged through houses, cellars, gardens, and parks. Reinforcements arrived at incomplete defensive lines with fragmentary intelligence and without the necessary equipment. Soldiers barely knew where the Germans were, let alone how to defend themselves. Confusion reigned in the Moscow editorial offices too. David Ortenberg, ordinarily a regular visitor to the Soviet military command in the Kremlin, was suddenly forbidden to meet Stalin. The editor could merely speculate that the situation at Stalingrad had "deteriorated" to such an extent that the leadership was panicking.[13] How could writers find any hints of heroism, let alone great *podvigi* or messianic turning points, in this chaos?

As the city's fate hung by a thread, mention of almost anything but Stalingrad disappeared from the newspapers. The time was right for one of Ilya Ehrenburg's invectives. "Stalingrad," the second work translated in this volume, is constructed around an interplay between the writer's own anger and official thematicism. Note in particular Ehrenburg's use of letters, diaries, and quotations from German troops. Ehrenburg had personally requested Aleksandr Shcherbakov's permission to add such materials unedited to his repertoire some months earlier. They provide a level of direct engagement with a human enemy lacking from almost any other author's Stalingrad works.[14]

After submitting his draft of "Stalingrad," Ehrenburg bumped into David Ortenberg in a corridor at the editorial office on Malaya Dmitrovka. Ortenberg prompted him to include reference to the *podvig* of the "Thirty-Three," which had recently cropped up in Sovinformbyuro's communiqués.[15] According to the story, a group of thirty-three Soviets had defended a small hill on the outskirts of Stalingrad against an overwhelming German force, destroying two dozen German tanks and 150 enemy soldiers without losing a single man. Ehrenburg, Ortenberg remembers, was delighted with the suggestion that he write about the Thirty-Three. Scurrying off to his desk, he had made the requested changes within minutes.

"Stalingrad" was even a hit with the story's real protagonists, who praised the work's "truthfulness."[16] Leonid Kovalev, a native of Vladivostok and one of the Thirty-Three, wrote to his wife that "a whole bunch of writers keep comin' to see us, and they write about our exploits against the fascist bastards in the papers, so, Lidochka my love, I'm gonna fight even harder now."[17] Kovalev then used language he must have read in the papers to tell his father that "your son is defending the City of Stalin."[18] Kovalev was evidently bursting with pride: "I'm gonna send you two copies of the paper, one for Papa too … The writers keep visiting and their photographers are taking our pictures all the time." In turn, thanks to Ehrenburg's story, Kovalev found himself fêted in letters from newspaper readers for months afterwards.[19] Writers, their subjects, and their readers all over the country, were – quite literally – on the same page. Reactions to "The Russian Anthaeus," the other early fall Ehrenburg story included here, were similar, even though its themes are drawn from a prewar Stalin speech that references a classical rather than wartime legend.[20] Bringing readers, writers, and the Kremlin into the same textual space was a powerful means to instil patriotism as Stalingrad's fate hung in balance.

At the front, Vasily Koroteev began to take increasing risks in the hunt for stories, throwing himself into gun battles and taking notes, under heavy fire, "mere metres away from the enemy."[21] "At Stalingrad," which is translated into English for the first time here, shows the author trying to frame a chaos of staccato sentences – the story's central battle scene rattles by in under two hundred fifty words – and unexpected attacks by drawing on allusions to the Soviet legend of Tsaritsyn, to Russian epic war poetry, and to Grossman's un-

Figure 1.2 Leonid Kovalev poses in uniform after the war.

published image of the "dead" city, which the two men must have discussed at Akhtuba or the front. Koroteev, the native Stalingrader, is in this quickfire text clinging to whatever ordering tropes he could to cope with the chaos of the front.

Meanwhile, David Ortenberg, who now believed that Stalingrad was the "centre of the war's events," had made the decision that, given the lack of direction coming from the befuddled Sovinformbyuro, a personal trip to Stalingrad would help muster and direct his writers. In the second week of September 1942, Ortenberg set off for Stalingrad, with his favourite correspondent,

Konstantin Simonov, in tow. In the coming weeks, Simonov would publish four stories – "A Soldier's Glory," "Days and Nights," "Battle on the Outskirts," and "U-2" – all of which appear in English translation for the first time here. Simonov's quartet of stories established a series of lasting images and tropes of Stalingrad as a heroic national turning point. Simultaneously, the author imbues his texts with echoes of his own, inner conflict between patriotic enthusiasm and increasing alarm at the horrendous events in Stalingrad.

Ortenberg and Simonov landed late on 8 September at Elton, a farming settlement one hundred miles east of Stalingrad on the border with present-day Kazakhstan. The pair were driven across the arid late-summer steppe at full tilt to Akhtuba, where they were met with an enthusiastic welcome. The two new arrivals knew that the Soviets' military and humanitarian situation had grown exponentially worse in the ten days since Vasily Grossman had been so shaken by his first trip across the Volga, but they had little idea of what they were about to witness.

Simonov and Ortenberg set to work immediately, following in Grossman's footsteps directly across the Volga and into Stalingrad proper. Just before crossing the river, they sought out Semen Shkolenko, a scout from the industrial city of Novoshakhtinsk on the Ukrainian–Russian border. Shkolenko would become the hero of Simonov's first Stalingrad piece, "A Soldier's Glory." Rumours of Shkolenko's feat had already made their way along the grapevine to Ortenberg.[22] Simonov, to his editor's chagrin, spent more than an hour interviewing the scout.[23] Nevertheless, the author cabled a story to Moscow mere hours later: "It just wrote itself," he joked to an astonished Ortenberg.[24]

"A Soldier's Glory" explains how Shkolenko had recently captured a German informer and saved a group of captured Soviets – just the sort of thing one might have expected from a man who had jumped at the chance to enlist on the second day of the war. Filled with details of life at the front and of Shkolenko's inner narrative, the sketch is a typical example of Simonov's skill at drawing together *byt* and a future-oriented temporality within a classic *podvig* narrative: Shkolenko's childhood is exposited as if this were an Orthodox hagiography; his slow, cautious approach to fighting links him with Socialist Realist positive heroes; his constant choosing of paths in a journey behind the lines resembles a fairy tale; and he is drawn into the world of the Russian national epic through comparisons to the Battle of Borodino.[25] Shkolenko's *pod-*

Figure 1.3 Vasily Koroteev (L), Konstantin Simonov, and David Ortenberg in Stalingrad, September 1942.

vig is thus expressed in Soviet-Russian saintly terms, which offered the reader a bridge from despair to hope. For all that Grossman and Koroteev were struggling with images of death, the myth of saintly Stalingrad was already beginning to take shape. Invincibility and immortality conjured up on the page, however, could not overcome real danger at the front: Semen Shkolenko was killed in July 1943 in fighting near the city of Kursk.

When Simonov was finished with Shkolenko, Vasily Koroteev and the visitors made their crossing at Lebyazhya Polyana, just northeast of Akhtuba.[26] The Volga was a sea of broken, burned, and battered bodies. Young men and women screamed out for help while shrapnel and bombs tore into their would-be rescuers. Simonov and Ortenberg were overcome: "They were bombing the length of the Volga's bank. The ground was constantly shaking from blasts big and small. Everything was jumbled up: ruined homes, destroyed huts, twisted rails, smashed iron barrels, wooden boards, bits of furniture, household detritus ..."[27] Only ruins remained of Stalin's city. Thirty years later, Simonov could still clearly picture his friend Koroteev on the crossing:

Riven with suffering, [Koroteev's face] bore the expression of someone who had watched their mother and father killed right in front of them ... Such an anxious, fearful face. He found it impossibly difficult to look at the city from the opposite bank and to see what had happened to it. The smoke, the ruins, the detritus. And even now it's tough for me to look at [his photograph]; a man who'd known the city when it was intact, and who had spent his entire life there.[28]

Koroteev's postwar memoirs deal with this scene in a brief interlude that through its sheer starkness reveals much about the traumatic aporia created by Stalingrad: "The steamer approaches the battered pumping-station on the right bank. The hulls of downed boats stick out of the water. Hundreds of civilians – women, children, old folk – are huddled together on the quay. Their faces are exhausted, tortured from lack of sleep. Their eyes are full of despair, woe, and terror."[29] The experience of physical destruction and the sight of the civilian population's suffering on the river crossing would run through Koroteev's and Simonov's depictions of Stalingrad for decades to come.

The visitors hurried off to meet the military commander Andrey Yeremenko and the then commissar Nikita Khrushchev at a command post dug into the Volga's banks.[30] While the commanders had made an effort to transform their headquarters into something resembling a home – Koroteev remembered "a rug spread over the wooden floor, a little writing desk in the corner ... and a bed made with a grey canvas blanket"[31] – even the most well-appointed bunker in Stalingrad was no place for rest: "Beams hung overhead willy-nilly; the pressure of the earth was making the walls start to cave in." The writers spent an uncomfortable night in the makeshift bunker. Simonov could not sleep. Troubled by his encounter with Khrushchev, who "was living with the weight of a great tragedy on his shoulders," and alarmed by "reports flooding in from every one of our positions," even the experienced *frontovik* was filled with dread.[32] The following day, Ortenberg and Simonov returned to Akhtuba, where they collated elements of Sovinformbyuro communiqués into an anonymous editorial that would appear in *Krasnaya Zvezda* two days later.[33]

On 10 September, Ortenberg left his travel companion to rest for a few hours in a bunker in Yamy, a hamlet just to the southwest of Akhtuba. Simonov seized the chance to slip away in search of another story to the northern outskirts of the city, where fierce fighting was taking place around the Stalingrad Tractor Factory.[34] Simonov's devil-may-care attitude on the journey to the Tractor Factory impressed even his seasoned journalist colleague Leonid Vysokoostrovsky:

> He and I had to cross a ten-metre expanse that the enemy had well covered. We would have to worm our way across slowly or make a dash for it. We'd already watched four other men give it a go: one man was killed, another was badly wounded. I said we should try going on our hands and knees, that it would be much safer. Konstantin Mikhailovich just said, "Not a chance. We'll run across. Did you stop to consider what the troops we're visiting will think?" I broke out in a cold sweat, but there was nothing for it.[35]

When they finally arrived at the Tractor Factory, the two writers walked into a firefight. Simonov, who wanted to observe the advancing Germans in action, refused to take cover. He seized a machine gun and opened fire on the Messerschmitts strafing the Soviet positions.[36] When the Germans had finally been repelled, the writer managed to interview Senior Lieutenant Vadim Tkalenko. Tkalenko, a Donetsk native, had enlisted in the army in 1938. By now, he was a rising star of his regiment and a recent recipient of the prestigious Order of the Red Banner.[37]

Tkalenko would become the hero of "The Battle on the Outskirts," in which we follow the protagonist's education from raw scout to hardened fighter and astute commander. The sketch is typical of Simonov's conversational style, which here leads us toward a frank discussion of the difficult fate of the nation's youth: Simonov was a talented interviewer who easily convinced men like Tkalenko to share their innermost thoughts.[38] Simonov combines the colloquial, confessional interview material recorded in his notebooks with language typical of a *podvig*.

However, where "A Soldier's Glory" finds some light in the gloom, "Battle on the Outskirts" is unremittingly, almost unprecedentedly, bleak. Tkalenko's *podvig* brings him no inner peace. The hero is internally tormented and physically aged by his experiences at the front: he has the "eyes of a man who's lived ten years and ten lives in a single year at war." The "merciless ... grief" of a nation is manifested in the protagonist's elevation – or, perhaps, descent – into the ideal Soviet soldier. Tkalenko's summary execution of a fleeing soldier invites the reader to read military discipline in and of itself as a form of *podvig* in which Tkalenko masters his own regret for the greater Soviet good: "This was a difficult moment for Tkalenko. He had just killed a man who, had he not proved to be a coward, ought to have been killing Germans himself." Tkalenko finds himself, like Simonov, engaged in a constant internal struggle to overcome personal and social tragedy. In these early days of the battle, it almost feels that the struggle at Stalingrad might be lost. Blithely positive 1930s-style Socialist Realism this is not.

The next day, Simonov and Ortenberg visited the Mamaev Kurgan, the strategically important hill in central Stalingrad. The heaviest fighting at the *kurgan* was still to come, but from an observation post on the hill's top, the two colleagues watched a pitched battle: "The battle was up close; the Germans were on our left and right flank ... When it got dark we could see the zigzagging line, [lit up by] tracers, shell bursts, and rockets going up. It was all criss-crosses ... The whole time, we were being heavily bombed." Worse than this disjunct hellscape was the scale of human loss: "When we finally left the observation post, coming back in the darkness, we could see the results of the bombing. Craters everywhere. Masses of dead bodies. Masses. The ground was literally blanketed in corpses."[39] This traumatic experience would stay with the author for years, cropping up in various forms time and again in Simonov's postwar Stalingrad work. At Stalingrad, however, Simonov was not deterred. He chomped at the bit to get to "the smoking city blocks and the line of fire ... He wanted to go further and further, until there was nowhere to go."[40] Ortenberg and Simonov had been treated to a taste of the frenzied and unthinkably perilous fighting that would characterize the coming months at Stalingrad.

In the following days, Simonov and Ortenberg braved the Volga crossing several more times.[41] Finally, on the evening of 13 September, Ortenberg gathered all the frontline journalists at Yamy and instructed Simonov to produce a summative piece:

Produce a panorama of the Battle of Stalingrad. Describe everything we've heard and seen with our own eyes without any embellishments. Write about the ruins of Stalingrad, about people's suffering, and about the hatred that is keeping us from sleeping and from breathing. Most importantly, write about the Stalingraders – the soldiers and the citizens who do not despair, who do not even think of surrendering their city, and who are selflessly holding steady to their last drop of blood and their last breath.[42]

Simonov took to the task with relish, staying up all night to write "Days and Nights." The story, in which Simonov tours the sites and sounds of Stalingrad, was finished the following morning. It proved one of the most influential pieces in the Stalingrad canon.

Vexed by the lack of female heroes in war stories, Simonov focuses on Viktoriya Shchepetya, a twenty-year-old nurse he had met on the first crossing into Stalingrad.[43] Simonov's sketch courses with Shchepetya's determination. Shchepetya's fictional proxy is desperate to return to the front after being nearly killed. The character's brush with death – a mirror of Stalingrad's own "death" – only emboldens her as she repeatedly crosses the Volga, each time being symbolically killed and reborn. Shchepetya's *podvig* is defined not by a glorious clash with the enemy in battle but by the mere willingness to go into battle across the Volga at all. To enter Stalingrad was, in and of itself, to transform oneself into a heroic figure.

The story's conclusion reflects its author's own brush with the horror of Stalingrad. The text bristles not with state-mandated platitudes but with the author's attempts to work through his own trauma: "At times like this, all the things you've seen in these last days and nights – the enraged and exhausted faces and the sleep-deprived and angry eyes of our troops – come to you all at once." Closing the story on an image of a drowned woman, "her face … disfigured … her torment … unimaginable," draws the writer and the reader closer to the human plight of Stalingrad's civilians. Simonov barely seems capable of bringing order to the tragic mess. As dawn breaks, we are told, the fighting in Stalingrad begins all over again, as if the battle might never end. Simonov was preparing the reader for a long siege that would make unprecedented demands on the individual and national psyche.

"Days and Nights" was an instant success. Vasily Koroteev wrote of the story's extraordinary effect on him to a friend, describing the work as "the apogee of Soviet war writing. Its greatest merit is its truthfulness. Simonov saw everything with his own eyes and heard everything with his own ears. He experienced absolutely everything himself."[44] In just a few days, Simonov had produced a trio of remarkable stories that would shape the Stalingrad story for decades (Simonov's fourth Stalingrad story, "U-2," was not written until the following month). For months afterward, Simonov received a flood of adulatory mail from ordinary readers, who praised him for the simplicity and empathy of his Stalingrad works.

✳ ✳ ✳

As September wore on, the Soviets' situation grew more precarious. Nine-tenths of Stalingrad was in German hands by the end of the month. The death toll was enormous: on the last day of September alone, 4,000 Soviets were killed, 10,000 were wounded, and another 900 went missing. The messages in the papers became desperate: "Turn every street into an impassable barrier and every house into a bastion" in a "sea of fire"; add to the "sea of [German] black blood" and to the "mountains of German corpses."[45] Writers began to ask how the Soviet defences had not disintegrated at Stalingrad as they had collapsed time and again in the preceding months.

To answer that question, Vasily Grossman ventured onto the open steppe to interview a group of young soldiers. "In the Gully on the Steppe," the last story in this section, was the result. By moving the action outside of the city of Stalingrad and onto the empty *prostor* – the flat expanse that rolls thousands of kilometres across Russia – Grossman strips away the distractions in the landscape of Stalingrad and the Volga to explore the psyche of the young gunners. Turning to *War and Peace* for inspiration, Grossman suggests that soldierly intuition and camaraderie were more important than grand strategy and leadership for keeping the Germans at bay. His protagonists' first battle would not at all have been out of place in Tolstoy's work. It is a clash of unseen enemies, dust, and blinding sun, and victory stems from "big toothy grins," "joking," and "laughter" – not from Soviet leadership, Party discipline, or military *nous*. These historical-literary comparisons could explain how, as Russians had in the past, the Red Army was now surviving a battle of untold ferocity and steadfastness.

By late September, however, literature was one of the few weapons the Soviet defenders had left to rally their hopes for victory. Observe the turn in severity between "Days and Nights" and "In the Gully on the Steppe": Simonov's heroine is tortured as she undergoes repeated deaths by crossing the Volga, yet she becomes ever more emboldened; Grossman's protagonist, Zholdubaev, is killed for good and buried in an almost unremarkable grave on the steppe. The significance of the fight at Stalingrad was, finally, crystal clear. The poet Vera Inber ended the month's run of *Pravda* by throwing down the gauntlet in a short verse. Stalingrad, no matter the cost and the grim outlook, simply had to be "the beginning of the end for the Germans."[46]

Vasily Grossman – On the Volga
21 August 1942, *Krasnaya Zvezda*

The front line runs through forests, along the steep banks of a river, and past lakes, rye fields, and flowering meadows. By night the sky is filled by fire. Red and white rockets soar into the sky from the German lines. One wave barely has time to burn out before another static flicker hangs over the dark earth. "Those dogs must be afraid of the dark," says a sentry, before asking quietly, "How are things back in Moscow? Almost everyone in our division is from Moscow."

The Moscow Volunteer Division has been fighting the Germans since last winter. The division's first battlefield victory came in February. One of its regiments went into battle for the charmingly named village of Vasilki.[47] The troops stormed the German line in a heavy snowstorm. The battle lasted eight hours, but the division got the Germans out of Vasilki. The next day, they drove the Germans from another two villages, and thus were the German defences broken. Much blood was spilled in the towns of Vasilki, Bystrylevo, Buznepovo, Podsosenki, Zhaganovo, Rostovo.

Replacements – workers from Stalingrad, fishermen from Astrakhan, and Tartars from Kazan – soon joined the Muscovites. It was by sheer co-incidence that all the replacements happened to come from along the Volga. The famous sniper Yusup Sabirov was amongst their number. He had lived where the Volga was at its widest and most powerful, at the point it slips past Kazan and the mouth of the Kama River and just begins to sense the far-off expanse of the Caspian Sea. Many of our soldiers, commissars, and commanders have family links to the Volga.

A divisional rally was called for six in the evening. We went to the regimental headquarters two hours before the rally was due to begin. Driving along the road you see the upper reaches of the Volga: supple, slender, and nimble like a maid; bound over by white bridges built from fresh pines oozing with sap. The river dashes through hills grown over with young blue firs. The grass is particularly thick thanks to the summer's heavy rain. The supple Volga sparkles in the sunshine. The young, maiden beauty weaves through the masses of cornflowers, bluebells, clover, and tender flax that run rampant in the fields and meadows around.

The forests are lush with blueberries and blackberries. The raspberry bushes are so red with juicy fruit that their leafy greenery is lost behind a bright saffian haze. The dark pine forest is packed with red and white mushrooms. At dawn, the young birds fill the forest with the noise of an enthralling concert. The rolling land of forests and lakes where the Volga begins is more beautiful than ever before this summer.

Yet this land is sad as never before. The heavy heel of war has trampled this beautiful land. The Germans were here. The famous, charming towns of Russia's glorious past have been turned into ruins. The blue sky peeks through the windows and roofs of burned out brick houses, which now resemble enormous white skulls washed clean by the rains. In the villages, thick grass has grown up around fences and wells. No more do mothers and daughters go to fetch water, and no more do old ladies gossip by the wells. The paths and tracks village lads would run down to catch roach and perch are overgrown. Grass has sprung up all over gardens and allotments. Great black char stains from fires mark the places where our peasants' simple, spacious huts – their pride and joy – used to stand.

As you drive along the road, you might suddenly see a pale outline amongst the wild grass: the lush, red flower of a dahlia. You might suddenly realize that there used to be a village here. Women tell terrible, tragic tales of the Germans' three-month reign over the Volga's left bank.

✳ ✳ ✳

The regimental commissar Nakhabin was telling us about his troops. Moscow had sent good, honest people – metal and textile workers, and coach and streetcar drivers – to join the division. There were also many – teachers, scientists, and artists – from among the intelligentsia.

A cook brought some lunch into the bark-covered hut. He was a big man of around fifty. The commissar told us his story. Cook Sokolov had enlisted as a volunteer, and his commanders have tried not to burden him with heavy duties. But he will not leave the army for anything – and takes great offence at even the slightest suggestion otherwise. Not too long ago he received news that his two sons had been killed in action. He broke down in tears; everyone tried to console him. A few days later, Sokolov received a letter. His eighty-five-year-old mother had apparently escaped from an area that had recently been liberated by our forces. The Germans had burned down homes and slaughtered people before her very eyes. She was so traumatized that by the time she was brought to Moscow she had lost her mind. And that is just one short story: the tale of a quiet, greying cook, a volunteer who flat-out refuses to leave the army.

We were not surprised to see Cook Sokolov at the divisional rally. The man's very soul was aching, yet still he had come to listen to his friends, the soldiers, at the end of a long working day. We were not surprised either by General Major Zygin's arrival at the rally. His soul was aching for his native South and for the whole Soviet land. At this difficult, terrible time he just wanted to share a few simple, truthful words with his friends, the Red Army's soldiers and officers.

The rally took place in a large forest clearing. The infantry arrived in wrinkled tunics and greatcoats. The submachine gunners arrived: they may be simple young lads, but they are the scourge of the enemy. The regimental and divisional heavy artillery's spotters, loaders, and horse and tractor drivers arrived. The anti-tank gunners, the mortarmen, and the chemists arrived. The machine gun crews arrived. The doctors and their orderlies arrived. The political instructors and commanders arrived. Every part of the great military brotherhood was there. The enemy was close, so the troops had come spread out in separate lines. Some had come from guard duty; others from trenches and dugouts at the firing line. They walked silently, but the heart of every last man was full of love for this beautiful land, for the Volga, for the forests and flowering meadows, and for the flax and rye fields. Every last man was full of the terrible sight of incinerated homes and ruined towns. Every last man bore a horrific, unspeakable pain on behalf of their defiled land and of the local inhabitants. Every man was wracked with worry.

The blue smoke of little cigarettes floated over the clearing, but it was surprisingly quiet. It hardly seemed possible that hundreds of Soviet troops could have been present. This great military mass had fallen silent. Every man was lost in thought. The division's soldiers had been through much and seen a great deal during the long months at the front. They had already long mulled over the fate of the Soviet people, the Soviet nation, and their loved ones. There was plenty of time to think when standing guard at night through howling blizzards, marching for hours along dusty military roads, arriving in towns destroyed by the Germans, bidding farewell to fallen comrades, and relaxing in the flower meadows along the Volga.

The rally began and the enormous crowd as one took a stride forward toward the truck where the speakers were standing. It was as if the forest clearing was taken up by one enormous warrior with one enormous heart who stood tall, breathing calm and even.

The rally was abuzz with the sense that a great battle was to take place. Every word spoken by the sergeants, privates, and commanders was about war and designed for war. Those who spoke from the truck, which was camouflaged amongst the foliage, were united by a single thought and a single feeling. Everyone – from the young, helmeted Lieutenant Buksin, who had taken part in the legendary battle of ninety Soviet troops against one and a half thousand Germans, all the way to Junior Lieutenant Baranov, who told his comrades-in-arms of how his wife had died terribly, defiled and murdered by the Germans – spoke of only one thing: a merciless battle against the enemy.

One of the speakers held out his arms to his comrades and said, "The fate of the nation is in these very hands, in *our* hands." Every last soldier glanced down at their own hands, and a light breeze rippled through the heaving throng.

Their responsibility is indeed great, their lot difficult! Fate has seen fit that these Soviets must, in their tunics bleached by the sun and the rain, resist the fascist horde's unprecedented, historical assault. In this forest clearing, surrounded by aspen, fir, birches, and rowan, standing shoulder to shoulder, and united in every breath, thought, word, and feeling, these men dressed in green tunics bleached by the sun and the rain declared: "We must resist. We must be victorious. The fate of the nation is in our hands."

Those same words resound here, where the hills are grown over with fir forest and where the supple young Volga flows forth, and they resound at Stalingrad, where the broad and mighty river of Russian freedom cascades onto the endless steppe: "The fate of the nation is in our hands. We must resist. We must be victorious!"

Ilya Ehrenburg – Stalingrad (I)
6 September 1942, *Krasnaya Zvezda*

The battle for Stalingrad has been underway for several weeks. What a terrible battle it is. The Germans intend to capture the city. They plan to slice through the Volga and suffocate Russia. Dozens of German divisions are being hurled at Stalingrad. Germany is on the rampage. Right here in the hot steppe, facing an indomitable city, are SS, Prussians, and Bavarians, sergeants, tanks, and soldiers sent from France, Dutch gendarmes and Egyptian pilots, and veterans and rookies. Here, though, the promised iron crosses are being turned into wooden crosses.

The heart of every patriot pours over whenever Russians surrender a Russian city. Each city is like a virgin forest that has taken years to grow. Each city is a web of lives and factories, of ebbing and flowing streets as complicated as a brain, of great squares where the will of the people is done, and of cozy little rooms where lovers exchange their passionate vows. Every city is like a great book, like a nation, and like an enormous family. Cities must not be surrendered. Cities must not be tossed away. A city is not just a name or a dot on a map. A city is a living being, a loved one.

Defenders of Stalingrad, Russia looks to you with hope. Remember that the enemy made it to Moscow and burned the dachas around the city. The enemy was strong and made rapid advances, yet he was stopped from entering Moscow. And who was it that stopped him? Soldiers. A year ago the enemy was making for Leningrad. He puffed and panted like an enraged beast; the Leningraders felt his fiery breath on the face of their city. But the enemy did not enter Leningrad, for he was not permitted to do so. Tula is no Moscow or Leningrad, but still Tula stood firm. The enemy surrounded it and squeezed it, but still Tula clung on.

Defenders of Stalingrad, the nation lives by your courage. The enemy is close, but he has fallen at the last hurdle more than once. The Germans may be decent at counting, but they make miscalculations all too often. Their calculations neglect the fact that the brave Russian is worth ten or even a hundred soldiers, that every last house can be a fortress, and that with every passing hour the whole outlook can change.

Stalingrad *is* the Volga. How can one describe the Volga's significance to Russia? There is no such river in Europe. She cuts through Russia and through the heart of every Russian. The people have written hundreds of

songs about "the mother Volga." They sing of the Volga; they live by the
Volga. Bustling cities and enormous factories sprang up by the Volga. Young
people in fragrant gardens used to gaze at the blinking lights of steamers
on the Volga and talk of freedom, of war, of love, and of inspiration.

Fierce battles are now being fought with the Germans in the Volga's
upper reaches; the river itself will tell Stalingrad's defenders about the heroes fighting for Rzhev. The Volga is Russia's bounty, its glory, its pride. Will
we really allow the despicable Germans to bathe their horses in our great
Russian river?

There is a line in an old song: "You, the steppe, have reached Tsaritsyn /
What colours, o steppe, are you painted in?"[48] Today the steppe is painted
in German graves, and the Germans are terrified to look around. "We suffer
from a unique disease: a fear of the vast steppe," said one captured lieutenant. There are only ashes behind them, but a glow lies ahead. The city that
will never surrender lies ahead.

The Germans already have many words to frighten each other to death
with in years to come. Now they have another: Stalingrad. One German soldier wrote to his mother: "Back home only someone with the most infernal
imagination could possibly imagine what we're going through. There are
only four of us left in the company. I wonder how many German cities have
to be completely emptied for us to take Stalingrad at last?" All those hateful
Stralsunds and Schneidemühls are already empty, but the Germans still have
not taken Stalingrad.[49]

Hitler keeps sending more and more divisions into the battle: "More soldiers! More aircraft!" The madman will stop at nothing. When people tell
him, "It's already September. What'll happen to us in the winter?," he just
waves them away. He must have Stalingrad, no matter the cost. So the Germans keep on at the city and the fighting goes on day and night. Stalingrad's
defenders are finding it unbelievably difficult, but they are holding on.

Who will ever forget the Thirty-Three? They were attacked by seventy
German tanks, but the Thirty-Three did not flinch. They attacked the tanks
with bullets, grenades, and bottles. They destroyed twenty-seven tanks. The
Thirty-Three were just ordinary Russians with ordinary Russian names:
Evstifeev, Strelkov, Khomichev, Kovalev. As ever, the Russian heart proved
stronger than iron. If a foreigner were to tell us that only a miracle could
save Stalingrad, we would ask, "Was the feat of the Thirty-Three not a

miracle?" The enemy still has no idea what the Russian is capable [of] when he is defending the motherland.

One can choose one's friends. Once can choose one's wife. But one cannot choose one's mother. A mother is unique; she is beloved simply by virtue of being one's mother. At Stalingrad, we are defending our mother: Russia. We are defending our motherland. Since ancient times the people have called "Mother Earth" their nursemaid and keeper. The earth is man's greatest joy and the site of man's eternal rest. Now blood, sweat, and tears pour into the earth; they kiss the earth with reverence.

Soldier, you tread on hallowed ground. Do not give it up! Do not allow the filthy German to touch it. In days gone by, when a Russian swore an oath, he would not be believed unless he swallowed a pinch of earth. Only then did others believe that he would not break his promise. They swore by the earth; so we too shall swear by the earth, by a pinch of it and by the whole of our vast country.

For Stalingrad, for the Volga, for the Russian land!

Konstantin Simonov – A Soldier's Glory
11 September 1942, *Krasnaya Zvezda*

At night a red glow hangs over Stalingrad. By day smoke covers the steppe: black columns from mortar blasts, thin trails from camp kitchens, and bitter smoke from soldiers' cigarettes swirl upward. Fighter planes leave white, feathery tracks in the blue and strangely clear September sky. The earth, though, is furrowed with trenches. The mounds of mass graves sit alongside the mounds of dugouts. On the steppe, glory and shame sleep under the same sky. One and the same nocturnal darkness envelops troops sweating and exhausted from battle and those who are fated never to see the sky again. Unnoticed fields, hillocks, and glades overgrown with wormwood have turned into places we cannot surrender. Often without even knowing the name of the village to the left or the stream to the right, we fight and die for these places. Yet we always know that Stalingrad lies behind us, so we must stand firm.

We must stand firm, whether the cost is life or death, whatever the cost. We may not yet be winning, but we fight on. The glory of divisions and armies, the glory of the entire Russian military, has not yet been born on these fields. But the soldier's glory, *our* soldiers' glory, is being born all over, every day and every night. The bravery and glorious deeds of man will never disappear, no matter how tough the going was or will be for the army or for the nation.

*** *** ***

I am sitting on the dry steppe with Semen Shkolenko. The wind, just as dry as the earth, blows into his calm, tanned face and fading red hair. I ask him what exactly happened.

"What exactly happened?" he repeats thoughtfully and, as if trying to remember something, gazes out onto the steppe. Suddenly, as if he wished to tell me that his miraculous feat did not happen just yesterday but a long time ago, as if to show that he'd been so deeply thoughtful his entire life, he slowly begins to recount the past.

"My father's name was Frol. He also fought here, at Tsaritsyn (Tsaritsyn's what they called Stalingrad back then), but he died in the fighting. He was a miner, like me. The mine's been flooded now. Or maybe it's been blown up; who knows? It was the Isaevskaya Mine Number Two. I was underground for a long time. I dragged a sled, I dug, and I was a foreman. The first time I went down below was a long time ago, back in 1924 when I was just a lad. How long has it been? Can it really be eighteen years? Today's my thirtieth name day, though, so I suppose it must be eighteen.[50] The commissar and I had a drink today; he treated me. I drank to my wife and my son, Yury Semenovich. I still haven't met the boy. He was born on 27 March."

Shkolenko loses himself in thought and repeats the words: "Yury Semenovich." Judging by the serious way he calls his son by name and patronymic, he feels proud that he has a son, a successor to a long line of miners – his son, Semen's son and Frol's grandson, is certain to become a man and a worker. And in the way that Shkolenko talks about his family, the mine, and every other facet of his tough, worker's life, I feel that you can't think his glorious feat is entirely unexpected. He's been driven toward it his whole life by all his experiences, by his *nous*, by his very Russian intelligence, and by his strong, Russian build. When he starts to talk of his feat, he does so unhurriedly, calmly, and deliberately. I see how he went about the thing: just as unhurriedly, calmly, and deliberately as he describes it now.

✳ ✳ ✳

It was morning. Battalion commander Koshelev summoned Semen Shkolenko. As they stood together in a thicket on the riverbank, the commander
explained what had to be done. As always, he was a man of few words:
"We need to capture a 'squeaker.'"[51]

"I'll get one," said Shkolenko. He ducked down into the trench, checked
his gun over, fixed three clips to his belt, primed five grenades (two ordinary
and three anti-tank grenades), and put them in his bag. Pausing for a moment to think, he took some copper wire from a sack and secreted it in
his pocket.

He would have to go along the bank. He set off slowly and cautiously,
shuffling along and looking about. It was all quiet. He quickened his pace
and, to reduce the distance he'd have to travel, cut straight across a hollow
through some shrubbery. Machine gun fire rang out. The bullets flew
close by. Shkolenko lay still on the ground; he didn't move a muscle for
an entire minute.

Shkolenko was disappointed in himself. He could have avoided that
machine gun volley. He ought to have gone through the thicker bushes; he
had wanted to save thirty seconds and now he'd lose ten minutes circling
around. He got up and, still crouching down, raced past the thicket. Half an
hour later, he had passed one and then another stream bed. Right past the
second stood three barns and a house. There was little cover bar wormwood
and grass. Shkolenko lay down and started to wriggle along on his stomach.
In a few minutes he had reached the first barn and was able to peek inside.
It was dark; the odour of dampness wafted out. Hens and a piglet were trot-
ting around the earthen floor.

Then right at the very last moment, Shkolenko suddenly noticed a shallow trench and an embrasure formed from two sawn logs by the barn wall.
A half-finished pack of German cigarettes lay by the trench. The Germans
were close; there was no doubt about it. The next barn was empty. By the
third, beneath a haystack, lay two dead Red Army men, their rifles next to
them. Their blood was fresh.

Shkolenko tried to picture what had happened: "Hmm, they probably
walked right out from over there without crouching down, and the Germans
shot them with submachine guns from that side over there." Shkolenko was

irritated by this needless death. "If they'd been with me I wouldn't have let
'em go like that," he thought. That thought in turn led him to an old but important thought: that our boys don't always do their reccies properly; that
they can be naive. But there was no more time for thinking now. There was
nothing for it. He had to find a German.

He happened upon a path in a hollow overgrown with vines. The ground
was still damp from the morning's rain, so it was easy to spy some tracks
leading off into the forest. A hundred metres farther on Shkolenko saw a
pair of German boots and a rifle. He had no idea how they had turned up
here, but just to be safe he shoved the rifle in a ditch, stamped earth down
over the top of it, then threw the boots into the brush. A fresh track led into
the forest. He had crawled barely fifty metres when he heard mortar fire.
A mortar fired off ten rounds in succession, pausing only briefly between
each shot.

There were thickets up ahead, so Shkolenko made to crawl to their left.
Then he spotted a pit with weeds all around and cinders at the bottom. A
chink of light glimmered in a gap between the bushes. Not ten metres away
lay a mortar and a light machine gun. A German was standing by the mortar. A little further on another half dozen Germans were sitting in a circle
and eating from mess tins.

Shkolenko immediately, instinctively, pointed his gun and aimed. But, at
the very next moment, he wisely changed his mind. He could not have killed
all of them with a single round, so he would have ended up in a one-sided
fight. He calmly began to ready an anti-tank grenade. He chose the anti-
tank grenade because the distance to the target was small and the grenade's
blast would be more concentrated. He was in no hurry. There was no need
to rush when the target was sitting right there. He braced his left arm on the
bottom of the pit, pressing hard into the ground so that it would not slip,
lifted his body up, and tossed the grenade. It landed right in the middle of
the Germans.

He saw that the big group of six were lying motionless. The other one,
by the mortar, was still standing there. He was looking with shock at the
weapon's barrel, which had been torn apart by a fragment of grenade.
Shkolenko leapt up and, without taking his eyes off the German, began to
approach. He motioned for the German to throw his Luger to the ground.
The German's hands were shaking; he struggled to take the pistol from its

holster. Then he threw it away from himself. Shkolenko, pushing the German ahead of him, went over to the machine gun. It was not loaded. Shkolenko motioned for the German to hoist the machine gun onto his shoulders. The German obediently bent down and picked up the gun. Now both his hands were full.

Despite the danger of his situation, Shkolenko began to laugh. He found it funny that the German was carrying his own gun, in his own hands, back to us. And that is how they returned: the German in front with the machine gun over his shoulders, and Shkolenko behind. The German walked slowly, constantly tripping. He did not resist, but it was obvious that he had not lost hope of finding someone who might help, so he tried to dawdle the whole way. Shkolenko, who had been so unfussed until this point, made haste. He was no stranger to the fearful sensation that someone hidden in the bushes might shoot him in the back at any moment. When he was getting down to business he had not rushed any more than he had absolutely needed to. Now, though, he wanted to get back as soon as possible, so he kept impatiently shoving the German in the back.

It was gone noon when Shkolenko made it back to the battalion command post. The regimental commander was there with Captain Koshelev. Shkolenko roughly shoved the German in the back one last time and curtly said: "There you are."

Only then did he give a full and proper account of how he had made it back. The regimental commander shook his hand, looked him up and down from head to toe, shook his hand firmly once more, then stepped away to confer with the battalion commander. They talked for a minute or so while Shkolenko stood waiting in silence.

"Good," said the regimental commander. "You've carried out the mission he" – he nodded at Captain Koshelev – "gave you. Now you're to carry out mine. You must find out where the remaining mortars are positioned."

"I shall," said Shkolenko curtly. "Can I ask, am I going alone?"

"Yes," said Koshelev.

"Right, so much the better." Shkolenko slung his submachine gun over his shoulder.

"Rest up a little before you go," the regimental commander said and left.

Shkolenko went over to a group of signallers sitting round a cook pot. He produced a spoon from his boot and began to slowly sup the cabbage soup,

savouring every mouthful. He was tired, but pleased he had been given
a break. He finished the soup and rolled a cigarette. Shkolenko had not
smoked all day, so it was delightful to do so, especially in the knowledge
that he likely would not be able to smoke again until the evening. Then he
sat down and rewound the footwraps around his gently aching feet. He sat
like that for half an hour or so, then picked up his gun and, without replen-
ishing his grenades, set off once more in the direction that he had taken in
the morning.

This time he headed to the right of the village, closer to the river, taking
cover in the bushes that had grown up along the path. He heard the first
mortar fire coming from 500 metres away. He would have to crawl through
a long hollow that cut through thickets of nut bushes that scratched the
hands and face. Mortar rounds were landing close and flying overhead. He
stopped for a moment, tried to estimate the mortar's flight trajectory, and
determined where the firing was coming from by its sound. After the bushes
he had to traverse a low hill and then enter another hollow covered with
thick brush. He had crawled another couple of hundred metres when the
shooting ceased. The last round had landed very close indeed. Suddenly a
German stood up, incredibly close to Shkolenko. Shkolenko clung close to
the ground, trying to hide, for a full ten minutes. When the German disappeared, Shkolenko crawled through the undergrowth and up to a large bush.
From behind the bush, he could see three mortars standing in a hollow.

Shkolenko lay flat and took out a paper that had been folded into a pipe.
He planned to use the paper to sketch out exactly where the mortars were
located. But at the very moment that he was about to begin drawing, the
seven Germans gathered around the mortars approached each other. They
all sat down next to the mortar closest to Shkolenko. They were just eight
metres away. There was one last German a little further away. The German
was lying on his side on the edge of a trench and trying to use the field
telephone, but he clearly could not get through.

With all but one of the Germans sitting together in close proximity,
Shkolenko was prompted to make a bold move. He was supposed to note
down and report on the mortars' locations so that the artillery could strike
the mortars. But the Germans were sitting right there all together and he
had grenades to hand. The decision was instantaneous. Maybe Shkolenko
took it so quickly only because he had been in almost the exact same situ-

ation earlier that day. In any event, Shkolenko decided to deal with the Germans himself. Still lying down, he took two anti-tank grenades and the little length of copper wire from his pocket. He wound the grenades together. Now all he had to do was throw them.

Just as before, Shkolenko braced his arm against the ground, took a deep breath, and lobbed the grenades. But the grenades were very heavy – there were two of them now – and he was exhausted – it was his second sortie of the day, after all. The throw fell half a metre short of the Germans. He saw what was happening before he had even got up. He almost instantly felt a sharp pain in his shoulder. He grabbed his shoulder with his hand and his fingers felt blood.

He leapt up, stood tall, and held his submachine gun at the ready. The explosion was incredibly powerful. Just like before, the Germans lay dead, but this time not a single one remained standing. The German who had been on the phone began to stir. Shkolenko went over and prodded him with his foot. The German turned over, held up his hands, and began to speak. In the heat of the moment, Shkolenko could not make out what he was saying. The telephone lay next to the German. Sholenko had no intention of carrying it back, so he struck the phone several times with his heavy, steel-capped boot, smashing it. He turned around, wondering what to do with the mortars. Suddenly there was a loud rustle in the bushes 10 metres away. Shkolenko pressed his gun into his stomach and strafed the area.

Instead of a German, though, out from the bushes jumped his old second battalion friend Satarov. He had been captured by the Germans a few days earlier. Satarov, unkempt, barefoot, and wearing only long johns, turned around and cried out in a strange voice: "It's our lot! Our lot have come!"

From the bushes emerged another sixteen people, each as dishevelled and woeful as Satarov. Three were covered in blood. Another had to be carried.

"Was that you shooting?" said Satarov.

"It was," said Shkolenko.

"You wounded them." Satarov pointed at the bloodied men. "Where are the others?"

"It's just me," answered Shkolenko, "what happened to you?"

"We were digging our own grave," said Satarov. "There were two submachine gunners watching us, but they ran off as soon as they heard the blast. So you're on your own?"

"It's just me," repeated Satarov. He looked at the mortars. The first thing that occurred to him at that moment was that there was no time to lose, so he made a quick decision. "You need to take the mortars," he said matter-of-factly. "Do it quick. Quickly now. Don't waste time. We're going back to our lines."

Several men seized the mortars and hoisted them over their shoulders; the others carried the wounded. Shkolenko tried to make it back even quicker than the first time. He wanted to get these poor men back to our lines and, what was more, he could barely believe his own luck. He worried that if they were to waste even the slightest bit of time, his luck might suddenly run out and the whole thing would fall apart. He went last, covering the procession, listening carefully, and turning around with his gun to look back.

It was only now, following the men he had released from imprisonment and seeing the bloodied bodies of the wounded, that he came to from the rush of battle. "It's a good job they weren't killed," he thought about his comrades, "it's a good thing I didn't kill anyone." He reassured himself: "I didn't know, did I? I thought they were Germans." Then he repeated that thought aloud to Satarov, who was walking alongside:

"I didn't know, did I? I thought they were Germans."

"I know," said Satarov, "I understand."

The captured German who had been manning the telephone limped along, clutching his wounded head, in the middle of the freed Red Army men. He held his head in his hands, groaning from time to time and looking around in horror at the bloodied men walking with him. Five minutes earlier they had been digging their own grave, now, like corpses back from the dead, they terrified him. They terrified him even more, perhaps, than Shkolenko did.

They reached the battalion after another hour and a half walking barely visible paths. Shkolenko made his report, received some gruff praise and a firm and friendly handshake from the captain, and walked a mere five paces before collapsing to the ground face down. The overwhelming exhaustion of a long day had finally got to him.

Shkolenko opened his eyes and looked at the blades of grass growing all around. It felt terrifying that it had all transpired and it was all over, but here he was, alive, with grass growing around him, and everything was just the same as this morning. The sun, red and dusty, was dipping below the steppe. The sudden southern darkness was just beginning to draw in from all sides.

* * *

"You know," said Shkolenko after several minutes of intense thought, "you know why I told the regimental commander it'd be better if I go on the sortie alone? You think it's better to go on a sortie alone? Not at all. It's more frightening to be alone. It's better to go on a sortie with a comrade, but only if you really know your comrade, only if you know what sort of a person they are. If you don't really know their character, it's better to go it alone. If I'm being totally honest, if I was to speak from the heart, then I'd say this: we're in such a desperate bind that sometimes people don't think what it means to go off on a sortie with someone you don't know. When I head into a bloodbath, I can't do my job properly if I don't know the other lad. Going on a sortie means going to face death with someone. I have to know his character like I know my own. That's the only thing keeps me calm deep down inside. But I suppose people don't get it. They don't think about our soldierly friendships and camaraderie much. They split people up for no good reason: one of you go over there, and the others over there."

Shkolenko was getting into it and began to share his most intimate thoughts: "Speaking from the heart, I have to confess it's terrifying when death is walking right there alongside you. I've been fighting with my tail between my legs for a year already. I've got this idea that when the German has a gut feeling that someone's coming at him, but it's someone who doesn't scare him, then the German begins to frighten his opponent. But if I start to scare him, then he stops scaring me. It's a rule of thumb in war that one person is always more scared than the other. So I want the other guy to be more scared than me." Shkolenko gazes at length at the evening steppe. An expression of bitter sadness comes across his face.

"What are you looking at?" I ask.

"I'm looking at how far they've driven us back. They've pushed us back a long way indeed."

And in those words I suddenly sense the two thoughts that constantly torture and gnaw at the brave heart of the soldier: they've driven us back;

they must be stopped. And the braver the soldier – the more he resembles
Shkolenko – the more distressing are those thoughts, and the harder it is
to retreat.

✳ ✳ ✳

The earth is furrowed with trenches. Dugout mounds loom over them.
Mortar fire howls away. The land around Stalingrad has no name. But at one
time, even the word "Borodino" was known only around Mozhaisk. It was a
local word, but then our whole nation learned it. The positions at Borodino
were no better or worse than many of our positions between the Neman
River and Moscow. Borodino became an impregnable fortress, though,
because the Russian soldier put his life on the line and refused to surrender.
That was how a shallow stream became impassable, and how the trenches
hastily dug through hillocks and copses became unassailable.

On the steppe around Stalingrad, there are many unknown hills and
streams and many villages whose names are unknown even a hundred *verst*
from here.[52] But the nation waits and believes. The nation believes that the
name of one of these villages will, like Borodino's, resound through the centuries, and that out on the steppe one of these rolling fields will become
the scene of a great victory.

Vasily Koroteev – At Stalingrad
12 September 1942, *Krasnaya Zvezda*

From the *kurgan* where the battery is stationed, one can see the whole of
Stalingrad and the Volga stretching out like a broad blue ribbon. The front
has reached the city, which has been wounded by bombs and burned by
fires. The enemy is losing blood, so, vicious as an animal, he is taking out
his anger on the city's population. He is bombing residential areas, kinder-
gartens, libraries, and hospitals. Yet this proud city, raised on stories of
Stalin's defence of Tsaritsyn, is a warrior city. It will not yield to his blows.
Thus it was during the Civil War, thus it shall be in today's battle.

The enemy has sent its elite divisions and the cream of an air force infa-
mous for its monstrous bombing of European cities into the fight for Stalingrad. The enemy has thrown hundreds of tanks into battle. The Germans

have been on the brink of taking the city for days. Nevertheless, the city, imbued with an iron fortitude, waves the Red Banner still – and the city is shattering the enemy's ferocious onslaught. The wings of glory are now embracing the warriors who are defending Stalingrad with their very bodies.

Senior Lieutenant Timofeev's battery had just taken up positions on a small hill by a road. The battery commander was almost immediately on the phone to Lieutenant Colonel Gorelik: "Ten enemy tanks are approaching!"

"Open fire!" ordered the lieutenant colonel. Three tanks were hit right away. The others turned back and took cover behind the neighbouring hill.

Barely ten minutes had passed when Timofeev was on the phone again: "Fifty tanks are surrounding the battery from the left and the right." Back came the order: "Don't let them reach the road. Hold out to your last round." The battery replied, "Yes, sir! Hold out to the last round!"

The battery duelled the enemy tanks for four hours. When the Germans came at the hill from the rear, the artillerymen flipped their guns around and began to pour fire into the tanks. The gun barrels strained with the heat, but neither the tanks' ferocious fire nor an aerial bombardment could break the artillerymen's will. On the artillery's left and right flank, smoke poured from eight tanks. Another eleven lay battered, twisted, and motionless.

One by one, though, the guns were knocked out of action. Their last round was fired. The battery fell silent. Of the fifty tanks, twenty-nine were sprawled out on the hill like corpses. The remainder were advancing fast along the road. At that very moment, our tanks went on the attack. The enemy vehicles stopped, then turned back.

Our troops are fighting with total determination all over the city. A German company attacked Sergeant Ievlev's unit. The Fritz were advancing head on and from both flanks. Our lads let the German company get close before they mowed down the first row. The Germans hurled themselves to the ground and returned fire, killing and injuring several of our troops. The Germans attacked again. This time Gunner Fyodoryako and Privates Krylov, Bondarenko, and Filyuk met them with heavy fire. Machine Gunner Garkush, meanwhile, kept quickly shifting positions, giving the Germans the impression that there were several machine guns in action. The Germans had failed. They retreated.

In the neighbouring sector our mortar fire repelled the German onslaught. Fifteen tanks had joined the fifteen carriers of infantry sent on the
attack. Our mortars opened fire, destroying a tank and seven trucks. The
enemy retreated into a ravine. Another enemy attack followed; another
six vehicles were incinerated in the mortar fire. The Germans dared not
attack again.

Konstantin Simonov – The Battle on the Outskirts
18 September 1942, *Krasnaya Zvezda*

Stalingrad is behind us. That's not just because you can make out the contours of the city, the roofs of houses, and the chimneys of factories. Those
words are in the very air of battle and on the faces of everybody you meet
up and down the front line. People's facial expressions show a special sort
of firmness and stubbornness. Their lips are pressed together tightly, while
their tired eyes, red from insomnia, glimmer with excitement.

At first glance, Battalion Commander Senior Lieutenant Vadim Yakovle-
vich Tkalenko has something of Chapaev about him. Perhaps the similarity
comes from the upward twirl of the light, flaxen whiskers, the bright intent
of the eyes, or the cap sitting gently askew on red hair. Whatever it is, he's
just like the Chapaev we know from the silver screen. It's only when Tkalenko emerges from his dugout and stands up tall that you suddenly perceive his almost boyish lankiness and his jerky movements. Tkalenko is still
young, and his whiskers are more youthful whimsy than veteran's grizzle.

Tkalenko is just twenty-three. You can see his youth in his gait, in his
movements, and in his build. But there is no youth left in his eyes. Senior
Lieutenant Tkalenko has the intent, heavy, merciless eyes of a man who's
lived ten years and ten lives in a single year at war. Experience has made
those eyes intent, brushes with danger have made them heavy, and the grief
of a nation has made them merciless.

Last fall, Tkalenko had a beard instead of a moustache for a time. He'd
been leading a group of scouts behind enemy lines to make raids on enemy
command posts and to link up with our partisans. One time, in the village
of Khristinovka, not far from Uman,[53] he was about to launch a raid on a
German command post. He was in disguise, hiding in a group of peasants,
when he found himself witnessing something he will remember until his
dying day.

A German death squad was at work in the village. The Germans were hunting down "Uncle Vanya," the commander of a partisan brigade, who had been born and bred in the village. Tkalenko was standing in the crowd alongside one of Uncle Vanya's partisans. The Germans knew that Uncle Vanya had to be somewhere close. They seized his father, a decrepit old man. After interrogation proved fruitless, they tied two ropes around him – one under his armpits, another around his legs – and tore him apart using a pair of light tanks. The crowd, who had been driven into the streets, watched on in grim silence.

Then the Germans marched from woman to woman, tearing their children from their arms, and demanding, "Where's Uncle Vanya?" The women remained silent.

The Germans started taking children off to the side. When they'd gathered more than two dozen, they tied the whole group together with ropes, fired up a tank and, as the crowd cried out from the sheer inhuman horror, crushed them. They crushed every last one. With a tank. At that moment, Tkalenko fished for the grenade he was carrying in his pocket. He clutched it tight, but a heavy hand squeezed his arm. The partisan standing alongside Tkalenko as quietly as anything whispered right into his ear, "My child is there. I'm still just standing, watching." He relaxed his grip and let Tkalenko's arm go. Tkalenko didn't throw his grenade. He threw it – and many more – that night when they destroyed the death squad's command post.

Since then, Tkalenko has witnessed much more of our people's grief: more, one feels, than the tough steel heart of an old soldier, let alone a young heart, can possibly bear. Yet that rope wrapped around the children, that silent village square, and that quiet intake of horrified breath, overshadow everything he has seen since.

Since then, whenever he hears the word "Germans," he sees that square; and whenever he is ordered into battle, he sees that square. He will never forget it. Since then, it's as if everything he's seen – every battle, every day and every night, and every victory and every defeat – he has seen through the lens of that square. His twenty-three-year-old's eyes have become merciless. Shining youth has given way to an implacable hatred. It is only the angry flame of hatred that lights up those eyes.

Tkalenko was heavily injured in the winter and spent the spring recuperating in hospital. He almost died. For just one quiet moment in the white hospital ward, he had felt that there wasn't a war on, that it was nice to just quietly lie down, that he didn't need to move a muscle, and that everything was happening somewhere else, far, far away from him. His injured body must at that very moment have been deciding whether to live or die. The next second, a sharp pain in his lung, which had been pierced by two bullets, made him groan. Through parched lips, he asked the doctor if he would survive, and if he would be a cripple. The doctor, with military directness, answered:

"If" – he paused at the word "if" – "*if* you survive, you won't be a cripple."

Tkalenko knew that his moment of tranquil indifference had come from the certainty that he would die. But he no longer believed that he would die. He wanted to live. He furiously wheezed through his tattered lungs. He wanted to live, to live at any cost, so he could kill more Germans – just like he had killed them before.

After his discharge from hospital, Tkalenko ended up in a newly formed detachment. He was anxious to recover so that he could get back to killing Germans, but he was also a disciplined soldier. He wasn't sent to the front straight away, but Tkalenko found a use for his hatred behind the lines: he taught it to others, inculcating it in his troops. Tkalenko taught his troops to kill as wisely, cunningly, and resourcefully as possible.

The long-awaited day came at Stalingrad. Tkalenko had waited with the cool calm of a man whose fate was war and war alone. He had been resentful that, having been hospitalized at Rostov in the winter, he would now have to fight at Stalingrad in the summer instead. He felt that way during the crossing from the left to the right bank of the Volga. However, when he saw houses on fire and homeless women and children wandering the streets in Stalingrad itself, that feeling was replaced by a familiar, cold hatred of the Germans.

It was a difficult day. The Nth Rifles battalions one after the other made contact with the enemy. Tkalenko's battalion, which had only just crossed into the city, was the first to be sent to fight. The battle on the northern outskirts began at dawn. By evening, the Germans had seized the neighbouring village. By morning, it looked as if they were preparing to advance further. The battalion would have to shape itself up to repel the Germans and drive them back to the north.

A bloody attack was in the offing. However, Tkalenko knew from experience that beginning a military career with a retreat was tough, so he was glad that his soldiers would begin theirs with an attack. Bayoneting a German, seeing him dead before your feet, and stepping over his warm body: that's the stuff that gives a soldier strength, that's the stuff that a soldier needs more than anything else in his first battle.

The attack began at dawn. The hollow leading to the village was strewn with anti-tank mines. The battalion's support tanks did not dare go on ahead of their sappers, so they fired from static positions. The infantry advanced alone. Three hundred metres later they were met by a hail of mortar fire. They scrambled up a hill.

Tkalenko, advancing with the battalion, suddenly and with a hint of bitterness realized that his old injury had left its mark. Climbing the hill was tough going when he was breathing through only one lung. However, long experience meant he did everything judiciously and accurately. He did not go to ground for no reason – unlike his novice troops – when the German artillery overshot or undershot. It was only thanks to his frontline experience that he could advance, just like he always used to, at the head of the attack. Those alongside him kept on too, and perhaps even better than he had expected. True, they threw themselves to the ground frequently, but he never had to convince them to get up again. Up they quickly leapt and marched on ahead.

The Germans met the battalion with machine gun fire at the edge of the hollow. The first houses, however, were already close. Within a few minutes, hand-to-hand fighting had broken out along the village's edge. Submachine gunners opened fire from inside the houses and from behind gates and fences. With a short, point-blank burst from his own gun, Tkalenko killed a German who had poked out from a house on the edge of the village. It was here by the house right on the edge that he stopped. He and his battalion had made that first and most terrifying leap in their very first fight together: traversing three hundred metres of open ground, head first, in order to reach the Germans. Now they had been initiated into the art of battle.

Tkalenko stopped by the house on the edge of the village, weighed up the situation with a glance around, and calmly gave further orders. The sappers cleared two paths for the tanks. Four tanks crossed the hollow and, entering the village, opened fire along the street. The battle was at its most intense.

Suddenly just on the edge of Tkalenko's eyeline, a crouching figure honed into view: "Halt!"

The man stopped two paces away from Tkalenko. He was not wearing a cap or holding a rifle, but had a bag with grenades slung around his waist. He had done a runner from the battlefield – the first and, thank God, the only one today. As soon as Tkalenko had issued the command to halt, he took a look at the man's face and tried to remember his surname. Yet he could not remember the name: the coward's facial features were so horrifically distorted that he was unrecognizable. His face had not been contorted by fear but by a completely abhorrent expression that revealed the man's obsession with his own fate. The runner's eyes searched the ground as if looking for a chasm into which he could disappear.

"Where are you off to?" asked Tkalenko coldly, tapping his submachine gun.

The man gave no answer. Instead, crouching down low, he tried to run straight past the senior lieutenant. Tkalenko held his gun steady and, in one short movement, brought it to bear. The runner crumpled over, clutched at the wall of the house with his fingers, and fell. Tkalenko looked him over for a second and then, just as calmly as he had begun, continued giving orders to the sapper standing alongside. This was a difficult moment for Tkalenko. He had just killed a man who, had he not proved to be a coward, ought to have been killing Germans himself.

But Tkalenko did not want to reveal his sorrow to the sapper or to anyone else. He did not want to admit his own feelings. He wanted people to see how calm he was and to understand his thinking: it was not he, Tkalenko, who had killed the coward, but the merciless law of war.

By midday they had captured the village. Tkalenko and his messenger went off to its northernmost outskirt. The village was theirs for now, but to hold it they would have to capture the hillocks that lay a kilometre beyond. Tkalenko remained in the village with Third Company. He sent the Second Company commander, a nippy little man by the name of Kashkin, and his burly and merry Third Company counterpart, Bondarenko, on ahead. The men knew Bondarenko as "the Decembrist" on account of his thick and beautifully sculpted black sideburns.[54]

Both companies advanced quickly and easily overcame sporadic fire from the Germans, who were still in a muddle after the first attack. Two hours had passed when messengers informed Tkalenko that Bondarenko had captured four German autocannons close to a ravine by the Volga. Tkalenko was pleased with how the fighting was going, but experience told him that the Germans would not let up so easily.

He ordered two anti-tank guns that were behind the lines to be brought across the ravine, which now lay behind them. It had just rained. The steep paths leading down into the ravine were slippery, so the guns would have to be lowered into the ravine, then dragged out again, all by hand. The artillerymen slowly and methodically went about the work of lowering the guns.

It was about five o'clock. Suddenly fifteen heavy German tanks appeared in the hollow that lay between the captured village and the hillocks where First and Second Company were positioned. The battalion broke off its march to begin the fight, but things looked very tricky: the battalion had very few anti-tank grenades or rifles at its disposal. Moreover, the tanks were carrying assault troops and, just as the tanks appeared, the Germans also opened fire with long-range mortars. Mortar fire peppered the two forward companies all over.

Sergeant Roistman and Sergeant Cheboksarov's pair of anti-tank guns opened fire on the tanks. Two tanks burst into flame, but the rest kept on rolling forward, their caterpillar tracks crushing the anti-tank crews. A quarter of an hour later two more tanks were blown up by bundles of grenades. They too burst into flame. The remaining tanks rattled forward, flattening the battlefield and trying to crush the infantry. German submachine gunners leapt from the tanks and began a counterattack. The farther the tanks advanced, the harder it was to hold them back; they had our troops' heads pinned to the ground.

Behind First Company, a bluff ran down to the Volga from the steppe. Beyond that were the tanks. Lieutenant Bondarenko bore that in mind when he gestured ahead and behind, and hoarsely called to the soldiers lying beside him: "We fight them or we die."

Tkalenko watched everything that was happening. The two companies had been separated and were in an increasingly dangerous predicament. His first instinct was to rush off to the spot where people were dying. But he immediately made the cold-blooded decision that that would not save them. Their salvation would come from the cannon, which were still being hauled up the slippery escarpment.

Cutting short his observation of the battlefield, Tkalenko went to help. He did so, as with all things, without hurrying or unnecessary fuss. As a result, the operation instantly started to speed up. At last, they pulled the guns out. There was no time to find a better position, so they opened fire right from the edge of the escarpment that they had been dragged up. They were side on to the tanks. They hit two right away. That was the turning point of the battle. Only nine of the fifteen tanks were left, and it was getting dark. The remaining tanks evidently had no desire to face the guns head on. They turned around and made to leave the battlefield. The submachine gunners set off after them. The battle carried on in the darkness until morning, when those who were still alive retreated beyond the hills.

They buried the dead in the morning. The battalion had incurred losses; Tkalenko was despondent. It certainly was not unexpected – he had prepared himself and his men for it – and the number of German dead was twice as large. He might have been satisfied with two German dead for every one of our own at the start of the war. But now, into the war's second year and after so many battles and so much suffering, it seemed too much to bear. After everything the Germans had done on our soil, they ought to pay not with two, but with four, five, even ten deaths for every one of ours. Yet things hadn't worked out that way in the previous evening's fighting; hence Tkalenko was despondent.

I found him in that same mood later in the day, when things were relatively quiet. When I arrived, he was sitting in thoughtful silence in his dugout. As he told his story, I could detect something like a smile on his face. Afterward, we went outside into the sunshine. I looked at Tkalenko's face and thought, perhaps, that his whiskers gave him a look of uncharacteristic seriousness for his age. I asked him: "Do you ever plan to shave your moustache off?"

At this he smiled – sadly, bashfully – for the first time. "I can't, you know," he replied. "I made a vow. When we went on our final sortie behind the lines last year, four men perished on the way back. Three died on the spot. The fourth, Khomenko, died in my arms as I was dragging him back to our lines. When the two of us who were still alive buried him, the sixth member of our group, a Georgian by the name of Samkharadze, said to me, 'Lieutenant, let's shave our beards off in their memory. But let's leave our moustaches until the end of the war, while we're still fighting for them.' That's how I made the vow." Tkalenko smiled his sad, bashful smile for a second time.

"Ah, here comes Bondarenko. Do you want to go over to his company? That's the man himself."

The tall, red-cheeked "Decembrist" Bondarenko came up to us. He had clearly wanted the sideburns to make his jolly, round face seem more severe, but it had not really worked out. He did have, though, the booming bass voice of an old soldier.

I bade farewell to Tkalenko, then Bondarenko took me to his company. He gave me a cordial tour of their positions, dugouts, trenches, and a cunningly constructed observation post from which you could easily see the German positions 600 metres away. It all made you feel that this man and his company were so well dug into the soil that they simply had no intention whatsoever of allowing themselves to be moved.

Then he and I clambered down the Volga's steep embankment. Women, children, and old men from villages that had been torched were sheltering here in the bluffs and the caves along the Volga's bank. All around you could hear the crying of children. The women's mortally tired eyes followed us pleadingly.

I turned to Bondarenko. Suddenly, I saw on his jolly face the same look of implacable, ineradicable hatred I had seen on his battalion commander's face.

"Scum. Look what they've brought us to," said Bondarenko, "just look what they've brought our people to ..."

There is indeed a limit to human patience. Beyond that limit only one feeling remains – hatred for the enemy – and only one desire remains – to kill the enemy. Those who have been in Stalingrad and seen what is going on here have, like Tkalenko, like Bondarenko, and like every last one of the city's defenders, crossed that limit.

Ilya Ehrenburg – The Russian Anthaeus
20 September 1942, *Krasnaya Zvezda*

The Germans are stumped by the bravery of Stalingrad's defenders. All they can do is speculate: "Why won't the Russians capitulate?" As 6 September's *Berliner Börsen-Zeitung* observed,[55] "The enemy does not seem to follow any logical rules in battle. The Soviet system created the Stakhanovite and now it is creating Red Army Man, who fights ferociously even in the most hopeless situations.[56] The Soviet industrial complex, which is continually churning out an unbelievable quantity of arms, is driven by the same frenzy. The Russians seem to resist when there is no sense in resistance. They leave the impression that they are lunatics for whom the war is fought not in the real world but in a world of imagined fancies."

Berlin's stock traders are not as wise as they think. Every Red Army soldier knows that the war is unfolding not on paper but on the ground. It is taking place on our very own, Russian land. For the Germans, our steppe is a battlefield. But it is only for us that the steppe smells of sagebrush. Only for us is it our native soil. For the Germans, Stalingrad is a major population centre, a point of strategic significance. But our nearest and dearest live in Stalingrad. We took pride in its schools, homes, and factories. We built it, like a mother gives birth to her child, driven by joy and ecstasy. For the Germans, the Volga is a mere boundary, just a river. Need I explain what the Volga means to us? The Germans saw it and shrugged: "A-ha. A big river." But us Russians have known her as the Mother Volga for five centuries.

For the Germans, our fields are "an expanse." But for us, they are the motherland itself. For the Germans, our riches are trophies. But for us, they are our sweat, our blood, and our history. For the Germans, Russian women are slaves. But for us, they are our wives, our loves, and our whole lives.

The Germans at the *Stock Exchange Times* ask with surprise: why do Russians carry on fighting in "hopeless situations"? For Russians, there is no such thing as a hopeless situation. One can compare units of measurement: one can say that a regiment is larger than a battalion, and a battalion larger than a company; one can weigh different sorts of shells; and one can test the thickness of different types of armouring. But a human heart can never be measured against a tank, a human brain can never be measured against a mortar, and human courage can never be measured against a bomb.

Sergeant Ivan Bobrik made it into a German tank that had been taken out of action near their front line. He spent thirteen days inside, manning a field telephone and directing our fire. He found that the tank had a machine gun emplacement, but the gun itself was not there. One night, Ivan Bobrik decided to leave the tank and find a gun. He found one, then cleaned, oiled, and loaded it. On the fourteenth day, the Germans figured out where the Russian observer was. They made for the tank. The sergeant met them with heavy machine gun fire. The Germans began to shell the tank. Ivan Bobrik slipped out and made it back to our lines. That very night, he announced that "I feel bad about the machine gun." He crawled over to the tank and fetched the German gun and its ammunition. There are no words to describe it. Ivan Bobrik was stuck in a "hopeless situation" for fourteen whole days, but he had courage on his side, so he found a way out.

Radio operator Ruvim Spiridon and three of his comrades were surrounded by the enemy as they directed our artillery fire for five days. They did not rest, they did not sleep, and they did not eat. When the Germans got close to the ruins where the radio was located, Ruvim Spiridon calmly gave the signal: "Fire on us." It seemed that there was no way out. But the artillery fire had shaken the Germans. Ruvim Spiridon and his three comrades burst forth with their submachine guns and set to destroying the Germans.

Boris Golubev's plane was shot down. The pilot ended up stuck behind enemy lines. He spent four days making his way back to our line. At last he made it. He was bandaged up and immediately asked for pen and paper. His hands shook as he wrote: "Hello, Comrade Sorokin. It's me, the fellow you lost on the 9th. Mission accomplished. The kite went up in flames. My right hand's broken. My face is burned." The bravado is obvious, but what could be more sublime than those humble words, "mission accomplished"?

Another time our troops were on the attack, but the enemy fire was so strong that the infantry had to take cover. Senior Artillerist Tolstopyatov called out to his friends: "Come on!" A dozen of them made it to the barbed wire, cut an opening, and broke through to the German position. Senior Sergeant Reshetov broke into a bunker and turned its machine gun against the Germans. That is how twelve brave lads managed to annihilate a battalion command point. The infantry went in after them.

A group of our scouts went in search of a "squeaker." Deputy Political Instructor Kunikbaev spotted three Germans and looked to see which of them was in charge. He shot the first two, then dragged the third out of the bunker by his breeches. More Germans ran over. Kunikbaev fought them off with his legs, since he had his hands full. Then off he dragged his German. Before he knew it, the German had come around and was proffering cigarettes at him: "*Bitte … bitte …* please …" Kunikbaev did not take a cigarette, merely replying: "Now, now. We know we've given you a hiding, but don't worry, we're done for now …"

This is the day-to-day life of battle. They do not write about it in our communiqués, but such is the everyday bravery of our troops. Can those Berlin stockbrokers really comprehend the Russian heart? They look with bewilderment at the smoking ruins of houses. How can the brave Fritz not capture them? Why does their spidery little flag not fly over Stalingrad? Because there are not just stones there. There are people. People who fight on. Russian people. Our love for the motherland is, like a river at high tide, overflowing, pouring forth. Individual fates are no more; there is only the fate of the motherland. Every soldier's life is now inextricably linked with the lives of his hundreds of comrades. Together, they are the life of Russia.

As he falls to the ground, the Russian Anthaeus finds new strength. He rises up and charges at the enemy. Anthaeus cannot be struck down. The Germans have reached the Volga; the Germans wish to take us by the throat. But for us there are no "hopeless situations." We have hope. There is only one hope, but it is a reliable hope: we must beat the Germans. And beat them we shall.

Konstantin Simonov – Days and Nights
24 September 1942, *Krasnaya Zvezda*

Those who were here will never forget it. In many years from now, we will look back and remember. When the word "war" passes our lips, an image of Stalingrad – the flash of rockets and the glow of raging fires – will appear in our eyes, and the endless, heavy roar of bombing will again ring in our ears. We shall sense again the suffocating odour of burning and we shall hear the rumbling collapse of burning iron roofs.

The Germans have besieged Stalingrad. However, when people here say "Stalingrad," they don't have in mind just the city centre, or Lenin Street, or even the outskirts. They have in mind the entirety of a massive 65-kilometre-long strip of land along the Volga. They have in mind the city and its settlements, the factories and workers' villages. Together, all these smaller towns form a single city girding the entire bend of the Volga.

But this is not the city that we used to gaze upon from pleasure steamers on the Volga. The jolly patchwork of white houses rising up the slopes of the hill is gone. All the little jetties are gone. The rows of bathhouses, kiosks, and homes running along the Volga's embankments are gone. The city today is smoky and grey. Flames flicker and ashes whirl over it day and night. This is a soldier-city, scorched in battle, a city of many separate strongholds and bastions, a city of heroic ruins and stones.

Nor is the Volga at Stalingrad the same river we used to gaze upon. That Volga of water coursing deep and blue through sunny channels, of streams of racing steamers, of rows of pine rafts and caravans of barges, is gone. The Volga here in Stalingrad is a military river. Its embankments are furrowed with craters. Bombs fall into the water, spraying dense columns of water into the air. Cargo ferries and light craft travel back and forth into the besieged city. Gunfire rattles over the river. The bloody bandages of the wounded are visible against the dark water.

During the day, houses first in one spot then another burst into flame. At night, a smoky glow envelops the horizon. The roar of bombs and artillery barrages hangs over the trembling earth day and night. There has been no refuge anywhere in the city for some time, but as the siege has gone on, people have grown accustomed to the constant danger. There are fires all over. Many streets have simply ceased to exist; many more have been totally deformed by bomb craters. The women and children remaining in the city have taken shelter in basements or dug out caves in the bluffs leading down to the Volga.

The Germans have been attacking the city for a month already. They want to capture the city, whatever the cost. Bits of downed bombers litter the streets and anti-aircraft shells burst in the sky, yet the bombardment does not let up, not even for an hour. The besiegers are trying to turn this city into an unlivable hell.

Here, where the sky burns overhead and the ground beneath your feet constantly shakes, it is difficult to exist. Your throat seizes up with a convulsive hatred when you see walls with gaping holes and burned-out windows in what were recently ordinary homes. The charred bodies of women and children set alight by the fascists on a steamer lie on the Volga's sandy embankment, crying out for revenge.

It is difficult to exist here, yet to live in Stalingrad and stand idly by is impossible. To live here and *fight*, to live here and kill the Germans, is not just possible: it is necessary. So that is how we shall live. We shall defend the city amongst the fire, the smoke, and the blood. The threat of death may hang over us, but glory is within our grasp. Amongst the ruins of the city and the weeping of orphaned children, glory itself has become a sister to us.

It is evening. We are on the city's outskirts. The battlefield is spread out before us. The hills are smoking; the streets are on fire. Darkness, as it always does in the south, falls quickly. Everything is shrouded in the blue-black smoke of our guards batteries' fiery mortar rounds. An enormous ring of white German signal flares shoots upwards, marking the frontline.

Nightfall does not interrupt the battle. We hear an immense rumbling: German bombers have again dropped bombs on the city behind us. A moment earlier we had heard the roar of planes move from west to east. Now we hear a roar from east to west. Our planes are flying west! They string out a chain of bright yellow flares over the German positions, then bombs explode along the illuminated ground.

It is relatively quiet for a quarter of an hour. I say "relatively," because a deafening cannonade to the north and the south and the dry chattering of machine guns ahead are still constantly audible. But people call that "quiet" in Stalingrad because real silence has not fallen here for a long time – and you've got to call *something* "quiet"! At times like this, all the things you've seen in these last days and nights – the enraged and exhausted faces and the sleep-deprived and angry eyes of our troops – come to you all at once.

We crossed the Volga in the evening. The specks of fires grew ever redder against the black evening sky. The motorized ferry we crossed on was overloaded: there were five vehicles with materiel, a company of Red Army soldiers, a handful of girls from a medical battalion, and us. The ferry sailed under cover of a curtain of smoke, but the crossing still seemed to go on a long time indeed.

Next to me, on the edge of the deck, sat a twenty-year-old girl by the name of Shchepenya. An orderly from Ukraine, I thought her first name, Viktoriya, rather beautiful. She was crossing into Stalingrad for the fourth or fifth time. Here, under siege conditions, the normal rules about evacuating casualties have been changed: there's no room for treatment points in the burning city, so the nurses and orderlies gather the wounded right at the frontline, transport them across the city, then load them onto boats and ferries. Having crossed to safety, they go back for the newly injured, who are already waiting for help. Viktoriya and one of my travelling companions turned out to be from the same area.[57] They spent half the crossing trying to outdo each other's stories about Dnepropetrovsk, chattering about the city's streets, about the building my companion had lived in, and about the building where Viktoriya had studied. They recalled every last detail of their hometown. It felt that, in their hearts at least, they had refused, and would always refuse, to surrender Dnepropetrovsk. It felt that, come what may, they believed that their town could never belong to anybody else.

The ferry was already getting close to the Stalingrad side.

"It's still a little frightening to disembark each time," said Viktoriya suddenly. "I've been wounded twice already – once heavily – but I still didn't believe I'd die because I haven't really lived yet. I haven't experienced much of life, so how could I just die?"

Her eyes were large and sad as she spoke. I knew she was right: it's terrifying to be barely twenty and to have been injured twice already, to have been fighting for fifteen months, and to be crossing here, into Stalingrad, for a fifth time. So much lies ahead: life, love, perhaps even – who knows – a first kiss? Yet now, tonight, accompanied by the constant rumbling and with the fiery city ahead, this twenty-year-old girl is entering Stalingrad for a fifth time. And go she must, even though she is terrified. In fifteen minutes' time, she'll traverse the burning houses and, on some street in the outskirts, amongst the ruins and the shrieking shrapnel, she'll gather up the wounded and take them back across the river. And if she makes it, she'll return for a sixth time.

Now we approach the quay, the steeply inclined bank, and the terrible smell of burning houses. The sky is black, but the frames of the houses are blacker still. Their mutilated eaves and half-destroyed walls cut into the sky. When the distant flash of a bomb turns the sky red for just a moment, the ruined houses look like fortress battlements.

For the houses here really are fortresses. In one, an HQ is operating out of a basement. Here, underground, there is all the usual hustle and bustle of an HQ. Telegraph operators, pale from lack of sleep, tap out their dots and dashes. Communications officers, dusted with dislodged plaster as if covered in snow, hurry in and out. Numbered hills, heights, and defensive lines do not figure in their messages, though. Instead, one finds the names of streets, suburbs, villages, and sometimes even houses.

The HQ and communications installation are hidden deep underground. They are the brains of our defence, so their safety cannot be chanced. The men are tired. Faces are leaden and eyes heavy with sleeplessness. I try to light a cigarette, but my matches, one after the other, instantly go out. There is not much oxygen down here underground.

It is night. We are driving a clapped-out truck, practically blind in the dark, from the HQ to a command post. Amongst the stream of broken and burned living quarters, a single housing block remains whole. Creaking carts loaded with bread rumble out of the gates. There's a bakery in the

surviving building: the city lives, and it will keep living, no matter what.
The carts creak along the streets and suddenly stop when, somewhere on
the corner ahead, a mortar round explodes with a blinding flash.

It is morning. The sky is blue and square overhead. The brigade command point is located in one of the partially constructed factory buildings.
The street running north from the factory, toward the Germans, is covered
by mortars. Some time, perhaps, a policeman might have stood there indicating where people were and were not allowed to cross the road. Now, behind the cover of ruined walls, stands a submachine gunner, gesturing at
the spot where the street dips gently down and one can cross unseen by
the Germans and without giving away the command point's position.
One gunner was killed an hour ago. Now there is a new one at his post,
"directing the traffic."

It is already light. Today is a sunny day. Midday approaches. We are sitting
on soft, plush armchairs in an observation post. The post is located on the
fifth floor in a well-appointed apartment that had once housed an engineer.
The flowerpots have been taken from the windowsill and placed on the
floor. A stereoscopic telescope is clamped to the sill itself. The telescope is
used to look at objects in the distance, but the frontline positions are visible
to the naked eye from here. German vehicles drive by the houses on the edge
of the town. A motorcyclist leaps out onto the street; next come the Germans on foot. A handful of our mortar rounds explode. One car grinds to a
halt in the middle of the street. Another car darts out of the way and clings
close to the village houses. Now the response comes howling back. German
mortar rounds fly overhead and into the next-door house.

I step back from the window toward a table standing in the middle of the
room. A vase of dried flowers, some books, and a few school exercise books
are scattered on it. On one book, a child's hand has neatly written out the
word "Composition" between the lines. Just as in many other homes, life in
this apartment was cut off in mid-sentence. But life must continue. And
continue it will, because it is to this exact end that our troops are fighting
and dying here amongst the ruins and flames.

Another day and another night pass. The city's streets are even emptier,
but still its heart beats. We drive up to some factory gates. Workers in
overcoats and leather jackets wound round with belts stand guard, looking
for all the world just like the Red Army men of '18. They rigorously check

our documents before we find ourselves sitting in a basement. Those who have stayed put to defend the factory and its workshops – the director, the duty men, the firefighters, and the workers who joined the militia – are at their posts.

There are no longer any ordinary civilians in the city. Every one of those who have remained has become a defender. Come what may, and however many pieces of machinery are removed from the factory, a workshop always remains a workshop. The old workers who have given the best part of their lives to their factory will defend – to the very end, to the limits of the humanly possible – these workshops with their smashed windows and their smell of recently extinguished fires.

"We still haven't managed to mark it all out." The director nods toward a plan of the factory's lot hanging on a board. He starts to explain how German tanks had broken through the line and made for the factory a few days earlier. The factory got word about what had happened. Something had to be done there and then to help the soldiers plug the gap before nightfall. The director summoned the repair shop manager and ordered that several tanks which were close to being repaired should be made ready in the next hour. His people fixed the tanks. Then, despite the imminent danger, they climbed inside to man them. On this very spot, right in the factory yard, the workers and inspectors of the militia formed several tank crews. They got into the tanks, thundered through the empty yard, and charged out of the gates right into battle.

It was near a stone bridge across a narrow river that they were the first to intercept the Germans who had broken through. An enormous ravine, which the tanks could traverse only via the bridge, separated them from the Germans. The German tank column and our factory's tanks clashed right there on the bridge.

A savage artillery duel began. At the same time, a group of German submachine gunners made to cross the ravine. The factory matched the Germans with its own infantry: two squads of militiamen had followed the tanks to the ravine. One squad was led by a Dean from the Mechanical Institute and Police Chief Kostyuchenko. The other was led by the toolshop foreman Popov and the old steelworker Krivulin. Fighting, much of it hand-to-hand, broke out on the ravine's steep slopes. Several old factory workers – Kondratyev, Ivanov, Volodin, Simonov, Momotov, and Fomin, and many more – died in the fighting. Their names are now being constantly repeated in the factory.

On the same day, the edges of the factory district were transformed. Barricades appeared on the streets leading to the ravine. Just about everything – boilerplates, armour plates, even the hulls of dismantled tanks – was thrown into constructing the barricades. Just like they had in the Civil War, wives brought ammunition to their husbands, and girls went straight from the workshop to the frontline, where they tended to the wounded before dragging them away from the fighting. Many perished on that day, but thanks to these sacrifices, the workers' militia and the soldiers were able to hold the Germans off until reinforcements arrived that night.

The factory yards are empty now. The wind whistles through broken windows. Whenever a mortar explodes nearby, shards of broken glass shower down onto the asphalt. But the factory, like the rest of the city, fights on still. If it is possible to grow accustomed to the bombs, the mortars, the bullets, and the danger, then they have certainly grown accustomed to them here. They have grown accustomed to them like nobody else.

✳ ✳ ✳

We are crossing a bridge over one of the city's ravines. I shall never forget the image unfolding before my eyes. The ravine stretches far out to the left and right. It is teeming – it is riddled, everywhere, like an anthill – with caves. Whole streets are dug into it. Charred boards and rags cover the caves: women have used whatever they could find to protect their young from the rain and the wind. Words can barely express how painful it is to see these rows of sad human nests in place of streets and crossings and in the place of a once bustling city.

We are out on the outskirts again, right at the frontline, which is the name given to the fragments of houses swept off the face of the earth and the small hills peppered by shells. Out of the blue we meet a man, one of a group of four anti-tank gunners to whom many front pages were dedicated a month ago.[58] The four gunners – Aleksandr Belikov, Petr Samoilov, Ivan Oleinikov, and Petr Boloto – who turned up out of the blue here had destroyed fifteen German tanks. Though on second thoughts, why should it be "out of the blue"? Of course a man like Boloto would turn up in

Figure 1.4 Homeless women and children shelter in a cave in the Volga cliffs, September 1942.

Stalingrad. It is men just like him who are defending the city today. And it is precisely because the city has such defenders that it has stood firm for an entire month, in spite of everything, and amongst the ruins, the fire, and the blood.

Petr Boloto is a beefy, muscular man. He has an honest face and twinkling, rather brilliant eyes. Recalling the battle when he destroyed fifteen tanks, Boloto suddenly smiles and says: "When the first tank was coming at me, I thought, by Jove, the end of the world is nigh! It got closer and then it burst into flame. That was it for him and not for me! What's more, you know, I'd rolled five smokes for that battle. I smoked them all right down to the butt. Well, tell the truth, maybe not quite to the butt. But I smoked all five. Battle's like that: you put your gun down and have a smoke whenever you've got a chance. You can smoke in battle. But whatever you do, don't miss. If you miss, you're not going to be smoking at all. That's how it is in this business …"

Petr Boloto smiles calmly, widely in the way only a man set in his views of the soldiering life can. It is a life where you can take a smoke break, but you just cannot miss. There are all sorts of people defending Stalingrad. Many – a very many – have that same wide, confident smile. And they have those same relaxed, heavy, soldier's hands: the sort that don't miss. Thus fights the city, even when in many places it seems almost impossible to fight on.

＊＊＊

We are on the embankment, or at least what is left of it. The chassis of burned-out cars, bits of barges thrown onto the bank, and the skewed re-mains of surviving houses. Midday heat. The sun wrapped in thick smoke. The Germans are bombing the city again this morning. Right in front of us, the planes dive in one after another. The sky is filled with anti-aircraft fire exploding into the mottled, blue-grey skin of some sort of beast. Fighter planes circle and squeal overhead. The intense dogfight does not let up even for a moment. The city is defending itself whatever the cost. The cost may be high, the great feats of our people may be frightful and gruelling, their suffering may go unheard, but there is nothing for it. This is not a battle for survival. It is a fight to the death.

The Volga's water gently laps against the shore, bringing a charred log right onto the sand at our feet. A drowned woman lies on the log, clutching it with burned, crooked fingers. I do not know where the waves have brought her from. Perhaps she is one of those who perished on the steamer, or perhaps she is one of those who perished in a fire on the quay. Her face is disfigured. Her torment before death must have been unimaginable. The Germans did this. They did this before our very eyes. May they never beg for mercy from those saw it. We will show them no mercy after Stalingrad.

Vasily Grossman – In the Gully on the Steppe
26 September 1942, *Krasnaya Zvezda*

One evening the submachine gunners were lying in a gully on the steppe. Almost all of them had taken their shoes off and were bending their heads to examine tired, red-raw feet. Some had even thought to wash their foot-wraps in the shallow stream that ran along the bottom of the gully. The footwraps were left to dry on the branches of wild cherry and pear trees as the troops massaged their toes and sighed: "There's nothing for it but to give your feet a break after a march like that."

Lazarev, a woodturner from Naro-Fominsk, with red hair that gently clung to his sunken temples and to the nape of his neck, voiced his frustration:[59] "I warned the sergeant major that my boots were too tight, but he said they'd loosen up. Look how they've loosened up; my feet are all mashed up and bloody."

"Dust. Sun. But no sign of salvation," said Petrenko. "There's no end to this steppe. It's not like Ukraine was, all fields and gardens."

Lazarev laughed: "Don't start having a go at the steppe. Zholdubaev gets the hump when people do that."

The Kazakh Zholdubaev and Lazarev were true comrades. They had become friends when they were doing training in the reserves. They would chat away in the breaks after training sessions. In the long march across the steppe, under the cruel sun, and in whirlwinds of dust so thick that the next man over would suddenly disappear, Lazarev would cry out, "Hey, Zholdubaev, are you there? I can't see a damned thing!"

Their conversations on the march were always brief, but they would walk side-by-side. Sometimes Lazarev would ask, "Tired are you, mate?" Zholdubaev would pull the stopper from his flask, which was wrapped with sodden wet newspaper, and offer the round glass bottle and its dark cloudy water to his comrade. "You first," Lazarev would say, and Zholdubaev would reply: "Not at all, not at all. Drink, please."

Indeed, the whole submachine gunner company was extremely close. Perhaps it was because they were, to a man, young. The strapping company commander Drobot, his second in command Berezyuk, the platoon commander Lieutenant Shut, and the rest of the gunners were all about the same age – somewhere between twenty and twenty-two. However, some, like Drobot and Berezyuk, had already been at war for over a year. Others, like Romanov and Zholdubaev, were about to go into battle for the first time.

Drobot kept them in line strictly. He insisted that they treat their weapons with respect and regularly check over their submachine guns. But the soldiers already knew – they somehow felt – that the PPSh had a special significance.[60] Every one of them cleaned and oiled their gun with unusual diligence. Drobot and Berezyuk were Ukrainians, and their families were still in occupied territory. The two men's particular composure and vengefulness caught on with the men.

Berezyuk had been injured in fighting in the fall; now his cheek bore a large pink weal. He was always on the back of his platoon and its detachment leaders, but it was obvious he never acted out of spite. He did it for the love of the army, so nobody resented him. The young Lieutenant Shut had already proved to be a good and reliable comrade back in training. Now, as platoon commander, he would tell his men: "The main thing, lads, is to keep up the camaraderie. Don't mess with that. It's the most important thing for us submachine gunners."

While the footwraps were drying, the gunners could smell the smoke coming from the kitchen. They were yawning. They desperately wanted to eat but, after the 50 kilometre march, sleep was an even greater temptation. However, they would have no time to rest.

Earlier that day, German tanks and motorized infantry had broken through in a sector near Stalingrad. The Germans were making for the Volga. They could feel the great river's moist breath and sense the approach of winter, so they had mustered all their strength in order to make it to the immense city.

The regimental commander was given the order to attack that very night. He walked around the battalions as they rested, looked over the troops' exhausted faces, and listened to snippets of their conversation. He walked past the submachine gunners and looked inquisitively at the boys' thin faces. They had become even more boyish. Many had never fought in battle. Could they resist the might of the German onslaught? Could these boys in vests bleached white by the cruel sun really hold the great line along the Volga?

A few hours passed and the regiment went into a battle that would last more than ten days. The men passed their first test.

Another chance of a breather on the steppe. The roar of friendly and enemy planes alike fills the warm evening air, machine guns and artillery fire high in the blue sky overhead. The fighting is taking place on the ground too. Black and white clouds from explosions burst up from the flat steppe; semi-automatic guns chatter in short, neat bursts; heavy artillery shells explode with deafening blasts. Sometimes the fighting quietens down so that you can hear the dry grass rustle and the crickets chirp. But in the deep gully on the steppe, the submachine gunners are utterly calm, so at ease that it is almost as if they were relaxing at home and not sitting just a few kilometres away from the enemy. They lie on the ground, grunting with pleasure as they stretch themselves out. Several have taken their shoes off; others have removed their vests and hung them on the bushes.

I look at the fighters' youthful faces. There is a terrible contrast imprinted on them: there is both a jolly sense of humour and the mark of men who have stared into the dark eyes of death. Their stories, like their faces, also reflect this mix of a youthful, almost childish, interest in the twists and turns of battle, and serious, sombre thoughts of losses, of their wartime fate and the burden they bear, and of their immense responsibility to the Volga and to Stalingrad.

Company Commander Drobot speaks calmly and thoughtfully. It is a good thing when a young commander is not satisfied with himself after a battle. He reflects on his mistakes – those that prevented the submachine gunners from operating at their absolute best – and anxiously picks apart his own blunders. It is an equally good thing when a commander speaks of his troops with pride and delight. The company had lived through a great trial and come out with honour. The gunners' camaraderie had only grown in these first battles at Stalingrad.

This is how Lazarev describes his first battle: "They sent us ahead of the rifles. We were ordered to take some pillboxes. There were five of us: me, Romanov, Petrenko, Belchenko, and my good mate Zholdubaev. It was already evening – the sun was going down – and they were firing on us something awful. Mortar after mortar. Smoke. Dust. Now, mortars don't go deep into the ground. They kind of spray it up, like a chicken scratching with its feet. But we just kept on forward.

"They almost got us a few times. You think you've drawn your last breath – the shell's blowing up five feet away – and your ears are ringing and ringing. But us lads have strong legs, so we'd leap off to one side – some of us one way, the rest the other. They can't keep track of that; they lose their target. So we'd dust ourselves off and keep on forward. We were getting pretty close. There were maybe two hundred metres left. Suddenly five tanks come out from behind a hill and bear down on us. We get down on the ground and take a look at them.

"Do we go back? Not a bit of it, it didn't even cross the lads' minds. The tanks sat there, firing over our heads, then went off back over the hill. We looked around and said, 'Well, lads, let's get going!' We had a job to do, and that's that. So off we went. Tell the truth, though, there was less joking then, especially after those tanks. We didn't think we'd make it out alive.

"So we got right close to the Germans, so close we could see 'em clearly. We counted about twenty-five of them with submachine guns. There was an officer in an unbuttoned greatcoat. We could see the little holster on his belt underneath the coat. He's going back and forth, looking right at us. Twenty-five of them, five of us. They've got submachine guns, we've got submachine guns. We lie down, every man for himself, and open fire. We fire off our first rounds and Zholdubaev pokes me and says, 'I got him!' I'm pretty surprised and ask, 'Really?' He looks at me, big toothy grin and all, and says, 'Really.'

"When he said that we felt a whole lot better and began to laugh. But a minute later a German sniper got Zholdubaev. Bullet went right through his forehead. He slumped down next to me. Didn't say a word. And then he was gone. He lay there dead, and I was covered in his blood. That left four of us to fight. I couldn't tell you how we managed to fight off those twenty-five men, how many we killed, and how many just ran away. I don't want to lie, and it was in the evening after all. But it was them and not us who retreated. I was left on the steppe with Zholdubaev. Dug him a grave and lay his body in it with my very own hands. I said goodbye and I buried him ..."

Lazarev's comrades listened to the tale, chipping in here and there. When he'd finished, Romanov said, "I used to wonder what the scariest thing about battle would be. But now I know for sure. The scariest thing is losing a comrade in battle. Having a comrade next to you in battle? It's better than if your mother and father were there ..."

The steppe was bathed in the pink light of the sunset. It was twilight in the gully. The soldiers' boyish faces seemed stern in the dusk. During this brief moment of respite, each man could feel the great power of military camaraderie.

2

1 OCTOBER–18 NOVEMBER

Torment

An unseasonably warm October was cold comfort to the fatigued frontline writers, who spent day after day scrabbling through rubble, eking out sleep in damp trenches and stinking dugouts, and dodging an enemy hidden in Stalingrad's every nook and cranny. Vasily Koroteev and Vasily Grossman, who had been on the Volga the longest, were exhausted. The latter was nonetheless still working late into every night to "neatly and totally fill lined pages with the scratchy little words, phrases and paragraphs that would in turn be set onto linotypes then stamped out onto the pages of *Krasnaya Zvezda* and *Pravda*."[1] A lucky few, including Grossman, left for brief periods of leave.[2] Many, however, had to stay put, toiling away as hopes faded.

The strategic outlook was dire. The fighting stretched hundreds of kilometres from Stalingrad down toward the mountains of the Caucasus. Stalin's pleading messages to his allies grew bleaker.[3] A stalemate had set in. Streets were captured and recaptured, houses occupied and reoccupied, but neither side could land a decisive blow. The budding author Viktor Nekrasov, then a sapper on the Mamaev Kurgan, remembered: "The first shell lands long before the sunlight. Must be ours. The echoes shimmer across the sleeping Volga. Another shell. A third, a fourth. Then they all coalesce into the magnificent morning barrage. Thus begins the day."[4] This was, he remembered, "the toughest period of the defence. All we did was defend and defend."[5] The idea that the battle might never end took hold. Konstantin Simonov's coda to "Days and Nights," in which one day of fighting simply rolled into another, had proved to be prophetic.

Terrible events exacerbated the sense that Stalingrad was a hell on earth. On 2 October, a group of fuel silos on the banks of the Volga was hit. Waves of burning oil poured through the streets and across the Volga's surface. Troops

Figure 2.1 Destroyed trucks and buildings in Stalingrad, late fall 1942.

and workers, desperately hoping to swim to safety, leapt into the water and were rapidly engulfed by flames. The scene induced such desperate pain that one witness "felt like I was going out of my mind."[6] The papers made no attempt to hide the scale of this destruction, permitting ever more graphic descriptions of soldiers' death and sacrifice, and printing photographs of fires, civilian corpses, and the devastated city. All the *podvigi* the newspaper writers could summon threatened to be overwhelmed by this torrent of misery.

The writer's task by this time, Konstantin Simonov explained, was straightforward: "Look how the writers [in October] used every means available to let the reader know: victory will come."[7] The resulting efforts to project the hope of a warless future onto the bloody status quo are reflected in this section's translations of works by Anatoly Nedzelsky, Boris Polevoy, Evgeny Kriger, Vasily Grossman, and Vasily Koroteev.

The first, Anatoly Nedzelsky's "Tales of Stalingrad's Defenders," introduces two typical heroes – one a novice machine gunner, the other a liaison officer – in a pair of unconnected miniatures. They show how an ordinary soldier like the forty-year-old Nedzelsky, a captain in one of Stalingrad's guards regiments, was able to share his writing on the pages of the national newspapers during Stalingrad. Nedzelsky had already written for a local newspaper and was now recruited by Vasily Koroteev to write for *Izvestiya*, becoming one of many such lower-ranked writers drawn into the central papers' fold.[8] Thanks to this new writing commission, Nedzelsky was able to leave his regular post to interview his subjects: Viktor Leontev, a twenty-six-year-old from the town of Vladimir who had been desperate to sign up in December 1941;[9] and Kuzma Makarov, a telephony worker who had become a liaison officer of particular renown.[10]

The "Tales" are poised between witness and literary account. Each of the heroes completes a *podvig* of sorts: Leontev's is a typical feat of battlefield bravery; Makarov's is a product of his positive hero-like *nous*. Both heroes are typically Soviet in background. The description of Makarov's past work in radiotelephony and municipal transport is an elegant nod to the Socialist Realist hero of the 1930s. These ordinary men are inserted right into the now familiar heart of literary Stalingrad. Nedzelsky suffuses the text of the "Tales" with observations about everything from the makeshift construction of dugouts to the breathless rush of entering battle and gruesome frontline injuries. These notes are sandwiched between allusions to prewar Russian patriotic tropes of wounded soldiers battling through adversity, to *War and Peace*, and to Konstantin Simonov's Stalingrad work. The Socialist Realist agglomerative method was not a hindrance but a crutch that enabled writers like Nedzelsky to bring textual order to their *own* soldiering experiences.

Meanwhile, Konstantin Simonov had spent several weeks working on the Central Front and mulling over the shock of visiting Stalingrad. The author now found time to write up material from a brief visit to the 596th Night Bombing Squadron he had made before leaving Stalingrad. The squadron, who worked with a relentless pace – they completed seven hundred sorties in the fortnight before Simonov's visit alone[11] – flew the unfancied U-2 plane. The flimsy machine was, put simply, a clunker: "One direct hit and it caught fire and burned up completely in the air, before it even hit the ground. Like a match."[12] The plane, though, turned out to be useful for precise bombing in cramped city blocks.[13]

The 596th squadron's workhorse pilots and their unlikely bombers were the perfect against-all-odds heroes for the difficult month of October.

Simonov depicts his aviators with a jocular familiarity, but the protagonists are no fools. They cannily turn their unbecoming jalopy into a phantasm that haunts the Germans. Through cunning, good humour, and hard work, the squadron conquers the skies and even seems to conquer death itself: it "sustains almost no losses," claims Simonov. If even the absurd U-2 could become "terrifying," then historical contingency and Soviet ingenuity, Simonov suggests, could turn the tide in even the most unpromising situation. While "U-2" might have reflected some newfound positivity in Simonov's mood, the U-2 pilot's lot was a tough one. Almost half of the 596th Squadron's pilots perished at Stalingrad. Of the three pilots named in Simonov's sketch, only Captain Ovodov survived the war. Lieutenant Georgy Osipov never returned from a sortie in May 1943, and Aleksandr Poklikushkin was shot down by a flak gun in March 1945.[14]

As October marched on, the bad news did not let up. David Ortenberg sent telegram after telegram imploring his writers to work faster. Above him, the Kremlin demanded that every page of every newspaper be filled with nothing but stories of Stalingrad.[15] The battle was accorded ever greater importance in a series of new axiomatic claims printed in *Krasnaya Zvezda* and *Pravda*: Stalingrad was now a "hero-city," a "warrior-city," the scene of a "miracle" to come, and "the greatest battle in the history of humanity."[16] When it seemed like the fighting might last forever, everyone from the Kremlin and David Ortenberg down to ordinary soldiers like Anatoly Nedzelsky was hoping that literary assertion alone might shape reality. Faith became ever more important: as Ilya Ehrenburg put it, "I *needed* to believe: back in those days, for me and every other Soviet citizen, there was no alternative."[17]

Evgeny Kriger was the man for the hour. Arriving in early October, the bespectacled Kriger – "the most peaceful sort of fellow" and an actor by training – was an unlikely *frontovik*.[18] Kriger felt much more at home ensconced in a chair in *Izvestiya*'s Moscow editorial office, which he laconically christened "the barracks," than at the front.[19] So unused to war was the writer that, when he enrolled in 1941, he would absent-mindedly forget his rifle in all sorts of places. Born soldier he may not have been, but Kriger was an affable fellow and a popular addition to the crowd at Akhtuba.[20]

Kriger was no soldier, but he was certainly no coward. Determined to see the "hero-city" for himself, he put in a special request to travel to Stalingrad. On his arrival, he was shocked by the contrast between how he had imagined Stalingrad before the war as a verdant and utopian Soviet city and the vision of obliteration that unrolled before him. Kriger noted in his diary a reaction to this dichotomy: "War doesn't just mean death. It means life."[21] His ability to find hope in the bleakness led him to pen a series of works – the first two, "This Is Stalingrad" and "The Streets of Stalingrad," are translated here – that shrink the fighting down to a human scale even as they crystallize the motif of Stalingrad as resurrection.

In these works, the city and its defenders are ritually slaughtered by gleeful Germans but rise from the grave to punish their tormentors. Kriger opens "This Is Stalingrad" with an extended Homeric simile, describing the Germans attacking and torturing "the city's tattered and burned body." The personified city survives to defend the starving and parched inhabitants, who, Kriger tells us, are forced to live in sewers: the *podvig* here belongs more to the city itself than to its human defenders, who function as sacrifices to enable the city's vengeful assault on the Germans. On the one hand, Kriger's tribute to the Stalingraders' destroyed homes and lives – their "peacetime city" has been totally erased by a new, "wartime city" – is convincing and elegiac. On the other, the suffering of 23 August – mentioned here in print for the first time – is transformed into a moment necessary for the city to be "reborn in battle." While the purpose of the *podvig* was purportedly to offer salvation to ordinary people, only civilians' suffering creates a Stalingrad that can save those very civilians. The circular logic suggests that any and all mistakes made before the battle, and any tragedies occurring during it, were necessary for victory: this line of thinking would, within weeks, come to dominate a Stalinist narrative of Stalingrad.

In "The Streets of Stalingrad," Kriger captured the Soviet hopes for resurrection in a new motto that would be used repeatedly for years to come: "Stalingrad lives!" While the phrase might seem to flatten the nuances of the Stalingrad narrative into a two-dimensional battle cry, readers lapped Kriger's material up. David Ortenberg was as taken by Kriger's Stalingrad stories as the other writers at the front.[22] Kriger might be largely forgotten even in Russia, but his Stalingrad stories were in the coming months more widely disseminated at home and abroad than any others.

Vasily Grossman, meanwhile, was in his element as he searched for ways to link ordinary soldiers' actions with a mythical narrative of Stalingrad. In mid-October, David Ortenberg sent Grossman and a fellow reporter, Efim Gekhman, to visit the troops under Aleksandr Rodimtsev, a thirty-six-year-old veteran now leading the defensive efforts in Stalingrad. Grossman and Gekhman stole across the Volga and into Stalingrad under heavy fire. Stationed just a couple of hundred metres from the German positions, Grossman spent three days interviewing Rodimtsev's soldiers and officers. The rank and file were delighted by this attention, but the sardonic Rodimtsev was rather more dubious: "I'm a superstitious fellow. You did an article about [Lev Mikhailovich] Dovator. He got killed the same day. They printed a photo of [Nikita Vladislavovich] Panfilov. He got killed the same day ..."[23] Nonetheless, Grossman gathered what he needed and began to write a new story while still in the thick of the action.[24]

Grossman finished "The Battle of Stalingrad," translated into English here for the first time, in just a couple of days back in Akhtuba. The work was, according to Ortenberg, a superlative piece in which Grossman "looked ahead to the future" at a time when the battle seemed endless.[25] The work is filled with Tolstoyan allusions to spirited soldiers and Rodimtsev's instinctive and inspirational leadership, as well as packed with mythical devices that draw great elemental forces onto and into the battlefield. The terrifying threat of a "sun [that] hung like a dark axe over an earth drowning in darkness" is conquered in two ways. First, by moments of exemplary sacrifice: the soldiers who perish during the crossing of the Volga seem at least as heroic as those who survive. Second, each of the soldiers' tasks are "connected to a single, greater task": the cohesion of the Red Army turns the individual into an all-conquering hero. Grossman's battle is simultaneously elemental and human, universal and bounded, apocalyptic and demiurgic. The martyrdom of Soviet man seems capable of bending reality away from war and back toward peace. "The Battle of Stalingrad" caused an unprecedented stir among readers. General Rodimtsev is even today fêted as one of Stalingrad's greatest heroes.[26]

Kriger's and Grossman's works provided a trove of ideas for other frontline writers. Boris Polevoy, *Pravda*'s leading correspondent, who was almost as popular as Simonov among ordinary Soviet readers and even more popular among the country's elites, was one of those inspired.[27] In a late-night conversation at Akhtuba, Grossman showed Polevoy his drafts of "The Battle of Sta-

Figure 2.2 Boris Polevoy writing at the command post of the 284th Rifles in Stalingrad, October 1942.

lingrad." Polevoy could barely contain his excitement as he pored over Grossman's notes. He too raced to visit Rodimtsev's troops on the Mamaev Kurgan, where he would write "House 21a."

The work leans heavily on Grossman, Simonov, and Kriger for inspiration, but Polevoy was no mere imitator. "House 21a" was the first of the "house defence" stories in which any building could stand in for the entire war, and which came to dominate the Stalingrad story in the 1960s and 1970s. The plight of the house's residents – we read a graphic story of rape, infanticide, and the murder of elderly residents – invites readers to map their own experiences of war against Stalingraders' tragedies while also filling Polevoy's soldiers with vengeful rage. The *podvig* of the house's defenders is linked, through the image of civilian suffering, to the salvation of the whole nation. Moreover, the interplay between Grossman's and Polevoy's work (and the similarities in the descriptions of prewar Stalingrad in the Kriger, Grossman, and Polevoy texts in this chapter) reveals how writers at Stalingrad were collectively placing ordinary people at the centre of a battle, and a war, that was expanding on ever greater scales. The act of reforming and recycling others' written material was becoming central to coping with the tragedy of Stalingrad.

As October ended, hopes of holding out at Stalingrad were all but gone. Leonid Kovalev, the guardsman who had been proud to feature in Ilya Ehrenburg's "Stalingrad," was losing himself in a furious depression:

> The Hitlerite scum have wrecked our beautiful city on the Volga, Stalingrad, every house and building. Our Red Army and me are defending things and getting at the enemy, all over in the basements and up in the attics, etc., everywhere we find 'em. I've seen our boys dying, I've seen our wounded in fires and on burning haystacks, I've seen it all with my own eyes, but my heart grows firmer and my hatred stronger.[28]

Kovalev incorporates language from the newspaper stories – references to a "beautiful city," to defending "every house," and to hearts growing "firmer" and hatred "stronger" – to make sense of his own psychological state and to explain events to the recipient of his letter. Soviets like Kovalev were beginning to parse and rewrite their own experiences at Stalingrad as part of a collective martyrdom.

Despite the tense strategic situation and their own fatigue, Vasily Koroteev and Grossman managed to produce some almost celebratory material in early November. Their co-authored story "In Stalin's City," which has never before been reprinted or discussed in Russian or English work, parallels Simonov's "U-2" as an attempt to describe Stalingrad in uplifting tones. The sketch focuses on the anniversary of the 1917 Revolution on 7 November. The date had always been an important Soviet celebration; now Aleksandr Shcherbakov's office distributed a series of talking points for editors to include to mark the twenty-fifth anniversary.[29] David Ortenberg used this prompt to call for pieces from his writers. In response, Vasily Koroteev secured invitations for both himself and Grossman to attend Stalingrad Party Secretary Aleksey Chuyanov's speech at an anniversary gathering.[30]

"In Stalin's City" combines the poetic hallmarks of Grossman's writing – the opening paragraph, which is filled with extended, elemental metaphors, is equal to any of his postwar output – with Koroteev's knowledge of the city and its political figures. The piece links the heroes of the recent present – Rodimtsev and Chuyanov are, among others, assumed to be known to the reader – with the "strength of the Great Socialist October Revolution" and the bringing of light to darkness. Through suffering and strife, Stalingrad's heroes had ascended to a place of vaunted historical and quasi-religious privilege; the reader is invited into this space with the jovial and straightforward descriptions of ordinary Stalingraders attending an upbeat holiday gathering.

Coverage of the anniversary celebrations clearly met with some success. Lidia Medvedeva, a young tank lieutenant and regular reader of the newspapers, wrote a letter home showing how she had completely absorbed the lessons of her regular newspaper reading:

> My beloved and dear mama, papa, Lyuba, Viktor and Genochka. My felicitations on the day of the great festival, 7 November, which is inspiring us to new heroic feats and the total destruction of the enemy. I know you've ended up celebrating the big day behind the lines, but we at the front aren't missing a thing today. We're going to go on the advance and liberate our country and our people from the enemy's yoke.[31]

Even in the bleakness of late October, Medvedeva was using her reading to help imagine the future: "I don't think I'll go back to the Far East after the war; I'll stay somewhere here out west ... But after the war and the defeat of the enemy, I'll come home and give [my brother] Genochka a pistol as a souvenir."[32] Amidst the exhaustion and danger, and even knowing that Stalingrad and the nation with it might fall at any time, the stories written at the front offered a sliver of hope. Perhaps Grossman, who wrote to his father on 13 November 1942 that "I think this winter will bring us many good things," found as much comfort in the writing emerging from the front as his readers did. A mere six days later, the Soviets began their counterattack. The hypothetical *podvig* of Stalingrad was about to become very real.

Anatoly Nedzelsky – Tales of Stalingrad's Defenders
3 October 1942, *Ivestiya*

The Birth of Courage
"That's right, I am indeed the same salesman you met in Vladimir. My name's Leontev." A pale and tall Red Army soldier stood before Lieutenant Chuprikov, the commander of a company of submachine gunners.

"And what can I do for you, Comrade Leontev?" asked Chuprikov with a smile, as if he were talking with an old friend.

"Permission to make a request, sir?"

"Go ahead."

Leontev explained his request. It transpired that he was supposed to be joining the rifles, but, as he put it, he "had wanted to be a gunner for a long time."

"Not a problem. We can sort that out," said the lieutenant, "only don't let me down." And so, thanks to what he jokingly calls his "old chum," Leontev joined the company of submachine gunners.

Viktor Leontev did not let his lieutenant down. He tried as hard as possible to get up to speed with his gunner comrades, who had already completed their training. He wholeheartedly embraced the submachine gun. Leontev liked first that the company was tasked with special and important jobs and second how the submachine fired, "like a machine gun," with glorious fury. That was a perfect match for his spirited character.

When Leontev first arrived at the front, he found it odd that the line was right there, just beyond that gully. It was really very close indeed. Beyond the gully out stretched the steppe. There was not a soul to be seen. The Fritz were in the gully itself. Leontev's platoon was asked to cover the battalion's left flank while it drove the enemy from the gully then took the high ground that dominated the surrounding area. The gunners fanned out and began to make their way through a hollow toward the gully. Past the hollow they would find themselves on ground that was, save for the odd weed, entirely open.

The Germans spotted the advancing soldiers. The steppe burst into life as volleys of artillery fire rang out. Three shells exploded, one after the other, just to the rear. The Germans added automatic fire to this assault, then machine gun fire clattered in from the left flank. Our soldiers threw themselves to the ground and began to dig themselves in. Leontev quickly raked himself out a shallow trench. His body disappeared underground, while his head was well protected by a little mound of earth. He grew tired of lying in the same position, so he rolled over and looked around. Spotting the smoke from a gunshot about a hundred and fifty metres away, Leontev rattled off a short burst.

The battle was raging. The smoke-filled steppe was shaking. Waves of soldiers sallied forth along the great expanse held by the battalion. The left flank, where Leontev's unit was situated, was pressed more and more by submachine gun fire. The Hun had taken up position in a destroyed tank and were now combing the approach to the gully with assault weapons.

Leontev found himself lying next to Lieutenant Danilov. Danilov motioned at the tank.

"How did they get there, the buggers?" cursed the lieutenant. "D'you see how they're having a crack at us?"

Leontev nodded in confirmation.

"Go and capture that tank and hold it until our comrades get here," said the lieutenant.

Leontev's reply was simple: "Capture the tank. Yes, sir." He still did not really understand how that could be done in practice, but he knew he would find a way to carry out the order to a tee. He grabbed his submachine gun, two magazines, and two grenades, and began to crawl up the side of the hill.

The tank was situated seventy or eighty metres from the near side of the slope. Leontev hugged the ground so tightly for the last fifty metres that his body seemed to leave a trail in the earth. Our gunners then began to fire at the tank with pinpoint accuracy. The Hitlerites, afraid that they would be encircled, fled the tank in a hurry.

Leontev suddenly found himself right next to the tank. It was no more than 20 metres away, but just then little fountains of sand and dust began to shoot out from the sun-scorched grass. The Germans were firing on the tank. Leontev kept on moving forward. When no more than 5 or 6 metres separated him from the tank, he burst forward and threw himself against the stationary black hulk. The Germans were so surprised that they could barely make sense of what was happening. By the time they managed to make their explosive bullets rain down on the tank, Leontev had already slipped inside through the open hatch. For a second he thought that the tank must be heavily riveted on the inside. Then he felt something warm run down his leg: blood! He had not felt the pain in the heat of the fighting a moment earlier.

Leontev tightly bandaged his leg just above the knee, then sat and listened carefully. The tank was in a ring of fire. The artillery was thundering away, the machine guns stuttered on, and the rifles fired endlessly. A serene and blinding blue sky glimmered through the open turret hatch. Then the shadows of some Junkers flickered across the sky. They were roaring toward our front line.

Leontev was seized by anger. For the first time he felt clearly, with his whole heart and being, the woes that the pack of German dogs – whose shadowy bombers and thousands of armoured monstrosities were now attacking his friends – have brought to our people. It was only by a stroke of luck that one of those very same monstrosities was now covering him from the enemy's bullets. Leontev forgot about the danger. He forgot he was alone. He could hear his comrades' voices not far off; they were close indeed. He suddenly wanted to be among them, to press the trigger tight, to lob his grenades, and when he had no ammunition left, to let the enemy have it with the butt of his rifle and with his fists.

"For the motherland! For Stalin!" The cry rolled out across the steppe in a fearsome wave. Leontev could restrain himself no longer. He emerged from the hatch, braced himself, and fired off a long burst toward the enemy. His finger was still on the trigger when he saw some figures advancing. He cried out, his voice cracking with the tension: "Kill them, the devils! No mercy! Forward, for Stalin!"

Then something happened that shocked the soldiers watching on from behind the tank. Leontev leapt down from the turret and tore off in the direction of a self-propelled gun. The Fritz abandoned the gun right away. Leontev began to imagine that he might capture it, roll it a little closer to the enemy, then fire on them with their own weapon. This courageous young gunner, who this morning had not so much as sniffed gunpowder, seized the gun.

※ ※ ※

Our boys picked the wounded man up that evening. Leontev recognized his friends – at the front one makes friends right away – and tried, in vain, to smile. The day's exertions were telling on him. A military doctor carefully inspected his wound: "It's bad, but it's not fatal," he said. Then he added, "I promise you'll be alright."

The Liaison Officer

A deep gully whose bottom is dark and damp, just like the bottom of a well. A moonless and blustery night. You can't see two feet ahead. The stars, alone in the black sky, are twinkling. If you draw back the cape tightly covering the entrance to the commander's dugout just enough, you might see a thin, faint strip of light across the gully's ridge.

Someone lifted the cape just for an instant to exit the dugout. A quiet voice sounded out: "Liaison officers, to your positions!" A group of hitherto invisible people suddenly emerged from the darkness and gathered around the thin strip of light.

"Come and get your packets!" The men moved quick and silent as shadows.

A few minutes later and the gully was empty again. The packets, which contained urgent military orders, had gone off to their destinations. They would end up with the various divisions, ready to be sent on to regiments, battalions, and companies. Then, in just a couple of hours, vital and decisive operations would begin on the basis of these orders.

It was the liaison officers who would deliver these packets. We were to accompany one of their number. Our travel companion introduced himself: "Technician, 2nd Class, Makarov."

The war effort requires people with all sorts of expertise. Kuzma Matveevich Makarov, who had worked in the administration of the Moscow Municipal Radiotelephone Network before the war, found a place for his skills in the military. His first army job had been to manage a radiotelephony workshop for an airborne regiment. Then he headed the signals operations for a rifles division for half a year. Then, just recently, this man of many talents, this intelligent commander, was made a liaison officer.

It is no coincidence that liaison officers are often referred to as "the commander's right hand." The liaison officer is always on his feet and always on the move, but he is no mere messenger or errand boy. He is given many tasks, and much is asked of him. It is no mean feat to deliver an order, in the face of all sorts of dangers and difficulties, on time, come what may. And then the liaison officer has to bring back documents detailing the situation on a particular sector of the front and report everything going on at that moment to his commander. The liaison officer's reports frequently inform serious operational decisions.

Makarov had been promoted to liaison officer on the eve of an offensive operation in one of our sectors. The objective was to capture a strategically important railway junction. Makarov soon found himself right in the thick of the action. Those were difficult days. The artillery did not fall silent and the mortars did not cease fire for four whole days. The area around the junction was the scene of fierce, bloody skirmishes. The enemy clung on to every last scrap of land and every last hill. They had built a complicated defensive system, dug themselves in deep, and set up firing lines along every approach to their strongpoints.

Late one afternoon, a car raced up to our headquarters. Out leapt Makarov. The general hurriedly tore open his packet with a single motion. The division had made its report: "The junction has been captured."

Night was approaching. Our general knew that the Germans would make repeated counterattacks in the hopes of retaking the little scrap of land they had given up. So off Makarov hurried, through hollows and gullies and along dusty roads ground down by war, back to where the fighting was taking place. His bag contained orders. Every moment of delay in delivering them meant putting today's operation in jeopardy and risking the gains that had already been made.

You can recognize a liaison officer's car without even looking at its markings. They race past tanks and guns headed for the front and coat the infantry's vehicles in a thick layer of dust as they speed by. Their drivers barely notice the alarmed cries of "Watch out!"

When an enemy plane dropped a bomb fifty metres or so behind him, Makarov simply touched his chauffeur's elbow and quietly said: "What a good thing we didn't stop! Best not to ever stop, if you ask me." The chauffeur could not have agreed more, which is how Makarov's order was delivered almost twice as quickly as it should have been.

However, Makarov's car did not succeed in making it all the way back again. A Heinkel got the vehicle while it was in a gully. Four bombs, one after the another, thundered down right next to it, a piece of shrapnel hit a tire, and the car screeched to a halt. The Heinkel made a second approach, ripping tracers through the windshield. Makarov and his driver just managed to take shelter in a crevice. Makarov had to return on foot.

The sector had not been in such a difficult position for quite a while. Every day was so packed with events it became like a stream bubbling over its banks. Makarov felt as if he were being carried along in the stream. He lost track of how one day turned into the next, and his only rest was an hour or two of sleep here and there. Once he almost fell asleep after handing his latest packet over at the divisional command post. He leaned against a log holding up the dugout, and a heavy fog descended on him. Makarov was awakened rudely. Something collapsed with a bang and twisted him around, throwing him back into the dugout. It was the shockwave of a bomb that had fallen nearby. Shrapnel had torn into a pair of horses that now lay palpitating in pools of blood.

That was how Kuzma Matveevich Makarov from Moscow began his career as a liaison officer. For a time he had led the technical propaganda division at Moscow City Transport. Now he looks back on those days with relish: how handy that he had learned about all the different City Transport vehicles back then! Should something happen to his chauffeur, Makarov will not have to stop en route, as he can easily drive any car. He knows how to ride a motorcycle, he handles a bike superbly, and he is strong in the saddle. When needed he can defend himself – and the secret packet tucked away in his bag – courageously in battle. He is a good shot with a pistol, a submachine gun, and a rifle, and he even knows how to use a machine gun.

✳ ✳ ✳

We entered the gully where the divisional command post was located.

"It's three o'clock," said Makarov, "Do you see how Ursa Major has covered the dipper?"

This man has even learned to tell the time by the stars, since the war has smashed time itself into pieces.

Konstantin Simonov – U-2
9 October 1942, *Krasnaya Zvezda*

Down here in the south, the Germans have ironically christened these planes "russky boxes." What exactly is this plane made of wood and covered in canvas? What kind of a speed is a 100 or 150 kilometres an hour? What kind of a motor makes a sound like a little motorbike bumping along a bad road? And, worst of all, what kind of a mad idea is it to bomb the German forces with such an archaic contraption?

That, though, was back in the beginning, when these improvised bombers' pilots had little experience of nighttime flying, when they did not have flares to light up the German positions, and when they were lining up bombs in the cockpit and chucking them overboard by hand.

The Russians are a stubborn people. When they have come up with a good idea, they will make it work someway or another, in a way that only Russians could. Yes, the plane may be made of canvas and plywood glued together. But it is light, so it can land and take off again anywhere at all – even in total darkness. Yes, its top speed may only be 150 kilometres an hour. But it can hit a target at night with accuracy other dive bombers can only dream of.

In the autumn, the pilots learned to bomb at night. In the winter, they got new planes. The new models were still light and still made of plywood, but they came with a few simple improvements. By the spring, our "russky box" squadrons were dropping hundreds of tons of bombs a night on the Germans. The words "russky box" acquired a new meaning. The Germans had been using them ironically. Now they used them in fear.

As soon as darkness falls at Stalingrad, signal flares shoot into the sky like fireflies, marking out the frontline. An unceasing little growl begins to sound over the German positions. Searchlights comb through the sky, with the German anti-aircraft fire in pursuit. Multicoloured machine gun trails from every direction meet, converging into a single sound. Those little airborne motorbikes, though, keep on growling away over the Germans' heads as if there was nothing doing.

Away go their flares and bombs, falling on German troops in ravines, falling on columns marching along streets, and falling on command posts in houses. The Germans cannot spend a single quiet night anywhere at the front. The bombs just keep raining down, all night long.

It took a long time, but the German anti-aircraft gunners did come up with a new approach. They figured out the speed of the "russky box" and started to fire more accurately. Our pilots kept their heads, though, and adopted a new method of bombing. Having ascended to their maximum altitude and latched on to their target, they would glide down noiselessly so as to drop their load on the unsuspecting Germans in total silence. The anti-aircraft fire would almost always begin after the first bombs had fallen. That is when the German soldiers' letters home first began to mention fantastic ideas about the Russians having some bizarre kind of aircraft: their engines weren't just silent; they *didn't have engines at all.*

On autumn nights the steppe smells of sagebrush and a cold wind whips in off the Volga. The stars are barely visible through the clouds obscuring the sky black, mute, impenetrable. All that is visible is a long, red glow growing clearer as it stretches out for kilometre after kilometre on the horizon. Stalingrad is burning.

We are walking across an airfield. Somewhere close, invisible airplanes buzz overhead. The buzzing was coming from the ground moments ago, but now it is in the air. Following some path visible to him alone, my companion leads me across the field toward the command post. In the distance, some 15 or 20 kilometres off, a searchlight suddenly flares up. Its beam points in our direction then suddenly disappears.

"Our boys are headed back. They're about to land. The light's guiding them," explains my companion.

At last, after an hour and a half's walk, we make it to the command post, which lies underneath one of the many haystacks scattered around the steppe. We crouch down and squeeze through a small door covered with a couple of capes. A spacious room is inside the haystack. Two tables are neatly set up in a T shape, so that they resemble a landing marker more than tables. The squadron's commissar and commander are sat at the table beside a "bat" lamp.[33] We have arrived at the busiest of times: planes are coming in and going back up again one after another. It smells of hay and nocturnal freshness inside the haystack. The lamp casts a red glow onto the flushed faces of the pilots as they report on their bombing runs.

Tonight, the squadron is bombing an air base taken by the Germans and where several sizable enemy units are now stationed. The base has been subjected to heavy bombardment for several nights running. Many of those doing the bombing used to live and work there, so their mission reports are detailed and accurate.

"What did you hit this time?" Captain Ovodov asks a strapping pilot who has just returned from a mission.

"Building No. 3," replies the pilot.

"The one where you lived?"

"No, I was in No. 4."

"That's where you're going now." After a moment's pause, the commander asks, "And where's Poklikushkin?"

"Still off flying, keeping those German boys dying!"

"Flying well, is he?"

"He is indeed."

The commander now wants to know what is happening at the frontline. "How's the battle progressing?" he asks.

"They're going to keep fighting all night." The pilot bends over the map: "There's a fire here, here, and here too."

"Right here?," asks the commander, and falls into silence for a moment. "Well then," he says, as if shaking off some or other thought, "that means my house is either on fire or it's already burned down. Righto then – on your way!"

The arrivals and reports follow one after the other. The time between landing and taking off again is down to ten, and sometimes even five, minutes. Even as a plane lands, a truck loaded with bombs is already approaching it. The plane will be ready for take-off as soon as the crew has made its report and gets new orders. That means the reports are made rather succinct: "Flight – one hour, thirty-five minutes. Altitude – 860 metres."

Airborne for seven or eight hours and flying five or six sorties every night. Our little "russky boxes" drop tons of bombs on the Germans every night. Sometimes they manage as much as the heavy bombers, and sometimes even more.

"Six times a day, and barely a day off," says Captain Ovodov, "especially in the summer. We might get a day off if there's a really heavy fog."

There is a break in the command post's work. Taking advantage of the chance for a breather, the captain relates some details about the squadron's activities.

When the squadron was formed and began to learn to fly at night, half of the pilots were from military schools and half were from the Civil Defence Society.[34] At the start, some of the men who had wanted to become fighter pilots turned their noses up at being posted to the U-2 squadron. That all changed very quickly. Within two months, they had become great proponents of their art: they grew to love it, and even found it had a rather romantic side.

The analogy is of course not quite perfect, but just as an assault rifle cannot do the job a rifle does in the hands of even an experienced sniper, the ponderous old U-2 is best at what it does. You just have to squeeze everything you can out of the plane, and then its shortcomings – its lack of speed, for example – can become advantages in the right circumstances. And those advantages can be put to use against the Germans.

Here, where the front runs zigzagging, spiking, and swirling, from house to house and village to village, no modern night bombers could be given the U-2s' missions. They can bomb any house – the *exact* house, not one bit to the left or right, but right where the Germans have taken cover. They can bomb the German half of a block while leaving our half unscathed. Thanks to their slow speed and impressive accuracy, they can float over a target and strike without errors or mix-ups. They can bomb in the places where German pilots, afraid to drop bombs on their own forces, dare not go.

The pilots have already grown accustomed to their planes. They have grown to love the accuracy of their bombing, the simplicity of landing and take-off, and the reliable mechanics. They love that these puny-looking planes have actually turned out to be fearsome weapons. They can fly six times a night in any weather, wherever they are ordered, and they know that the infantry on the ground do not have such tender feelings about any other plane. The infantry might call them "woodsmen," "crickets," or "foresters" (that all depends on the landscape) when they spot them flying low overhead, but the humorous nicknames come of genuine warmth!

The pilots have flown hundreds of hours since the squadron was formed. Every last man of them has become an expert nighttime flier. Thanks to their experience, they sustain almost no losses: just two planes have failed to return from a mission in the past six months of action. They take off and land in total darkness, and the Germans cannot bomb their airfields, because the only illumination comes from the flashes of two hand-held torches. The squadron's members joke that soon they will be able to land a plane to the light of a burning cigarette.

Today is a red letter day for the squadron because the pilots and navigators are receiving military medals. Almost the whole squadron, almost every one of those pilots and navigators, went airborne with a medal on their chest today. The very best of them, Flight Lieutenant Osipov and Pilot Officer Poklikushkin, received the Order of Lenin. Now, as dawn approaches, they are off on their sixth sortie.

The cape covering the door starts flapping again. An hour has passed, so the crews must be returning after that sixth sortie. Since it is the last of the night, they are not in such a hurry when making their reports to the commander. They crack jokes and, shivering in the sharp morning chill, rub eyes red from exhaustion and the blasting wind.

The last of the returnees had been complaining that the sky was clouded over for half the night, "But the moon was out for the first sortie, so I could see exactly what I'd done!"

"You're saying the bomb went right through the attic window where the Germans had hung out their laundry?" jokes the commissar.

"That's it, Comrade Commissar," the pilot jokes back. "We watched them hop out in the buff!"

The commissar and I walk out onto the aerodrome. It is still dark, but far off to the east, on the edge of the steppe, a narrow strip of the dawn light is visible. Invisible planes left and right taxi back to their ranks with a hum. The pilots have come outside to smoke. They chat away next to us. Their cigarette ends burn bright red. The men joke wearily but good-heartedly. After a dangerous, tough night, they want to speak frankly, to stretch their legs, and to reminisce about their homes and their loved ones. The night's work is finished. Dawn breaks. Time for sleep.

✳ ✳ ✳

Someday, when they begin to write the story of the war, a historian ought to pick out these men from all the unnoticed heroes. Because of these brave and humble men, the courageous workers of aviation, the words "russky box" no longer sound funny. They are terrifying.

Boris Polevoy – House 21a
14 October 1942, *Pravda*

The broad street lined with large houses and lawns and young, slender poplars would seem calm and tranquil were it not for the pavement and asphalt riddled with shell craters, barricades, and a pair of burned German tanks jutting up against the rubble of a concrete wall. This is the frontline.

One four-storey building's moulded pediment, broad staircase, and rows of bright, clean apartments would be particularly fine were it not for an entire corner flattened by bombs, for the yawning gulfs of empty windows, and the doors blown in by explosions. The battle for this house, defended by a handful of brave souls under the command of Junior Lieutenant Tsvetkov, is into its ninth day.

The house diagonally opposite is held by the Germans. From time to time they rattle off submachine gun fire. The bullets scream off the windowsills and tear into the plaster, which rains down onto the floor. The room looks like it was an engineer's office until recently: some classic novels and *Hütte's Handbook* stand on some bookshelves;[35] there is a desk, an oilcloth sofa, and a framed photo of the Tractor Factory with just a single shard of glass remaining.

The room has two thick walls; a single small window looks out onto the courtyard. Junior Lieutenant Tsvetkov has requisitioned the room for, as he jokingly puts it, an "HQ." In a hoarse, cracking voice he enthusiastically tells the story of how his troops have defended House 21a out in the outskirts of Stalingrad.

In the middle of September, the Germans assembled a mighty strike force on the city's outskirts. After a heavy aerial bombardment, the tanks and infantry took the street and the Germans immediately started to fortify their positions. The lieutenant takes me to the window and instructs me to carefully peer out from behind the jamb. He shows me the sinewy, venous trenches that cut through the courtyard and points out a bunker camouflaged under a pile of wood in the middle of the courtyard. A solid fortification indeed. The Germans, though, did not manage to hold out for long. One night, one of our Guards units launched a heavy flanking attack and cleared out the Germans from this and the adjoining streets. After the fighting, our guardsmen found heaps of German corpses in trenches, in House 21a's courtyard, and in the basement boiler room.

The guardsmen encountered a terrible sight on the threshold of apartment No. 3 up on the second floor. In the open doorway, sticking halfway out into the stairwell, lay a grey-haired old lady. She was using her body to shelter the corpse of an eighteen-month-old child. The woman had been shot three times through the chest. Before she passed, she managed to utter a little about herself: Anna Kapustina. Pensioner. Mother of a planner in a Tractor Factory workshop.

She told a horrific tale to the troops. She, her grandson Igor, and her youngest daughter, fifteen-year-old Vera, had been alone in the empty house when the Germans captured it. Soon, our units began to hem the Germans in. A German officer burst into Kapustina's room in a drunken rage. He screamed something, grabbed his revolver, and shot at the bed where the little boy Igor slept. Kapustina leapt to her grandson's defence, seizing the executioner's arm. He shot – once, twice, a third time – right at her chest. Vera was dragged off by some soldiers.

At this point in the story, the lieutenant leapt up off the couch and paced furiously around the room. Rummaging around in his pocket, he pulled out a colourful little celluloid parrot: "Here's what we found in the little boy's hand when we went to bury him. I'm keeping it. I'll keep it forever so that I never, ever forget him."

That, however, was just the start of the battle for House 21a. When our guardsmen had captured the house they set up a perimeter defence, covering the intersection with machine guns. In the morning, the Germans launched a counterattack. Shells howled down into the street; wave after wave of bombers swooped in. The steadfast guardsmen knew the attack was coming. They held fast in their trenches and from behind barricaded windows.

Next, the German tanks raced into battle and a dozen armoured cars carrying submachine gunners rushed onto the street. A fierce battle was starting to rage within the confines of this little street. Anti-tank gunners waited calmly until the tanks grew level, then shot right at them. Five tanks burst into flames. The others continued to advance, calmly negotiating the burning fires. The gunners' ammunition was running low. They began to scurry from window to window, dodging the tanks' hail of fire, rapidly changing positions, and picking the perfect moment to cast grenades high into the air. The tracks of another three tanks were mangled. They ground to a halt, but four more were still coming at them. The guards' submachine guns mowed away at the tank group from the lower windows, but soon the anti-tank supplies were exhausted.

Then, a tall soldier – a hero whom the troops talk of in reverent tones but whose name remains unknown – cried out: "You won't pass, you reptiles! I

Figure 2.3 Scouts of Rodimtsev's division in street fighting, October 1942.

won't let you!" He seized an anti-tank mine, clasped it to his chest, and
threw himself under the leading tank's tracks. There was a loud bang.
The steel vehicle seemed to stagger, then its mangled body stopped moving.
Three tanks were left. They broke through the barricade and drove right
up to House 21a. Now the house's defenders put to use a tried and tested
method: flaming bottles began to fly out of the house's front door.

The German submachine gunners, however, managed to leap clear of the
tanks. They gunned down two soldiers who were blocking their path and
burst into the hallway. A furious fight broke out on the staircase. There were
three Germans for every one of ours, but our troops steadfastly repelled
every attack. Private Chepurin positioned his gun on the mezzanine leading
up to the second level. He held back the Germans with short bursts of fire
while his comrades erected a barricade made from assorted household chat-
tels behind him. The Germans only managed to take the corner apartments,
Nos. 9 and 10. Chepurin fired off one last round and, staggering from
wounds in the shoulder and hip, made to head upstairs. His comrades
dragged him over the barricade.

At that very moment, German reinforcements were arriving. Low-calibre mortar fire hit the stairwell windows as the Germans began to storm the barricade. The five defenders had no more grenades or bullets, so they could only get at those Germans who actually tried to mount the barricade. They held the barricade right up until a second group of Germans climbed up the fire escape and attacked them from behind. Yet still they managed to get away and entrench themselves on the third floor. They laid the wounded Chepurin by the balcony doors in the kitchen, ready to stop any more attempts to sneak up the fire escape. Fierce back-and-forth fighting took hold again. The Germans threw grenades at the barricades, but the defenders managed to catch them and throw them back – right onto the heads of the fascists – before they exploded.

"That's for Stalingrad! That's for Mother Ukraine! And that's for my collective farm, Wormwood Way, back home!" shouted Comrade Klimuk as he deftly lobbed German grenades.

The Germans could not hold out. They ended their siege and went back down to the lower floors. At dawn, they again renewed their attempts to clear out the house. This time, the mortars fired at the stairwell windows for a good ten minutes. Everything was covered with a veil of tawny smoke and chalky dust from the explosions, but when the Germans tried to make it upstairs, they were once more met with sporadic but pinpoint fire from behind the barricade.

The guardsmen had waited out the bombardment inside the apartments, but now they were in position once more. They fired off every last one of their rounds and prepared for a hand-to-hand fight. Suddenly a cry of "Hurrah!" rang out from above. The cry grew louder and louder. The troops from the neighbouring block had climbed up onto the roof and were coming to the rescue. Grenade after grenade rained down on the Germans' heads. The stunned Germans began to flee, leaving behind their dead and wounded. Apartments 9 and 10 had been recaptured. The entirety of House 21a was in our hands once more. The failed assault had cost the lives of fifty-two German soldiers and two German officers.

Every night, our troops are now adding to the fortifications by building brick embrasures into the windows, constructing battlements, and digging trenches around the house.

"Our house is just one house in Stalingrad," says the lieutenant, as he gives me an insider's tour of what is really a bunker, but which just a month ago had been a home for civilians. Ordinary people's possessions, albeit now sprinkled with chalky dust and shards of glass, still lie all over the place. In one room – what must have been somebody's dining room – two anti-tank crew soldiers are sitting in armchairs by a bricked-off window. They have thrust an anti-tank rifle's barrel through the window.

They sit, fashioning cigarette holders from the remnants of a German Messerschmidt by the light of an oil lamp. Gunners Zhukov and Evtifeev are manning a medium machine gun in the room on the corner. Inside the room there is still a children's play area with some fine miniature furniture and small rugs depicting animals hanging on the wall. The junior lieutenant looks at them, pulls the colourful little parrot from his pocket – the memento for the murdered boy – and says ruminatively: "I've a four-year-old girl, Sveta, and a son, Georgy, who's two." He suddenly marches up to the machine gun and rattles off two rounds at the Germans in the house opposite. They fire back. The floor shakes from bursting mortar rounds. The lieutenant says: "That's how I'll remember the Germans. Everything shaking, and me with hands itching to shoot, to throw a grenade, and to get stuck in with a bayonet."

✳ ✳ ✳

I am minded of his phrase about how these men are defending just one of the houses in Stalingrad. Just as the sun is reflected in a drop of rain, the great, epic fortitude of Stalin's city's defenders, a struggle for every street, for every house, for every window and apartment, for every step on every staircase, is reflected in the fight for this house. And in every part of this fighting, this battle, and this heroic city, the Germans are hated just as implacably and just as heatedly as in House 21a.

Evgeny Kriger – This Is Stalingrad
25 October 1942, *Izvestiya*

Two months have passed since the fighting penetrated the city's tattered and burned body. The Germans plunged the knife of war right into the city's very heart, yet still the city lives. The Germans readied the drums to announce the city's death, but now they are burying the drummers. This Russian city arose from the flames and the blood to drive the enemy back to its outskirts and deep underground, into trenches, cellars, and crevices.

The Germans came to realize that they could never take the city alive, so they decided to murder it. They would slowly torture it to death. They took flight with thousands of tons of bombs, then they dropped them onto the very streets and squares where not long before girls had sold flowers, onto the boulevards and parks where gardeners had once tended young trees, and onto the bazaars where housewives had noisily hurried about their business. They even dropped them onto schools, hospitals, and ordinary people's homes. The bombing was planned meticulously and carried out with German precision. They methodically bombed block after block, only moving to the next square marked out on the map when not a single wall or roof remained standing, when there were no more signs of life, and when the residents had lost all hope that they would ever again return to their homes and their hearths.

When the bombs had ground the city's very stone into dust, the Germans threw themselves into the attack. The ruined city met them with bullets, shells, and grenades. The Germans dug themselves in and again set fire to the city. Stalingrad burned for many days and many nights. The glow was visible from 50 kilometres away across the steppe, and the wind from the Volga drove the fire from building to building. Once again the Germans went on the attack, but once again the city – blackened, scorched, infernal – arose from the ashes. It lived. It fought.

Once again the Germans went to ground and hid in basements. Now they speak of Verdun. Verdun is dear to the heart of every one of Stalingrad's defenders. The defensive line here is not deep. In some places there are only 600 or 700 metres between the frontline and the Volga's water. For two months, tanks and Junkers in their hundreds have been trying to pierce this narrow strip of land in the city. The land has not the bastions or the fortifications that Verdun did. Very different defensive measures are needed now. Eight hundred metres is usually a paltry distance in modern warfare. In this city, though, Russians have chosen to stand firm and hold fast, so the depth of the defensive line has become infinite. It could only ever be measured in terms of the strength and persistence of the Russian heart.

Who are these soldiers defending Stalingrad? The Red Army soldiers who stand firm for week after week on ground constantly trembling from explosions. The dust-covered and bloodied boat, raft, and steamer crews. The captains and mariners on the Volga crossing. The workers who fix up guns and tanks in workshops riddled by shellfire. Those workers even went into battle when the Germans concentrated all their forces on taking the town and there were not enough people on the burning streets to man the tanks they had been repairing. They will fight and fight until the Germans are expelled from the city! The city's defensive line can only be measured in terms of these people's nerves and self-control; it cannot be measured in metres.

The war in Stalingrad is being fought at close quarters. Defensive positions are squeezed into the space between the same heaps of rubble where the homeless shelter. On an empty street, an iron manhole cover suddenly pops open. A pale, thin girl wriggles her way out. Her home is right there, underneath the manhole cover cut into the pavement. She is living there with her mother. The girl thought that things had got a bit quieter and the ground was not shaking quite so much, so she darted out in search of water. Other people are living in holes dug into gullies and ravines. They dare not leave; they are waiting until the Germans are gone from the city. I saw an old man walking across a square. A shell fell and exploded, enveloping him with smoke. By the time the smoke cleared, the old man had got up and was walking along, clicking his cane, just the same as before.

"Hey, uncle," we said, "how did you get out of that one alive? Are you made of iron?"

"That's right," he answered, "I must be made of iron. They can't kill me now. I've already been dead once." He was silent for a moment, then continued. "The Germans killed my son, an army man. Right here, near the city. Now I'll bury them."

"Where are you fighting?" we asked.

"I'm a guard at the factory."

Off he went, clicking his cane, to his factory and its battered walls. The city was living through a time of the most terrible danger, but still he relieved a younger man and stood guard, holding his rifle, by the gates. Like many other people here, he has no fear of the shelling after two months of the ceaseless roaring and rumbling of the defence. Shrapnel rains down even in the brief silences, tapping away on stone like acorns falling from

an oak. Then again come the howls, the whistles, and the roars. Walls
are torn down, but the will, the patience, and the tenacity of the locals are
immovable.

The factories are right at the front. In spite of the constant bombardment, nobody leaves and they never extinguish the furnaces, at least where
they can still physically be ignited. When things were at their most perilous,
the factory's director, Hero of Socialist Labour Gonor,[36] summoned everybody – even the old folks – to the workshops. They worked right through
twenty-four hours of bombardment. Many were wounded. The factory sus-
tained just as many casualties as the military at the front, and the factory
fought just like the military at the front did. After a full night and day's
work, the factory's tool-wielding workers eventually sent two hundred guns
back to the defensive line. However, there were not enough gun crews, so
the the foremen and armourers went to the line and shot their own guns.
The Germans began to understand the depth of Stalingrad's defensive line.

The factory continued to take in damaged tanks, gun tractors, and engines from the front. Several hours later, back to the front they would go,
ready for battle. The workers armed themselves. In three days flat they
formed a unit nine hundred strong and went to man the defensive line. The
unit filled a breach, completing a chain that prevented hundreds of German
tanks breaking through to the Volga. Women, children, and seniors upped
tools and built barricades. The barricades were set on fire and the people
driven away. The fire was extinguished, and back they went. Those who lived
through the bombardment of 23 August have absolutely no fear. The city
was gone. But the city wanted to live, so it survives, it fights, and it is being
reborn in battle.

The fighting is taking place in cellars, in stairwells, in ravines, on steep
hills, on the roofs of houses, in gardens, and in courtyards. The war is being
fought at close quarters in Stalingrad. The Germans send in division after
division. They hold many of the roads, but there is always space for more
graves on the steppe. The divisions are destroyed as soon as they arrive.
The German drummers who were sent to the victory parade now rot underground. The city, though, still stands. It stands in ruins, in ashes, its walls
now right against the Volga, but it lives. This is a Russian city! Russia!

There are no forts or concrete bunkers here. The defensive line passes
through empty spaces, through courtyards where housewives have hung out

laundry, through the truncated railway, through the home where an accountant, his wife, their two children, and his elderly mother used to live – through dozens of homes just like it – through an empty square whose tarmac has been torn up by shells, through factories where armourers are working, and through a park where lovers sat on green benches whispering sweet nothings to each other this very summer. The peacetime city has become a wartime city. The logic of war has placed it at the very centre of the front, at the very point where a battle crucial to the outcome of the entire war is being fought. The defensive line passes through the very hearts of Russian folk here. The Germans have, after six hundred days of war, discovered what that really means.

"Verdun," they mutter. But this is not Verdun. It is something entirely new in the history of warfare. This is Stalingrad!

Vasily Grossman – The Battle of Stalingrad
27 October 1942, *Krasnaya Zvezda*

A month ago one of our guards divisions – three rifles regiments, artillery, a wagon train, a medical and other rear echelon units – arrived at a fishing village just across from Stalingrad on the Volga's eastern bank. They had completed their march unusually quickly using motorized transport. Day and night the trucks had rumbled across the flat steppe toward the Volga. Kites sitting on telegraph poles had turned grey from the dust kicked up by the movement of hundreds and thousands of wheels and tracks. Camels looked around in alarm, thinking that the steppe must be on fire. The mighty expanse of the steppe was in motion, smoking and humming. The air became cloudy and heavy. A rust-red shroud covered the sky. The sun hung like a dark axe over an earth drowning in darkness.

The division barely made a stop en route. Radiator water boiled and motors overheated; the troops would barely manage to gulp down some water and shake the thick layers of soft dust from their vests before the command again rang out: "Back on the trucks!" And off to the south the motorized battalions and regiments would again roar.

The intensity of the journey amazed everybody from the soldiers and drivers to the artillerymen. General Rodimtsev alone thought that his division was still travelling too slowly. He knew that the Germans had already

reached Stalingrad, so the general urged his division on ever faster and
further curtailed the brief stop-offs. His intense, wilful drive caught on
among his men in their thousands. It was as if their whole lives consisted
of nothing but marching, on and on, all night and all day.

The road turned to the southwest. Pussy willows and maples with slender
red branches and thin silver-grey leaves soon started to appear, and large
orchards planted with squat little apple trees began to dot the landscape.
As the division approached the Volga, they saw a tall, dark cloud overhead.
Sinister, heavy, and dark as death, there was no mistaking it for a cloud of
dust. This was the smoke from burning oil silos floating over the northern
reaches of the city. Enormous arrows nailed to tree trunks pointed toward
the Volga. A single word was written on them: "Crossing."

The division made it to the Volga at what was a terrible time for Stalingrad. There was no time to wait to cross at night, so the men took to hurriedly unloading crates of weapons and ammunition from the trucks.
They were issued grenades, bottles filled with petrol, and bread, sugar,
and sausage.

It is no mean feat to transport a division across the Volga in a hurry,
especially when the sky is swarming with yellow wasps – Messerschmitts –
and when the German bombers are going at the banks. The spirit that had
seized the division on their rapid march and the troops' yearning to get
up close to the enemy, though, helped them get to grips with the task. The
men boarded barges, steamers, and rowboats.

"Ready?" asked the oarsmen.

"Full steam ahead!" cried the boats' captains.

The grey strip of rippling water between the boats and the bank began to
grow broader. The waves gently lapped against the boats' bows. Hundreds
of eyes turned their anxious gaze from the water to the bank downstream,
which was covered in greenery just starting to turn yellow here and there,
and then over to the towering, scorched city blanketed in white smoke and
accorded a terrible but heroic fate.

The waves rocked the barges. The men of the rifles were not much used
to the water. They had fleeting pangs of anxiety that the enemy could be
anywhere, that they would make contact without the calming firmness of
the ground beneath their feet. The air was unbearably clear and transparent,
the sky unbearably blue and clear, and the sun mercilessly bright. The cours-

ing water seemed treacherous and unreliable. Nobody took any pleasure
in the fresh air, in the freshness of the river as it hit the nostrils, or in the
Volga's tender and moist breath as it caressed eyes weary from dust. There
was total silence on every barge, steamer, cutter, and rowing boat. Suddenly
heads turned to gaze into the sky, and somebody cried out: "Dive bombers
incoming!"

A slender column with a frothy crest suddenly shot high out of the water
some 50 metres away from the barge. The column collapsed, drenching the
men. At that very moment a second column shot up even closer, and then
a third. Then the German artillery opened rapid fire on the parts of the
division that had begun crossing. Shells tore into the water's surface. The
Volga was covered in frothy lacerations, and shrapnel hammered against
the barges' hulls. The wounded began to cry out, ever so quietly, so quietly
it felt like they were trying to hide their injuries from their friends, from the
enemy, and even from themselves.

There was a terrible moment when a large-calibre shell struck one of the
smaller ferries. Up leapt the flames; the boat was engulfed in dark smoke.
You could hear the sound of the explosion and the soldiers' drawn-out
screams coming right from within the thunderous blast. Thousands of
people at that exact moment caught sight of the heavy green helmets floating among the wooden debris in the water. Twenty of the forty guardsmen
on board the steamer had perished.

The crossing continued into the night. For as long as light and dark itself
has existed, people have perhaps never been so delighted at the darkness of
a September night. General Rodimtsev spent the night in a state of intense
activity. He had been through many trials during the war. His division had
fought at Kiev and repelled SS regiments from Stalinka. Several times they
had turned defence into frantic attack by breaking out of encirclement. The
young general's military character was marked by mettle, calmness, a strong
will, the reaction speed and wisdom to attack when nobody else would have
dreamed of doing so, by military experience and guile, and by fearlessness.
The general's division took on the general's character.

In the army, I often encounter people with great enthusiasm for their
own regiment, battery, or tank brigade. But perhaps nowhere have I seen
such devotion to one's unit, such patriotism, as here. It is almost touching.
The division are above all proud of their military exploits, their general,

and their equipment. But if you were to take the commanders' word for it, nowhere else can a cook bake such a perfect pie, nobody else has a barber who can give you the perfect shave and just so happens to play the violin exquisitely to boot. When they want to rib somebody, they say, "But heaven knows what you're doing in *our* division!" And you'll hear them say things like, "I'll tell the general," "the general will be pleased," or "the general will be disappointed." When the "veterans," as they like to call themselves, tell stories of their great military exploits, they'll always slip into the conversation, "Well now, our division *always* fights in the most important sectors." The wounded lie in hospital, fretting they will be transferred to another unit and writing letters to their comrades.

As the last units were crossing into Stalingrad that night, it may have occurred to the general that his men's camaraderie and strong bonds would lead him to victory in this uniquely difficult situation. Indeed, it is difficult to imagine a more unpromising picture at the start of a battle. As the division entered Stalingrad, it split into three. The rear echelon units and the heavy artillery remained on the eastern bank, cut off from the fighting regiments by the Volga. Meanwhile, the Germans occupied the land between the two regiments which had crossed into the city – one regiment had crossed into the factory district and the other a little further downstream – so they could not form a continuous line.

I am certain that the sense of "patriotism," the love and familiarity that bonded the division's commanders, and that particular unity of military thought and character across the division and its general, contributed greatly to the divided units' ability to act as one, strong whole and not at odds with each other. They linked up, worked in concert, and ultimately – brilliantly – managed to fulfil their order to create a frontline running between all three regiments that would ensure a supply of materiel and resources.

The situation in the city was dire. The Germans reckoned that they would capture Stalingrad within the day, perhaps even in a few hours. As is often the case during these difficult moments, our artillery turned out to be the mainstay of the defence. The Germans sent their submachine gunners to deal with it, since the street fighting conditions permitted men to steal up to the guns and unexpectedly take out the crews. They planned to make it

Figure 2.4 Soviet troops on the offensive in Stalingrad, October 1942.

to the riverbank and thus drive us back into the Volga. However, our vehicles had not driven day and night through clouds of dust, and our regiments had not advanced so far, to give up now.

✳ ✳ ✳

The next morning General Rodimtsev crossed into Stalingrad on a motorboat. The division had joined the ranks of the forces defending Stalingrad;
but what was it to do now? This was, after all, a division whose support was
on the other side of the Volga, whose HQ was just five metres from the
river's water, and whose regiments had been separated from the others by
the Germans. Should they stay on the defensive by digging in quick and for-
tifying themselves in houses? No, that was not it. The situation was so dire

that Rodimtsev turned to a different – a fearsome – strategy that he had
already tested at Kiev: he went on the attack!

He attacked with every regiment, with all his firepower, with the whole
extent of his knowledge, and with every urgency. He attacked with the full
force of that bitter rage that was gripping thousands of men at the sight
of the red sun rising over the heavily wounded city; a city of once white
houses, marvellous factories, and wide streets and squares. The dawn sun,
like an enormous eye overflowing with the blood of sorrow and rage, gazed
down onto the bronze statue of Kholzunov,[37] onto the eagle with a wing
stretched out over the ruined children's hospital, onto the white figures of
nude children juxtaposed against the black velvet, soot-covered Palace of
Physical Culture, and onto hundreds of silent, blinded homes. The thousands of men who had crossed the Volga now beheld the city the Germans
had mutilated through eyes overflowing with the same blood of sorrow
and rage.

The Germans were not expecting an attack. They were so confident in
their ability to methodically press our forces back and into the Volga that
they had not properly secured the areas they had already captured. Three
regiments, led by Yelin's guards, carried out an assault on some of the city's
captured streets. The primary aim was not to link up with one another but
to strike at the enemy and thus deprive him of the best positions. When
Yelin's regiment attacked, they could not even see the other two regiments.
However, the regiment felt – they believed – that they were not facing their
fate alone. They felt the breath of the two other guards regiments close, almost alongside, almost touching. They felt their comrades' heavy steps. The
thunder of their own artillery sounded like brotherly voices. The dust and
smoke of battle whipping high into the air testified to the guardsmen's forward progress.

Yelin's regiment successfully stormed the German strongholds in some
large buildings. Never before had they seen this sort of fighting. Every rule
of war was turned on its head. It was as if forests, gullies, mountains, and
streams had come to the city on the Volga, as if the particularities of every
theatre of war, from the White Sea to the mountains of the Caucasus, had all
been gathered here. In a single day, a unit might leave thickets and trees that
called to mind a Belarussian glade and enter a mountainous crevice formed
by walls rearing over a narrow alleyway, where they would scramble through

the stone blockwork of a collapsed firewall. A mere hour later the unit would be on an enormous, asphalt square a hundred times flatter than the Don steppe. By the evening the unit might have to crawl through the tilled soil and burned down fences of allotments like those found in villages near Kursk. Those sudden shifts put constant pressure on the commander to quickly alter his combat techniques.

Sometimes, though, an assault on a single house would go on for hours at a time. The fighting would take place among the scattered rubble of half-destroyed rooms and corridors. The soldiers' feet would get tangled up in broken wiring and among the broken skeletons of iron beds and home and kitchenware. That sort of fighting was quite unlike anything else anywhere from the White Sea to the Caucasus.

The Germans had lodged themselves into one building so firmly that it was decided to blow the whole building, with them inside, ten metres into the air. Six of our sappers would use ten pounds of explosives to set up the blast. The Germans, scenting blood, trained heavy fire on our men. Picture the scene for a moment: Lieutenant Chermakov, the two sergeants Dubovy and Bugaev, and the sappers Klimenko, Shukhov, and Messerashvili. They are crawling along the ruined walls under heavy fire, all sweaty, dirty faces and tattered vests, each carrying one and a half pounds of pure death, then Sergeant Dubovy shouts:

"No flagging now, sappers!"

Shukhov sucks his lips in, blows out the dust, and answers: "No time for that right now! If we were going to flag, we should have done it back there!"

While Yelin was victoriously claiming one building after another, the other two regiments assaulted a hill that has been deeply linked with the history of Stalingrad ever since the Civil War.[38] Children used to play here. Lovers would wander here. People would sled and ski here in the winter. The site is marked with a thick ring on German and Russian maps alike. General Gott must surely have dashed a delighted radiogram message off to the German command when it was captured! German HQ knows the hill as a "domineering height from which both banks of the Volga and the entire city are visible." And in war what gets seen gets shot. That phrase – "domineering height" – is frightening indeed.

Thus the guards regiments stormed the hill. Many good men perished in the fighting. Their mothers and fathers, wives, and fiancées will not see them again, but their comrades and loved ones will remember them. Bitter tears will be shed all over Russia for those who died in the fighting for the hill. The battle took a great toll on the guards. Henceforth this place will be known as the red hill, or perhaps the *iron* hill, for it is covered by the prickly scales of shrapnel from mines and shells, by German bomb stabilizers, by cartridges charred black, by ribbed grenade fragments, and by the heavy steel carcasses of overturned German tanks. Yet the glorious moment when Private Kentya tore down the German flag, threw it to the ground, and stamped his boot down on top of it did eventually come.

The division's regiments had linked up. An attack of unprecedented scale had concluded successfully, as if putting an end to the first phase of the division's work in Stalingrad. It had created a front made of one strong, continuous, and advantageous line. No academy in the world could teach the great wealth of invaluable experience that the men had gained in the fighting.

Thus began the battle's second phase: a defensive war. Dozens of times over, German tanks would attack suddenly and powerfully and dive bombers would make their runs, then our units would counterattack. This was a sniper's war. This war involved every type of weaponry, from the rifle to the heavy cannon and the dive bomber. Day-to-day life became surprising, strange, and quite unlike anything else. Not mere hours but whole days and weeks passed in this smoking hell where the artillery and mortars did not cease fire even for a minute. The howl of tank and airplane engines, the coloured fire of flares, and the explosion of mortars became as familiar as streetcars' rattles, cars' horns, streetlights, the Tractor Factory's polyphonic roar, and the Volga steamers' busy chatter had once been.

The battle's participants have created their own day-to-day life here: they drink tea, cook meals in mess tins, play guitars, make jokes, inquire after their neighbours, and chat away. Those living here are as one with the nation. They share a character, habits, a mindset, and a soul. The nation has sent its sons to complete an arduous task.

✳ ✳ ✳

We went to the divisional command post at nine in the evening. Multicoloured rockets hanging from invisible stems over the tattered embankment lit up the Volga's dark waters. The water was first silky green then turned blue-violet. Suddenly, it would become pink, as if all the blood of the war was flowing into the Volga.

"Hey, is dinner here?" asked the private sitting at the dugout's entrance. A voice from the darkness answered: "They came a while ago, but they're not back. They've either taken cover somewhere or they're not coming at all. The kitchens are in the area that's really getting it."

The command post is in a basement deep underground. Lined with stone and reinforced with wood, it resembles an adit in a coalmine. Water runs along the bottom just like in a real mine. In Stalingrad, where gaining a metre is as much effort as gaining many kilometres in field conditions, and where the distance to the house an enemy is occupying might only be a couple of dozen paces, all our preconceptions have changed. That of course means that the relative positions of divisional command posts have changed too. The division's HQ is close to the enemy, so regimental and battalion command posts are relatively close too.

"In the event of them breaking through," jokes one man from the HQ, "it'll be easy to keep in contact with the regiments. Just holler and they'll hear you! Then they'll pass it on to the battalion."

The atmosphere of the HQ, though, is the same as ever. Wherever it is located – in a forest, a palace, or a hut – the HQ is always the same. Even here, where everybody scampers about all aquiver from the mortars and shells, the divisional commanders sit hunched over maps. Even here the signallers call out, as if in a clichéd sketch from the front, "*Moon calling! Moon calling!*" Even here, messengers sit in the corner with thin cigarettes trying not to blow their smoke in the commanders' direction. And here, in this adit lit by oil lamps, one senses right away that all the cables and wires carrying commanders' questions from the destroyed houses, factories, and mills occupied by our guards lead to one man.

The adit, as if it were the base of a dam, holds back the terrible tide of enemy forces rushing toward the Volga. The floor, the walls, the ceiling – absolutely everything trembles from the force of exploding bombs and shells. The phones tinkle, the lamp flames flicker, and great, dark shadows frantically play across the wet stone walls. Yet the people are calm. They were in this crucible yesterday, they were here a month ago, and they will be here tomorrow.

The Germans broke through and attacked here a few nights ago. They lobbed hand grenades into the escarpment around the dugout. Dust, smoke, and shrapnel blew into the adit. From the darkness came commands shouted in a strange language, a language that sounded wild here on the banks of the Volga. Even at this perilous moment, Rodimtsev remained as calm as ever. Speaking almost derisively, his every word was carefully chosen to replace one more stone in the dam that the enemy had punctured. Thus was the enemy drained of his strength.

I spoke with General Rodimtsev. He said, "The division has got into the rhythm of battle." During our conversation, the phone rang a good ten times. Rodimtsev would turn his head a little to one side and say a couple of words to the on-duty operator. His short, softly spoken, rather routine orders coursed with the triumphant power of a man who had mastered the rhythm of war's whirlwind and was now dictating the rhythm of his division.

The general's deputy gave some final orders before an assault on a German-occupied house. The five-storey building had particular significance as the Germans could see the Volga and part of its banks from the windows. I was struck by the detail and complexity of the planned assault. Both the house and surrounding buildings had been accurately sketched out on a schematic. The provisional reports suggested that there was a light machine gun in the second floor's third window, that there were snipers in two of the third-floor windows, and that a heavy machine gun was in another. Every floor, every window, and the front and back entrances: the entire house, in a nutshell, had been scoped out.

Men with grenades and mortars, snipers, and submachine gunners took part in the assault. Even the divisional artillery and the heavy guns situated on the Volga's other bank joined in. Every weapon had a particular role connected to a single, greater task. All were to be linked in a network of signals, radios, and telephones.

✳ ✳ ✳

We were traveling along the Volga by motorboat in the dead of night. Six kilometres and an hour or two on the Volga's broad waters.

The Volga was boiling. The blue flames of German shells flickered over the waves. The wailing shrapnel promised death. Our heavy bombers woefully hummed in the dark sky overhead. Hundreds of luminous, winding tracers in shades of red, white, and blue reached out to the bombers from German anti-aircraft guns. The bombers spewed white machine gun fire at the German searchlights. On the other side of the Volga, it felt was if the whole universe were shaking from the mighty rumble of our glorious artillery's heavy guns. The land on the right bank trembled from the explosions. Exploding bombs flashed over factories. Everything – the land, the sky, the Volga – was on fire. I could feel it deep in my heart: a great battle for the motherland was taking place, but here our people were carefully, triumphantly fighting through the flames.

Evgeny Kriger – The Streets of Stalingrad
1 November 1942, *Izvestiya*

People here can still remember what Stalingrad was like before 23 August, before that first, most horrific day of air raids. Seventy days have passed, and some of our troops troops have crawled into a recently bombed city block. Some dazed and confused former local is looking around at the lumps of broken stone. He picks up a brick blown apart in the fighting and mutters:

"God only knows what street this is. I could've walked around here with my eyes shut: there was a building with a whopping display window over there, a toyshop where I used to buy a doll for my daughter every week. She used to mother them so much their arms and legs would come off, she'd beg for a new one, so I'd head off to the shop again and … Mortar! Get dooown!"

Everybody dives for cover among the rubble. Even on an open battlefield, a mortar explodes with a hysterical, piercing, ringing, wild sound, a sound so powerful it feels as if your eardrums are being sawn in two. In the city, though, it feels like your entire ear is being torn off. The city amplifies the overbearing noise of war. The sounds echo from stone to stone, swelling up and growing louder as they strike walls and smash into people with a wailing that totally annihilates one's consciousness.

For a moment, the soldiers lie still, their faces pressed into the stone. One survivor suddenly realizes he is alive, gets up, and says: "The battle's getting really ugly. It's really screaming out there! Is everything okay? Hold on a second lad, let me bandage that up. That better? Right, off we go!"

They set off crawling again. When the opportunity to take a breather for a couple of minutes comes, the former resident again starts to talk about the city where he studied, built factories, and loved. He grows angry that even during this, a scouting mission, he cannot recognize the streets where he spent his guitar and flower-filled youth ...

"This must be it," says one of the soldiers, "this is the street." He tugs a tin street map out from a pile of a rubble. Two months earlier the map had hung on the wall of a building on the corner, "Solnechnaya. That's the street, right?"

And this is the street. The former resident remembers it well: the newly plastered walls, the sidewalk softened by summer heat, a kiosk on the corner. Now there is no corner, no kiosk, and no street. Just chunks of tin with names in faded paint and rusting letters. *Solnechnaya ... Krasnozavodskaya ... Respublikanskaya.*[39] These are the streets of Stalingrad.

Most of the scouts find things a little easier, since there is at least something left here. But the former residents, their palms tearing at deafened ears, always succumb to their memories. It was such a beautiful street, such a very beautiful street! The residents look at it today as if it were still alive. And again they press their faces into the crumbled brick. Mortar!

Once upon a time the Americans made a film called *In Old Chicago*.[40] A third of the film – the most important part, a real masterpiece of trick cinema – depicts the great fire of Chicago back when it was new. You have to give the American cameramen their due. It is shot so well that the viewer really feels like they are in the fire, like there is and could be nothing more terrible. It is beyond theatre, beyond cinema, beyond art. It reveals, without embellishment, the truly horrendous nature of life at the very limits of existence. Beyond lies only death. Whole walls collapse. Hundreds of people are buried. Yet the viewer forgets that these are just extras in fancy costumes who will walk off set alive and with a paycheque in hand. The viewer leaves the cinema totally pale, just barely audibly muttering: "Horrific! But nothing like that could ever really happen. It's just a movie."

When I left Stalingrad and went out onto the steppe, I found it tough to describe the fighting on the Volga city's streets. Words seemed to pale into insignificance. Then it came to me: "Have you seen *In Old Chicago*? After seeing Stalingrad in the flesh – something real, not some director's make-believe – that film is nothing. It might scare children. But a child who'd spent even a single day in Stalingrad wouldn't bat an eye at it."

The fighting is entering its third month already. An aerial bombardment accompanies every single German attack. Junkers and Heinkels launch attacks among the densely packed city stonework just like they do at the frontline. They work over every block for hours on end so that, by the time the tanks appear, the planes have already bombed the houses into nothing but a pile of rubble lying on top of a basement. Then, just when it seems like not a single soul could be left alive, in go the ground forces. Just stone, blood, emptiness, death. Once, the Germans dropped two thousand tons of bombs and conducted 1,850 sorties over a single one-and-a-half kilometre patch of Stalingrad in a single day. The German tanks rolled into what was practically a cemetery. Who could make it out alive from a scrap of land that the entire German air force had descended on? Who would be left to fight? The German tanks approached the edge of the block, but then our anti-tank rounds, our grenades, and our petrol bombs flew at them from behind heaps of incandescent stone – from the cemetery, from the kingdom of the dead. The Germans will not forget how we defended either that Stalingrad street or the Volga itself.

Here is a story about a different night. You could even call it an ordinary night, given what has transpired these past two and a bit months. These sorts of nights are a daily occurrence all over the city and around the factories. This is just one of them.

One of our motorized infantry units and some tanks were preparing to drive the enemy out of a bunch of two- and three-storey stone and timber houses. Senior Lieutenant Samoshchenko led the infantry forward under cover from the tanks. German submachine gunners opened fire from windows, roofs, and basements. Our infantry took cover and dug themselves into piles of rubble. The scouts were sent on ahead. They could not stand up, so they crawled. Street fighting is subject to unique and cruel laws. There is no open field, nor are there any sweeping manoeuvres. The enemy is always close: sometimes ahead, sometimes to the rear, and sometimes to the right or the left. A whole battle can be bottled up in just half of a city block, and filled by constant explosions, whizzing rockets, voices speaking a foreign tongue, and the groans of the dying.

The scouts dove into the darkness, crawled past the front and then around the back of some houses. They heard German whispers and some muffled invective, then let off a submachine gun round to draw fire on themselves. They pressed themselves to the ground to take a breather, which frightened some of the faint-hearted novices who had not yet seen live fire. Then they headed back and made their report: "It's not just submachine gunners. There's anti-tank guns. Some other guns too, but we couldn't tell which in the dark."

The Germans had been taking potshots at the river crossing from the third floor of one of the houses, which had got our commanders' backs up. The river crossing is the most heavily defended spot in Stalingrad. It has been filled up with shells, overrun with broken barges, and bombarded hundreds of times by the Germans, but the crossing is still functioning. It lives. Stalingrad lives.

Samoshchenko ordered the troops to move in closer to the houses. The tanks rolled on after the infantry. The occupied houses sprang to life and a heavy gun opened fire. Samoshchenko wanted to protect his tanks, so he gave the signal: "Reverse!"

The Germans dragged another gun out of a cellar. Its fiery maws had not yet time to open when the gun was struck by a tank round. The gun was silenced, so the tanks opened rapid fire on the houses. The Germans grew quiet then fell silent. You could not tell whether they were alive or dead, though surely, buried in the stone, they would not die quickly.

The battle fell silent for the time being. A silent battle is like a quiet spasm. It is a terrible thing. Opposing troops are forced to sit side by side. They can hear each other as they await death. They ready themselves to cut the throat of anyone who leaps out of the darkness. In this wary quiet, Sergeants Kinzhaev and Barannikov crawled forward once more, wriggling over the stone and squeezing through the narrow gaps they found in ruined houses. Then they came back. They still had not managed to gather enough information, though: when it comes to street fighting, it is best to measure twice and cut once. Sergeant Ponomarenko crawled off on his stomach toward the same houses again. He got closer still. He was just ten or so metres short of the Germans. They were smoking; the bitter tobacco smoke stung his nose. He could get no closer.

The sergeants summarized everything they had seen and heard in a short note. The battle-hardened Private Ershov set off to take the report to the commander. On the way, a German submachine gunner opened fire on him from a ditch. Ershov threw himself to the ground and paused to catch his breath. Then he suddenly launched himself into the darkness. Quick and furious as only a man under threat of death in darkness can be, he managed to avoid the bullets skirting to the right.

Hearing a movement ahead, he cried out in a strange voice, a voice that seemed wild and terrible even to him: "Hands up!" Up ahead somebody leapt backward and began to run away. Ershov was joined by the other soldiers in hot pursuit. Suddenly, they spotted a skirt flapping and realized that they were chasing a woman and not a soldier at all. Whoever had fired at Private Ershov stopped and cried out: "I'm a woman, I'm a woman!" This was, like many things when fighting at night, wholly unexpected. Yet when they seized the woman, they spotted the unshaven cheeks of a German soldier. The skirt was covering grey-green trousers and steel-toed boots, and a woman's headscarf hid the sharp cap of a fascist. It was yet another German scam: a plan to take Stalingrad not in open battle, but through cross-dressing, deceit, and lies.

When morning came, the Germans in the houses were still holding out. A group of our boys were stuck in the same spot, hemmed in by rubble. At dawn, the Germans began to pour artillery fire onto the area. Then it fell silent. Then a sudden rustling and stamping came from one side. Samoshchenko got up to see forty rifle-wielding men in Red Army uniforms emerge from a hollow. Someone next to Samoshchenko leapt up and shouted – "It's our boys!" – before collapsing as a bullet struck his temple. Samoshchenko immediately ordered the troops to fire at the men emerging from the hollow. They were not our boys. They were Germans in our uniforms.

The Germans were repelled, but it was not easy. Some managed to run away, while others remained lying on the ground. Not ten minutes later, a full battalion launched an all-out assault, crashing noisily forward and firing signal flares everywhere, just like every other German attack. Were this an ordinary battlefield, Samoshchenko would have spotted them from afar and could have freely engaged in all sorts of manoeuvres. He could have opened fire just when the timing was right. But on this occasion the Germans suddenly appeared up close, so just when they needed their full firing strength, there was nothing for it: it had to be sheer fury; the sheer fury of Samoshchenko and his troops. They fired away, taking cover in the ruins, hiding in basements and sewer pipes, and nestling their bodies among the ruins of that same familiar, beloved street that they had discovered yesterday night; the street where residents used to open their windows in the morning and make small talk between the peaceful houses. Now there were neither houses nor windows. There was only frenzy, rage, death, and the need to fight off the attacking battalion. Samoshchenko forced the Germans to take cover. He looked at his soldiers' faces, hollowed out, blackened, dripping with sweat. Was that the lot for the day?

Things do not work that way in Stalingrad. As soon as morning comes, the Germans always appear again. And appear again they did, right from that same hollow. They were supported by mortar fire from the rear. Samoshchenko was holding them off. A direct mortar hit took one of his machine guns out of action. Senior Sergeant Markin fell to the ground. He was wheezing and could not get up – he had been wounded in both arms, in the leg, and in the stomach. He asked for water, but how on earth could they get water here? Someone picked Markin up and carried him off. But this is no ordinary battle. This is Stalingrad, where the Germans attack on the ground and from the air. Markin was hit by shrapnel from a bomb while in his comrade's arms. Orderly Khutov was wounded in the head.

The daily bombing had begun. It would continue until nightfall, and then the nocturnal street fighting would begin again. There would be no breaks. The Germans had to be repelled, and nobody would forgive Samoshchenko if he were to retreat. Yet that small group of our boys clung like limpets to the stones of these ruined houses. They repelled a whole battalion's attacks and the attacks from the hollow the Germans in our uniforms had emerged from. The street was still in our hands.

All that happened on just one street on one night, in a city that stretches along the Volga for 56 kilometres. There are many such streets in Stalingrad. For three months, the fighting has been taking place all over this city.

Vasily Grossman and Vasily Koroteev – In Stalin's City
10 November 1942, *Krasnaya Zvezda*

A holiday rally attended by representatives from Stalingrad City Council, from party, civil, and agricultural organizations, and from the military units defending the city was to take place in one of Stalingrad's factories. People made their way to the rally individually and in small groups. They carefully negotiated the darkness of the November night, stepping over rails and warped metal frames and skirting huge black craters dug out by high-explosive bombs. The deep darkness was rent asunder by exploding shells and mortars; the red threads of tracers shot into the sky like sparks from an invisible fire. German searchlights heard the howl of our heavy bombers and began to frantically grope the clouds. For a split second, sheets of heat lightning from exploding bombs, as broad as half the sky, would light up the black waters of the Volga, the endlessly long walls and broken windows of factory workshops, and the steamers hanging motionless between cranes.

The guests travelled carefully, lighting the way with electric torches. The sentries challenged them, then pointed the way toward and down a darkened staircase. An armed worker checked invitations by torchlight.

After the long darkness, everyone reflexively blinked when they entered the brightly lit hall. They smiled at the sight of the electric lamps. Everyone understood how brave the workers and engineers had been to rig up bright festive lighting for the rally during the street fighting and under artillery and mortar bombardment. Men and women alike wore the same boots and cotton bodywarmers. Everybody had a revolver, and many even held submachine guns. Soldiers and commanders of the Red Army and workers and factory directors sat side by side.

A glass placed over the top of a decanter on a table rang out in alarm with every explosion. Over the high table hung large portraits of Lenin and Stalin and a red banner declaring, "Long live the heroic defenders of Stalingrad!"

Pigalev, the Chairman of the City Council's Executive Committee, opened the rally:[41] "Two generations of Soviets are today defending the victories of October with that same level of heroism and dedication. The older generation, the veterans of Tsaritsyn, are those who fought for Soviet power; the younger generation are the sons of Stalingrad. As we celebrate the twenty-fifth anniversary of October, we remember those who gave their lives for the fatherland. We remember the glorious heroes of Tsaritsyn and Stalingrad. The nation shall never forget those who fell in the fight for freedom. We bow our heads before their sacred graves." Pigalev suggested that the assembly honour the memory of the fallen heroes. Everybody rose.

Members of the All-Union Communist Party's Politburo – Comrade Stalin in first place – were elevated to the honorary presidium to vigorous applause and cries of "Hurrah!" Among others, the head of the city's Defence Committee and Stalingrad Regional Party Secretary Chuyanov, the city's Party Secretary Piksin, the commander and several members of the army's military councils, the soldier Kondrashev, and the factory directors Suvorov and Zemlyansky were chosen for the presidium.

Those at the rally chose to send a brotherly greeting to the troops and commanders – the heroes of Stalingrad. "When defending Stalingrad," said Comrade Chuyanov, "we are defending both the fruits of the October Revolution and humanity's future freedom. The enemy intended to seize Stalingrad in short order, but that plan is in tatters. You and I are celebrating the 25th anniversary of October in Stalingrad. Our city has stood firm as a *bogatyr* and resisted three months of the enemy's furious blows."

Chuyanov described the marvellous courage and tenacity of Stalin's city. He recited the names of those brave men in Rodimtsev's Guards division and Gorokhov's brigade whose miraculous feats have amazed the world. He spoke too of Stalingrad workers' total dedication.

"Is it not the case that turbine mechanic Skotnikov is a true warrior?" exclaimed the speaker. "A bomb fell through the roof and struck the ceiling joists. Shrapnel hit the control wheel. Skotnikov was showered with hundreds of tiny shards of glass. Blood poured from this mechanic's hands, but he did not leave his post until a replacement arrived. He fell unconscious as soon as he finished his shift. And what about Kharitonov, the stoker? A shell hit the boiler room and smashed a steam line. Clouds of burning steam filled the room, but this stoker managed to shut off one boiler and drain the other. He saved the day."

In closing, Chuyanov said the following: "Stalingrad has halted the Germans' advance. Comrades, we must swear to our nation and to Comrade Stalin that we will spare no effort – we will give our lives if we have to – to defend our beloved hometown." The holiday rally's attendees as one rose from their seats and applauded these words. After that, a letter to Comrade Stalin was read out.

The rally's attendees had not gathered in some grand theatre, nor had the Stalingrad factories' delegations arrived from streets lit up in celebration. They had come from dark, half-destroyed workshops, and from basements, bunkers, trenches, and dugouts. Yet the glory of wartime Stalingrad had lent this rally a great beauty and summoned a great celebratory mood among these armed workers and Red Army men. And in the harsh appearance of their faces and clothes, in their gleaming weaponry, in the total unity of the workers, soldiers, and mariners sitting shoulder to shoulder, in all of it shone the eternal, invincible might of the Soviet people and the strength of the Great Socialist October Revolution.

3

19 NOVEMBER–31 DECEMBER

Resurrection

Even as the Soviets at Stalingrad came perilously close to losing the city after German attacks in early November, and while both armies sank into ever deeper fatigue, Stalin's generals were hatching an audacious plan to encircle the German army. On 19 November, Soviet tanks went on the advance outside the city. By the end of the following day, the German 4th Panzer Army had been sliced in two. Soviet divisions were moving toward Stalingrad and along the left bank of the Don River to the southwest. The deadlock had been broken.

The corpus of writer-soldiers remained unaware of events until late on 19 November. When they heard the news, they were delighted. Vasily Grossman thought the events at Stalingrad were a "miracle."[1] As Ilya Ehrenburg put it, "up until then one believed in victory as an act of faith, but now there was no shadow of doubt: victory was assured."[2] The troops on the ground too were jubilant. Lidia Medvedeva, the tank lieutenant who had enjoyed the October Revolution celebrations earlier in the month, could barely contain her excitement: "I feel marvellous now. Don't worry about me!"[3] Medvedeva was right to be excited.

The Germans struck no blow in return – even though, as Viktor Nekrasov recalls, the Soviet troops in Stalingrad got so drunk to celebrate that "the Germans could have taken our positions without firing a single shot. The only sober ones were the two nurses Lyuda and Zhanna, and the cripple Tuska, and even they were a bit tipsy. But those dumb Germans took our drunken shooting for real fighting and shrank like violets."[4] The Wehrmacht might not quite have been shrinking violets, but in the following days, the Red Army snapped shut a ring of encirclement at Kalach, to the west of Stalingrad, trapping 250,000 German troops. The Soviets would hold the whip hand all the way to Berlin. The promise of resurrection now seemed like it might be made reality.

Figure 3.1 Red Army troops enter the attack near Stalingrad, fall 1942.

Stalingrad would live. Any death or tragedy could now be read as a necessary precursor to victory.

The big news was kept under tight wraps for several days until Stalin was certain of success.[5] The newspapers of 20–22 November were notably – perhaps even deliberately – tedious: headlines such as "Political Work at the Front Line" and "Winter at the Front" were hardly soul-stirring. But word spread rapidly. By the time readers saw Vasily Koroteev's "The Man from the Volga" published in 22 November's *Krasnaya Zvezda* (translated here), many of them would have been ready to interpret the story as a celebration of a wider victory. Read without this knowledge, however, the sketch is one of the most pointed reflections of the exhaustion of mid-November.

"The Man from the Volga" at first appears to be a generic Socialist Realist tale of a stoic Civil War veteran and construction worker at the front. However, the piece is a deeply personal reflection of its author's own wartime grief. Koroteev had met Polyakov, a fellow Stalingrader, with David Ortenberg and Konstantin Simonov two months earlier. Polyakov, remembered Simonov, was "an old fellow in a cap and with a goatee. [He was a] civilian who'd been thrown into the war, and was now risking his life from morning 'til night, day after day." Koroteev, like Polyakov, was suffering from the exhausting pace of work at Stalingrad. The two men soon bonded over their shared anguish and met regularly at the Volga. The painter Boris Efimov observed the two locals sharing a moment of joint sorrow in October: "The captain and our Koroteev, both Stalingraders, looked on at the smoking, burned city. An unspeakable grief came across their faces. It was tough for all of us, but even more bitter for these men, who had seen the bustling city full of life so recently."[6]

Transformed into an artillery man in "The Man from the Volga," Polyakov is a composite of Soviet and Stalingrad literary and historical tropes: he is a Civil War veteran, a veteran of Tsaritsyn who has even had a brush with the glorious Stalin of the past, a labourer, a father figure, and a man of the great Russian river. Yet Polyakov also seems to embody Koroteev's own wartime experience. He toils away while desperately wondering how a better future can possibly emerge from the devastation of his hometown, aiding civilians at the front even as he has to demolish buildings he has built. Koroteev was using his column inches not to write stock propaganda but to write about himself: formulaic materials offer a setting for an exploration of personal grief. When "The Man from the Volga" was published just as news about the successful Soviet advance broke, however, Polyakov's – and Koroteev's – torments were accorded a heroic sheen. Anguish was made worthwhile by the counterattack.

In the days that followed, the pages of *Krasnaya Zvezda* and *Pravda* were flooded with odes celebrating the breakthrough. Editorials, mastheads, and articles breathlessly listed the number of German dead and described the rapid advance through German territory. The "character of the nation" had been "baptized."[7] The "epic" battle of Stalingrad had become a "time of biblical miracles," a battle to rival Carthage and Troy in importance, and a clash that would go down in world history.[8] The front pages made increasingly extravagant claims about Stalingrad's significance: "These days, the word 'Stalingrad' has become a sort of greeting for decent people all over the world"; "all those who hate Hitler's Germany and its barbarous behaviour think of the courageous 62nd Army with delight." The Red Army's glory would "live on for centuries."[9] The martyrdom and resurrection of a personified Stalingrad was being portrayed as the ultimate *podvig*.

Even the most cynical readers could now dare to believe, as one postwar Soviet refugee put it, that "the Germans might lose."[10] Petr Borisov, an NKVD officer stationed in the 25th Rifles Division in November 1942, reacted to the news by imagining a joyous future:

> Mitya, you must have already heard the latest. Our boys at Stalingrad and Vladikavkaz have gone at the enemy. Just think, it's just the start and soon we're going to be walloping 'em on every front all over the Soviet Union, we'll smash that ring that's encircling us right now, it's happening very soon and so hard that nothing can stop us and there'll be a celebration on our street too. It's coming soon!"[11]

Borisov's words flow so fast they seem carried away by the very thought of victory. Yet he draws not just from an internal well of thought; even in this moment of emotional abandon Borisov draws on a phrase, "there'll be a celebration on our street too," that had recently been used in an order issued by Stalin.[12]

The phrase, an old Russian exclamation, would become central to the portrayal of the victory at Stalingrad. The front page of *Pravda* on 23 November saw the publication of the second text included in this section, "There'll Be a Celebration on Our Street Too!" Although the text was not attributed in print, David Ortenberg and one or two others had toiled in their offices on Malaya Dmitrovka through the night of 21–22 November to write up news of the Stalingrad counterattack for the next day's papers; their efforts almost certainly resulted in this piece.[13] A work marking such an auspicious occasion would, of course, have been read by Stalin. Indeed, the piece marks the start of a sharp Stalinist turn in the Stalingrad story. Its first paragraphs hail the usual array of "Stalingrad's defenders" and "the Soviet people." The sketch climaxes, however, by suggesting that Stalin's 7 November message to "sweep the Soviet soil clean of the Hitlerite scum" had been the catalyst for victory. Only "under the leadership of ... the great Stalin" could Stalingrad have been won. Hitherto mostly absent from Stalingrad, Stalin was now declared victory's architect.

Stalingrad had been the leader's brilliant strategic ploy to entrap the Germans, a "gift" from a beneficent leader to a purportedly grateful people.[14]

Aleksandr Shcherbakov's Sovinformbyuro went into overdrive. Having been left with little but between-the-lines hints to interpret for weeks, David Ortenberg passed on increasing numbers of direct orders to "show soldiers' bravery and fortitude, military *nous* and skill; to show commanders' ability to affect the outcome of battles, operations, and offensive; [and to show] the international significance of Stalingrad."[15] Stalin was, naturally, to be at the pinnacle of this new hierarchy. The increasingly assured dictator would exert ever greater control over the Stalingrad story. The contents of the 23 November editorial translated here would be widely quoted and redistributed at home and abroad in the coming months.[16] The discursive unity between state and people around Stalingrad would never again be quite as evenly balanced as it had been until 19 November.

✳ ✳ ✳

By early December, Viktor Nekrasov remembered, everything seemed to be swinging the Soviets' way:

> The Volga froze over at last, so the supply line from the left bank was more or less functional. The food got better. [Supplies] were forthcoming, so I didn't have to fuss over every last spade and pickaxe. We laid a lot of mines, mostly anti-personnel mines. Nobody had any tanks – not us, and not the Germans. The cold didn't scare us – we had winter boots, warm jackets, fur bodywarmers, and hareskin mittens on strings to make sure they didn't get lost.[17]

The Red Army drove deeper into and beyond Stalingrad. The Wehrmacht could do no more than stall as they haemorrhaged troops and equipment. Soviet commander Nikolay Vatutin reported that on 28 December alone, his forces had seized 60,000 POWs, killed 60,000 of the enemy, and destroyed seventeen divisions while repelling Manstein's attack. A single tank corps reported destroying 84 German tanks, 106 guns, and 431 planes and killing 12,000 Germans in December alone.[18]

The battle may have been in the bag, and everybody may have been exhausted – "my nerves," Vasily Grossman wrote to his father, "are shredded" – but nobody wanted to depart Stalingrad: "I don't want to, I *can't,* leave now."[19] In a brief flurry of activity over the next month, the writers at Stalingrad eagerly began to pen stories reflecting on the broader significance of what had transpired. The frontline journalists now had time and space to think big – and to think of the future. Like Petr Borisov and the other troops at the front, the soldier-writers countenanced pasts and futures that had seemed beyond imagination mere days earlier. David Ortenberg was deluged with – and delighted by – this new material.[20] As the bitter cold of the Russian winter froze the Volga solid, Akhtuba was alive with relief and wonderment.

Boris Gorbatov's "The Mountains and the People," the third story in this section, is one of several stories illustrating how the idea of a "Stalingrad spirit" spread across the front: the story of the counterattack was beginning to inspire Soviet troops everywhere to, as one tank commander put it in a letter to his fiancée, "get at the Fritz in a hurry."[21] An experienced journalist who had worked everywhere from the Donbas region to the Arctic before the outbreak of war, Gorbatov had been one of the first writers to volunteer in 1941. "The Mountains and the People" is filled with examples of Socialist Realist *podvigi* that will now be familiar: the isolated unit relying on spirit and verve; the older, wiser troops assisting their juniors; and self-sacrifices made in the name of both nation and Party. Writing from the Caucasus, Gorbatov suggests that the "Stalingrad spirit" – shorthand for a mix of Tolstoyan spirit, Soviet heroism, worthwhile sacrifice, and glorious *podvig* – could provide inspiration for a military readership that had long awaited a miracle.

Meanwhile, Anatoly Nedzelsky found himself continuing to report from pitched battles on the Volga. "Before the Attack," the final text in this section, brings Stalingrad back down to earth. In it, nervous soldiers waiting for an attack draw on the knowledge of Stalingrad's resurrection to counter fear. In his previous month's effort, "Tales of Stalingrad's Defenders," Nedzelsky had turned to literary models to structure and order a harsh frontline reality; now the literary model of Stalingrad's resurrection summoned a utopian future close to the present, in this textual space at least. In reality, however, hundreds of thousands of Soviet troops would perish later on fighting the Axis armies. Company Captain Nedzelsky himself would barely make it out

of Stalingrad. He would be killed in action close to his hometown of Zapo-
rozhe in August 1943.[22]

As 1942 drew to a close, the danger in Stalingrad continued to recede. Viktor
Nekrasov remembers:

> The fighting where we were on the Mamaev Kurgan was no longer so in-
> tense. The Germans were no longer threatening the Volga; they just sat
> back and bared their teeth a bit. We weren't especially active, either. The
> real fighting was down to the south, where the Germans were trying to
> break out of the encirclement. There were tanks and planes there, but we
> were only seeing "skirmishes of local significance," as they called them in
> the Sovinformbyuro communiqués.[23]

Since stray bullets and sudden firefights no longer posed such a risk, writers
and soldiers could wander relatively freely about the front. David Ortenberg
even briefly returned to take in the breathtaking scale of destruction.[24] The
leading writers at Stalingrad at last requested leave. Vasily Grossman asked
Ortenberg to send him back to Moscow. Simonov, who had been at the Central Front since departing Stalingrad, was granted time in Central Asia to
start work on what would become the first novel about Stalingrad, *Days and
Nights* (1943).[25]

The newspapers were flooded with more and more testaments to Stalin's
personal brilliance. After printing Sovinformbyuro's material and masses of
letters from readers lauding Stalin, there was little space for any other writer.
Stalin's presence squeezed out everyday heroes – the Shkolenkos and the
Shchepetyas – and everyday writers like Anatoly Nedzelsky. The equilibrium
that had briefly existed as the nation's fate hung by a thread in the fall was gone
for good. Nonetheless, nothing could suppress Ortenberg's high spirits: the
night of 31 December 1942 "was the starting line for our new, peacetime life."[26]

Vasily Koroteev – The Man from the Volga
22 November 1942, *Krasnaya Zvezda*

The other battery crew respectfully referred to Battalion Commander Ivan
Polyakov as "Father" – but not because he was any older than the other
troops. "Father" actually looked relatively young for someone in their

forties. Only the wrinkles that cut across his face suggested that he might have led an eventful life. More than a quarter of a century ago he had fought the Germans at Pinsk and Slutsk.[27] Then in 1918, he had enrolled in the 2nd Tsaritsyn Regiment and defended his besieged hometown. It is really quite a story!

Many years have passed since then, and much water has flowed down the Volga. To Polyakov, though, it sometimes felt as if all that happened just yesterday. He liked to compare the past and the present. Much about the situation in the present – the town shaped like a squashed horseshoe, the cold October wind, the artillery's thunderous peals – reminded him of '18. The Volga, just as broad as ever, flowed on past the city; blood was again streaming all over the city. Back then Polyakov had been in the rifles, but now he was a mortarman. But back then there had not been the terrible fires, there had not been the "musicians" (our troops' nickname for the howling German dive bombers), and there had not been the inferno that raged all over the city.

Polyakov knew the site of every past battle. He knew Stalingrad's centre and its suburbs like the back of his hand. There was barely a building in the city that this skilled carpenter had not hammered a nail into or fitted out with framing or doors. He was proud that he worked on almost every major workshop in the Tractor Factory and had received two commendations as a reward. He had built homes in every last nook and cranny of Stalingrad: in Balkany and Dargora, in Beketovka and Yelshanka, in "Little France" and "Big France,"[28] in the upper and lower Tractor Factory villages, and in the Red October settlement. For Polyakov, the whole city felt like one gigantic house. He knew every room and every floor. He was fighting the Germans in his own home.

Polyakov had loved his civilian work. He would often tell his fellow soldiers with great relish about the beauty of the carpenter's trade, about how happy you were when you put up the scaffold for a new building and climbed up to the roof to gaze at the expanse all around! You would survey the city and see how many factories had been built and how many gardens and parks had been planted up. Alongside it all onward would flow the deep and bright Volga.

Polyakov in turn knew his mortarmen by their peacetime professions: Ignatov, the loader, had been a machinist; Kurdyukov, who carried the

shells, a woodcutter; and Private Yunkin had been a fitter. "Father" viewed
war as he viewed any other manual labour. A tough job required hard work,
skill, and *nous*. They would often have to move the mortar's heavy barrel
and base plate along with cases of shells. It was almost impossible to bring
shells up to the firing position during the day, since doing so had already
cost too many lives. Instead, they stocked up on shells overnight. They
would usually need a hundred, but Polyakov always got a hundred and fifty
or even two hundred.

"You're so greedy, Father," the lads would say. His greed, though, was
understandable. Polyakov knew from experience that the next day might see
intense fighting, and if they did not have enough shells they would have to
bring them up under enemy fire. That would lead to avoidable casualties,
so the whole crew would spend almost the entire night stocking up on ammunition. They were unable to sleep for more than three hours at a time, so
occasionally the exhausted men would simply keel over on the spot. The ferocious fighting would strike up again in the morning and last until nightfall.
But nobody complained about the exhaustion. The men knew that there
was no other way.

In battle Polyakov sometimes felt as if he were on a construction site: dust
clouds would billow, the clatter of iron was deafening, and rock crushers
and cement mixers would rasp away. But this was no construction site. This
was war – a war that had caused total devastation from which the glittering
edifice of our life must soon arise once more.

No other crew managed to build a dugout as snug and solid as Polyakov's.
Dug into the side of a wide and steep ravine, its floor was four logs thick.
It provided good shelter – inside one was almost completely safe from
German mortars and bombs – and made a comfortable nest for the mortar.
"Father" had pinned up a newspaper cutting showing a Suvorov quotation
that he had liked very much: "Fight the enemy. Show no mercy to him or
yourself. Fight cruelly, fight to the death. He who shows less pity for himself
will win."

When there was a quiet moment, the troops would gather in the dugout
to listen to the old soldier. To them, Polyakov had seen and done it all. He
was like a living history of the Defence of Tsaritsyn. He embodied the biography of the city they were now defending. "Father" would show the troops
the sites of past battles and tell of how the Krasnovites' attacks had been re-

pelled,[29] of how there had not been enough bullets and shells to go around, and even of how Stalin had come and made the city's defenders feel ten times stronger.

"But did you get to talk to Comrade Stalin?" one of the younger mortarmen asked Polyakov.

"I shan't boast, lads. I didn't get to talk with Stalin, but I saw him up close in the town, and again in the trenches with Kolya Rudnev. I did end up talking to Parkhomenko a few times, though ..."[30]

Ivan Polyakov loved to wax lyrical about his prewar life in Stalingrad. He had been a brigadier with a decent wage in the Red October factory. He even had his own little house with a cherry orchard. His children grew up. The oldest, Yury, studied at the Tractor Factory technical institute, and his daughter, Taisiya, at the chemical institute. The city – *his* city – grew as if in a fairy tale. He had been right to fight for the good life back then, a quarter of a century ago, and it was worth fighting for even more now!

Polyakov simply adored his hometown. He was proud of its history, its accomplishments, and the work done in it. He was pleased that his battery's mortars were homegrown, made right here in Stalingrad, and that their shells were produced in his own factory. Most of the battery's troops were also locals, taken from Stalingrad's Barricades, Tractor, and Red October factories. Every last one of them – the pockmarked machinist Ignatov, the bald fitter Yunkin, the strapping Chetverik, the burly Sergeant Tokarev, the glazier Savin, and the woodcutter Kurdyukov – was an honest and smart lad, and a brave, disciplined warrior to boot. It was not too long ago that they first slipped on the Red Army greatcoat, which led the divisional commander Major Tsygankov to call them the "Workers' Guard." Their heavy mortars would always hit the target, crushing the enemy with lethal fire from on high.

The young troops learned a lot from Polyakov. He told me with a chuckle how his lads had only ever been frightened once, and even then not on account of a German attack but because one of their own rounds had stuck fast in the mortar's barrel. Someone had to get it out.

"So I took the barrel off the base plate, tipped it over and gently teased out the shell. I'm looking over at the lads, and they're lying down, looking like deer in the headlights, not moving a muscle. Well then, I think to myself, they're not a timid lot, they're not a bit afraid of the Germans.

But they're terrified of their own shell! I got it out alright, then I loaded it into the mortar and fired it off at the Germans so it didn't go to waste.

"Then I ask, 'Why are you lot all trembling?' Yunkin goes: 'We don't even know how powerful it is – if it goes off we're bloody well in for it!' Then they all start laughing too."

A narrow stream trickled along the bottom of the ravine. On the edge of the ravine had once stood a wooden pavilion where Polyakov used to have a glass of beer after work. The battery had not changed its firing position for four days. The Germans had pinned it down now, though, and were peppering the ravine with mortar fire and bombs. But they could not change position. There were Germans to the left, and the Volga was right behind them. Any attempt to get out of the ravine up onto the flat expanse to the right would mean losing the mortar. They would have to sit tight. Those "squealing musicians" flew at them once more and dropped several dozen bombs. The barges on the Volga's banks lit up. A column of thick smoke rose high into the sky over the ridge of the ravine.

One after the other, the mortarmen – Polaykov's and the neighbouring crews' – were being taken out of action. Polyakov had seen many deaths in his years as a soldier, but still every death wrenched at his heart. Kabakov was suddenly fatally wounded when a piece of shrapnel pierced his chest. Pink blood bubbled from his lips. Sergeant Tokarev was hit. He did not want to be taken to the field hospital. "I can still fight," he protested. Still the mortarmen did not leave their posts. They had to repel the German attack.

"See that big white house behind the grain elevator?" Junior Lieutenant Motorin asked Polyakov. "And the house with the red roof past that? Fire at the red one. There are German machine gunners and an artillery piece in there. Make sure to hit it, that gun's nailing our boys good."

Polyakov the carpenter of course knew the red house past the grain elevator very well. He had helped to build it not two years past. Who can understand the emotions of a man who must destroy a building that he himself has built, a building that had remained intact until now only by some miracle? But the enemy was in the building, so there was no time to think. Polyakov calculated the distance to the target, set the sight, and loaded the mortar himself. An instant later the building with the red roof disappeared in a cloud of grey smoke.

❊ ❊ ❊

The divisional commander ordered Polyakov to take four men to fetch extra rounds from the factory. Polyakov sat up front with the driver in the truck. With a deep sigh he looked on at the terrible picture of a disfigured city before him; at the vast conflagrations, at the houses blown to smithereens, and at the crater-riddled streets. He saw the central department store, whose green sign was miraculously still in one piece: "Opening hours: 9am to 6pm." And there was the great white house, destroyed by the direct hit of an incendiary bomb. He remembered how quickly they had managed to build it. There had been no hoists, so they had carried the lumber and rafters themselves. It was exhausting work, but how satisfying to know they had "knocked up" an entire building in just two months!

The fighting was taking place in Stalingrad engineers' apartments, in workers' houses planted all around by cherry and maple trees, in ravines and parks, and on great asphalt squares. The mortarman looked on and thought to himself: "So much wealth will be lost. We shall have to spend so much on account of the Germans." He felt that he and the town were one and the same, and every German bomb and shell was striking his own body. The city's life and death were his very own. Now the city resembled an enormous cemetery, and its every house a skeleton.

It was a clear afternoon, but clouds of smoke from the fires were hanging over Stalingrad. The city's residents had not seen the clear light of day for three months already. The closer he got to the factory, the more rage and anguish gripped Polyakov's very soul. He saw his own street and recalled the night when a German bomb had destroyed his little house. He was asleep in the small cherry orchard, but he had put his wife and two younger sons in the cellar. When the sirens sounded in the night the carpenter had woken up his son and said, "Yury, let's go into the cellar?"

"Not the cellar again," his son grumbled and drew his blanket around himself. At that very second there was a whistle overhead and a bomb fell somewhere close. The shockwave tossed them both against a wall.

In the morning, the carpenter found a family photograph under a bed inside the destroyed house. He hid it in his pocket. He was seething with rage. On that very day, Polyakov left for the front to become a mortarman.

Ivan Polyakov, formerly of the 2nd Tsaritsyn Regiment, fired his first heavy
mortar close to the very same cemetery where that regiment had once repelled the Germans' attacks.

✳ ✳ ✳

While they loaded up the car with shells, Polyakov dashed off to see where
his family had got to. On the corner of Granitnaya Street, he met a tanned
young boy walking barefoot with a sack over his shoulder. Polyakov immediately recognized the son of one of the factory machinists.

"Where are you off to, Tolya?" he asked the boy.

"We're crossing the Volga!"

"And where's your father?"

The boy lowered his eyes. It was obvious he was trying hard as he might
not to burst into tears. His father had been killed by shrapnel from a bomb.

"It's alright, Tolya," said the old soldier, "don't cry, I'll give 'em what for!"

He was just wondering how best to console the boy when an old lady
walked up. It was his neighbour. She was dragging a large bundle with her.

"Ivan Semenovich, the Germans burned my house down! I stayed put,
I didn't want to cross the Volga. I felt sad to leave my home and hearth. And
now there's nothing left of the house. This is all I've got left!" The old lady
hoiked up her bundle. Then she said, "But your family crossed the Volga.
I saw them myself."

She hoisted the bundle, which was so large it was almost twice her size,
onto her back. The orphaned boy and the homeless old lady left together.
The mortarman watched them for a few moments then hurried off when he
remembered that he was expected back. He urged the driver to make haste
for the whole journey. Polyakov's soul ached with a single desire: to kill the
Germans, to avenge the tears of children, and to fight for his neighbour's
burned down home and for the wounded, burned Stalingrad.

Polyakov delivered the shells to the firing position that evening. He had
not slept for three days, but still he could not fall asleep. He tossed and
turned, mulling over his trip to the factory and thinking of his family. Then
he was seized by another thought: how long would it take to heal the city's
wounds and to reconstruct it? If there were enough supplies available, he
was sure they could do it in two or three years.

Figure 3.2 A Red Army private gazes across the Volga, fall 1942.

Yunkin, the former fitter, was on sentry duty. He gazed at Polyakov and nodded: "Sleep, Father. It'll be morning soon, and the battle will start again."

There'll Be a Celebration on Our Street Too!
23 November 1942, *Pravda*

The Soviet nation is full of joy as it hears of our forces' successful advance at Stalingrad. Soviet forces broke through the enemy's defensive lines and, three days later, have advanced between 60 and 70 kilometres. Kalach, situated to the west of Stalingrad on the eastern bank of the Don, the train station at Krivomuzginskaya, and the station and settlement at Abganerovo have all been recaptured. Both the railway lines that were supplying the enemy to the east of the Don are out of action.

The fascist invaders have been dealt a serious blow. Our troops have totally destroyed six enemy infantry divisions and one enemy tank division. Another seven infantry, two tank, and two motorized divisions have suffered heavy losses. We have counted the corpses of some 14,000 soldiers and officers on the battlefield. An enormous quantity of prisoners – more than 13,000 – and valuable trophies have been seized.

The three months of fighting around Stalingrad have been unprecedented in world history. The glory of Stalingrad's defenders will be eternal. The whole world followed the titanic clash taking place on the Volga's banks with bated breath. The Soviet warriors defending Stalin's city have shown the world an incomparable example of valour, fortitude, bravery, and military skill.

The enemy sent dozens of their best divisions and thousands of tanks and aeroplanes into the battle at Stalingrad. The Soviet people erected an unassailable wall to block the path of the fascist bandits. The Stalingrad defenders' heroics smashed the enemy's frenzied, rabid onslaught. The defenders knew that there was nowhere to retreat. They knew that the advancing enemy must be stopped. They heard the call of their beloved motherland; she was crying out for a boundless strength of spirit, for the greatest of self-sacrifices, for enormous courage, and for supreme military skill.

Stalingrad's defenders saw the fight for every brick of every ruined building as a fight for the freedom of hundreds and thousands of kilometres of Russian land and for the freedom of millions of Soviet citizens. Fighting in trenches torn up by German bombs and in ruined houses, they understood that they were engaged in a battle for what the Soviet people had spent twenty-five years constructing: the mighty, proud, and impregnable edifice of Soviet society.

Hitler's bandits thought they could take Stalingrad with tanks. In just two months, they lost eight hundred of their steel machines at the foot of the city walls. The Germans wanted to pave the way to Stalingrad with bombs. In just two months, they lost more than a thousand of their planes on the Volga steppe. The Germans wanted to drive Stalingrad's defenders into the Volga with infantry divisions. In just two months, more than a hundred thousand of their soldiers and officers were buried. *Unteroffizier* Erich Muller had good reason to write in his diary that, "We should call our route to Stalingrad the Road of the Dead."

The bravery of Stalingrad's defenders grew ever stronger in the flames of battle. Our Soviet soldiers' and officers' will was tempered in the smoke and fire of combat. Our response to the fascist hordes was forged in fierce fighting. Stalingrad's defenders brimmed with the knowledge that they were certain to defend Stalin's city and to beat the German swarm back, far away from the Volga. "Our spirit is higher and our will firmer than ever," wrote the city's defenders in a letter to Comrade Stalin. "Our arms have not yet tired of striking the enemy. We have chosen to defend Stalingrad's walls to the death!"[31] And hold firm they did! They waited for that joyful, radiant hour of retribution: the advance of our forces at Stalingrad.

This is not the first time the enemy is facing the Red Army's mighty blows. The successful actions at Rostov, Tula, Kaluga, Moscow, Tikhvin, and Leningrad have already shown how our troops can not just best but smash the German army. Back then, the Germans did not just have to go on the defensive. They actually retreated more than 400 kilometres, abandoning guns, vehicles, and supplies on the way. The events of last winter showed that, as Stalin said, "the Red Army and its fighting cadres have grown to become a force to be reckoned with and capable not just of resisting the fascist forces but also of beating them in open battle and driving them into retreat."[32]

In his missive of 7 November, People's Commissar for Defence Comrade Stalin explained that the day when the enemy discovered how strong the Red Army's new attacks would be was not far off. The German armies are now experiencing the might of these new attacks. Sovinformbyuro published a communiqué announcing the German defeat at Ordzhonikidze, near Vladikavkaz, just three days ago. The enemy had counted on taking the city with tanks and creating a bottleneck on the Georgian military road that would divide our forces. The enemy miscalculated and suffered terrible losses. More than five thousand soldiers and officers and a great quantity of equipment were abandoned on the fields of Northern Ossetia.

Both our successful offensive at Stalingrad and the operations conducted at Vladikavkaz show how the Red Army is becoming braver, tougher, and mightier with every passing day. It is ready to dutifully carry out its every task needed to crush the hateful enemy, the fascist invaders, and their bloody accomplices for good.

The Soviet people know that the enemy is not yet broken. There can be no doubt that the German invaders will again embark on new exploits to make real their bloody dreams. Crushing the enemy once and for all will require every last bit of the army's and the people's strength at the front and behind the lines.

"Comrades of the Red Army, commanders and commissars, partisans! The defeat of the fascist army and the repulsion of the Hitlerite invaders depends on your tenacity and fortitude. It depends on your military skill and your readiness to do your duty to the Motherland! We can, and we must, sweep the Soviet soil clean of the Hitlerite scum!"

Thus spoke People's Commissar for Defence Comrade Stalin in his November missive. Our forces' attacks at Stalingrad and Vladikavkaz prove that we can and must sweep the Soviet soil clean of the Hitlerite bandits.

Our forces' advance at Stalingrad continues. It is just one more demonstration of the Red Army's might; it reveals our forces have the military skill to win. The Soviet nation is following the developing military operations at Stalingrad with the greatest excitement and joy. The heart and mind of every Soviet citizen is with the valiant fighters and commanders fighting fierce battles with the German invaders and their accomplices on the steppe around the Volga.

The Soviet nation warmly congratulates its valiant sons. The nation is certain that under the leadership of our beloved commander, the great Stalin, our courageous troops will crush the fascist bandits and sweep the Soviet soil clean of the despicable enemy.

There will be a celebration on our street too!

Boris Gorbatov – The Mountains and the People
6 December 1942, *Pravda*

1.

There's rain over the Black Sea. Rain over the mountains. Rain over a road. Heavy, driving rain. What could possibly be making this wet road seem jolly, the Black Sea blue, and the murky mountains cheerful?

I remember what this road was like in August. There had been no rain for some time, so the highway sweltered in dry clouds of green dust. The dust settled on tormented faces, dead leaves, and motionless cypress trees. That only happens on roads of retreat along which a dense stream of vehicles, horses, carts, people, and herds of animals flow. There is nothing worse than the road of retreat!

Bounteous natural landscapes sumptuously unfurled around us, the sea was a blinding turquoise, and the white-stone holiday villas were drenched in the greenery of vineyards. Yet the more sumptuous nature became, the more painful it was to behold. It was terrible to think that the war had even come here. It was terrible to see bomb craters even at these resorts. The lily-livered thought the time had come to part with our beloved Black Sea, that the mandarins were ripening for the Germans, that the gardens were not to bloom for us, that the palatial seaside sanatoriums were to be taken by the Germans, and that it was to be those Germans, not us, who would take their strolls through the local parks …

But the mandarins were not to ripen for the Germans! Our military kiosks are now selling them for four roubles a kilo in this very spot, and our soldiers are now impatiently recuperating in the sanatoriums right here.[33]

The language of the frontline road is rather eloquent, but if you were curious, the street itself could explain what is happening here at the front without words. There is a sense of cheery alarm – a furious flurry of activity – on the roads of an advance, and a sense of calm, confident strength on the roads of a defence. People have returned and life is back to normal here. Cars travel at the posted speed limit. There are signs – a whole library of banners, slogans, and information panels – at every turn. Special care has been taken to ensure that you can easily find water for drinking and to fill motor cars, the bathhouse for the soldiers passing through, or the way to the gorge you are looking for.

At every major intersection there are stern-looking traffic controllers. Many of them are young women who will give you a regulation salute and flag the way as you pass through. The only people that can make them raise a smile are the mariners. They really are an incorrigible bunch! Their response to the girls' proper greeting is anything but regulation: they put their hands to their lips instead of their caps, and they blow air kisses. The girls blush as the mariners chuckle.

The heavy spring rain falls, beating down on the road, on saddles and windscreens, and on heavy gun carriages. The cars stream ever on, until those cheery mariners are lost behind the bend, carting happy memories

of their shenanigans off to the frontline. They will remember the girl and
the road before some fearsome battle and smile a heart-warming smile.

2.

Towns, just like people, have personalities. Some people, picked out by fate
for heroic deeds, are *bogatyri*, while others are quiet, peaceful, and entirely
civilian. Nobody ever expects them to accomplish anything heroic. Leningrad, Stalingrad, and Sevastopol are *bogatyri*. History, the Revolution, and
war have made them so.

Tuapse, meanwhile, is a small and very civilian, mostly a tourist, town.
Yet there is something touchingly great in Tuapse's unexpected bravery.
The war made its demands, and Tuapse, like so many dozens of other Soviet
cities, was transformed into a warrior.[34] The Germans had been racing forward toward the sea and Tuapse. Hitler even named a date for the town's
capture. That deadline has passed and the city still holds out.

The road to Tuapse is shielded by mountains that the city's inhabitants –
real warriors – defend. It was the people who tore up the so-called Führer's
plans and who buried his Black Sea dreams – and thousands of soldiers and
officers to boot.

What halted the Germans at Tuapse? Mountains? There are higher mountains in Greece, but none at all near Mozdok.[35] Soldiers forged from a miraculous metal are fighting here today. They alloy the persistence and courage
of Sevastopol with the bitter experience of Kerch and the difficult lessons
of Rostov. Miners, mariners, gunners, artillerymen, infantry, and pilots are
hammering the Germans all along the road to Tuapse. A fierce, merciless, and
difficult war is being waged in mountain gorges between tiny units and in
one-on-one combat. Skirmishes break out in gloomy ravines and on un-
trodden paths; nighttime clashes are fought in dense forests. The people fight
for peaks, slopes, ridges, for every last stone and path along this pass.

This incomparable and difficult war demands of our warriors great spirit,
immense tenacity, and inhuman stamina. We need brave and resourceful
warriors, men with initiative and no fear of close-quarters combat. We need
our warriors to possess ardent belief in our victory and absolute trust in
both their weapons and their comrades in the trenches.

On the approaches to Tuapse, the fascist meat is being inexorably, inces-
santly pulverized as if in a bloody meatgrinder. The Germans may be trying

to worm their way from the mountains to the sea, but every last one of our soldiers is doing everything they can to stop them slithering anywhere at all. They take pleasure in burying German corpses in the mountains.

The Germans know that they are suffering terrible losses. One German *Oberleutnant*, a battalion commander, forgot his place and angrily told his commanders that he could not carry out their order to advance. He had nothing to attack with; his losses were already innumerable: "I absolutely cannot," he exclaimed, "conquer the Caucasus and the Black Sea with nineteen submachine gunners!"

Oberleutnant, you shall not take our Soviet Caucasus or our Soviet Sea with nineteen submachine gunners. You could not do it with nineteen divisions.

3.

If you were to discuss the people fighting here in the mountains, you would have to mention the unit commanded by Comrade Arshintsev. You would have to talk about its banner, which is decorated with four commendations and a medal for Chongar.[36] You would have to state that the unit is a stickler for military tradition and that the troops' camaraderie has been forged in the fire. You would also recall Skulen, Floreshti, and Dubossary. And Prut, who was baptised in the blood of the enemy. Nikolaev the same, under heavy fire. And how in winter '41 the unit added a medal for Rostov to the one from Chongar in fighting on the frozen Don crossing.

One would have to mention the scorching, difficult summer of '42. Rostov, Krasnodar, Maikop. Dark days. As difficult as they may be, one can be a hero on dark days too. The thousands of crosses on German graves on the Kuban and Don steppes are testament to how Arshintsev's unit did its banner proud during those dark days. Not one of Arshintsev's troops wavered as they fought in the ring of death. When the order to retreat came, though, they openly wept. Colonel Arshintsev, pale from sorrow and rage, gathered up all those who had retreated from the surrounding units. He and his eagles threw themselves back into the fray.

That was when Arshintsev met Shtakhanovsky. There are so many things to be said about that meeting. Shtakhanovsky was the commissar of a militia regiment from Rostov. A plump old fellow, he had been with the security services and worked as a personnel director on the railways before the war.[37] He never could say no to a good fight, so he enrolled in the militia. One day people will pen songs about that regiment, which captured Rostov in winter 1941 and was wiped out on the barricades in the same place in summer 1942. Now Shtakhanovsky is Arshintsev's political deputy.

One could go on and on about that friendship, but the time has come to tell the tale of Bald Mountain and the Wolf's Gate Gorge. It all happened very recently, right here in the mountains. In a single day, the Germans fired 8,000 shells at the mountain and conducted six hundred air raids. Yet the eighty-four-strong garrison stood firm in the way that only Soviet warriors can: they stood to the death.

To understand and explain this tenacity, one would have to describe the Soviet warrior's love for and immense pride in his unit – and discuss his happiness at advancing under a tattered old banner that reeks of gunpowder. One would have to describe how the wounded lie in infirmaries pining for their battalion as if for their own home, writing letters and trying to secretly slip away back home, back to their company. Commander Maloletkov, a veteran of the division, puts it like this: "They'd have to carry me away, actually drag me off. I won't go of my own accord!" Puffing at his fluffy whiskers in the dugout, he grills his radio operator "daughter" about her work with a pretend strictness, wagging his finger and telling her, "Daughter, just you mind not to disgrace our family name and our unit!"

One would have to describe the dugouts too. These mountain caves have hearth-like stone ovens that emit a warm, bittersweet smoke. The smoke, as from a hearth in a real home, warms and stirs the soul. And one would need to describe the gorge, with its rapid running rivers, and the mountain peaks, where lonely garrisons proudly serve, and every part of this bloody and muddy daily life at the front. Iron falls on the people like rain; the rain beats down, malicious and biting, like iron.

And then one would need to describe the road leading over the ridge. Two months ago the road did not even exist. There was just a path surrounded by a fearsome forest. So the people cut a road through the trees, and off went packs with food, fodder, and arms to the front.

Do you know what it really takes to feed a unit? What it takes to feed hungry cannon and machine guns? What it takes to supply a whole battle? Caravans travel through the pass day and night. Cars cannot get through.

Horses proceed with trepidation, snorting and afraid to lose their footing. Donkeys clamber up slopes. Oxen harnessed to carts issue drawn-out cries. Pack horses move slowly and laboriously. The lead horse's tail is lashed to the bridle of the one behind so that the caravan travels in a long train. And with them, spattered with mud, wet and exhausted, go the pack handlers – about whom barely a word is ever spoken or written – making their way through the mountains.

One could go on and on about these mountain warriors, from Hero of the Soviet Union Esaulenko all the way down to the most ordinary baker, but here you will find the story of the garrison defending that nameless mountain in a battle that happened just the other day. The battle did not make it into a Sovinformbiuro communiqué. It will not even be noted in the unit's own history.

✳ ✳ ✳

It was a red letter day for the unit. Celebrations are a rarity at the front, and those that do occur are spent under fire, just like every other day. But this was a special celebration, their very own celebration: it was the unit's twenty-fourth anniversary. After a short political meeting was held, Deputy Political Instructor Yeronin said to Senior Sergeant Lomadze, "Right then, Lomadze. We'll get you enrolled in the Party tomorrow."

It was a murky, rainy morning. All was quiet at the front bar the noisily flowing river in the gorge and the cries of damp birds in the forest. On the nameless mountain the soldiers were waiting for their breakfast. It was being brought up from the canteen at our defensive front line, which was far behind the unit. The nameless mountain stood like a lonely sentry in no man's land. The mountain's garrison was doing guard duty.

They waited silently and impatiently for breakfast, as is always the way when it comes to hot food in the trenches. Suddenly, somewhere close, up went a loud cry: "Hurrah!"

"Our lads having a rally, are they?" asked Yeronin with surprise. But there was something suspicious about this Russian "hurrah." It did not really seem very *Russian*, as if it lacked a Russian spirit, a Russian joy, and a Russian anger. This was a foreign "hurrah."

"Prepare the machine gun!" yelled Yeronin, wanting to be on the safe side.

But there were already shots thundering out from the neighbouring emplacement. The un-Russian "hurrah" gave way to German groans and curses. The Germans had failed to trick the garrison, so they were waging an all-out attack.

There were thirty-six soldiers on the nameless mountain. Three hundred Germans were attacking from all sides. The garrison's commander Lieutenant Sinelnikov knew that regulations permitted a unit on guard duty to withdraw in such circumstances, so long as it fired at and held up the enemy so that our defensive lines would have time to prepare for contact.

Today, though, was a very special day. The unit had been formed precisely twenty-four years earlier somewhere in far-off Siberia to fight Kolchak.[38] Now this man, the young Lieutenant Sinelnikov, was lucky enough to serve and fight in its ranks. This was an important day, and absolutely everybody on the nameless mountain felt it.

The crew of anti-tank gunners that had borne the brunt of the Germans' first attack preferred death to retreat. Every one of them died in an exchange of grenades. Only Party Organizer Palishko, heavily wounded as he was, found just enough strength to crawl over to the neighbouring emplacement. He did not crawl off to lie down and die. He did it so that he could fight, and fight, and fight some more.

When he had reached the emplacement, he did not ask for bandages, water, or peace and quiet. He asked for a rifle. "Rifle!," came his angry cry. So he was given his rifle.

Now the Germans turned their attack to Lomadze's heavy machine gun. The telephone cable had been severed, but not before they had managed to signal to Junior Lieutenant Rybakov: "We need mortar cover!" The response was inaudible over the telephone, but the mortar rounds now flying toward the Germans suggested that Rybakov had understood.

Two German attacks from the front and two from the rear were repelled, but the ensuing quiet did not last long. Lomadze had managed to feed a new belt into the machine gun, but it was Koshubyak who fired it off as Lomadze was wounded. Blood was gushing from his hands, but he was almost crying at not being able to fight on. A desire to fight still boiled inside him, and only Yeronin's order to go back behind the line made him leave. Koshubyak fired off the cartridges from Lomadze's belt, inserted a new one, then suddenly slumped over. Yeronin began to fire Koshubyak's belt. Now only two men, Yeronin and Gridchik, remained at the gun. The gun's fire kept on felling Germans, but a new wave would always crawl out from the forest. A bullet pierced the gun's housing. Water poured forth. Yeronin opened the top of the munitions casing and continued to fire. The hot iron burned his hands. Another armour-piercing bullet cut through the casing.

"Gridchik, grenades!" cried Yeronin. An intense exchange of grenade-throwing began. The two soldiers were fighting dozens of Germans in communications channels and trenches. Only when all the grenades were gone did they begin their retreat to Sinelnikov's command post.

But the Germans had got there already. Sinelnikov got up and waved a grenade, but he had not managed to throw it before a submachine gun pierced his chest. Sinelnikov's grenade slowly fell from his hand before exploding like a salute over a hero's grave. The battle was now taking place right at the peak of the mountain. Rybakov's mortarmen were up there fighting to cover the retreat of the wounded. The wounded were fleeing along an overgrown path. Lieutenant Subbotin quietly moaned as he was carried along on a cape. Those with heavy wounds leaned against the stronger troops. Everyone walked in silence, knowing that they had done their duty to the last. They would be able to bravely look other frontliners right in the eye.

Back on the mountaintop, shots still rang out and the battle raged on. The wounded Party Organizer Palishko's bunker was completely surrounded but still fighting on. There were three other men with Palishko: the burly, jolly, and ruddy accordionist and singer Shevchenko; the aged Koshevets; and little Sergeant Serezha Voinitsky, a lad from the next village over who was almost lost in the folds of his oversized greatcoat. Palishko and Shevchenko were firing while Koshevets and Voinitsky reloaded the rifles. Palishko shot with a furious anger, but Shevchenko did so with good cheer. Koshevets was muttering under his breath, and sighing, huffing and puffing, but Serezha gave himself over to the task completely. He was terrified he would not reload the rifle fast enough and Shevchenko would scold him: "Come on, you little wimp."

When the Germans had them completely surrounded, Palishko turned to Shevchenko and said, "Right, brother, let's go and meet our guests." They grabbed some grenades and ran out of the emplacement. Serezha heard the grenades explode, the Germans screech, and Palishko shout something. Then everything fell silent. Neither Shevchenko nor Palishko came back. Serezha seized a rifle and threw himself against the embrasure.

"Now you and I are going to do some shooting, old chap," he said. An intense joy began to burn within him. At last he would get to start shooting, at last he would be waging war. He grinned broadly as he spotted a redheaded German officer standing right in front of the embrasure. The second Serezha spotted him, he fired. The officer fell. "It was my bullet that got him," thought a delighted Serezha, but at that very moment he was shot in the hand.

The Germans rushed into the bunker. Serezha was dragged out of the trench. He could see German corpses splayed out all over the battlefield. Serezha counted hundreds of them. The groans and curses of the wounded came from all over; the medical orderlies had no chance of collecting all t he injured. There were Germans wandering all over the mountain, loudly shouting their *Heils* about something or other, but it looked like they did not intend to advance any further. Their battle with the mountain guard had proved too costly. Chaos, as always after a tough battle, reigned. Serezha took advantage of the chaos to throw himself down a cliff. He rolled head over heels through a prickly bush. Stones came clattering down after him and bullets whistled past. Serezha heard nothing.

He only came to his senses down below, in some sort of dried-up stream bed. He found a path and began to follow it. It was here that he discovered Palishko. Palishko was crawling slowly and awkwardly and, what was strange, in silence. His leg had been fractured; it was leaving a bloody trail behind him on the path. When Serezha bent over him, Palishko said: "That's quite alright. It's all fine now."

"What's fine, uncle?" asked Serezha.

"Don't carry me, there's no need," said Palishko. "My time's up. Take my Party Card. Take it back to the unit, have them give it back to the man who gave it to me. They'll know what to do." Serezha took the Party Card.

That is all you need to know about this battle on the nameless mountain that took place on one unit's twenty-fourth anniversary.

✳ ✳ ✳

On the very same day, a group of scouts – those masters of the mountain paths, the scourge of the enemy's rear – returned from a raiding mission. They were exhausted, hungry, and smothered in mud but still in high spirits. Back came Filipp Kononov, who describes himself as "a fan of a good fight," back came the miner Ivan Kazakov, and back came big Bayuk, who thinks that there is no weapon better for a scout than a sharp knife. These were Lomonovsky's fighters. They greedily threw themselves at the pans of steaming oatmeal. Their comrades surrounded them. The scouts, wolfing down their hot porridge, revealed everything about their latest incursion, showing off trophy lighters and boasting about captured weapons.

The others listened on with envy. It means a great deal to any fighter to be a part of a tough but successful mission and – like Kononov did – to attack and destroy an execution unit, or – like Lomonovsky had – to break into a German-occupied village and make hay there. It means a great deal to turn back a supply train, to try foreign wine, or to boast about a trophy trinket. Indeed, many soldiers now pleaded with the scouts, imploring them, "Take me, teach me, let me go on a raid." Kononov looked at them for a long time. He did not need brave men. He needed sensible ones. A brave lad would only let them down and get people killed. Scouts need to be a clever kind of brave. So Kononov spent a long time explaining to the people surrounding him how being a scout is a cunning and interesting, yet still rather cheerful, profession.

Now Lomonovosky's troops are taking their platoon commander to hospital. Lomonovsky was injured in the very next mission. It is not a serious injury, but he has to go to hospital all the same. Lomonovsky gives his command to a new man, explaining everything necessary and dawdling before going to hospital. The whole platoon has gathered around his stretcher. Everyone is worried. Tears glisten in the eyes of many of them. Lomonovsky is worried too – even when facing death he is sad to part with his lads. In a quivering voice, he speaks to the new commander: "Take my boys, take my kids, and keep going just the same as we have been."

The new commander promises to do so. "As you are my witnesses, I promise," he repeats, with concern in his voice. Suddenly, Lomonovsky breaks into a cheerful smile, and says, "Kill the Germans, like we have been killing them. Show them no mercy!"

"Right," shouts Lomonovsky to the rider, "tally ho!"

4.

The echoes of the Stalingrad offensive can be heard in the mountains of the Caucasus. They bring joy, pride, and even a kind of envy – a good, a *military* kind of envy – into soldiers' hearts. "Gah, how come I'm not there?," everyone exclaims. "Gah, when will it be our turn?"

The desire to advance has never left the Russian soldier's heart. The same question is always on his lips: "Will it be soon? Will it be soon?" Ukrainians in bunkers drink to future meetings in Kiev, and young Soviet officers dream of marching to the west. You will not find a single warrior who has no faith in our victorious procession over liberated land, nor one who would not be overjoyed at the order to advance. To advance means to liberate. What could be more holy?

Our envy is understandable. Everyone wants to tread, like the Stalingraders, that ground covered in snow, smoke, ashes, and blood. "Yes," say the frontline soldiers in their dugouts, "there's already a celebration on the streets of Stalingrad. Look how joyfully they are killing the enemy. Well, we're waiting for our celebration in the mountains. We too will kill the enemy on the streets of Maikop and Krasnodar!"

Anatoly Nedzelsky – Before the Attack
10 December 1942, *Izvestiya*

The divisional artillery commander's observation post is on the crest of a large *kurgan*. Looking down, there's a clear view in every direction. Through the stereoscopic telescope, one can easily make out the roads on the other side of the Don a good 15, maybe 17, kilometres away. A white ribbon of road twists its way upward and disappears over the horizon, vanishing into a thin cloud of freezing grey smoke.

The front line is right here on the Don itself. The Germans here are clinging on to their defensive emplacements. It is only at night that they can take the chance to use their only, albeit painstakingly camouflaged, crossing. During the daytime, no matter where you look, you cannot see a single living soul on the German side. The Hitlerites have disappeared deep underground, digging themselves into foxholes, pillboxes, and bunkers, laying minefields, and blanketing the space in front of their line in a tangled web of barbed wire.

It is early morning. A vicious wind rips over the steppe, tearing the barely fallen snow out from gullies and hillocks and chasing it back into ditches and hollows. Cold, snowy clouds creep along so low they almost touch the ground. Little strips sometimes detach themselves from the clouds, float to the ground, and kick up squalls of snow that obscure the outline of the hills beyond.

It is appalling weather for the artillerymen, and it's making the mortarmen curse everything under the sun. Imagine trying to locate the enemy's guns, which wander about like nomads, in conditions like this! Correcting the line of fire is impossible; triangulating new firing lines is even harder.

However, the closer the clock hands get to midday, the clearer both the sky and the artillerymen's faces become. It seems like nature itself has timed it perfectly to coincide with plans made, revised, and finessed long ago: the preparation for an attack scheduled to begin at twelve o'clock.

It is no coincidence that artillery fire is often compared to music. The music of the artillery can tolerate no false notes. A false note – over- or under-shooting – could prove fatal here. A spotter is atop the observation point to ensure that the vast, multi-calibre orchestra of the artillery plays ogether in perfect harmony. The spotter is like a conductor, but he holds a telephone receiver instead of a baton; phone cables strung along wooden pegs and stretching out in every direction along the ground convey his voice.

The divisional artillery commander, Lieutenant Colonel Pavlov, is standing at the stereoscope. The lieutenant colonel is a veteran artilleryman: in 1915 he had manned a cannon. He is facing down the Germans for the third time in his life. "More fire!" cries out the former gunner brusquely. He has at his command the whole firepower of the "cooperative" – the mighty clenched fist that is tasked with dealing a crippling blow to the enemy, breaking his defences for good, and piercing the frontline. That task in turn exists only for one reason: to clear a path for our infantry's advance.

The lieutenant colonel's brusque command is heard loud and clear. A few minutes later and the steppe is covered by the smoke from explosions and glittering flashes of fire. The air shakes as if reverberating from a mountain rockslide. Black plumes of smoke float up over the length of the frontline. The plumes grow wider then, blown by the wind, clump together to form a dense and all but impenetrable wall.

The cannonade grows yet stronger. Heavy guns and howitzers howl away with a deafening roar; mortar rounds fly up, almost vertically, and away into the clouds. Dry yelps like whipcracks can be heard from the frontline as the anti-tank guns begin their fire.

A battery of howitzers commanded by a certain Prokopenko is positioned on the sector's left flank. The battery's crews pose a real threat to the enemy. Prokopenko is a real master of "working over" the opponent's frontline. Everybody here has heard about how his battery managed in just one day to demolish two enemy bunkers, clean out two trenches defended by machine guns and submachine gunners, and scatter and almost totally destroy a whole company of the Fritz.

Senior Lieutenant Kameko's battery is closer to the centre. Kameko is from Belarus. Here at Stalingrad he is taking revenge for the destroyed towns and villages of his motherland. People here would tell you about how a mighty German unit came under his battery's fire and – so heavy and dense was the fire on them – simply ceased to exist.

Battery Commander Lieutenant Bulich, a Ukrainian by birth, is another artilleryman with a sterling reputation. His battery is right in the middle of the line. In no time at all his battery have notched up a decent tally by destroying four observation posts, six infantry trenches, and five heavy machine guns, and sending a fair portion of three or so Hitlerite units off to meet their maker.

Just to the left is a gun commanded by the boundlessly brave Senior Lieutenant Mishustin. His observation post is right under the enemy's nose, but Mishustin is at his post, keeping track of what the enemy is doing a mere 600 metres from our line. It is no trouble at all to find Mishutin's observation point under a ring of artillery and mortar fire during the battle right now, but I promise that tomorrow – as always – you will be overjoyed at this battery's impressive score. Their guns hardly ever miss!

The artillery thunder grows louder. The explosion forms a dense wall ahead of our line. Now the battery's music is interrupted by some or other dissonant sounds coming from behind our positions, from the rear. They are getting louder and louder and ever easier to hear. Here come the strike planes! The aircraft are flying in two echelons. They dip low and, almost touching the ground, roar over the enemy positions.

Lieutenant Colonel Pavlov is rubbing his hands together – not because they are chilled by the bitter wind, but because that is what he always does when a job is going well. He cannot hold it in; he lets out a shout: "Top job, pilots!" Looking up at the sky, he smiles at the strike planes as they return home.

There are mere minutes until the attack begins. Yet another crushing blow awaits the Hitlerites. An overwhelming roar, as if a waterfall were striking the ground from a great height, suddenly comes from the left flank. That is the long-range artillery, so beloved of our frontline troops, striking up a tune. The artillery plays its motif four times, and four times fierce explosions rock the enemy's line. The anointed time, the moment when the infantry will sally forth, ticks ever closer.

Now the anointed hour – a time of fire, smoke, and thunder – is upon us. A mighty overture, performed splendidly by our artillerymen, has preceded it. To the left, the tanks race at full speed through a gully. The artillery redirects its fire deep into the enemy's defences. Machine guns cough their way into the music of battle; non-stop waves of rifle fire pepper the field.

The attack has begun!

4

1 JANUARY–2 FEBRUARY
Forward, Life

Viktor Nekrasov, still stationed on the Mamaev Kurgan, saw in the New Year with raucous celebrations:

> The party happened in [a] spacious dugout. My sappers had made it into a palace. They'd got hold of some cardboard with a black marble pattern among the ruins and stuck it on the walls. The table was covered with a white cloth. We had the lot, even oranges and Armenian cognac. The scouts took care of that. We ate, we drank, we sang, and then we went outside to salute the German positions. The Germans mustered some sort of response. But barely. The end was near.[1]

The pages of the new year's papers were packed with odes to Stalin: "The path to victory is clear," intoned one editorial on 1 January. "Comrade Stalin, in all his genius, has laid it out for us. It was under his leadership that the Soviet nation overcame, and will overcome, every possible obstacle in its path."[2] David Ortenberg, who always had a finger on the reading public's pulse, tried his best to limit the more formulaic stories. In a terse meeting at the Kremlin, Ortenberg suggested he should use his limited column inches for material from the front. Aleksandr Shcherbakov responded with silence, glaring at Ortenberg "as if I were mad." The editor got the point. Stalingrad was now Stalin's victory.[3]

Readers of *Krasnaya Zvezda* who picked up the New Year's Day paper were treated to a triumphant front-page editorial. The article, titled "The Results of Our Forces' Six-Week Attack around Stalingrad," summed up the counterattack at Stalingrad thus far. It, of course, lauded Stalin as a strategic genius, suggesting that the Germans' plan to cut off the Ural and Volga regions from European Russia was always destined to be trumped by the Soviet leader's cunning ploy

Figure 4.1 General Rodimtsev's troops attend a victory meeting on the Square of Fallen Fighters, 4 February 1943.

to encircle and crush the Wehrmacht. The text was padded out with a large map indicating progress to the end of 1942 – the first map published for months – and lists of Soviet military achievements: thousands of planes and guns captured, division after German division destroyed, and dozens of villages and towns recaptured.

Leafing past the new year's greetings to Stalin and on to the last page of the day's *Krasnaya Zvezda*, the reader would have found a pair of celebratory but stylistically antithetical stories, which are both translated here: Grossman's "Today in Stalingrad" and Ehrenburg's "On the Verge." As he contemplated leaving Stalingrad for good, Grossman had wandered through the city to produce one more piece on the ground. In "Today in Stalingrad," the author, so terrified of the crossing in August, now elegantly captures a lively scene close to how Viktor Nekrasov would later remember it: "The Volga was frozen solid, but it had come to life ... Trucks painted white bounced over paths worn into the ice [and] the bank, so recently completely empty, now felt more like the Nevsky Prospect or Kreshchatik. People were sprinting, rushing, sliding and falling all over the place, sleds dragged their loads, and vehicles were honking their horns constantly."[4]

In "Today in Stalingrad," this burst of activity is the most explicit manifestation yet of Stalingrad as a turning point from death to life. The Soviets have "fought to see the sun, fought for the very light of day," which illuminates every aspect of their apparently newly safe *byt* in Stalingrad, which is described as a city humming with activity and ordinary life. Meanwhile, the Germans, "hidden away from the sun and the daylight under the cruel stars of a Russian December night," starve and contemplate death. The turning point of Stalingrad is thus presented as a series of inverted tropes: up/down; light/dark; life/death; past/future. Order is asserted through this steady counterpoint: life, crows Grossman's narrator, awaits the Soviets.

Six weeks after the November counterattack, Grossman's unease had given way to calm confidence. Indeed, David Ortenberg thought that "Today in Stalingrad" showed a "new Grossman, maturing in the war."[5] Perhaps no work of the period more calmly and personally allows us to follow an author's response to seeing Stalingrad at peace. Indeed, Ortenberg described the work as a "panorama of the city, but as if you too were walking along its street and into its dug-outs." The reader follows Grossman's path through Stalingrad so closely that it is impossible not to share the narrator's own relief at Stalingrad's rebirth and the sense that the *podvigi* described throughout the Stalingrad period have birthed a future without war.

Ehrenburg's "On the Verge," meanwhile, is a boisterous pendant to Grossman's quiet confidence. It was, as David Ortenberg put it, "simply unthinkable" not to ask the author to produce a showstopper to mark the new year.[6] The "joyous and trepidatious" Ehrenburg relished the task his editor had set.[7] "On the Verge" is typical of Ehrenburg's stylings: the author patches together themes from the front page's editorial, righteous – almost religious – preaching about the Germans' historical errors, and a series of choice insults that paint the Germans as callous monsters about to get what was coming to them. Ehrenburg had no thoughts of magnanimity: "I was in high spirits: it was clear that the turning point had been reached; up till then one believed in victory as an act of faith, despite everything, but now there was no shadow of doubt: victory was assured."[8] Stalingrad proved that Ehrenburg's faith had not been misplaced. Reading the calls to enact revenge on the enemy in "On the Verge" and thinking of the end of the war, what Soviet would not, like Ehrenburg, have delighted in the results of the 19 November offensive?

Clever editing by David Ortenberg's team made the 1 January edition of *Krasnaya Zvezda* the best example yet of each day's newspaper as a collection of complementary works. The reader could revel in the weight of numbers on the front page, delight in Ehrenburg's contemptuous wit, and indulge with

Grossman in tranquil reflection that promised internal and mythic transformation. Little wonder that Viktor Nekrasov thought January 1943 to be "the most jolly month of the Stalingrad defence. And I mean jolly. The whole thing was drawing to a close, and everybody knew it. People were smiling, laughing, joking. I'm not sure the Germans found it quite so jolly."[9]

For all the revelry at the front, orders from Moscow were increasingly constraining. The Kremlin began to express discontent about perceived transgressions in everything from the work of local newspapers to that of the Soviet Union's book distribution networks and of Fotokhronika, the central photography service.[10] Some in the creative industries felt moved to complain to their superiors. In January 1943, for instance, the filmmmaker Mikhail Romm was frank in his criticism that his colleagues were receiving "not leadership but direction, bureaucratic whimperings, and torrents of incomprehensible and hostile commands."[11] Those in the newspaper milieu seem to have been temporarily shielded from the worst of these vagaries thanks to Ortenberg's skills as a go-between. Nonetheless, two things had become clear: Sovinformbyuro was turning the screws harder than at any point during the war; and the regime was turning its gaze away from inciting defeat of the invader to stage-managing Soviets' understanding of the war and the government's role in victory.

The public and the journalistic corps, however, remained widely positive as yet more strategic successes were reported. The Soviets ran rampant in the few operations that were conducted, while the Germans were gripped by despair. After rejecting a demand to surrender, the remaining Germans were struck by a massive Soviet attack on 12 January. A fortnight later, no Germans remained in the Stalingrad region outside of the encirclement. News of the avalanche of successes gave rise to "whispered rumours" about the end of the war: "The nearness of liberation was conveyed by the ceaseless flow of retreating German forces and in the cowardly and slippery attempts by German pamphlets to hide their catastrophic situation."[12] Both sides knew what the end of the Battle of Stalingrad meant.

As mid-January approached, the writers' barrack in Akhtuba grew ever quieter. Journalists departed for short periods of leave – an exhausted Vasily Grossman at last returned to Moscow – or followed the advance toward the west. Evgeny Kriger stayed put, producing "Stalingrad's Answer," another chunk of invective suffused with mythic and biblical metaphor. Unlike the crowing Ehrenburg, Kriger finds a place for sympathy in his work: the author draws on Grossman's "Today in Stalingrad" to imply how his Germans have been so thoroughly vanquished that they, "howling out in fear," are almost pitiable.[13]

Readers were gripped by the papers' stories of new life and future victory.[14] Ortenberg was overwhelmed by the quantity of material coming from the front, but still asked for more. Editors were now taking material about Stalingrad from anybody who wanted to chip in. The writer Vsevolod Ivanov decided to try his hand at a Stalingrad tale in "A Russian Field," the third story translated in this section. Ivanov had met and interviewed Ignashkin, a fighter ace who would complete a total of 180 sorties in the war and go on to high rank in the postwar air force, when the pilot was in Moscow to receive a commendation for his bravery at Stalingrad.

Even in this most triumphant period of writing about the war, Ivanov's story still centres tragic humanity. The story accords much space – which was in short supply in the Stalin-heavy papers of January 1943 – to lamenting the death of an elderly peasant trying to escape the Wehrmacht. For all of Ignashkin's brilliance, the pilot is helpless to save the man, who pleads for assistance from the ground. The resulting effect is open to interpretation: is the peasant a tragic figure who emblemizes the suffering of a nation, whose fate drives the Soviet military to feats such as those of Ignashkin? Or is he a tool, whose personal suffering is being leveraged now that Stalin is being written into the centre of the Stalingrad narrative, to suggest that such deaths are the price of victory?

The troops at the front were thrilled by the new turns in the Stalingrad stories. The newspapers' inspirational material now fuelled the heavy fighting and long marches of what was a rapid advance. One soldier, Pavel Mikhnov, a twenty-one-year-old from a village just outside of Vladivostok, described the phenomenon in a letter home:

> When you read the papers your heart quivers with joy. You just feel full of joy. It's nice to read that the Red Army is making successful advances. When I send you this cutting ... you'll cry with happiness. You won't be able to stay calm when you read the article ... I wasn't at all worried when I saw a line of 1,500 fascists coming at me, and neither were my men. We met them heroically, like Bolsheviks, and we kept firing to the last bullet.[15]

Reading about the advance in the papers filled Mikhnov with zeal. He even uses language taken almost verbatim from newspaper stories ("We met them heroically …") to explain his battlefield experiences, imagining them as a heroic *podvig* of his own. That *podvig* is, in the letter writer's conception, steeped in the Russian tradition of sacrificial historicism: Mikhnov seems open, indeed almost *eager*, to sacrifice himself within the scope of a historical event like Stalingrad.

As the final victory approached, many other Soviets in Stalingrad spent time imagining their own heroic status. Leonid Kovalev, the member of the Thirty-Three who had been in the lowest of spirits in the fall, delighted in lording it over the Germans. In a letter home from late January 1943, he related a story that bears a striking resemblance to the tale of the cross-dressing German from Evgeny Kriger's "The Streets of Stalingrad": "We got 'em unawares. They was running out of houses in their drawers but they didn't give themselves up, Lidochka … all dressed in their caps and worn out boots, freezing and wrapped up in girls' jumpers and shirts and that. Then they were snivellin' and saying *Hitler Kaput*."[16] Did Kovalev, who had been reading the papers throughout the battle, see Kriger's story and embellish his own tale with details taken directly from it? It is certainly plausible. Many soldiers at the front, like Mikhnov and Kovalev, were looking to the papers for models of triumphs and revenge as the German monster was turned into a mouse.

✳ ✳ ✳

The final victory at Stalingrad came on 2 February 1943. The trumpeting of "100,000 German dead, and 46,000 prisoners, including 16 generals" on the next day's front pages was accompanied by the announcement of total surrender – good news always made it into the papers much faster than bad news. The writers and editors of Stalingrad could, at last, breathe easy.

Troops, writers, and many of the remaining residents rejoiced at a victory rally on 4 February on the central Square of Fallen Fighters. Surrounded by destroyed streetcars, collapsed apartment buildings, and the skeletal ruins of the city's bombed post office, the attendees listened to speakers including Aleksandr Rodimtsev, Aleksey Chuyanov, and Nikita Khrushchev. The leaders applauded those who had "stood to the death," promising that death would bring a rebirth. Chuyanov swore "to our Motherland, Party and government that we will resurrect our beloved city!" The story of resurrection had left the pages of the newspapers and entered public discourse. The speeches were received with adulation.[17] Viktor Nekrasov remembers how he and his comrades celebrated by drinking well into the night: "To victory! To their defeat! To *kaput!*"[18] The celebrations continued all night at the Red Army shipyard canteen on the bank of the Volga.[19]

Ilya Ehrenburg was again the man called on to produce a piece summing up the victory for the next day's newspaper. "Stalingrad," the penultimate story in this section, mirrors Ehrenburg's story of the same name from September. This new story encapsulates the turn from terror to euphoria. Ehrenburg describes how Stalingrad has inspired victories the world over; thus, readers could now project their own sacrifices, losses, and deeds onto a canvas stretching from the Eastern Front to the battlefields of North Africa and into Hitler's bunker. Stalingrad had been transposed from individual houses and individual sacrifices across the Caucasus and the Don, on to Moscow, and now the whole world. Thinking back to the vast natural sweep of Grossman's "Today in Stalingrad," there is little wonder that readers were taken with the multilayered temporal significance of this messianic story.

All the same, sorrow was never far away. Any mention of Stalingrad was still as likely to conjure images of "air-raids, pychological abnormalcy, and corpses" as it was of glorious, resurrected futures.[20] Vasily Koroteev was the last of the major writers to leave Stalingrad. "Goodbye, Stalingrad!," his final despatch from the city and the final work translated in this chapter, sums up the contrasting moods of sorrow and delight. Exaltation and relief as Stalingrad "returns to life" are interspersed with memories of death, observations of destruction, and ever-present grief. The serenity of surrender must have deeply moved Koroteev, the man who had watched his hometown engulfed by bombardments and conflagrations and seen many of his acquaintances perish. Ortenberg was delighted by the personal inflections in Koroteev's tale, lauding his friend's ability to write only of "what he had seen himself, and of what he had himself experienced" in spite of the abstract, mythical turn the Stalingrad story was taking at the Kremlin's behest. Ortenberg, ever empathetic, thought the story a "touching" work of final parting.[21]

The flood of news, photographs, and stories printed in the days following the final victory at Stalingrad had an enormous impact on readers. Viktor Nekrasov, like many others, would remember "leafing through the pages of the newspapers over and over again" when victory was announced.[22] After reading the news, one teenage reader wrote to Aleksey Chuyanov from her hometown to ask for permission to travel to Stalingrad:

> When I saw you on the front page of the newspaper, I cried tears of joy, I laughed, and at the same time, I was furious that I didn't get to take part in the Great Patriotic War ... I'm helping on the home front, but what kind of help can I really give there; it's all talk there ... I want to go to Stalingrad, and I won't have a moment's peace until I do. I await your response with excitement.[23]

All across the front and for months afterward, exhausted troops' morale was boosted by the victory at Stalingrad. In June, Leonid Kovalev recalled how at a meeting with a general he and his comrades "swore, naturally, that we'd keep fighting like we fought at Stalingrad."[24] Stalingrad had become the yardstick for spirit, stubbornness, and success.

Just six months had passed since the German bombing raid on 23 August had razed the city, but Stalingrad's significance had been etched deeply into the public consciousness. Readers were using the stories and language they had read to explain what had happened to their loved ones at home and in their private writings. Lidia Medvedeva, for example, now borrowed language verbatim from the newspapers to tell her parents on 9 February about "our phenomenal successes, so many villages and towns captured."[25] Troops, civilians, workers, children, and adults alike would react with joy to any mention of the word "Stalingrad." But this was no propaganda trick. The authors of the story felt just as strongly about their work. Konstantin Simonov later explained:

> The thing that's etched in my very soul from 1942 is the word "Stalingrad" ... The image burned in my retina is of the smoky haze stretched over the Volga's banks for dozens of kilometres. The sound that still rings in my ears is the crunching of Hitler's war machine as it began to break down. [Stalingrad was] a recognition of the victory of good, embodied in our country, over the forces of evil embodied in fascist Germany at that time.[26]

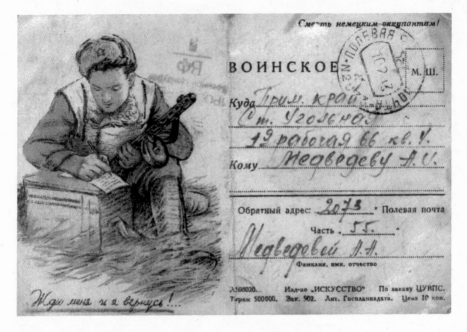

Figure 4.2 Lidia Medvedeva's postcard home from 9 February.

The language Simonov uses here is instantly familiar to those who have read the Stalingrad stories from *Pravda, Krasnaya Zvezda,* and *Izvestiya.* The victory at Stalingrad, offering up its visions of martyrdom and rebirth, had just as much semantic and cultural significance as it did strategic importance for the battle's writers and for their millions of readers at the front and at home.

Vasily Grossman – Today in Stalingrad
1 January 1943, *Krasnaya Zvezda*

A strong northeasterly wind was blowing throughout 16 December. The dark, dank clouds began to lift and brighten as they shed their heavy moisture. The fog began to freeze over and coat the military telegraph cables and the trees by the river, which had already been pruned almost to the ground by mortar shrapnel, with a layer of white down. Sheets of white ice encased the puddles in shell craters. The dark bodies of the one-pound mortar and the heavy artillery shells buried in pits around the crossing's eastern jetty were covered in a light frost. The frozen ground had become sonorous. Off to the west, a red sunset of incomparable beauty rose over the tattered gossamer stonework of the dead city.

The wind and the current drove an enormous block of ice, three *sazhni* in length, down the Volga.[27] It crawled past Spartanovka and on past the ruined Tractor Factory, which had been desecrated by the enemy. It started to slowly turn and finally came to rest by the Red October factory. Then, among the ice floes running down from the Volga's eastern and western banks, out it stretched its wide arms.

The moon carefully brushed the stars aside and rose high into the clear sky. All that had been white now turned a dim blue. The moon alone – as if it had sucked in all the whiteness of the steppe's snows – remained bright and white. The wind – cold and vicious, yet so close to thousands of hearts – kept on blowing. Held back by the block of ice, the current sought out new paths closer to the riverbed. The thinnest, most fragile of icy crusts coated the water's surface. Within a few hours, it had thickened and crystallized.

That very night, Titov, a sergeant in a sapper battalion, became the first to walk from the Volga's left to the Volga's right bank across the sagging, bullet-pocked, 3 centimetre thick layer of ice. As he reached the shore, he looked back across the Volga and out onto the steppe, then began to roll a cigarette. Titov chuckled in response to the other army lads' question, "How was the crossing? Well, I just upped and went. Easy as anything!"

Yet at that precise moment, time was turning a page in the great and tragic book of the battle for Stalingrad. This was a page written by great, dark hands with skin cracked by icy water, by the hands of sergeants and privates of pontoon and sapper battalions, by the hands of mechanics and truck drivers, and by the hands of all those who had held onto the Volga crossing for a hundred days, crossing the dark, grey, and icy river and staring a quick and cruel death in the eye. Some day, a song shall be sung of those who sleep at the bottom of the Volga; the song shall be as simple and righteous as the labour conducted and deaths met among those sheets of black nocturnal ice, occasionally illuminated by the sudden dark flame of a thermite shell or the cold blue eyes of a German spotlight.

✳ ✳ ✳

We are walking down the Volga at night. The two-day-old ice no longer gives under the weight of our steps, and the moon illuminates a network of countless trails and sled tracks. An army messenger marches ahead as quick and confident as if he had spent half his life navigating the criss-cross of paths. Suddenly, the ice begins to crack. The messenger halts at a large hole and says, "Whoops-a-daisy! Wrong path, that is. Need to head right." These messengers always seem to utter that same soothing phrase, no matter where they have taken you off to in the middle of the night. We set off to the right and come back out onto the trail.

Little round clouds start to sail smoothly across the moon, enveloping the Volga in a grey gloom and making it grow dark. Barges hit by shelling have frozen into the ice. The ice-covered rigging, the sterns jutting high above the water, and the prows of stricken cutters and sunken motorboats all twinkle a light blue.

A battle is taking place in one of the factories. The pink-white flame of gunfire illuminates dark, destroyed workshop walls. Booming cannon fire echoes away. Mortar blasts resonate with a dry bang. The punching chatter of machine and submachine guns is unceasing. This music of destruction is strangely like the factory's peacetime work. A steam hammer could for all the world be beating away to flatten a steel ingot; metal may as well be being riveted or broken up ready for the furnace in the scrapyard; molten steel and slag could very well be flowing into buckets and illuminating the fledgling Volga ice with their quick pink light.

The sounds of nocturnal fighting in the factory also point to a new page in the Battle of Stalingrad. This is no longer a battle of elemental thunder, flaring high into the sky and falling back to earth to deluge the vast landscape around the Volga. This is a battle of short, sharp shocks. Shells and machine gun tracers fly quick and direct through the cramped spaces between the workshops. These are nothing like the languorous, shining hyperbolas of an aerial dogfight. Like shining spears and arrows cast by a warrior cloaked in darkness, these lines dart out from behind one cold stone wall only to pierce and disappear into another.

Shells and mortars pound German bunkers in search of German machine gunners buried in camouflaged dugouts and slicing razorlike through the ceilings of communications trenches. The Germans have dug themselves deep underground, vanished into stone burrows, and slipped off into the deepest cellars. They have slunk off into concrete tanks and water and sewage pipes and driven themselves into underground tunnels. Only a well-aimed artillery shell or a precisely thrown grenade or thermite bomb can hurt them or flush or burn them out of their deep, dark burrows.

Morning breaks and the sun rises into the clear, frosty sky over a Stalingrad that has been put to death by the Germans. The sun rises over the bare yellow sandstone of the Volga bluffs. It illuminates stone ruins ground up by explosions. It illuminates factory yards that have become battlefields, sites of mortal combat for entire regiments and divisions. It illuminates the edges of massive craters blown out by one-tonne bombs. A gloomy darkness constantly lingers in the bottom of these pits; the sun is afraid to touch them. The smiling sun gazes down on factory chimneys blasted apart by shells. The sun illuminates hundreds of sidings where tankers with mangled undercarriages lie like slaughtered horses. The shockwaves from blasts have tossed hundreds of goods wagons into a great heap; they butt into cold locomotives like a herd, driven mad by terror, pressing against its leaders. The sun illuminates heaps of iron turned red by rust and heaps of metal meant for the factories and the military. The metal, slain by writhing explosions, is preserved forevermore in its death throes. The winter sun illuminates mass graves and the makeshift monuments placed where those who died in the fighting along the main line of attack now lie.

The dead lie sleeping in knolls beside the ruined factory workshops, in gullies, and in hollows. They sleep right where they fell. These tombs are the greatest of testaments to the simple, bloody loyalty that stopped these trenches, bunkers, and stone embrasures from being surrendered to the enemy.

This is a holy land! How I wish I could keep this glorious new city, a city that grew out of the ruins, the city of our people's freedom, in my memory forever. I wish that I could absorb in its entirety this city, with its underground dwellings, its chimneys smoking in the sun, its criss-cross of new paths and roads, and its heavy mortar barrels rearing up from dugouts. I wish I could absorb those hundreds of people dressed in padded jackets, overcoats, and fur hats who, sleepless from battle though they may be, carry mortar rounds tucked under their arms like loaves of bread, peel potatoes to the intense howl of a heavy gun, and quarrel or quietly sing as they tell tales of last night's grenade battle. These are marvellous, everyday heroes. I wish that I could commit to memory every last detail of this miraculous, moving panorama of the defence of Stalingrad; I wish I could remember every last minute of this great day, which will go down in history forevermore.

Everything is changing. Just as today's river crossing is different from yesterday's and tonight's factory battle is different from the enormous, elemental attacks of November, the day today in Stalingrad is utterly different from those of October and November. The Russian soldier has emerged from underground. He has emerged from the stone to stand tall, and now he goes forth with calm certainty. Out on the Volga's ice, glittering in the brilliant sunshine, soldiers drag sleds and artillery men bark at horses gingerly pawing the smooth ice. Truck drivers unloading supplies are outlined, as if engraved, on the snowy crest of the left bank. A postman carrying his leather bag slowly meanders, enjoying the sun, over to a battalion command post. Two messengers stand tall, striding up a hill just 40 metres away from the German trenches, on their way to deliver soup thermoses.

Our troops have fought to see the sun, fought for the very light of day, and fought to win the great right to walk tall about the earth of Stalingrad and under blue skies! Only the Stalingraders know the true cost of victory, yet they chuckle at the sight of troops and vehicles moving around in the sunshine. For long months the slightest movement or the tiniest speck would draw heavy fire from the German forces. For long months thousands of people awaited the night so that they might emerge from the stones and the earth, gulp down the fresh air, and stretch their numb legs.

Everything is changing indeed. Those same Germans who in September would tear into a street, install themselves in its houses, and dance away to their raucous harmonica music – those same Germans who would drive around with their lights on at night and deliver supplies in the daytime – have now secreted themselves underground, hidden away among stone ruins.

I stood for a good long time on the fourth floor of one heavily damaged house, peering through binoculars at the blocks still occupied by the Germans. Not a single puff of smoke. Not a single person moving. There is to be no sun and no daylight for them here now. They are receiving twenty-five, maybe thirty, rounds a day and have been ordered to fire only when

Figure 4.3 Troops eat lunch in Stalingrad; in the background, civilians pull a sled.

fired on. Their daily rations are limited to a hundred grams of bread and horsemeat. They sit and choke down their horsemeat in smoky darkness like grizzled savages in caves. They sit in the ruins of the beautiful city that they have destroyed and in the dead factory workshops of which the Soviet nation was once so proud. They crawl up to the surface at night. Terrified by the mighty Russian force slowly throttling them, they cry out: "Hey, *Russ*, shoot me in the legs! Why are you shooting at my head?!"

They blew up the water supply with their six-barrel mortars, they fired five hundred shells at the Stalingrad Power Station, they set fire to everything that would burn, and they destroyed schools, pharmacies, and hospitals. Now a time of terrible days and nights is upon them. By the law of history and the will of the Soviet soldier, they are fated to meet retribution, right here in the cold ruins and the darkness as, hidden away from the sun and the daylight under the cruel stars of a Russian December night, they go without water and choke down their horsemeat. Everything is changing indeed. Everything has already changed in Stalingrad. The law of history is just and terrible. The will of our Stalingrad armies is unbreakable.

Ilya Ehrenburg – On the Verge
1 January 1943, *Krasnaya Zvezda*

We have found the past year difficult. The green steppe of the Don was like the green baize of a gambling table onto which a desperate player throws his last chips. That madman threw them all at us. We had the Kaiser's grey-haired grenadiers and the German whelps. We had workers and technicians – those "irreplaceable specialists" – taken from arms factories. In his dash for meat, Hitler even forgot about blood, so we had soldiers "with less than twenty-five percent Aryan blood." Indeed, as one miserable Fritz mongrel put it: "They've given me the chance to 'earn' my missing Aryan grandmother on the battlefield. Of course, I might have to pay for that grandmother with my life …" We were confronted with French tanks, Czech guns, and Belgian rifles. We fought alone throughout those difficult months. We resisted.

The spring of humanity came in the late autumn. To the Germans, Stalingrad had seemed like a good stop-off on the road to victory, but that road became more like a mountain pass as Germany careered faster and faster downhill. The Germans have tried to explain away last year's failures: it was all due to an unexpectedly early winter; they were not familiar with conditions in Russia; some or other German general made an error. But winter came late this year, the Germans are no rookies, and their commander is not some scapegoat but the Führer himself.

One German, Erna Krauss, wrote to her husband: "The children are asking you to send them a military victory for New Year. I shall be more modest and ask you to send soap and, if it's not altogether too much, some fur to make a jacket like Betty's." Major Krauss is now one of thousands upon thousands of German corpses lying on the steppe around the Don. Bottles of French cognac and a trampled German banner lie next to him. Erna will not get her jacket and Germany will not get its victory.

The Germans still thought they were headed for victory in September. In the villages of the Caucasus, the older Krauts were nervously asking how far it was to Baku while the younger ones hastily gnawed on their chicken. They had to chew quickly, they explained, as they were in a rush to get to India. Hitler, who had already been photographed at the Eiffel Tower and the Parthenon, dreamed of being immortalized on film at the Egyptian pyramids too.

November changed everything. The Germans tried to laugh off the English offensive as "just another African quadrille." They were wrong. It was a German galop.[28] How unsurprising of the Italian paper *Il regime fascista* to write that "Field Marshal Rommel has proven himself to be a brilliant strategist by unwaveringly avoiding all contact with the advancing enemy." And who does retreat better than the Italians? Then, on what would turn out to be a not entirely wonderful morning for Germany, the Germans woke up and discovered that America had set sail for Africa. Italy went into a panic, France reared her head, and people in Europe began to speak of liberation.

Münchner Neueste Nachrichten tried to keep its readers calm:[29] "The long winter nights have always dented Germans' confidence … Germans start to see ghosts whenever they encounter the slightest difficulties. It has been difficult to endure our state of suspense for the past two months; people say one thing today and the opposite tomorrow." The nights will soon grow shorter, but the Germans' confidence will not grow.

On New Year's Eve, a Germany that is now terrified of ghosts will catch sight of its fate. It will be visited by those who were hung at Volokolamsk.

It will be visited by those who were shot at Nantes. It will be visited by the children of Lidice.[30] The Germans write that "it has been difficult to endure our state of suspense." We can help to lighten this burden. We can tell the Germans that we already know history's verdict. Germany has lived by the sword, and it shall die by the sword.

Even the dimmest of the Germans is starting to understand that they are told one thing today and another thing tomorrow. I read recently in one of the Berlin papers that "the pincer movement, the envelopment, and the encirclement are uniquely German ideas." What must the Krauts languishing in their little triangle at Stalingrad think of those boastful words? Not that they are likely to care much about strategy now; they are praying for manna from heaven. Neither transport planes nor Goebbels's lies will feed them.

In fits of despair, that clubfoot Goebbels dictates his communiqués: "The encirclement of the Russians in the bend of the Don continues." Using the same logic, can the inhabitants of the German island of Heligoland not thus declare that "our island has surrounded the sea"? The commander of the German 6th Army told the troops that they were encircled on 27 November. He promised "the Führer's help" to those in the encirclement. And where has that help got to now? The hapless saviours are beating a hasty retreat from Kotelnikovo. "It was all so unexpected," splutters Kurt Küller, a captured German major. Rubbish! The entire human race has been waiting for this moment for years. Right was always going to prevail, and now it *is* prevailing.

When the clock strikes twelve at New Year, the German men and their lady friends will stand up and raise glasses filled with the last drops of French wine. They might even try to smile, but their smiles will look more like grimaces! The vineyards of France are already running over with anger. Those German men and women will hear the fatal words: "The court is in session." That means the Red Army is coming. It matters not that the judge wears camouflage instead of robes, for the law is borne in our hearts. We shall write the verdict in black and white and in German blood on the snow. Germany's ragged jackals and mangy hyenas quiver at the sound of the Russian warrior.

Our offensive is neither cheerful nor enthusiastic. We gaze ahead sternly. The new year is dawning amidst the roar of battle. Great battles and great trials await us in the new year. Germany knows that it has become the focus of the world's hatred. Germany will fight back in desperation. The Germans will force their vassals to send more divisions, and the Germans will assemble new legions in their occupied countries. They will fortify every town and village, and the fear of atonement will fuel their bravery. We know that many of our own will die, but our great spirit drives us forward.

Ukraine and Belarus await us. Mutilated Russian towns await us. An exhausted Europe awaits our allies. Way back in childhood, we would read about selfless doctors hurrying through a blizzard or a sandstorm to a patient's bedside in the dead of night. When it comes to the life of a loved one, the striking of the clock is ominous. Every single day means thousands of lives saved. Have no doubt that the Germans will defend themselves. They may even counterattack. But ours is a desire stronger than any armour. A mother defending her child is one thing; a thief who does not wish to part with his loot is quite another.

We have drunk the cool water of hatred from the soldier's flask. It burns the mouth, stronger than any spirit. Damned Germany has interfered in our lives. Europe dreamed of flights into the stratosphere, but now it is forced to live like a mole in bomb shelters and bunkers. The devil and his followers have eclipsed our epoch. We do not hate the Germans merely because they so abominably, so abhorrently, murder our children. We hate them because we must kill them in return, and because, out of all the words that were once dear to us, only one word remains: "Kill." We hate the Germans because they have stolen life itself. Of all life's aromas, they have left behind them only the smell of war: the smell of fires, of burning petrol, and of blood. Of all life's many colours, they have left behind only one: military green.

We used to build our towns, till our gardens, write our poetry, and mother our children. The Germans tore us away from all of that. They declared our cornfields, Ukraine's cherry trees, Burgundy's vineyards, and Norway's fjords to be one indistinguishable "expanse." They have turned the whole of Europe into bunkers and pillboxes on one great battlefield. They have taken the best years from our younger generation, tearing them from their mother's embrace and destroying their hearths.

Now the year of retribution is come. We do not want to torture them. We want to destroy them. We want to wipe this great stain from our epoch. Such is our desire, such is our oath, such is our vow.

Russia is at the frontline of liberation. An oil lamp in a bunker might be
seen as a beacon, a torch, or as a star lighting the way. The soldier lying at
his machine gun seems to stand tall. The scout stealing silently across the
snow seems to speak aloud. We have long fought alone, but the first shots
from our brothers in arms are now reaching us. We witness the spirit of
England. We witness how America sends reinforcements in defence of freedom. The world says, "It is time!"

The new year might be the year of victory. Victory cannot just be won. It
must be earned. Victory means exhausted hands and bloodied feet. Yet as we
see in the new year, still we say to ourselves and our military friends: "This
must be the year of victory."

At new year, we used to wish one another good health, good fortune, and
success at work. The meanings of many words, however, have changed. The
Germans buried people – perfectly healthy people – alive at Vitebsk. The
children of Smolensk and Coventry, the hostages of Paris, and the girls of
Serbia were perfectly healthy. Our work is for a great cause. Did the Germans not destroy the vineyards of Champagne, the dams of Holland, and
the towns of Russia? What prosperity is there to speak of now? Bountiful
France dreams of simple turnips. No, there is only one thing that people and
nations can wish for one another now: victory.

In our darkened towns, bunkers, and trenches, we shall declare: "Welcome in the year of victory!" We used to see in the new year with our loved
ones. It is strange to think that there used to be streets, clubs, and parties
awash with light and the twinkling of festive trees. Now there is only the oil
lamp's dull light. Perhaps its flickering might remind the soldier at the front
of the eyes of a loved one, so that on New Year's Eve he might remember his
family. He will see another light at the same time: the beautiful, shining eyes
of our beloved, eternal Russia. She birthed us, so for her we go to our
deaths. We shall liberate the motherland. We hear those wonderful words:
"This just in: the offensive continues."

Happy New Year to the Army! Happy Year of Victory!

Vsevolod Ivanov – A Russian Field

16 January 1943, *Izvestiya*

This extraordinary series of events happened near Stalingrad at the tail end of summer 1942.

Lieutenant Gavriil Ivanovich Ignashkin, the twenty-five year old commander of an attack aircraft squadron, had just received his orders. His squadron was to destroy an airfield behind enemy lines. According to the scouting reports there were at least a hundred transport and fighter planes at the airfield. Ignashkin took to the skies with two echelons of "Il" fighters.[31]

They could have flown in a straight line from his regiment's airfield directly south toward the target. However, Ignashkin decided to trace an arc so as to come at the enemy out of the sun. He descended down low toward the Volga. As Ignashkin left behind the willows and steep ravines of the river's right bank and ascended over the steppe, he noticed a light fog. Looking at the fog more closely, Ignashkin started to grow anxious. His cockpit had filled with an odd smell from an unknown source. Where could the smell have come from?

The lieutenant remembered the festivals in the peasant village where he had lived in his youth and where his father and grandfather before him had lived. They had been very poor, so they could only ever bake pies for the most important festivals. Even then, there was never much firewood in Orlov Province, so their pies were never quite cooked right: they would try to save fuel and the pies would come out underdone, or they tried to bake them too fast and the pies ended up overdone. The odour filling Ignashkin's cockpit smelled like burning bread. The lieutenant knew his plane very well. All sorts of odours emanated from it, but never the smell of burning bread.

The fog grew thicker. The smell of burning bread intensified. The lieutenant started to gain height to escape the fog. "Where's this stuff coming from?" he wondered. "The weather forecast didn't say anything about fog! Our forecasts are never wrong. There oughtn't to be any fog anywhere over the Volga or the Don." A sort of sorrowful, secret anxiety began to grip him inside. What on earth was going on?

Ignashkin kept ascending. He gained another 800 metres in height. His squadron members, though, were not trained to fly at such high altitude.

What was worse, that odd fog was spooking them. The planes bunched up closer to their leader. The fog was still no thinner. Wherever they looked – 100 kilometres ahead or 100 kilometres to either side – the fog was totally cloaking the ground.

Neither Lieutenant Ignashkin nor any of his comrades had ever taken their "Ils" above 3,000 metres. Yet they kept ascending, for even 3 kilometres up, the hot and still summer air was saturated with fog right down to the ground. When the planes had finally escaped the cloak of fog, the lieutenant looked down. He finally realized where the feather-like clouds of fog had come from. The cornfields were ablaze. It was smoke!

So it *was* burnt bread! The corn was burning all over the vast expanse between the Volga and the Don. The fruits of our people's, our peasants', labour were going up in flames. The Russian land, the Cossack land, and the entirety of the Don were going up in flames. And it was the German forces that had lit the kindling.

Flying over this smoke made the lieutenant distraught. He was brought up to work out and about on other people's land while his father tended to their house. It was tough going for a nine-year-old to dig and weed for somebody else and to tend cattle grazing on someone else's land. In spite of all these difficulties, Ignashkin loved being on the land to watch how the grain grew and the corn matured.

The ground was invisible; the lieutenant was still flying at a high altitude. Time ticked on. By Ignashkin's estimates he must have been approaching the Don. He could now just about see through the smoke. No matter how bitter the smoke, Ignashkin could not turn back. His mission was as urgent as it was vital. He crossed the Don. The far bank was free of smoke, so he descended. He flew past a little river, some mountains, and a forest. Beyond the forest he caught sight of an open field – a Russian field, a field of the Don.

Now the lieutenant was hedge hopping. The sun's eastern rays lit up the motionless field from the east. The lieutenant caught sight of his own plane's shadow as it crept toward the enemy airfield. There was silence all around. Silence to the left and silence to the right. The lieutenant could hear nothing but the whir of the propeller, but he was so accustomed to that sound that it hardly interrupted the quiet. He looked to the left and right and saw broken tanks, smashed-up guns, abandoned carts, and German corpses. The minutes and the kilometres passed by, but wherever he looked there was nothing but trenches and destroyed tanks, guns, and carts. German bodies lay uncollected as if they had been deliberately positioned that way. There was nobody to bury them.

The lieutenant spotted a large road ahead. The wide road was marked by potholes and ruts; its edges were covered in white dust. It lay empty. Motionless. The lieutenant flew along the road at a height of 20 metres, so close to the ground that he could see the tire tracks.

He suddenly spotted a peasant walking from west to east. The peasant walked with a cane and carried a sack on his shoulders. Catching sight of a Russian plane, he stopped, removed his hat, crossed himself, then gestured to the east as if to say: "I'm headed that way." The lieutenant waved, pointed to the west where he was headed, then looked back. The old man had already donned his hat and was again walking along the dusty and hot empty road to the east.

The lieutenant thought, "Doesn't he know the front's that way?" He made a note of the spot where he had seen the old man: "I'll have a look where he's got to on my way back." And on he flew.

Half an hour, then an hour passed. Ignashkin estimated that there would be a railway 20 kilometres away. He soon passed the rails. And then – there was the frontline. That meant the airfield should be just a little off to the right. He saw the field, and then the enemy planes stationed on it.

The lieutenant gave the command: attack! He was at 300 metres. He strafed the airfield with his cannon and machine guns, then dropped a bomb. The German anti-aircraft guns let go with a barrage so intense it felt that every inch of the ground must be covered with enemy guns. The lieutenant, with his squadron in tow, clung low to a ravine. He began to ascend. He could see three enormous conflagrations on the airfield. That meant the fuel trucks were on fire. Then up went the munitions dump with a huge blast. The job was, in short, done. The lieutenant was satisfied.

It would have been quicker to return to base from the destroyed target in a straight line, but his thoughts turned to the smoke on the cornfields and the old peasant. He wanted to see him. Where was it that he was going? The lieutenant returned to his earlier bearing.

The peasant was no longer on the main road, but the lieutenant soon spotted him. He had made it to the front and was trying to crawl across.

The old man was crawling back to the east, back toward his people, his loved ones, his wonderful army and its young soldiers, his evacuated children, and his cattle-herder friends. He was crawling from the west to the east!

Seeing the Russian planes approach, the old man got up on his knees, threw down his hat, and raised his hands. He was trying to say, "Take me, pilots! Pick me up! I can't stay here surrounded by Germans!" The lieutenant understood. But he had no orders to land, and how could he have landed there anyway? The lieutenant's hands and face were wet with tears. He ascended with a jolt, as if trying to wipe the tears away with his plane.

When the lieutenant landed, his comrades clamoured around him and asked, "Comrade Commander, did you see the old man? How he begged?"

"Of course I saw him."

✳ ✳ ✳

Even when he is in a rage, the Russian rarely uses grandiloquent language, and is even more rarely given to making grandiloquent gestures. Instead, he just screws up his eyes and clenches his teeth so tight that steely lines protrude from his jaw. He might even use the sort of strong word that could shake a pine to its roots. But nothing more. Yet the Russian's anger lingers, and its consequences are terrible. Driven by the memory of the burning fields, the destroyed villages and, above all, the old man crawling to the east, Senior Lieutenant Ignashkin's squadron performed innumerable great feats.

There is a little town by the name of Gumrak near Stalingrad. The German tanks had formed up in a line a couple of kilometres long there. Lieutenant Ignashkin got his squadron together – eighteen "Ils" and twelve fighters – and took them over to Gumrak. Ignashkin's lads were consumed by rage. They dropped their bombs and watched fires spring up below. Was it time to leave then? No! In went the planes again, hugging the ground to strafe the Germans with machine gun and cannon fire. Again and again they went in! Ignashkin could not drag them away. They destroyed more than forty tanks, but still it was not enough! Ignashkin tried to round the lads up for three quarters of an hour, but he could not do it. He left alone, and they came back on their own afterward. Not a single plane was lost.

They were flying four or five sorties a day.

"Aren't you tired?" asked the regimental commander.

Of course they were tired, and they had barely eaten to boot. Yet still they replied: "No. How could we be tired? This is just what we do."

The commander knew they were exhausted. But he also knew that you cannot quench the Russian's anger, so he just said, "Off you go."

❊ ❊ ❊

For his flying at Stalingrad, Lieutenant G.I. Ignashkin became a Hero of the Soviet Union. He has successfully carried out every mission he has been given. G.I. Ignashkin has flown ninety-seven sorties. Multiplying that figure by the amount of enemy planes and tanks he destroys, you come out with a figure that perfectly enumerates Lieutenant Ignashkin's hatred for the enemy.

I met him just after he had received the gold star of the Hero of the Soviet Union and the Order of Lenin. He stood before me in a fur coat and hat. The room we were in was long and, on account of the dark furnishings and wallpaper, gloomy. It was filled with folders and books about Russian history and the Russian people. This too was a field of Russian history! And I must say that, in spite of his boyish face, Ignashkin did not seem out of place here.

"Will you be in Moscow long?," I asked him.

"I'm leaving for Stalingrad first thing tomorrow. My pilots are still convinced that the Germans haven't yet paid for that old man who crawled across the field and toward the front. We have work to do."

Evgeny Kriger – Stalingrad's Answer
17 January 1943, *Izvestiya*

I shall never forget the late September night when I first saw Stalingrad, besieged by the Germans, from the Volga's left bank. The city was in torment but it refused to die. Its angry, bloody sky, visible even 50 kilometres off, loomed over the road we were travelling. The human mind is incapable of painting a picture of that night on the river crossing. The entire right bank was ablaze, as if gigantic lava flows were gushing from the very depths of the earth to drown the living flesh of Stalingrad, as if all the earth's great heat had poured forth so that every last part of the city – the walls, rubble,

streets, alleyways, and embankments, right down to the soil under burned-
out buildings – burned red-hot.

Stalingrad was not in that state for just one night. The flame of war
tormented it for many weeks. There was not enough compassion in our
hearts to fully understand the inhuman suffering of the people of Stalingrad. Pain turned to an anger as dry and sharp as gunpowder thrown on
an open wound.

The Germans did everything they could to kill the city. They bombed it
methodically, block by block. They moved on to the next block only when
the walls of the very last house standing collapsed. Then, as they sent their
tanks into the breach, steel tracks would crunch their way over stone already
ground to dust by bombardment. It was as if human bones on a rack were
being tormented and cracked.

The Germans assumed the city was already dead. They thought that no
soul could have survived such an infernal bombardment, so they prepared
for the city's capture. The people of Stalingrad turned out to be stronger
than the stone their houses had been built from. They did something that
terrified the Germans, something like a miracle that they simply could
not comprehend. The city rose from the dead, stood tall, and strode forth
into battle.

Grenade-wielding workers defended their factory gates. Women repaired
anti-aircraft guns in battered workshops in the shadow of German bombers.
Even watching through chinks in the roof as death soared above them, they
did not abandon their machines. The warriors of Stalingrad crossed a Volga
raging from bombardments, then took up positions among the rubble of
ruined homes. They burrowed into cellars, using their bodies to seal up
every last aperture through which the enemy might slink. Our troops would
hold the first floor of a building even when the Germans had already taken
the attic. There were even houses where the frontline, piercing the very body
of the city, bisected staircases. The troops would drive the Germans from a
cellar all the way to the roof and throw them onto the street below.

The frontline went right through houses and the fighting took place deep
within the stonework. Our command posts were in concrete drains and in
derelict sewage pipes. They were in every hole that could provide shelter
from shrapnel and dim the thunderous roar just enough so that the commander could hear the telephone operators' messages. Every stone seemed

to be shooting at the Germans. Every wall loomed over them like a heavy tombstone.

Then the Germans thought to conclude their attack with a new assault. They began to assail the defenders' will, their psyche, their inner strength. The howl of German planes overhead did not cease for even a moment. The first rays of sun brought German bombers that would depart only as darkness fell. The Germans planned to capture the city by hammering away again and again and again, by hammering until the Russian nerves were totally frayed. After all, even drops of water falling for hours enough can pierce the human skull and reach the brain! Never before has there been an assault which continued without pause for minutes, hours, weeks, months on end.

The defenders of the city on the Volga resisted that assault. They clung on to a patch of soil that could not be surrendered, where the Germans could drop two thousand bombs in the course of a single day. Our people did not give up that soil. They resisted the most monstrous assault in the history of warfare. They stood firm, awaiting the moment when they could avenge the Russian blood spilled by Germans, avenge the tormented, tattered city, and avenge the children slain by German bombs.

Decent people the world over prostate themselves in astonishment before the miraculous feat completed at Stalingrad. Far, far away from fiery Stalingrad, few would have thought that dozens of German divisions would end up in encirclement, resorting to eating horsemeat, burrowing into the ground, trying to save themselves from the counter-assault, and howling out in fear. They saw how the tormented, scorched, bloodied city arose, in all its immortal human strength, and wielded the heavy sword of revenge against its would-be murderers.

The Germans wanted to kill Stalingrad. Now the enemy, trapped in an iron ring, fated to perish but unwilling to surrender, hears Stalingrad's answer: "Death!"

Ilya Ehrenburg – Stalingrad (II)
2 February 1942, *Krasnaya Zvezda*

Hitler used to make a speech every year on 30 January to mark the day when he seized power. After all their defeats, Germans were trying to guess what

he might say this year. But the Führer wormed his way out of it: he said
nothing at all. The cannibal had balked.[32] He did not dare show his face
before the German nation. Hitler preferred to play the role of deserter.

Instead, German's clown-in-chief, that two-bit Marshal of the Reich
Hermann Göring, gave the anniversary speech.[33] Four times he cleared his
throat and opened his mouth to speak, and four times he had to scurry off
into a bomb shelter. The English bomber pilots turned out to be a lot more
forthcoming than Hitler. They did not hesitate to congratulate the Berliners
on the cannibal's tenth anniversary! In the shelter, Göring had the chance to
reflect on his erstwhile claim that "I guarantee that not a single enemy bomb
shall land on German land." The howl of high-explosive bombs marked the
opening of the celebrations.

Göring behaved himself like a sort of ersatz Führer and got in a pickle.
He tried to assure the dunderheaded Germans that "the Red Army is made
up of nothing but sixteen poorly armed teenagers." That did not stop him
from going on to claim five minutes later that "the Germans are facing a
serious opponent. The Russians are succeeding in making inroads all over."
Those German dunderheads should have guessed why the "poorly armed"
Russians were breaking through their front and why the Marshal of the
Reich also called those same teenagers a "serious opponent."

Göring shed a tear and said: "The Russians have fallen to a new low of
cruelty, and now they are advancing across the front." The bandits are really
irate this time: they went pillaging without a second thought, but now they
are all of a sudden being chased off. Is that really the treatment they deserve?

Germany is in mourning. She weeps over the Germans who have perished at Stalingrad, on the Don, in the Caucasus, in Voronezh, in Velikiye
Luki, and in Shlisselburg. That clown Göring thought he would try his hand
at a spot of wit: "A shiver runs down my spine when I think of the Russian
losses." Germany did not smile at the joke. A shiver runs down Germany's
spine on account of the Russian offensive, not because of Russian losses.

Göring was even forced to utter that fateful word: *Stalingrad*. The
Marshal of the Reich had to explain to Germany why hundreds of thousands of German households had lost their children. He said: "History de-
creed that the defenders of Stalingrad should die so that our race might
live." These cattle breeders even want to think of race in death! The pure of
blood are wailing out now, though, as they ask: is the continuation of the

Aryan race worth three hundred thousand German graves? Göring makes reference to "history." No. It was not "history" that sent the Fritz to Stalingrad. It was their wicked and capricious *über*-jobsworth, that coward and cannibal Hitler, that man who dared not face the Germans to explain his great defeat.

Then the Marshal of the Reich decided to try and instil some optimism in the Germans: "Our soldiers' resolve is ever firmer in the fight for Stalingrad." Let's change the tense. The soldiers have already *firmed right up*: some are firming up six feet under; others are firming up in prisoner of war camps.

Now the Germans are trying to ring their defeat with a halo. Göring, lousy director of affairs that he is, compared the Germans at Stalingrad to the "heroes of Sparta." The German generals are quite unlike the Spartans. Firstly, the generals ordered those Krauts who meekly dared to dream of being taken prisoner to be shot. And secondly? Secondly, these Germans waved their own underpants instead of a white flag! Göring said that "the defenders of Stalingrad are the descendants of the von Nibelungs." Well I never! The "descendants of the Nibelungs" indeed![34]

At 4 p.m. on 31 January, Hitler's command announced the following: "For the valiant defence of Stalingrad, Colonel General von Paulus has been promoted to the rank of Field Marshal." At the very same time, the newly minted Field Marshal, with all his baggage – his baton, his iron crosses, his oak leaves, and his Romanian 3rd class Order of Michael the Brave – was being taken prisoner.[35]

The "Nibelungs" are surrendering en masse. More than a dozen generals are in captivity already. This is a cautionary tale for the Germans, who do not much enjoy facing the music. Hitler was afraid to make his speech, and his generals know perfectly well what is coming. With their backs against the wall, the Nibelungs are putting their hands up.

It is not hard to guess the impression the Germans' defeat has made on their vassal states. The master has disgraced himself and now his lackeys are in a panic. Mussolini could not fire his chief officer, General Cavallero, fast enough.[36] Cavallero, though, does not matter one bit. Mussolini cannot fire Hitler. The Italians, Hungarians, and Romanians sent to Russia by Germany are all asking the same question: how can we save ourselves?

Göring said: "A thousand years from now Germans will speak the word 'Stalingrad' with reverential awe." He is right. In a thousand years the Germans will still be uttering that fateful word with "awe." There are more than just hundreds of thousands of Krauts buried in graves at Stalingrad. Their criminal dreams of a "new order" and of the "master race" have been buried for good on the Volga.

Stalingrad. Every true son of Russia will keep repeating the word with pride. Justice has triumphed at Stalingrad. Retribution has begun at Stalingrad. Those who lived by the sword have died by the sword. Stalingrad: the word will live on in Russian chronicles alongside the names of Chudskoe Lake and Kulikovo Field.[37] The city has done justice to its name. Our great-grandchildren will read the Epic of Stalingrad and think of the courage and foresight of the man who led our army to victory.

Stalingrad is just the start. Now we know how those those Spartan sausage munchers can scarper. Now we know how the Nibelungs of every rank can surrender into captivity. Tremble in Kuban, you brigands! Tremble in Oskol! The Red Army is on the march. Russia is on the march!

Vasily Koroteev – Goodbye, Stalingrad
11 February 1943, *Krasnaya Zvezda*

An unusual quiet hangs over the ice-covered Volga. It is disturbed only by the occasional muffled explosion as sappers blow up the last mines left in the city, clearing them from paths, streets, and homes. The artillery has fallen silent, the fires have been extinguished, and the clouds of heavy smoke that blanketed the city for five and a half months have dissipated. Stalingrad is deep behind our lines, and the front has disappeared far to the west and southwest.

With every passing day, the city is returning to life and being filled up with people. Stalingrad's residents – workers, women, and children who sheltered for months in bunkers and barges along the Volga's banks – are returning to their homes. They embrace one another joyfully and congratulate one another on the Red Army's victory, which has delivered them from trials, from torments, and from death itself. They look over the ruins of their homes and their factories with tears in their eyes.

The Stalingraders are getting down to business, since there is much to be done in the city. Half-destroyed businesses, smashed water mains, and the streetcar network must all be rebuilt; the Red Army must be helped to gather trophies; streets and houses must be cleared of rubble and detritus. The task of clearing enemy corpses will take substantial time and effort, since there are tens of thousands of bodies that will have to be removed before the spring.

Even as civilian life is returning, the troops are marching out of Stalingrad in snaking columns. Now the battle on the Volga is over, our soldiers are moving onward, toward the frontline. Regiments and divisions, buoyed by the eternal glory of Stalingrad, are off to find new battles. Every last one of them is thinking the same thing: "We did our part."

And they did their part most magnificently indeed. The artillery played a truly invaluable role in the great battle for Stalingrad. Now Stalingrad's artillerymen hurry off to the front. Their tractors nimbly and swiftly haul anti-tank guns along the snowy road. The infantry marches on. The burly lads – our heroes – are as affable on the march as they are in battle. A cannon has stuck fast in a ravine, so a group of soldiers sprint up and drag it back onto the flat road. Knives and daggers – souvenirs from battles at Stalingrad – hang from their belts.

Stalingrad's inhabitants bid the departing troops a fond farewell. They thank their beloved defenders with all their hearts, wishing them luck in battle as they gaze on at the departing columns. The home of Nazarenko, a fire brigade chief, has miraculously remained intact through the bombing and shelling. The home's inhabitant stands by the road, waving his hat cordially at the passing troops. His wife, Taisiya Fyodorovna, is alongside. Wiping away the tears with her headscarf, she says:

"We lived under the Germans for three months. I'll never forget the first of our soldiers who came into the house. I don't know his name, though. Now I'm standing here and looking, I hope I might recognize him. I just wish I knew his name, so I could remember it forever ..."

For their part, the soldiers have loved with ardour this wounded city that they were defending. Burned and littered with debris it may be, but the city has somehow become even closer to them, even more their own. Many regiments and divisions covered themselves in glory right here. The soldiers have sworn to live up to that glory into future battles. As they leave the city, they proudly proclaim themselves to be Stalingraders. Many add that, when the war is over, they plan to return to rebuild Stalingrad.

The sun dips down to the west. Commander Sukhov's glorious regiment is passing an elevator chewed up by shelling. Several days ago, they were engulfed in fighting right there around Tar Hill and the elevator. At the head of the column rides a horseman in an Astrakhan hat with a bright crimson top. This is Captain Sokolenko, the battalion commander. He halts the horse, stands up in the stirrups, and intently stares at Tar Hill and the elevator, as if trying to commit them to memory forever.

Half the city is visible from the top of the tall elevator building. This was the site of especially intense fighting. Then one night, Sokolenko's battalion broke through at Tar Hill. In spite of heavy German fire, his troops doggedly advanced. Senior Lieutenant Viktorov's company managed to storm the elevator. Eight hundred German soldiers and officers gave themselves up after the fierce battle.

Captain Sokolenko dismounts and lights up a cigarette. "It's a shame to leave," he says thoughtfully. "We've grown attached to the city, and these streets will always be something like memorials for us. My command centre was just over there, by the brick factory's chimney. And I lost two brave lads over there by the institute building. When the war ends – if I survive – I'll bring my son here. I'll show him where we fought and what it was like. But for now, goodbye, Stalingrad!"

Sokolenko's grey mount races off in pursuit of the battalion. The horse's hooves kick up a snowy mist. The captain's Astrakhan hat glimmers red from afar. More and more battalions and regiments file past the elevator.

Goodbye, Stalingrad! Goodbye, city of glory!

The troops look back as they pass. Every last one feels as if they are leaving their own home.

5

1952, 1965
Utopian Lives

For all the promises of Stalingrad as the dawning of a new day, victory did not bring utopia to Stalingrad or Stalingraders. The city's population had been decimated. Those residents who remained or returned struggled to house and feed themselves.[1] As Stalin seized control of the narrative of Stalingrad after 19 November 1942, so too his proxies exerted an unpleasant and familiar control over life in the city. A paranoid search for "deserters" and "looters" in Stalingrad now began.[2] Provision of rations to hungry civilians in the Stalingrad of spring and summer 1943 depended on NKVD searches for anti-Soviet elements. The government worked thousands of German POWs to death clearing and reconstructing the city.[3]

As ever, these wrongs of the present were rarely permitted to breach the walls of the Stalingrad story. Instead, past sufferings were reimagined as essential sacrifices on the road to victory. The 23 August bombing, for example, became a canonical part of post-battle depictions of Stalingrad. Its depiction took on absurd forms in many artistic works. Leonid Varlamov's 1943 film *Stalingrad* seems almost to luxuriate in depicting the bombing of the city's population, layering image after image of the destruction onto the narrator's triumphant description of Stalingrad's survival. The following year, Iosif Pospelsky's *The Rebirth of Stalingrad* again mobilized the image of civilian hardship in the service of an authoritarian myth of postwar nation-building by depicting women and children living in bunkers, crashed planes, and basements as heroic achievers of their own sort of *podvigi*.[4] Whatever unity of purpose had been channelled into the Stalingrad stories between August 1942 and February 1943 was now rent asunder in favour of justifying the state's symbolic and physical power. The old regime was back.

Figure 5.1 Vasily Koroteev examines the remnants of the Stalingradskaya Pravda offices, summer 1943.

✳✳✳

Despite the Kremlin's narrative smash and grab, Soviets from top to bottom continued to seize on the language of the Stalingrad story. In an interview conducted just as the end of the fighting at Stalingrad approached, Vasily Chuykov, commander of the 62nd Army at Stalingrad, explained the feeling of nervous uncertainty that had wracked the Soviet defenders in the weeks before 19 November: "Every day and every night, we didn't know whether dawn would come. We didn't know how it could possibly come."[5] The reference is unmistakable: intentionally or not, Chuykov was using language originating in Konstantin Simonov's "Days and Nights" to explain his experience at the front. The commander's choice of words, though, was not informed simply by the recency of Simonov's work. Almost forty years later, in his 1980 memoir *From Stalingrad to Berlin (Ot Stalingrada do Berlina)*, Chuykov continued to use language informed by frontline journalism. This time, the inspiration – almost certainly subconscious – was Vasily Grossman's "Today in Stalingrad": "The turning point approached as inexorably as the dawn comes after a dark night," Chuykov tells us of 19 November.[6] Chuykov here was suggesting, in a way that Grossman never did, that victory was preordained, but he framed the battle in very familiar terms.

Chuykov's recollections are indicative of a wider process of returning to the textual site of Stalingrad in the postwar years. First to revisit the battle were the writer-soldiers, each of whom turned his hand to writing longer pieces about Stalingrad in a race to pen "the *War and Peace* of our time."[7] Whether those stories lauded Stalin as omniscient leader, hailed the role of the ordinary soldier, or attempted to debunk the narrative of the battle as resurrection, the postwar return to the battle always meant summoning the words, phrases, and motifs produced at the front for the wartime papers.

Konstantin Simonov and Boris Polevoy approached the battle from the upper echelons of the Soviet literary world. Simonov was the most popular of the postwar Stalingrad writers – indeed, for a time, he was the most popular Soviet writer full stop – both at home and abroad.[8] His 1943 work *Days and Nights*, which develops the characters and themes from the September 1942 story into a full novel, was the first in the author's one-man production line of Stalingrad texts and among the most printed of all Soviet postwar novels.[9] The work describes a house defence story that clearly emulates Polevoy's

"House 21a." Simonov projects onto that framework the character of the nurse Shchepenya from the eponymous 1942 story translated in this volume, working the plot around the male protagonist's near-death and recovery from an injury – the hero here standing in for the martyred and resurrected Stalingrad. Alongside a slew of references to the hellish Volga crossing, to medieval literature, to Tolstoy, and to Kriger's and Grossman's works, these recycled tropes dominated a novel spliced together in a way highly reminiscent of Simonov's battle-era work.

Polevoy, meanwhile, had the honour of managing to get the first long-form prose work about Stalingrad, *The Hero-City* (*Gorod-geroy*), into the December 1942 edition of the literary journal *Oktyabr*. The work was warmly received by the editorial staff and by Sovinformbyuro – Stalin too probably read and approved it.[10] Polevoy would then pen the smash-hit novel *The Tale of a Real Man* (1946), which revolves around the idea of Stalingrad as a motivating force for a grievously wounded pilot's return to flying – an unavoidable parallel with Vsevolod Ivanov's "A Russian Field." In the postwar years, Simonov and Polevoy received hundreds of letters from readers expressing admiration for them and inquiring about their Stalingrad links and their knowledge of loved ones' fates. The pair remained close friends until their deaths in the late 1970s.

Our three Jewish protagonists – Ilya Ehrenburg, Vasily Grossman, and David Ortenberg – experienced rather different fates. Ehrenburg produced a widely distributed high Stalinist novel about Stalingrad, *The Storm* (1947), which was promptly forgotten when Stalin died in 1953. Ehrenburg went on to author a series of repentant, anti-Stalinist works before his death in 1967. Grossman's postwar career was even more sharply divided between official and non-official culture. The author was fêted after Stalingrad. On 8 February 1943, he received the Order of the Red Star for his exemplary courage and literary achievements.[11] He began work on a great Stalingrad novel. However, antisemitism and oppression in the late 1940s delayed publication of what would become *For a Just Cause* until 1952.[12]

In *For a Just Cause*, Grossman borrows liberally from his own Stalingrad sketches. The novel resonates with the sense of *podvig*. The protagonist, Vavilov, eventually sacrifices himself, saint-like, in a hopeless battle that seems to turn the tide at Stalingrad. At times, the writing in the novel is near identical to the writing in the stories translated here. The work's conclusion, for example, has its second protagonist, Krymov, crossing the Volga. The narrator comments:

A quick spear then flashed from the dark wall of the Soviet bastion and pierced the wall of the German workshop. A few seconds later, the air was full of fiery spears and arrows. There were bursts of tracer fire from machine guns; rifles were firing tracer bullets that seemed like incandescent flies. The dark walls were like great thunderclouds, with forked lightning flashing between them.[13]

The lines, slightly rewritten and moved in time from after to before 19 November, are from Grossman's "Today in Stalingrad."

The publication of *For a Just Cause* led to a wave of sharp antisemitic criticism. At a time when prominent Soviet Jews were facing increasing oppression, Grossman was almost arrested. Only Stalin's timely death in 1953 saved him. Grossman was appalled by this backlash and by his own complicity in propagandizing for Stalin's regime. In response, he penned *Life and Fate* (1961), a thorough excoriation of the epic tale of resurrection at Stalingrad that had, the author contends, only led to further suffering for ordinary Soviets. Grossman again reiterates the language of the newspaper stories, albeit purely to distance himself from that material: the novel's first battle scene, the vision of the flaming Volga, and the details of soldiers' almost humdrum *byt* as they defend a house for days on end have an immediate connection to the language of the wartime front. Grossman rewrites his own and his colleagues' material to summon the aura of the wartime "quickfire epic," pulling us into the time and space of the *podvig*. He then tears apart the idea of Stalingrad as a moment of worthy sacrifice as characters are arrested, destroyed, or betrayed. To hold such anti-Soviet views was blasphemy even under Nikita Khrushchev's comparatively permissive rule. *Life and Fate* went unpublished, and Grossman was all but excluded from literary circles. A broken man, he died of cancer in 1964. His Stalingrad novels would be rapturously received on their release in the 1980s, but it was clear that the Stalingrad story was increasingly an instrument of state power rather than a shared creation.

David Ortenberg's exit from the halls of power was even swifter. In July 1943, he was dismissed from his editorship and demoted without explanation – an early indication of the nation's antisemitic turn.[14] Ortenberg disappeared from public life. Konstantin Simonov, who always remained Ortenberg's close confidant, was barred from including even a brief mention of his former editor in a poem of 1946. Nonetheless, Ortenberg never lost his fighting spirit.

In 1949, he implored Stalin to reveal why he had been removed as editor of *Krasnaya Zvezda*,[15] and he continued to lobby on behalf of his former charges where he could. Even in the 1970s, when Ortenberg joined the flood of veterans publishing war memoirs, he battled the authorities to have material on Vasily Grossman included. When permitted, Ortenberg became a regular and much admired visitor to the *Krasnaya Zvezda* offices in the 1970s. Whatever stain of complicity his character might have borne for acting in collaboration with the Stalinist elites in the war years was far outweighed by respect for his wartime leadership.[16]

In spite of these travails, and unlike Grossman, Ortenberg never recanted his faith in the Stalingrad narrative. He finally returned to the city three decades after the war's end. Seeing the Mamaev Kurgan crowned by what was then the world's tallest statue, the Motherland Calls monument, Ortenberg turned to familiar words of resurrection to frame his emotions: "I didn't recognize the city at all. It really had risen from the ashes."[17] Ortenberg still parsed his experience in the language of religion and myth he and his colleagues had set down on paper in 1942–43.

Ortenberg's ability to reconcile his personal suffering and official narratives of the battle is indicative of a widespread phenomenon. In spite of the regime's very public capture of the Stalingrad narrative, Soviets continued to engage with and propagate the story. It was not just fêted regime propagandists and celebrity Stalingraders like Ortenberg who revisited the fighting on the Volga in person and in text after the battle's end. Ordinary Soviet journalists, workers, and civilians were desperate to go to the city and to discuss their relationship to the wartime past, using the wartime Stalingrad story as their axis.[18] In late 1943, for example, Aleksandr Kotov, a young teacher living in Kemerovo, wrote to the Stalingrad Komsomol – the nationwide Soviet youth league – about a novel he had apparently spent years working on:

> I'd got another three or four chapters to go when the Germans bombed Stalingrad. I had to bury the manuscript and all my notes under a willow in the yard … I ask that you invite me to Stalingrad so that I can find out what happened to my parents, then find the novel manuscript and finish it.[19]

Kotov was one of many who linked their own biography to the act of writing about Stalingrad. Kotov's fellow Stalingrader, the worker B.B. Panchenko, managed even to publish his Stalingrad piece, *Destruction Battalion* (*Istrebitelny batalon*), in a tiny print run through the local publishing house. The short documentary fiction, about the author's paramilitary unit formed at the Stalingrad Tractor Factory, reveals an ordinary writer and veteran drawing on language from *Krasnaya Zvezda* and *Pravda* to transform his own brigade into the participants in a great *podvig*:

> The ring around the city was ever tighter, but our Soviet troops stood firm, they stood to the death, in their efforts to defend every metre of burned and bloody land. Our [home] village was destroyed and became a battlefield ... The Volga was aflame. We could barely see our bunker and pillboxes through the smoke. We crossed the Volga on one dark night.

Panchenko inscribes his unit into a familiar – and famous – history of the battle. The evidently traumatic events of 23 August, the burning Volga, and the destruction of the unit's homes around the Tractor Factory are all framed and ordered within this greater story. The *podvig* of Stalingrad serves as a means to orient Panchenko's war contribution and suffering.

For ordinary Stalingraders like Kotov and Panchenko, "visiting" the narrative of Stalingrad was a means to participate in the shared discourse of the turn from death to life. The innumerable short stories, novels, and films that reworked lines written at the front in 1942–43 were vital to making sense of the wartime experience as the country strove to rebuild itself. As Konstantin Simonov explained in a letter from 1945, "It's not just cities we have to rebuild. We have to rebuild feeling itself."[20] For many Soviets, the idea of Stalingrad as a turning point from death to life and the act of recreating the *podvig* of 1942–43 in textual form were ways to rebuild feeling.

✲✲✲

In the final section of this volume, I present two stories of the return to Stalingrad: Vasily Koroteev's "Ten Years On" (1953) and Viktor Nekrasov's "An Incident on the Mamaev Kurgan" (1965).[21] Each repeats the form of the classic battlefield tour narrative and invites the reader to share a maelstrom of inner thoughts and feelings prompted by re-experiencing the battle. However, each narrator faces different challenges in a battle to resolve memory, the present, and the future into inner harmony.

After Stalingrad, Vasily Koroteev accompanied the Red Army to Prague. Once the war was over, he scaled the heights of the Soviet journalistic establishment, becoming secretary of the literary magazine *Literaturnaya Gazeta*, editing *Niva*, and working as a correspondent at both *Pravda* and *Izvestiya*. Thanks to his Stalingrad-era connections with Nikita Khrushchev, Koroteev's career took him to the Kremlin and even on trips abroad to meet world leaders.

In spite of this globetrotting career, Koroteev never quite left the war or Stalingrad behind. He married the renowned partisan Nadezhda Troyan and published two collections of stories about the battle. Koroteev even planned a great novel to rival Simonov's *Days and Nights*. Simonov, with whom Koroteev remained close until his death in the 1964, encouraged his friend to persevere. Koroteev, however, was beset by self-doubt. He wrote to Simonov:

> Those who were actually at Stalingrad will reproach me endlessly. Someone'll spot one little plot hole, then somebody else will spot another. Then somebody will say I've misplaced a street, and somebody else will say that their division didn't do such and such, and anyway, it wasn't the 13th, it was the 15th, or the other way around.[22]

Dealing with his own trauma, and with what he perceived as the weight of historical responsibility to capture Stalingrad correctly, proved too burdensome. Koroteev never did manage to produce his novel.

However, Koroteev was a master of the Stalingrad short story. The story translated here, 1953's "Ten Years On," is the finest example of Koroteev's postwar work. It carefully dovetails the author's personal response to memory of the war as his narrator returns to Stalingrad in 1953 with an account of the government and people's postwar reconstruction work. Koroteev's piece runs over with sacrificial historicism: for the author, the sacrifices of the past and present are all made worthwhile by his managing to piece together his experiences using the sights and sounds of another battlefield tour shaped around the textual heritage of Stalingrad.

Much had changed in the ten years since the end of the Stalingrad battle. Thousands of civilians and young Soviets were sent to begin a massive reconstruction project. News footage depicted workers on construction sites, women and girls carrying out domestic chores among the rubble, and schoolchildren returning to bombed-out classrooms. "Stalingrad lives!," proclaimed the newsreels, echoing Evgeny Kriger's pithy phrase to promise that "life has begun anew!"[23] Whatever the difficulties of life in post-battle Stalingrad, writers took up arms in the battle on the construction front. Vasily Koroteev, ever the hometown patriot, was as enthusiastic as anyone.

At first glance, "Ten Years On" simply reflects the author's delight at undertaking yet another battlefield tour and seeing his hometown reborn, as if this were any other Socialist Realist piece hailing Stalin's great achievement. However, memories of the destructive past intrude constantly on Koroteev's observations of the present. Assertions of the newly constructed city's glittering future threaten only to highlight the distance between reality and dream. Koroteev was giving voice to a widely held ambiguity of feeling – many Soviets thought of the war as simultaneously "beautiful" and "frightening."[24] However, he was also leveraging the idea of Stalingrad as a historical turning point to herald the coming of utopia in the (almost) present. As he had done during the dark days of fall 1942, Koroteev describes his own reactions to tumult. Here, he responds to what during the battle had seemed unimaginable, adopting familiar tropes of rebirth and new life verbatim to counter the overtones of destruction.

What seems at first glance to be an epic ode to centralized Soviet power sweeps us away with human emotion. The idyllic sublime of the story's climax contrapuntally expresses the loss and exaltation embodied in the Stalingrad story, painting the city as a site of abundant utopian potential. Nonetheless, the penultimate paragraph suggests that the newly built Stalin statue at the entrance to the Volga–Don canal "personifies our people's great and triumphant victories on the Volga at Tsaritsyn and Stalingrad": a reminder that, for all of the sense of shared enterprise coursing through the wartime stories, and Koroteev's evident delight in his tour of the reconstructed city, victory at Stalingrad in the early 1950s belonged only to one man.

Fast forward to 1965 and we again meet Viktor Nekrasov – the same lieutenant who had fought on the Mamaev Kurgan – on a tour of the city now known as Volgograd. Nekrasov had become one of the Soviet Union's leading war writers, yet his gritty Stalingrad stories stood out from most epic late Stalinist novels.[25] His masterful 1946 novella, *In the Trenches of Stalingrad* (*V okopakh Stalingrada*), which intertwines the author's experiences with tropes drawn in particular from Konstantin Simonov's Stalingrad stories, was first lauded, then criticized.[26] Nonetheless, Nekrasov's Stalingrad writing was hugely popular. Ilya Ehrenburg, for instance, named Nekrasov alongside Vasily Gross-man as the only man ever able to "convey the tragic nature and immensity of spirit of those who participated in the Battle of Stalingrad."[27]

In the 1960s, under the new Brezhnev regime, the wartime tale of ordinary people's heroism was being replaced by a monumentalized story of the old political guard's heroic leadership.[28] Nonetheless, Nekrasov was never afraid to suggest that soldiers, and not political leaders, were the real victors at Stalingrad – and, therefore, the real architects of the *podvig*.[29] He spent much of his time corresponding with veterans, offering support or guidance that the government would not give.[30] He and his correspondents won occasional victories, but for many veterans, homelessness, alcoholism, and poor medical and psychiatric care were the norm. The official portrayal of a heroic generation rewarded with a utopian existence thanks to Stalingrad's turning point was totally at odds with reality.[31] For Nekrasov, who had travelled abroad widely, the gulf between the resurrection promised by the achievement of the *podvig* and the reality of day-to-day life was particularly obvious. When the need to resist a destructive invader was gone, when the time to battle individual traumas came, and when the government's hold over memory of the war seemed to be becoming ever more absolute, cracks in the Stalingrad narrative inevitably began to appear. "An Incident on the Mamaev Kurgan" is a striking example of these fissures.

Driven by a desire to see the "real" story of Stalingrad shared with the public, and encouraged by letters of support from fellow writers and veterans, Nekrasov worked on "An Incident on the Mamaev Kurgan" for at least half a decade, and even planned to turn it into a film.[32] In the story, Nekrasov wrestles to resolve the tensions among his own recollections, the narrative of the wartime papers, and the various Stalinist and post-Stalinist versions of the battle now codified in Soviet public ritual and memory.[33]

Nekrasov's narrator again visits Stalingrad. By the mid-1960s, much of the construction work Koroteev had described had been completed, and the famous Motherland Calls monument was almost finished.[34] However, Nekrasov's narrator is interested in reflecting not on external reality but on his own relationship with the past. Nekrasov's narrator follows what should be an exemplary Socialist Realist method. Visiting the sites of construction and past victories ought to have catalyzed a rumination on a great future. Touring the textual sites of Stalingrad – both his own and those depicted by Simonov and Grossman, whom he now counted as a close friend – leads, however, only to cacophonic disarray.[35] The narrator is an insomniac and a drunk who falls into the past. He frankly discusses disease, starvation, and incompetence at the Stalingrad front, almost wilfully fails to enact any acts of heroism, wracks himself with survivor's guilt, and becomes lost in the differences between his own fiction and historical fact. The sublime harmony of Koroteev's climax in "Ten Years On" is replaced by a chaos that resembles the disorder of the early months of Stalingrad in 1942. Nekrasov's authorial control, and thus his control over his sense of self, collapses in on itself, spiralling away from the author and away from the myth of Stalingrad as site of creation and harmony. The text becomes bogged down in contradiction, conflict, and the author's spontaneous utterances. The figure that should be the hero of the Stalingrad story – the demiurgic soldier-writer – is rendered powerless to unravel this chaos.

Little surprise that Konstantin Simonov thought that the public would find such a complex and shocking work "baffling."[36] Indeed, when Nekrasov sent the text to Simonov as the idea for a film script, the older author refused to even countenance its production. Simonov praised "yet another ... addition" to Nekrasov's résumé but thought that what had to be the most bewildering but brilliant Stalingrad work yet written belonged in literary journals for intellectuals.[37] An exchange of testy letters ensued, but the film project never got going.

Yet not all readers found the work quite so confusing. Take Ilya Maryasin, a former classmate of one of Nekrasov's protagonists, Yury Benyash (who, coincidentally, happened to be a nephew of Vasily Grossman).[38] For Maryasin, the heroic portrayal of the dashing Captain Benyash was "proof" of "*our* participation" in the war:[39] a way to write Jewish experience back into Stalingrad after Vasily Grossman and David Ortenberg had disappeared from view. The Stalingrad story, even presented in the most subversive ways, offered an infinite capacity for readers to make sense of their own pasts and presents.

Nekrasov's story reveals a rupturing of unity between the government and Stalingrad authors. Yet it also suggests a bifurcation of authors' responses to memory of the battle. On the one hand, Koroteev as a native Stalingrader must have been aware of the use of forced labour and of the terrible living conditions in Stalingrad after the battle. "Ten Years On" still seems to suggest that the utopian promise of Stalingrad rendered the continued sacrifices made on behalf of the Soviet government worthwhile. The "new day" promised to the readers of early 1943 was still in the offing; Koroteev draws on textual models to resolve dissonances between reality and ideal. By contrast, Nekrasov's story intimates that a wartime pact of discursive unity between the state and the people had been broken. The utopian promise of the *podvig* had resulted in nothing tangible for those who had made great sacrifices at the front. Even then, Nekrasov *still* cannot escape the redemptive potential of Stalingrad; he re-experiences that potential endlessly, if only to constantly re-engage with the trauma of the wartime.

The return to Stalingrad, even when it was evidently traumatic, was compulsive.[40] Nekrasov forced himself to return in writing and in fact to Stalingrad, which he always described as the "defining event" of his life. He visited the city time and again and penned hundreds of pages of work about the battle.[41] Even when he was forced out of the Soviet Union and deprived of his citizenship in the mid-1970s, he still could not disentangle his life story from Stalingrad.[42] He would continue discussing the battle in émigré journals and on regular radio appearances until his death in 1987. Drawing again and again on the language of the wartime newspapers, the author seemed – just like the many of his fellow Soviets who tried their hand at writing Stalingrad stories or who drew on elements of the stories they had read to frame their own biographies – unable, unwilling, or both, to escape the idea of the battle as a great *podvig*.

When we read wartime, Soviet-era, or modern references to Stalingrad, we should understand that those references are not *historical* or *nostalgic*. Indeed, in some sense, readers and writers of Stalingrad are not discussing the historical battle at all. Their words are an interaction between the self and society, between an individual and the present. They are a means to resolve today's disorder, not to describe yesterday's past.

The Putin government has, in the twenty-first century, revived a Brezhnev-style cult of the war. The Second World War is portrayed as Russia's greatest achievement through a limited array of *podvigi*. Stalingrad as *the* moment of national resurrection stands at the centre of this web. The government's approach today imitates the tsarist past, when the military, the church, and the ruler were even more closely linked than in the Soviet era: in autumn 2021, Patriarch Kirill visited the Mamaev Kurgan, reaffirming the site's spiritual importance; images of Stalingrad have been inscribed on the facade of the vast

Cathedral of the Armed Forces in Moscow, a monument to the state and church's intertwined past and future consecrated in 2020. Stalingrad has become in this context a religious symbol.

Increasingly, however, individuals have been relegated to the status of being footnotes. At times, this has been almost literally true: 2020's Victory Day celebrations in Volgograd saw serried ranks of names projected onto the base of the Motherland Calls monument; elegiac and human tales of civilian suffering and ordinary troops' real bravery were nowhere to be seen. Individuals' real lives have thus been absorbed into a monumental state vision of Stalingrad. When it so chooses, the government can graphically, visually, and narratively subjugate the civilian and military dead in favour of its preferred visions of Stalingrad.

Nonetheless, even this ossified, monumental projection of state power still appeals. Thousands attend annual celebrations of victory in Volgograd, undertaking pilgrimages to the city to pay their dues. Their trips echo Vladimir Putin's 2018 pilgrimage to the Mamaev Kurgan and, of course, Vasily Koroteev's and Viktor Nekrasov's earlier tours. Social media are packed with posts from young, cosmopolitan Russians who document their own interactions with Stalingrad, drawing on the language of the frontline papers to describe trips to the sites of battle and the *kurgan*: "When I go to the Mamaev Kurgan, I read the inscriptions. I get goosebumps and weep"; "I got the chills when I stood on the spot where the soldiers fought and the eternal flame burns, and I thought of how they're no longer alive"; "The Red Army ground the Germans and their allies down over two hundred days and nights ... [The battle] changed history ... #Motherland #OntheMamaevKurgan."[43] In spite of the government's recalcification of the Stalingrad story and aggressive militarization of society, the diverging responses to Stalingrad that Koroteev and Nekrasov bring to their work live on – and the phrases and words of Stalingrad's journalists still widely reify and represent memory of the battle.

Vasily Koroteev – *Ten Years On*
1953

"When were you last in Stalingrad? Last year? Come again today. You won't recognize the city at all!"

My Stalingrad friends have been writing me letters just like this one for years. And now, at long last, I am on my way back to my hometown.

The Stalingrad veteran Sergey Fyodorovich Gorokhov, now a military academy teacher, bade me farewell in Moscow:[44] "Pass on my greetings to Stalingrad and say hello to my friends at the Tractor Factory." Aleksandr Adamovich Poshkus, another veteran who teaches in another military academy, said: "Visit the Verkhne-Kumsky Hill near Kalach and take a tour around the ring of encirclement. I'd like to know what's going on there now."

There are several Stalingraders in our carriage. Passengers who have never visited Stalingrad excitedly ask the veterans about the city. They may never have been, but they adore the city all the same, and they are fascinated by anything to do with Stalingrad.

The train approaches Razgulyaevka. The Tractor Factory chimneys are already visible: familiar places are getting nearer. What gives rise to that gnawing in your chest, that bitter feeling of regret, every time you arrive in your hometown, the place where you spent your youth?

I disembark from the train and rush off to the Square of Fallen Fighters in the city centre. The whole time I look around with intense excitement. As soon as you leave the train, the Volga rolls out ahead of you, as if the river were flowing directly toward the Square of Fallen Fighters and into the very heart of the city. And there it is: the hero-city's central square. Today, the square is surrounded by the Party school, a theatre, a department store, and some blocks housing a post office, hotel, construction workers' homes, and the Hydroelectric Station. You can go right out onto the embankment then descend a great granite staircase down to the river. Peace Street runs into the square then turns into the Alley of Heroes.

How everything has changed!

A bleak picture of this very square ten years ago, on 4 February 1943, suddenly comes to me. The square is surrounded by ruins, ravaged by bombs and shells, and littered with tanks, vehicles, and streetcar carriages. German helmets, tattered overcoats, and the corpses of Hitlerites protrude from the snow ...

I remember how we had celebrated our glorious victory with eager delight at a mass gathering on that very day – even as our hearts overflowed

Figure 5.2 The production line at the reconstructed Tractor Factory, 1948.

with sorrow at seeing our city so gravely injured. Shipyard labourer Comrade Sidnev had sworn on the residents' behalf to rebuild the city. Not everyone had believed that that would happen any time soon. "It'll take half a century," said many as they stared forlornly at the ashes and the ruins. Indeed, none of us who saw the city right after the Hitlerites' defeat could really have thought that just a few years later the chimneys of reborn factories and a crowd of new, whitewashed buildings – indeed, the whole city of Stalingrad – would rise up from the Volga's steep bank and even become the site of two great new construction projects![45]

Stalingrad has been reborn from the ruins and ashes thanks to the people's love and the Party's and government's leadership. Its famed factory chimneys have been improved; they are even more powerful now than they were before the war. Tractors, steel, excavators, and oil pumps are despatched from Stalingrad to every corner of our nation.

I remember the picture of despair at the Red October factory. Metal beams and frames had buckled from explosions and fires, the brickwork had crumbled, and the furnaces had been blown to pieces. Yet now, ten years on, the factory has undergone an extraordinary transformation. New chimneys and new workshops have been erected. Green alleys traverse the factory's grounds. Lightning seems to flash above the factory as steel for tractors, combines, and automobiles is produced. Stalingrad's metal and tractor workers are giving the country more steel and more tractors than they were even before the war. Stalingrad's industry has taken a huge step forward.

Construction work roils away in every last corner of this enormous city. Stalingrad is growing to the north and south, and moving ever farther onto the steppe, without restraint. The tenth anniversary of our victory was celebrated in the forests of this gargantuan construction site.

The contours of the new city – a Stalingrad its former residents would not recognize – are being drawn with ever more clarity. New factories have been added to the dozens that were already here, and civil engineering, agricultural, forestry, and cooperative technical institutes have joined the old pedagogical, mechanical, and medical schools. Stunning buildings now adorn the city: the "Victory" cinema, the regional Party school, the Tractor Factory's palace of culture, the Red October Factory's exhibition hall, and the multi-storey apartment blocks along the embankment, on the outskirts, and right in the city centre. The theatre, now rebuilt almost from the ground up, is even more spacious and beautiful than it was before. Soon, the palace of labour, the railway station, the planetarium, the large tuberculosis hospital, and the winter swimming pool will be completed too. Entirely new streets have appeared in the city centre. The workers' villages have been improved. The architectural face of the city has been totally changed. The shady parks and gardens, packed as they are with young and verdant trees, are simply splendid in the summer. I envy my Stalingrad friends and acquaintances their well-appointed apartments in new buildings along the Volga embankment. Since the residents receive gas service, they even have gas hobs at home.

Shortly after the fighting at Stalingrad ended, letters from soldiers, workers, collective farm labourers, and students in Siberia, Primorye, Kazakhstan, and Georgia began to pour into the city. The writers explained how much they wished they could see Stalingrad, a city that many of them had never visited. The letter writers had no architectural knowledge and knew nothing of engineering calculations, but how great was their burning love for the hero-city!

The last sounds of battle had barely died away when the entire country once more came to the ruined city's aid. Those who were in Stalingrad in 1943 and 1944 remember how tough it had been to survive back then. People lived in canvas tents and cellars, hastily constructed barracks, and even in dugouts and bunkers. Then more than 25,000 young men and women had answered the Komsomol's call for volunteers to rebuild Stalingrad. Their ticket to the city was inscribed thus: "The Komsomol charges you to raise the city, destroyed by fascists, from the ashes. You must not cease work, leave the construction sites, or come down from the scaffolding until our Stalingrad is beautiful and blooming once again!"

Every new house, every new workshop, and every new square is another shining example of Stalingraders' courage and of their love for their hometown. They have contributed more than fifteen million hours of their spare time toward their hometown's reconstruction. Every day, labourers, troops, engineers, artists, teachers, and students would clock off. Then they would take up spades, picks, and axes and they would clear sites for new buildings, plant trees, saw and plane timber, and haul bricks around.

The prewar resident and former woodmill porter Mikhail Danilovich
Zhavoronkov, now deputy director of the Stalingrad Reconstruction
Directorate, remembers how difficult it was to rehome those living in cellars.[46] Nevertheless, they solved that problem some time ago. Before the war,
there were 900,000 square metres of living space in Stalingrad. Now there
are 1.6 million.

The Stalingraders named their first cinema "Victory" and their finest
street "Peace." Through their heroic efforts they aim to achieve both victory
and peace.

✳ ✳ ✳

The city's construction workers are at a rally taking place in the theatre.
These workers are today the most esteemed of the city's residents. In the
theatre's foyer, we take the chance to look around an interesting exhibition.
The photographs and dioramas paint a splendid picture of the Stalingrad of
tomorrow. Regional Party Committee chairman Ivan Timofeevich Grishin
gestures at a set of plans and explains, "This is the agricultural institute
building. It's already under construction." Pointing toward another project,
he adds, "That one's under way too. And here's the planetarium!"

In Stalingrad, architectural ideas leap off the drawing board and into
reality at breakneck speed. The city has become the nation's biggest construction site. The skyline, with the blue sky outlining scaffolding and
cranes, is truly something to behold.

The plans for the new city were only agreed on after much discussion
and debate. Now they are being drawn out ever more clearly. Chief architect
Simbirtsev and Regional Secretary Grishin described something that
seemed like a fairy tale at today's construction workers' rally. Nevertheless,
it is not just those who were at the rally – all those bricklayers, carpenters,
crane operators, foremen, and architects – but every last citizen who firmly
believes that the plans will become reality!

Stalingrad sits on a group of small hills that form a terrace leading down
the Volga's steep banks and into the water. It feels almost naturally destined
to become the world's most beautiful city. The world's greatest arterial road
is currently under construction: the 60 kilometre Stalin Prospect will link
the city's southern and northern suburbs with its centre, snaking through
the city's various squares along the way.

The project's first stage is 18 kilometres long. The construction workers are cutting through deep ravines so as to avoid endless twists and turns. The prospect will be lined with magnificent apartment buildings five to seven storeys high. Boulevards and squares will adorn its entire length, and perpendicular streets will lead down to the Volga. Peacetime urban construction has never seen anything like it. Leningrad's famed Nevsky Prospect, for instance, is just two and a half kilometres long. Building the prospect is the most important part of Stalingrad's five-year plan. It starts on Dzerzhinsky Square, then passes the Stalingrad Tractor Factory's gates, the Barricades factory, and the Red October housing complex. The road seamlessly merges with a 2 kilometre long square, rows of large and elegant homes, and the Metallurgists' Palace of Culture, which is currently also under construction.

A monument to the steelworker Olga Kovaleva, a glorious patriot who fell in battle against the enemy at Mokraya Mechetka,[47] is planned for one of the squares near the Red October factory. Closer to the city centre, a park and a 40,000-seat stadium will sit at the foot of the Mamaev Kurgan. On Defence Square, the Stalingraders intend to erect a bronze monument to the Stalingrad Soldier. They plan to build a second monument, to the Heroes of the Stalingrad Crossing, at the nearby pump house.

An ensemble of important structures – to be linked together by the city's tallest building, the twenty-one-storey House of Soviets on the Square of Fallen Fighters – is already taking shape in the city centre. A collective of architects headed by Lev Rudnev has already completed designs for the House.[48] Meanwhile, at the end of Peace Street, right in the city centre, construction of the planetarium is almost complete. Its equipment has been supplied as a gift to Stalingrad from the workers of the German Democratic Republic. The Square of Fallen Fighters broadens as it intersects with the Alley of Heroes on the Volga side. Bronze busts of Stalingrad's heroes are to be placed among the alley's trees and fountains. At the prospect's southern end, right where it meets the entrance to the Volga–Don Canal, stands a most wonderful monument to Stalin. In addition to the Stalin Prospect, yet another thoroughfare, this one to be dotted with multi-storey homes, will later be added.

Victory Park sweeps from the Tsaritsa River valley up along the Volga's bank and all the way to the foot of the Mamaev Kurgan. A grandiose monument celebrating victory will stand at the park's centre, and there are plans to build a new Museum of the Defence of Tsaritsyn–Stalingrad in the park. The Stalingrad Panorama Museum will stand atop the Mamaev Kurgan.

The nation's leading architects are helping to build the new Stalingrad. Thanks to their creative efforts, the city will doubtless soon play host to a striking collection of Soviet architectural pieces. The people too are fixated on the wondrous future of their city. The future of Stalingrad is for them, after all, a very important business. Those working on the reconstruction view beautiful and precise building work as an obligation.

The construction of a second city on the Volga's left bank is a serious topic of conversation in today's Stalingrad. The idea is to build two bridges to link the left and right banks in the city centre. The city will thus be joined with the green expanse of the Volga steppe, as if that land had always been naturally intended to provide space for Stalingrad's dachas. In turn, the un-inhibited construction work in the northern and southern suburbs could be replaced by the building of two and three-storey homes on the left bank. This wonderful idea is born of genuine care for ordinary residents, though we are not yet certain when or if work on the project will begin.

The Volga–Don and the Hydroelectric Station, which is still under con-struction, have left a significant impression on the hero-city. The place is becoming busier and busier as new residents – construction engineers, hydrotechnical workers, and surveyors – arrive.

There are still many traces of the battle left in the city, and many build-ings have yet to be reconstructed. However, the most difficult period is in the past. Every year, more ruins and more wrecks, along with many more remnants of the devastation, are disappearing.

Stalingrad's postwar five-year plans have led to an incredible transforma-tion. Stalingrad is on the edge of the arid southwest, so it often experiences droughts. Today, though, the city contains six wooded areas. Oak groves, to be used by industry, are being planted, and the world's greatest hydroelectric station is under construction.

Plots have already been sown with rice and wheat on the irrigated land around the Volga–Don Canal. Very soon indeed the floodplain between the Volga and Akhtubinsk will become a valley of verdant gold, of rice, kenaf, gardens, and vineyards; and the Volga steppe will provide abundant grain harvests.

Stalingrad is at the forefront of the battle for communism, just as it was during the Civil War, just as it was during the first five-year plan, and just as it was during the fighting with Hitler's army. The hero-city bestrides the Volga's steep bank. Stalingrad has never forgotten the essence of its past glories, just like the soldier who understands that victory comes only after great military efforts.

***

Travelling along the flat highway past the Volga–Don Canal, one is endlessly astonished at the miraculous changes that have taken place in the arid, sun-scorched steppe between Stalingrad and Kalach. Endless new hills have changed the steppe's appearance. Cars dash along broad roads day and night, but it is easy to remember how, just a few years ago, camels would bellow as they strained along washed-out paths during muddy spring thaws. On the way from Krasnoarmeisk to Kalach one can see enormous concrete sluices, new groups of neat, cheery stone houses, schools and clubs, high-voltage electricity and telephone cables, new railway lines, and bridges crossing the rivers and ravines.

The first Volga–Don construction workers arrived on the steppe to the south of Stalingrad in summer 1948. Before long a gigantic front of construction stretched more than 100 kilometres along the plateau between the Volga and the Don. In the same place where Stalin and Voroshilov led the Red Army's regiments to a great victory over the counter-revolution, and where a decade ago the Soviet forces surrounded and destroyed a strike group of 330,000 Hitlerites, a civilian army of Soviet workers built the canal our people had dreamed of for centuries. The Don came to Stalingrad. The canal had united the two mightiest rivers of Russia.

The area around Kamyshin, to the north, is just like that in the south. Boundless steppe wastes away from lack of water. Bar the odd sagebrush or thyme, sometimes a tumbleweed, one does not see many trees or bushes here. Yet even here, the newcomer might now find something to wonder at. In this very spot, belts of bright green trees – young elms, maples, ashes, and acacias already as tall as a man – now rise above the Volga for some 250 kilometres.

Forestry workers arrived here several years ago, in 1948. Theirs was a tall order. They had been asked to create a new forest belt by planting half a million seedlings. Along the length of the new forest up popped the Gorodishchensky, Gorno-Balykley, and Kamyshin forestry stations. Each was equipped with powerful tractors, motor vehicles, seeding machines, and tillers. A great undertaking had been launched on the steppe. The Stalingraders gladly assisted the foresters: many thousands of workers, troops, Komsomol members, and schoolchildren took to planting trees. The foresters sowed corn to protect the shoots from the summer's scorching sun and fierce winds and from the winter frosts.

In May 1952, Stalingrad's forestry workers and Komsomol members were finally able to report that the planting and seeding along the "Road of Youth" had been completed not in the planned fifteen but in just three and a half years. One hundred sixty-eight hectares of apple, cherry, and pear trees had been planted. Stalingraders called the forest belt the "Road of Youth" both because its greenery had appeared so quickly and because the city's young people had created much of the belt themselves. Stalingrad's Komsomol members, pioneers, and schoolchildren are all helping with the great business of transforming and rejuvenating their native land. Now the planting is over, they are looking after the new forest and making sure that every last young tree is safe. The pioneers have constructed little nesting boxes all along the belt so that starlings will move in and destroy any voracious caterpillars that might threaten the forest.

Young maples, oaks, acacias, and elms now stand as testament to the transformation of the steppe's climate from Stalingrad to Kalach in the south and to Kamyshin in the north. A panorama of the great labour front on Peschanny Island is visible from the banks of the Volga at Rynok. Farther off, the very land around Akhtuba seems to smolder; smoke is rising from the concrete repair factory's chimneys. Not far from Rynok people are being rehoused, since this area will soon become the site of a dam. The women – workers' wives – are somewhat sad to leave the place they call home. That said, they are on balance more happy than sad, since they are due to receive apartments in newer houses.

Today's changes are just the start of the transformation. Soon, young forest and oak groves will blanket the Volga steppe and quench a centuries-old thirst. Bountiful cornfields will spring up, orchards will bloom, and vineyards will become ever greener.

* * *

If you are in Stalingrad you simply must visit the Stalin Museum. Pictures commemorating the past come to life in the museum's cosy little rooms. Visitors can admire the Military Council's command ordering a state of siege in Stalingrad as of 24:00 hours on 25 August and marvel at a photograph showing Georgy Malenkov and Aleksandr Vasilevsky's arrival in Stalingrad to organize the city's defence, which was such an important moment in the story of Stalingrad. They might inspect a photograph of Nikita Khrushchev – then a member of the Stalingrad Front's Military Council – speaking at a political meeting of soldiers, or look at a shot of Andrey Yeremenko handing a medal to a soldier, Ivan Polyakov.[49]

In another image, General Utvenko is congratulating a stocky, smiling soldier, who is receiving the Hero of the Soviet Union award. The soldier and four of his comrades had destroyed sixteen enemy tanks on their way to Stalingrad. I look at the shot and think to myself: "Where are you now, Gunner Petr Boloto? You proved such a reliable soldier in combat."

The museum director shows me a new exhibit, a lithographic stone for printing leaflets prepared by the Hitlerites. The following words are engraved on the stone: "Stalingrad has fallen. Moscow is the head of the Soviet Union, but Stalingrad is its heart." The enemy fully understood Stalingrad's importance. Then he shows me yet another document: a September 1942 issue of the Belgian newspaper *La Legia* with a white box left blank. The space was meant for a report on "the details of the fall of Stalingrad."[50]

Our holy relics – photographs, letters, and documents – are gathered in this museum. Thousands of pilgrims from all four corners of the country and from abroad come to visit Stalingrad. As they leave the hero-city, many take a pinch of Stalingrad's soil or some shrapnel with them as a memento.

There are thousands of entries in the museum's visitor book. To pick some out at random:

"The Stalingrad heroes' courageous example inspires us to make our Motherland even mightier – A group of soldiers."

Some Czechs write: "Without Stalingrad's heroism we would not have our freedom."

Some Hungarian workers: "We bow our head with a sense of thankfulness and love."

A delegation of Hungarian sportsmen: "Those who were victorious at Stalingrad freed the Hungarian people too."

Zhou Enlai writes about a feeling of brotherly friendship and deep gratitude to the hero-city's workers on behalf of the Chinese people.

The entries in the visitor book continue:

"I bow my head. - M. Sholokhov."[51]

"We have come to Stalingrad from a far-off outpost to bow our heads before the graves of the heroes of Stalingrad. We are proud of our glorious Soviet people's great deeds. – A group of soldiers."

"We looked around the hero-city of Stalingrad's museum twice with a feeling of deep respect. What we saw in the museum will stay with us for many years. We did not participate in the Battle of Stalingrad, but it has taught us about bravery and valour. We Soviet troops must demonstrate exceptional military skill and preparedness. We swear to follow in the footsteps of Stalingrad's defenders. – Senior Sergeant Kalinichenko, Sergeant Chudakov."

"Having visited the museum, I, a former soldier of the Soviet Army, will try to further strengthen our Motherland's might through my labour. – Malyshev."

"This city is a living page from our history. I swear that as I leave it I will do my utmost, I will give my all, to ensure that the torments documented in the museum are never repeated. My peacetime labour will defend the peace for which my military comrades gave their lives. I will remember their names always. – Former *frontovik* I. Sakharov."

"I am from Siberia. I took part in the defence of Stalingrad in 1942. I returned to the city in 1953. I am astonished by the great accomplishments of the hero-city. – N. Kosov."

"Having looked around the Museum of the Defence of Tsaritsyn-Stalingrad's exhibits, we as young soldiers of the Soviet Army are amazed by the valour and heroism of our older brothers and fathers, Stalingrad's defenders. We will stand guard over peace just as tenaciously as those troops defended the hero-city so that no aggressor country can destroy our peacetime work. – Privates Khanin, Kuptsov, Yakubin."

"We mariners take great delight in the fortitude of our troops and of Stalingrad's residents. We shall keenly defend the nation's peacetime work on the Motherland's naval frontiers. – Petty Officer, 2nd Class, Shchedrin, on behalf of a group of mariners."

"Glory to the city of Stalingrad, where our victorious attack on the fascist barbarians began. Everyone who comes to Stalingrad must visit this museum in order to remember the enormous cost at which our victory came. – Italian workers' delegates."

"Stalingrad has become a cherished symbol that will be eternally dear to the hearts of all free people. The defenders and builders of Stalingrad have a place in the heart of every honorable man and woman. – Endicott, Winner of the International Stalin Peace Prize."[52]

"Ten years ago, I served in the ranks of the Red Army at Stalingrad. I took part in the victorious fight against German fascism. I witnessed the fascist generals' surrender in the Stalingrad department store's basement. I was delighted to acquaint myself with the heroic defenders of Stalingrad. Ten years on, I have come back to Stalingrad and seen the marvellous city on the Volga miraculously reborn. It is a splendid symbol of victory and of the creative force of the unified Soviet nation. I am delighted to see what the heroes of Stalingrad have constructed and to observe their desire for peace. – Willi Bredel, German writer."[53]

"I am proud to be able to write in this book after visiting such a splendid museum. The museum sums up the great defence of this marvellous city, which was the most important event of all time. According to Winston Churchill, 'the Red Army at Stalingrad tore the guts out of the German war machine.' He was correct. The trunk of the fascist tree was felled by the Stalingraders at Stalingrad. All that is left for us to do is to destroy every shoot of the roots that still remain. We must destroy them one after the other, everywhere they appear. What the Red Army did at Stalingrad strengthens our labour. We move forward full of courage and with the truth of the Soviet nation and this great city on our lips. – Hewlett Johnson, representative of Canterbury Cathedral."[54]

✳ ✳ ✳

I could not leave Stalingrad without taking a trip around the ring of encirclement, visiting the most famous sites of the battle, and heading out to

Sarpa Lake, then south to Tsatsa and Barmantsak. That was where General Volsky's tanks and motorized infantry began their advance to the Don. By uniting with General Kravchenko's tanks near Kalach they snapped an iron ring shut around 330,000 enemy troops.

Behind me lies the ice-covered Volga–Don and its snow-covered sluices and pumping stations, where mirror-like reservoirs serve as skating rinks for young lads. Farther on are the Tinguta woods. It was here in fall '42 that our anti-tank gunners repelled a group of enemy tanks, but today the green shoots of what will eventually be an oak wood are already emerging. The steppe is covered with bristly grass and, just like in November 1942, a powdering of snow. Lakes cloaked by banks overgrown with reeds lie to the right and left. The older inhabitants say that vast herds of saiga antelopes used to roam the steppe here.

The road between the lakes peters out into blackness. This is the very road along which, following an artillery storm, General Volsky's tanks and motorized infantry drove into the advance. And now, ten years on, we remember how that time led to victory. We remember the tank crews who did not leave their vehicles for days on end and the exhausted artillerymen who dragged their guns by hand through the deep snows.

We remember the hour of the final reckoning, when the Nazi command refused to capitulate and was destroyed by our artillery's vengeful fire … and then came the order to cease fire and to send mediators with red flags from every battalion toward the enemy. Long lines of filthy, unshaven, and starving prisoners emerged from encirclement.

We remember the bright fires on that dark and frosty night. Our soldiers in their coats and white robes, fatally exhausted but exhilarated by the joy of their glorious victory, standing around them. They already knew how important the mighty clash at Stalingrad would prove to be.

General Volsky stopped near Buzinovka to pose a question to a tank commander whose head had popped out of a turret: "Where are you headed?"

The commander's smile sparkled against his soot-covered, exhausted face as he answered with almost total precision: "To Berlin, that's where!"

Another memory has stayed with me: the sight of hundreds of our doctors and soldiers saving wounded and frostbitten Germans and even setting up field hospitals for them. I remember meeting an elderly lady, a lumber factory worker, in the basement of a school at Dar-Gore. The Hun had captured Dar-Gore and shot her husband, an already wounded infantry soldier. Two months earlier she had been burying her husband in the courtyard, but now she was helping our doctors care for wounded Germans. Is this not the most shining example of the Soviet people's humanism?

In the village of Abganerovo, you can even see the ruts where trenches and the enemy's barbed wire used to be, though the village has grown over them now. You can see new buildings and heaps of lumber destined for Stalingrad's construction sites everywhere.

* * *

The Stalingrad–Moscow train leaves at night. For dozens of kilometres along what you suppose must be the Volga, the lights from new windows, multi-storey apartment blocks, workers' clubs, and factory buildings twinkle in the darkness. The passengers gaze at the lights of Stalingrad and slowly, earnestly talk of the city and of life today and tomorrow: "The things they are doing, what amazing things, in Stalingrad!" People only talk that way of things that are especially dear to them; things that have changed their life forever.

Talk of Stalingrad can be heard in every corner of our nation and abroad. People in every country know why they are indebted to Stalingrad. "What's happening there now? How do people live? How are they building the city?," ask people in China, Korea, Bulgaria, Czechoslovakia, Poland, England, and America. This unquenchable interest in Stalingrad is quite understandable, since Stalingrad means so much to our people and to all of mankind.

Think back, dear reader, to those days when our fate was being decided in the street fighting on Stalingrad's soil, when with nervous trepidation you would read Sovinformbyuro's communiqués about the battle on the Volga. The glow of the burning Stalingrad will appear in your mind as if it were right in front of you. Back then there was nobody dearer to us than the defender of Stalingrad.

Warrior-city. Hero-city. That is how we knew Stalingrad. It was our country's crucible, its test. It was the destiny of our fathers and older brothers, those who fought for Soviet power in the Civil War (after all, without Red Tsaritsyn, without the victory on the Volga in 1918, defeating the counter-revolution would have been unimaginable). During the Great

Patriotic War, though, the fate of the entire nation and the fate of the whole civilized world depended on Stalingrad. Without the victory at Stalingrad – the progenitor of our victory in the Great Patriotic War – the enemy would surely never have been destroyed. Even today, our fate is still bound up with Stalingrad, since the construction of the Volga–Don Canal and of the gigantic hydroelectric station is inextricably linked with the city.

I am sharing a compartment with a young technician working on the Hydroelectric Station construction site. He is going to visit his mother at home in Novo-Annenskaya.[55] The technician talks of Stalingrad with as much excitement as he talks of his hometown: "I wish we could hurry up and knock down the wooden houses so we can build solid stone ones that'll last a hundred years instead!"

As I listen to this young man's passionate speech, images from the past come to me: smoke over the burning city; the water on the Volga crossing boiling from enemy bombs and shells; barefoot nurses in charred dresses carrying the injured, the sick, and children across broken glass to the quay …

I remember too an image from the Tsaritsyn–Stalingrad museum depicting a dead Hitlerite lying on the bank of the Volga, right by the water. "He reached the Volga," went the laconic caption. The picture serves as a formidable lesson to all those who would follow in Hitler's footsteps! The glorious, proud name of Stalingrad is a threat and a warning to all those would light the touchpaper of a new war.

Images of the past turn to vivid portraits of today's Stalingrad: the broad Worker-Volga; the dozens of barges sailing down the river; the horns of steamers carrying far off onto the steppe; the green expanses of the left bank, where the gardens stretch from the Volga to Akhtuba; a vista of mighty factories on the northern and southern outskirts; the obelisk on the Mamaev Kurgan; the doleful face of a robed nurse offering laurels to the dead; the green T-34 tanks on elevated stone plinths standing guard over the fallen as they rest; the dozens of cranes over construction sites; the sight of *bogatyr* factories to the north and south and the high-voltage lines across the Volga; the small hydroelectric station that is serving as the prototype for the giant hydroelectric project; the powerful dredgers clearing the way for the Peschanny Island dam; the young belts of forest from Mokraya

Mechetka to Kamyshin; the grandeur of the theatre and its murals, spacious foyers, and red velvet armchairs ...

And over the whole gigantic city, over the Volga and Volga–Don's waters, over the great expanses of the steppe, a monument to a great man stands on a pedestal rising into the blue Stalingrad sky. The city bears that great man's name. The figure of this great and brave yet simple man, this military genius, is visible for dozens of kilometres around, from the streets of Stalingrad to the canals and deep into the steppe beyond the Volga. The monument to our leader personifies our people's great and triumphant victories on the Volga at Tsaritsyn and Stalingrad.

It is indescribably beautiful at the Volga–Don canal's entrance in the summer. The shining horizon continues for many kilometres toward Stalingrad and out onto the steppe. The sun floods the monument's chased copper with light. The waves, washing against the shore, sing an eternal hymn to the feat of Stalingrad.

Viktor Nekrasov – An Incident on the Mamaev Kurgan
1965

What meaning can you really find in an encounter with your past, with your youth? Are such encounters necessary? How would you feel, for instance, if some panting, balding fellow with a potbelly called out your name in the street? And then he turned out to be none other than Venka Shustroy, who back in the day would usually shimmy up the drainpipe and enter the classroom through the window? How would you feel?

Thinking of one such encounter fills me with sadness. A friend, born in Kiev but now a Leningrader, had thought to arrange a class reunion. Well, said everybody afterward, that was quite lovely, it was nice to see everyone after all these years and remember the past, our teachers, and all those shenanigans. Really, we've hardly changed at all. Not inside – not *spiritually* – at least.

And it really was quite lovely. We talked about the past, we leafed through photographs, and we grieved for the departed. Then when we sat down to eat, we realized that there had been no need at all to buy any vodka. That said, there was mineral water aplenty. At around eleven o'clock we clapped another on the back and went our separate ways. We had agreed to meet the following day on Vladimir Hill to take a group photograph.[56] I knew that the old duffers would take offence, but I didn't go. I simply couldn't.

Don't ever give in to the temptation to return to the places of your youth. Don't go wandering alone down alleyways where once you walked arm-in-arm with some girl. Don't try to forcibly resurrect old relationships, and don't try to meet up with the long departed. Humour's usually the saving grace in those sorts of situations, but it won't save you this time.

I knew all that when I was buying my ticket for the turbo cruiser *Russia* (Moscow–Rostov-on-the-Don with stops in the major ports of Gorky, Kuibyshev, Saratov, and Stalingrad). Stalingrad ... that's where I was headed, albeit with a certain dread. I'd been once before since the war ended, but that trip hadn't brought me any joy at all. I was subconsciously afraid of a second encounter with Stalingrad. Perhaps I just sensed that this time the remarkable story that's about to be told would happen to me. Anyhow, I ummed and ahhed for a good while before I bought the ticket. But this painfully tempting trip along the Volga had come out of the blue. How could I possibly refuse such a serendipitous chance to combine work and pleasure? I'd been holed up in the city for the whole summer, enduring the bustle and the heat without a chance to get down to work, but my deadlines were inexorably approaching. Sod it all. Cut a long story short, I got the ticket.

Do I regret it now? It's hard to say. Yes and no. Probably more no than yes. I'm the sort that doesn't like the unexpected. I prefer peace. A quiet, plodding life. But obviously that's exactly why I sometimes need a shake-up. Maybe nothing quite so inexplicable and exhausting as what happened to me, but I do need it. In a nutshell, I got the ticket and turned up at the boat when it was due to depart, trying not to think about the encounter with the distant past that awaited me.

That last encounter, the one I mentioned, had taken place in summer 1950, exactly seven years after the end of the fighting in Stalingrad. I had been on a business trip but, just as anybody in my shoes would have done, had raced off to the Mamaev Kurgan right from the airport.

It hadn't changed a bit in all our years of separation. Nothing around had changed much either. There was construction work going on in the city and the factories, but everything on the Kurgan was just as it had been. The dry and unattractive hill, grown over with weeds, looked just like it had before,

when I saw it first. It was just as it had been in July '42, when I first saw
Stalingrad after the retreat from Kharkov we all remember so well. Even the
tiny, reconstructed village at its foot looked just as it had during that stifling
hot summer.

I meandered up a familiar gully – the shortest and least dangerous route
to the front line – stopping from time to time as I went. I went out into no
man's land – that sorry 60 metres that separated us from the Germans –
and looked around. The war had never left this place. The trenches had
collapsed. They were shallow and overgrown with grass, but they were still
obviously there. So too were the rusty cartridges, cases, helmets, mess tins,
bayonets, bolts, machine gun belts, the waffle cloth towelling footwraps ...
and the bones ... skulls glimmered white here and there. But you couldn't
tell which were Russian and which German. We had buried the fallen before
leaving in March '43, but the ground was frozen, so we didn't dig deep.
Seven years of wind and rain had blown and washed the soil away ...

I had left the *kurgan* morose and broken. Down in the city below the
bulldozers were snarling, the cranes were whirling, and red posters and
loudspeakers were urging Stalingraders to reconstruct their beloved hero-
city with the utmost speed. But there at the forgotten frontline death still
reigned supreme. I was met with embarrassment and confusion at the
Regional Party Committee office: "Nothing doing, we can't get around
to everything right away, we can't do it all ..."

＊＊＊

I didn't tell this whole sorry tale to reopen old, healed wounds, but to explain why I was on the fence about getting the ticket and why, on the day before reaching Stalingrad – the *Russia* was due to dock at five in the morning
– I couldn't settle down. I fretted my way around the deck all night.

I spent the whole trip from Moscow to Stalingrad alone. I had my own,
rather splendid cabin where I could shut myself off from the world. The on-
board tannoy wasn't working for some reason. The crew were courteous and
affable, and the few other passengers were quiet. Mostly of advancing years,
they passed their time dozing in deckchairs or looking out to shore through
binoculars. In the mornings I would work a little, take breakfast, then settle
into a deckchair to read *The Thibaults*.[57] When we made land I wandered

the streets of unfamiliar towns alone or I lolled about on beaches in my
trunks and admiring the Volga. It was the end of September, but still as hot
as summer. I felt serene in the way that only somebody who has nowhere to
hurry and knows that nobody will bother him can.

After Saratov I experienced a sudden bout of anxiety. My work was at a
dead-end, *The Thibaults* was dragging on and growing dull, and the other
passengers were getting on my nerves. How did they not get tired of sleeping
all day long, playing bridge, and running off to the quay to pig out at
every stop?

After dinner I tried to sit down and write some letters, but they came out
all tortured – full of flat platitudes and sorry attempts at wit. I tore them
up and headed for the buffet. It was empty. The attendant, a flat and slow
woman wearing bright lipstick, was counting something behind the counter.
My attempt to strike up a conversation with her did not prove successful. I
didn't fancy talking to the old fellow who looked like an accountant and was
nursing a mineral water. But the arrival of two young soldiers just before the
buffet was due to close piqued my interest. They took some time to count
out their money, whispering and looking askance at me as they did so. At
long last they bought a bottle of port. And that sealed their fate.

Half an hour later we headed for my cabin with some sustenance from
the buffet. They turned out to be glorious lads. The pair of them were from
the Volga. They were in good shape, had their fair hair cut short, and were
still wearing their white army collars. They had been demobbed and were
heading home. They still kept self-consciously smoothing out the folds on
their tunics and they were very shy. But I did the talking – about the war,
and, of course, about Stalingrad.

I still blush at the memory of that evening. I prattled on and on. I talked
about various events and about my comrades, explained our strategic situation, and sketched out maps. But really, I was holding forth. The lads pol-
itely chewed on their sausage and listened carefully without interrupting,
but I think they really just wanted to get some sleep. On and on I went,
persuading them of something, proving something, and sometimes, issuing
a ruminative, "Hmm, yes ..."

The lads left rather suddenly. They just got up and said, "We have to go.
Thank you." I immediately felt ashamed, especially of how I had persist-
ently and repeatedly insisted that they should go to the Mamaev Kurgan

with me: "I was a regimental engineer there, so I know everything about it."
They looked at one another and thanked me. Then they just got up and
said they had to go.

I couldn't sleep all night. I wandered around the deck, tried to doze off in
a deckchair, and looked out at the shore. We passed Dubrovka and Pichuga.
Our reserve rifle battalion had arrived here in autumn '41; we ended up
staying put the whole winter. We dug into the frozen ground. We bayoneted
dummies. We took apart rifles and put them back together. Then they sent
the soldiers to Crimea and sorted us officers out into units getting ready for
the front. That was before the spring offensive in Kharkov ...

Everything was unrecognizable. The hydroelectric station had changed
everything. We arrived at Stalingrad at five in the morning, right on sched-
ule. Afraid to meet my soldiers, I disembarked in a hurry.

※ ※ ※

I was in Stalingrad before, during, and after the fighting. I remember the
city as it felt and looked at every stage. I remember the morose, snowy city
when it was deep behind the lines, the flea market where I bought mittens
for my troops, and, next to the department store, the officers' mess that
everybody thought better than any restaurant. I remember the city when the
Germans were approaching in July. There were cannon in the parks and a
downed Junkers on the Square of Fallen Fighters. Streams of the wounded
flooded in from Kalach and Abganerovo. I remember that famous day of the
first mass bombing, 24 August, when everything was exploding and going
up in flames.[58] I remember that final day when we left the city: the ruins,
the snow, the prisoners trying to warm themselves around the fires, and the
bodies. The bodies, the tens of thousands of bodies. We didn't have the
energy to clear them away ...

Now a hulking, unfamiliar, totally foreign city lay before me. Not a trace
of the old remained. Not even the department store, which had been totally
subsumed by the new city. Well ... I suppose that's how it has to be. Almost
a quarter of a century has passed. A new, living city of large but uncharming
houses, of new streets, and of new names and new people, had grown up
over the ruined, dead city.

Figure 5.3 Visitors to the Mamaev Kurgan, fall 1964; the Motherland Calls statue is still under construction.

I climbed the grand colonnaded staircase leading to the Square of Fallen Fighters. Between the overgrown parks I could make out the silhouette of the railway station's tower and spire in the distance. It was all very triumphal, built in that 1940s style. The square was empty. Too early and, what's more, a Sunday, so there were barely any people. It wasn't hot. And there was no wind, so that meant no dust too.

I went to the Mamaev Kurgan on foot since the streetcars weren't running yet. As it so happens, I'd have gone on foot anyway. I walked along the Lenin Prospect. It used to be the Stalin Prospect, but it wasn't there at all before the war. It's extremely wide and long and stretches all the way along the Volga right to the Tractor Factory. Left, right, all over – housing, housing, and yet more housing. "Grocery." "Haberdasher's." "Footwear." "Stationer's." Again "Grocery." T-34 defensive turrets on concrete plinths mark where the front line had been.

The Pavlov House. A very ordinary house painted in pink, like they used to build in the thirties. There's a memorial plaque and one of those T-34 turrets out front, right on the Square of Soldiers' Glory in the midst of new housing developments. There are no slogans daubed on the houses nowadays, although back then there were so very many. Now it's all smeared over with pink paint.

I stood for a while then set off again. I was getting close to the Metal Fixings Factory – the left flank of our defensive line. Then there would be a wasteland and the meat plant beyond. First Battalion's command post had been in the meat plant. To the right, closer to the Volga, were some burned-down buildings and the oil terminal. The terminal had burned for a long time, eclipsing the sun with a dense black cloud. To the left lay the railway and the Mamaev Kurgan.

You could only get through the sector between the burned village and the railway at night, since there were shooting positions ahead, to the side, and all along it. There were streetcar wagons standing a little to the left, closer to the Metal Fixings Factory. It was all such a long time ago ... twenty-three years ago ...

I got to the Fixings Factory and suddenly had a thought: why not go in? Just on the off chance something from the past had been preserved? In the basement, where the command post had been, perhaps?

It was the usual story at the checkpoint: "Who are you? What d'you want? What's your business?" The watchman was highly suspicious but called somebody up anyway. Something similar had happened on my last trip. I had gone to see the Tractor Factory's power generator, but it turned out I needed a particular pass. I shook my documents at them, and they let me through, but only after an hour and a half's wait. Funny thing out of all that is that in 1942, when the Germans had been racing toward the factory, the generator's fate had been – quite literally – in my hands. The circuit breaker for the wires leading to the explosive laid under the generator's various units was right under my pillow. The generator's life and death could have been decided by my making a single movement.

After a rather laborious process – they wrote out every last word from my passport in a heavy cursive – I was issued the necessary pass. I went to see the deputy director. A courteous middle-aged fellow, he (against all my expectations) at once recognized the feelings that raged within me. He summoned one of his assistants and said, "Show the comrade around, but don't bore him. Then show him down to the basement. The comrade has some heroic personal memories of the place." He smiled at me obligingly.

The assistant, a young lad in overalls, carried out the orders to a tee. He didn't bore me, inquired out of politeness what it was like to fight in the factory, offered me a torch in parting, and said, "It's a bit, not to put too fine a point on it, full of junk down there. I can come if you like ..."

"You what, why?" I objected. "They didn't exactly sweep the parquet for us every day back then either ..."

He smiled and we said our goodbyes. Armed with the torch I set off down the dark staircase. The stairs had been there back in the day, but we never used them. It was much easier to slip through a window and down through a trapdoor into the basement.

I didn't spot the trapdoor right away. The room it was in really was full of junk, so I had to tidy up a bit before I found the entrance to the basement. The trapdoor didn't open right away either, but I came out the victor by using a metal bar. I carefully descended a creaky wooden staircase; I reckoned it was the same one, preserved from back then. Then I had to traverse a long corridor lined by pipes. At the end there would be an iron door and, behind that, the basement where the battalion command post had been.

The command post had been there for quite some time: from August '42, when the Germans had taken the water tanks on the *kurgan*'s summit, right to the end of November. When we took to the offensive, they relocated our battalion toward another, unnamed hill off to the right. I'd come here fairly often back in the day. The battalion had been commanded by a devilishly brave and dashing captain, Benyash. He was a marvellously handsome, curly-haired, cheerful chap, the scourge of Germans and the local nurses alike. He'd arranged parties for us here in the basement command post. We inspectors would find any pretext to "inspect" this particular battalion.

Benyash passed away at the end of October, maybe the beginning of November. He died a stupid death. Got hit by a stray mortar in the courtyard of the meat plant, where he'd arranged to meet one of his admirers. We cried over him for a long while. We buried him on the banks of the Volga. Then when the fighting ended in Stalingrad, we put a monument on the grave. I sketched a design and the regimental sappers built it. It was the first monument in Stalingrad. You could see it clearly from the Volga. It was made from wood, so it's already long gone.

So. I descended the staircase and started down the long corridor lined by pipes. Curiously enough it was tidier here than up above. Well, there was less junk at least. At one point there were a couple of dozen of what looked a lot like munitions crates stacked against the wall. We had called them "zinkys" back in the day. I opened one up and, to my great amazement, saw that it was filled with rounds. Even more shocking, they looked good as new. They must have just brought them. The oil hadn't even dried up. Just think: all these years and no one had bothered to come down here. I imagined how the occupants of this basement had been in a rush to move out. Some pragmatic sergeant major had probably taken one look at those crates and waved his hands: "Nah, do we really need to haul any more stuff around? They'll just give us new ones when we get there." So they've just been sitting there for twenty-three years.

As I approached the iron door, which was also preserved just the same as it had been back then, I felt a frisson of quiet excitement. It was as if I'd been here just recently, as if it were just yesterday. As if I and Benyash, or his commander, were about to head off to the line to examine the firing positions, just like we did yesterday. Or maybe we wouldn't go anywhere at all; we'd just have some tea and wind up the gramophone (Benyash had a whole heap of records). I pushed the door ...

Everybody has little black-outs, periods that they don't remember. But there are some days where you remember every single minute, every tiny detail, every word spoken, and every passing thought. I'd wandered right into one of those days. It'll be clear in my mind, just as clear as if it were on the big screen, for my whole life, right up until I draw my last breath. But I'll never know when it all happened. Was it yesterday or twenty-three years ago?

At the exact moment I pushed the door there was a great crash overhead and plaster came raining down from the ceiling. It felt like a 152mm shell was exploding somewhere up top. I shook, or maybe I took a step or two backward: I wasn't used to it anymore.

"Ooh, you're a bit nervy, Captain!"

That was said in jest. It was just a bit of fun, and not meant to hurt my feelings. I recognized the voice right away. Stretched out on his wooden bunk and propping his head up with one hand – his favourite pose – there was Captain Benyash, looking over at me with cheerful, lively eyes hidden behind black curls that were falling onto his forehead.

"Come in, come in, don't be shy! We're giving you the royal welcome today. We've got our hands on something special!"

There was another explosion overhead, but nobody except me paid any attention. At first, I thought that I must be on the set of a movie about the Great Patriotic War. But there were no directors, no cameramen, and no lighting rigs. The basement was cozily lit by a big kerosene lamp with a green shade. It lit up a chessboard lying on a bunk between the commander and his commissar. The commissar was a fit, good-looking Georgian whose name I never could remember. I could see by the flickering light of a lamp made from an artillery casing that in one corner a young and pockmarked signaller was reading something into a handset held up to his face. In the other corner a sergeant major was sorting through his laundry. Two or three privates had laid a roll of felt matting on the floor and were now asleep underneath their overcoats.

The lamp with the shade stood on a little table next to the battalion commander. I remember the little table – an exquisite, delicate thing with curved feet shaped like lions' paws – well. Over the table hung a great mirror, its golden frame adorned with cupids and wreaths. A photo of some curly-haired girl was stuck onto the mirror. It couldn't have been Benyash's wife; I think he was a bachelor.

Even now I could describe every last detail of the scene in the basement. I could even name the date – 5 October – on the calendar that hung between the mirror and a portrait of Stalin in his marshal's uniform cut out from a magazine. But I don't want to digress from what's important. Benyash saw how Stalin's portrait had caught my attention. Right away he got off his bunk and casually mentioned: "Don't worry, don't worry, no judgement here … Fancy a drink?"

Benyash wasn't afraid of anyone. Not even his commissar. I'm sure he would have stood in front of Stalin just the same as he permitted himself to stand before his regimental or divisional commander: not drawn to attention, one leg lolling around, his head held high, with arms gently bent at the elbow and hands clenched into fists. Not once had he been dressed down about that – not even by Chuykov, who was not a man known to appreciate such laxity. Wobbling around like a sailor on shore leave, Benyash crossed the basement, dug around in the corner, and returned with a bottle of cognac. It was French – Martell – with a load of medals and crests on the label.

"I've been holding on to this for a real connoisseur."

He sliced the foil off with a knife, then knocked the cork out with a single blow.

"I've got some lemon too. Go on, slice it, Sidorenko. And fetch the sugar. You and I, my dear engineer, are going to do this properly. Knives, forks … We'll lay out the tablecloth …" He glanced over at the commissar with an ironic look. "What you smirking at? Not for you, mate. You can't. Got to be an example for the lads." He winked at me. "Sit yourself down, engineer. Why are you so down in the dumps today? You don't seem yourself. Got a telling off, did you?"

I must have looked utterly bewildered. I sat down at the little table, glanced in the mirror, and only then saw that I was wearing my vest and an unbuttoned jacket. I looked just like the photo on my officer's identification card: no stubble, no wrinkles, no bags under my eyes. I kept catching myself glancing at the mirror. Looking at my own face – especially at the barber's – hadn't been much fun for a while. Now it seemed almost pleasant. I felt a little rush of confidence.

What did I feel in those first few minutes? Somehow or other I had got used to this unnatural state by the end of the day (I say "somehow" because I simply can't think of the right word for it), but at first, I wanted to rush off, scramble up that creaky staircase, and find that lad in the overalls. I was, by the by, still clutching the torch.

"Go on, give us a look," said Benyash as he reached for the torch. "Where'd you get it? Look at that! Chinese …"

"Chinese," I said. It was the first word I had uttered.

"Meliton, look, a Chinese torch! As if we didn't have enough between ours and the German ones."

The commissar came and took the torch. They went back and forth with it, shining its light all over the room, and marvelling at its power. Then the sergeant major and the signaller had a look. I couldn't help regret leaving my little "Falcon" transistor radio in my cabin.

"Righto," said Benyash, "that's enough larking around. Time to get to work. These are my scouts." He nodded at the sleeping soldiers. "They went out on a sortie last night and 'dekulakized' an officers' bunker.[59] You've probably never drunk anything like this, eh?"

I'd had something like it, or similar at least, in Italy. But that had been five years earlier, or rather, fifteen years later.

"That's a decent cognac," I said. We had another.

Benyash took pity on the commissar and let him try some. Then the sergeant major and the signaller too. Everybody sang the cognac's praises and sucked on their lemons. We spent a while discussing various drinks, comparing their quality and strength.

God only knows what I was going on about. I'm babbling on about trifles, but I want to talk about something else. I knew so much, after all: how it would all end, how long it would go on for, and what would come after. But how could I just spill it out? Most importantly, how could I protect Benyash from what awaits him? How could I warn him, keep him safe?

HQ rang to ask about the situation.

"Nothing doing. All quiet." Benyash spoke into the receiver. "No signs of the rodents here. Tonight, I'm going to … incidentally I've an engineer here. Wait, don't hang up." He turned to me. "Listen up, have you got any mines? I need some laying in a spot where there's a gap in the line."

I was in total confusion: did I have any mines or not?

"Alright!," Benyash shouted into the receiver, "Get a sapper, find out about the spuds, then get him to ring here."

Thus began my second period of military service. I'd forgotten so much; it was completely awful. I'd forgotten the names and attributes of the mines, I'd forgotten how to map out a minefield, and I'd forgotten how to operate the detonators. In a nutshell, I'd forgotten it all. At the end of the day, it didn't really matter. My platoon commander, who could do absolutely everything – a man you could rely on – arrived with two sappers and a sack of anti-personnel mines that evening. Still, I felt a real fool. I was desperately trying to remember everything about October '42. I had spent the whole of September getting the Tractor Factory's demolitions done. Then they took us away from that and I spent a handful of days on the left bank. Somewhere toward the end of September I landed up at this division and regiment. That means I'd only just arrived; it had been no more than ten days ago. Everything on Benyash's calendar up to 5 October had been crossed off. How many sappers had I had then? A fair few still. I think they were meant to be digging bunkers in the steep Volga bank for the regimental and staff commanders. I talked to the platoon commander Lisogor and found that I was right about that. The sappers were nearly done the first bunker, which they were already lining with wooden boards, and had just started work on the other.

Lisogor told me that, apparently, a delivery of spades and pickaxes was due that evening. A liaison from the divisional engineer had arrived with the news. Lisogor explained how important it was to grab the tools before the neighbouring regiments snapped them up. I knew what he was getting at: he'd palm the mine-laying off to me so he could go back to the bank. He didn't much like being at the line. I went along with it and let him go. At the end of the day, he'd brought his two best mine-layers, Shushurin and Sagaydak, and he really was peerless when it came to these sorts of things. If we wanted more spades, it was him and not me who should go back to the bank.

Just as he was about to head off, he noticed the cognac bottle and began to hover around Benyash, who immediately made it clear that nothing would come of his efforts.

"There's one more bottle. But we'll open it once the minefield's laid. Got it?"

Lisogor circled around and around, but then he left. It was evening; eight o'clock or so.

I'd had a splendid sleep before that. I had barely slept at all on the steamer the previous night, so when Benyash's sergeant major – a particular, bewhiskered old sort – had offered me a blanket and a mattress, I jumped at the chance. Apparently, there was a short bombardment in the day, but I didn't hear a thing. I was dead to the world. I only woke up because somebody began shaking me gently but insistently by the shoulder. I struggled to open my eyes. There was Valega, my orderly.[60]

"I brought you a meal, Comrade Engineer. Time to eat."

I hungrily demolished some cutlets and half a pot of pearl barley soup from the officers' mess. Just as I was giving the pot back to Valega, I realized everything was getting even more complex. Valega hadn't even been with me at Stalingrad. That was Titkov. Valega only appeared in summer '43 when I left hospital and went to the sapper battalion. It was only after the war that I made use of my artistic licence to transport him to Stalingrad – strictly speaking, into the *Trenches of Stalingrad*. I even wrote a short story, "Three Meetings," about it for *Novy mir*. And now this little chap with his big head, just as gloomy and displeased with my behaviour as ever, was standing right before me. Why did I get posted to the first battalion without him? What a mess …

I was confused, but I still asked about Titkov in passing. Where had he
gone and what was he doing?

"What do you mean where?" Valega was surprised. "You sent him to the
medical battalion yourself! He had jaundice …"

Right, jaundice. Lots of people at Stalingrad had jaundice. Jaundice and
night blindness. Vitamin deficiency or something. But I really can't remember Titkov ever being sick. He was a strong lad, a hardy Siberian.
Never under the weather.

The appearance of some scouts – regimental scouts, not the battalion
ones – interrupted my train of thoughts. Four of them – three privates and
their commander, Fishchenko – had turned up. Their mariners' vests peeked
out from under their tunics, and the commander was even wearing a sailor's
cap. They all looked rather handsome, but Fishchenko was especially dashing: the vest cut off to three fingers' width below the belly button; the boots
all bunched up into an accordion; the German knife with a ribbed bone
handle by his side. On the other hip, hanging almost over his posterior, was
a Walther in an exquisite holster but without its little German ramrod. By
that time the ramrod had become entirely too fashionable, so connoisseurs
of frontline haute couture "removed it from their weapon." All four were
quite fabulous: The Fabulous Four.[61]

They put down their submachine guns and sat down on the bunks without a word. Me and Vanka Fishchenko were at odds over some trifle or
another at that point. I outranked him and I was older (Vanka was only
nineteen). I had given him a dressing down, done a bit of the old, "About
turn, quick march!" He didn't forgive me for that for a while. We were both
wounded at Golaya Dolina on the River Donets a year later and ended up
in the same hospital in Baku. He admitted to me that he and his scouts had
planned to give me what for, just to make sure "you wasn't such a smar-
tassed *interlechual.*"

Now he was sitting on a bunk, knees spread wide, while he scowled and
tried not to look at me. I thought it was funny. You, you absolute viper, you
and me, had lain around in hospital almost four months, thick as thieves –
thick as a whole bloody gang of them – and then you slept on my couch like
quite the fine one for three years while you studied in the technical institute.
And this year you sent me a telegram with the most splendid greeting for
9 May: "Drinking to victory stop your health stop you understand stop

Vanka." And now you and your ugly mug are sitting here and you won't even look in my direction.

Then Benyash made things even more complex. Turned out he'd summoned the scouts to update me on the minefield's position and to check the gap in the line between Second and Third Company. I couldn't help thinking that maybe me and Vanya had had our barney right there and then, and maybe we could skip doing it the second time around? Then I remembered that we hadn't argued on the frontline. It had been back on the bank.

Somehow or another all eight of us – the four scouts, me and the sappers, and Valega, who was indispensable in every situation – set off for the frontline around midnight. Up until then nothing much had really happened. The Germans were behaving themselves and keeping quiet. They must have given themselves the day off. HQ had called a couple of times. Lisogor had phoned too, boasting about how he'd sweet-talked the neighbouring regiments, taken more of the tools than he was meant to, and had already swapped three spades for a German submachine gun and some wire cutters since ours had got nicked.

Benyash clapped me on the shoulder just as we were leaving and said, "Return victorious and I'll lay on a real spread. Just remember that this spot between the companies is absolutely lousy; the Germans are pouring rockets into it."

Needless to say, I was nervous. I hadn't laid a mine in twenty-three years. Before we left, I'd made Shushurin and Sagaydak prime and unprime a few mines as a sort of training session, but I couldn't shake off a horrid sense of fear. I knew it was silly, that nothing could kill me, that I'd survived the war. As for getting wounded … that would come later, in June of the following year. But still, what can you do? I was as nervous as a rookie who'd never seen live fire.

Climbing the creaky staircase out of the basement, I couldn't help catch myself secretly wishing I'd come out into the meat plant, and everything would be just as it was in the morning: tranquil, quiet, with cars coming and going and that killjoy watchman having a go. Alas, there was none of that. Just walls peppered by shrapnel and craters from mortar fire.

We made it right to the line quickly. As was the custom, we stopped for a smoke break, this time by a bombed-out train loaded with salt. Five months later, on the way out of Stalingrad, the platoon lads, led by Titkov, would

stuff their kit bags with the salt that had lay there all winter. Then they'd do
a roaring trade in Ukraine in exchange for milk, cream, and cottage cheese
… and then, in 1950 – no, later, when we were shooting *Soldiers* – me and
some lads from the crew would light up by the same embankment. I had
told them all about this trip to the line and we'd taken photographs as
mementos up by the water tanks. Well there you go. And now – off to the
frontline to get those damned mines down! Ugh!

Strictly speaking I didn't have to go and lay the mines, since it's not really
an engineer's job. Maybe I wanted to prove myself. Or maybe I was just
confused and didn't know what to say to keep my dignity intact. I probably
hindered more than I helped. But by and large it all worked out well, and
we didn't suffer any casualties. We got the mines down, and even managed
to figure out the right layout (a tough task at the front when there are no
landmarks). Then the scouts headed off, as they always did, to the artillery.
I sent the sappers home and made a beeline for Third Company. I seemed
to have pulled my right ankle, so I wanted to get it bound up nice and tight.

A young nurse – pretty, couldn't have been more than eighteen, but I
barely remember her – deftly bandaged my leg.

"Where's the company commander?," I asked. I didn't give a surname
because I'd forgotten who the commander was back then.

"He'll be here any moment," said the nurse. She looked at me inquisitively: "Fancy a tea? The strong stuff?"

I couldn't refuse. While she brewed the tea, I phoned Benyash and let him
know we'd planted the spuds.

"Congratulations. A well-deserved reward awaits. No dawdling now."

Alas, I never did get that reward. And I never saw Benyash again. It still
gnaws at my conscience: we sat there for two whole hours chatting all sorts
of guff, but I didn't warn him about what was most important, what awaited
him in a month's time, or about how to stay safe. I didn't say a word about
any of it. How could I? What could I say? Don't date the nurses? Or only
date them in safe places? Look out for yourself? Transfer to another battalion? Move the command post? That was the only thing I had managed to
say. I just about stuttered it out, but Benyash just made me laugh.

"A nice bit of safe real estate? Are you mad? Even Chuykov doesn't have
one. He's off sheltering in some pipe in the bank, but we've got space for a

whole dance troupe in here! And our ceiling's concrete, thank God. Anyway,
I'm like a cat, getting all snug in here." What could I say to that?

Anyway, the tea was ready. Just as it was poured into little aluminium
cups the company commander turned up. In the hours leading up to his arrival, I'd been fretting over how the past didn't totally match up with what
was happening now. I'd already made my peace with the fact of my return to
the past (they're even doing cybernetics these days, so nothing surprises me
now). But the little imprecisions and those shifts in time (the simultaneous
coexistence of Titkov and Valega, for instance) were throwing me for a loop.
The company commander's appearance muddied the waters even more.

A tall, narrow-shouldered, and bespectacled lieutenant lumbered into the
bunker, getting his greatcoat caught on something as he came in. His every
movement revealed his innately civilian nature. I knew right away who it
was. I knew it. I was stupefied. It was Farber.

I'll have to digress a little here. I've already mentioned the short story,
"Three Meetings," that I wrote a few years back. The story was about my
orderly Valega. Strictly speaking, it was about three Valegas: the one who
really existed, his literary double from *In the Trenches of Stalingrad*, and the
one played by Solovev on the big screen in *Soldiers*. Each existed in his own
right and to some extent eclipsed and replaced the others. I tried to clear up
these relationships in the sketch, but I think I just jumbled the whole thing
up even more. I don't think you could ever make sense of it all.

What's worse is that I'm afraid of us three – me, Valega, and Yury Solovev,
that is – meeting. We'd never manage to sort out the whole tangled web
then. We'd probably only tangle it up even more. But that's not the point.
The point is that such a meeting could happen. It could, even if I still don't
know a thing about the fate of the real Valega (I do hope he's still alive,
though).[62] But our three meeting is somehow, theoretically, a real possibility.

Let me get back to Farber. There's no chance of my meeting him. There's
no chance of it for the simple reason that he's a composite of other people I
met at different times and in different places. Yet here he is right in front of
me. He lumbered into the bunker, wiped his glasses, and sat down at my
table – or, more accurately, he sat down at a munitions crate covered with
an oilcloth.

"Have you been waiting long?" he asked.

"Nah. Five minutes or so."

"I went to check on the machine guns. One of them's not working again. It'll have to go to the artillery workshop. That's the third time. Keeps getting jammed for some reason ..."

I felt goosebumps running down my spine. I recognized that voice and manner of speaking, those long fingers, those clever, sad eyes, that gaze that flicked from one of confusion to one that turned inward. All that was Farber, or at least, Farber as I had imagined him. Yet that was simultaneously somebody else: Smoktunovsky. That's right. Smoktunovsky, Innokenty Smoktunovsky, who had played Farber in *Soldiers*, was sitting with me.[63] There he was, melancholically stirring his tea with a spoon ...

I was so confused for the first few minutes that I couldn't utter a word. Farber was neither a sociable nor a chatty type. He sipped his tea in silence and stared off somewhere into the distance. The nurse had perched herself in the corner and was rolling bandages. A clock was ticking somewhere. A private went in and out. Grabbed a spade and left. Didn't say a thing. Everybody was silent for some reason. It began to get awkward. Truth be told I, or rather Kerzhentsev, had always felt uneasy around Farber.[64] But this wasn't Farber, it was Smoktunovsky – a cheerful, witty, funny man. And now he was about to push his mug away, give me a sly look and a wink, and say, "Right! Enough of this nonsense, we've had our fun, but that's quite enough! Let's head to the buffet!" But he didn't give me that sly look and he didn't wink. He just stared into the distance, sipped his tea, and absentmindedly drummed his fingers on the table.

I got up.

"I have to go."

I felt that it was, at last, time to get my thoughts in order. I could head to Benyash's, lie down, stick my head under a greatcoat, and try to figure it all out. The maps and the logbooks could wait until tomorrow – the divisional engineer would survive for a while yet.

"I have to go," I said.

"And your leg? What about your leg?" interjected the nurse.

"Are you wounded?" asked Farber.

"It's nothing. Just a sprain. An old injury."

Farber stood up.

"Then I'm coming with you."

"There's no need."

"Yes, there is. You can show me where you stuck the spuds while we're at it."

We set off. It was dark. There were no stars, just some muddy, fuzzy spots in the sky. It was all quiet. A machine gun chattered away somewhere in the distance. We traversed the shallow trenches (we never did get them to a proper depth, even by the end of the war) and came out into a gully. We began to slowly clamber down into it. We were both silent, but somewhere near the end of the gully, Farber said, "There are a lot of little craters here. Be careful."

We took a smoke break by a ruined bridge. That's the tradition: smoke break by the train wagons on the way out; smoke break by the little bridge on the way back. Farber used the light from his smoke to look at the time on his watch.

"There'll be a concert in a minute," he said. "They've put up a loud-speaker on the other bank. They broadcast the news and then a concert. They did it at the same time yesterday."

"From Moscow?"

"Guess so."

A line of a dozen or so soldiers walked past carrying mines and equipment. You could hear the crunch of the gravel underneath their feet. They were cursing as they stumbled. They'd be back twenty minutes later. Then, another half an hour later and back they'd go, stumbling and swearing in the darkness, swearing at the bits of iron scattered everywhere, at Hitler, and at the sergeant major who'd insisted they each carry four mines at once. They'd do somewhere between six and eight trips that night. All the ammo and equipment would be used the next day, then come sundown it'd be back off to the bank, from the bank to the line, and from the line to the bank.

"How are things in the company?" I asked.

"Fine. Nothing much has changed," answered Farber coldly.

"How many men've you got now?"

"Same as before. We'll never get more than twenty or so. There's almost nobody left from the original lot."

"What about reinforcements?"

"Pull the other one!"

"And the youngsters?"

"They're seeing a rifle for the first time. One of them got killed yesterday. A grenade blew up in his hands."

"Mmm," I said. "Lousy little contraptions, they are."

Farber didn't answer. He got out his tobacco box, rolled another smoke, and lit it from his own butt. Just for a second his thin face, his hollow cheeks, his bony nose, and the folds around his mouth were lit up.

"Has it never struck you that life is a funny old business?" he asked.

"Life or war?"

"Life. The whole thing."

"That's a tough question. A fair amount of funny stuff does happen. What were you thinking about, in particular?"

"Nothing in particular. I'm just philosophizing. Summing things up, in a way."

"Isn't it a bit soon for that?"

"Maybe a little. But you can still sum something up. Do you never think back, for instance, to your past life?"[65]

Stop! That doesn't need repeating! It's all there, in the book, and in *Soldiers*. The dialogue between Farber and Kerzhentsev was shortened and moved to right before the attack in the film, of course. But Smutnovsky and Safonov acted the scene splendidly – a real gala performance. Farber and I did the book version, not the one from the cinema, word for word. We repeated every word and phrase just as they were thought up and written twenty years ago – or, more accurately, we re-created them, just as if they had been spoken for the first time by the destroyed bridge at that exact moment on that dark and inexplicably quiet night. And then the *andante cantabile* from Tchaikovsky's Fifth reached us just at the same time as we heard the monotone drone of a three-engine heavy bomber we had nick-named the "Tuberculosis."

"Funny, isn't it?" said Farber.

"What?"

"The whole lot ... Tchaikovsky, the greatcoat, the Tuberculosis ..."

Then the concert ended. We sat in silence for a little while longer before heading back to Farber's. I didn't want to leave him. I don't know how other people feel, but for me, a person who can look at himself critically and see the bad even in his good side is always alluring. There's nothing worse than a man who's too confident. Or to put it bluntly, too *self*-confident. In war a lot of things become very clear, and war showed me that I'm right about that. The critical fought better than the self-confident because they de-

manded something of themselves before asking anything of their subordi-
nates. That's how Farber was. Smoktunovsky knew it too, and he played
it to perfection.

That's all well and good, but who was I with now? Who was with me as
I climbed the ravine up to the line? Does it even matter? It's just that I
wouldn't want to part with the man I'd just sat with by the destroyed bridge,
the man whose confession I'd heard. More important, now I had the desire
to start talking – up until then I'd mostly been listening – and to reveal what
I know now. I wanted to tell it all to him, to them, to the people sitting on
the Mamaev Kurgan, to the real and the fictional people, to the living and
the dead friends from what were perhaps the most meaningful years of
my life. Would I be within my rights to do that?

We climbed the slope slowly and in silence. Somewhere off to the right
another machine gun began chattering away. Several rockets – German, of
course – went up then slowly descended, trailing sparks behind them. It got
even darker.

Good God, how could I get my thoughts in order? Just give me ten minutes to lie down, close my eyes, and think. I'd lain down at Benyash's, lain
down, closed my eyes, then fallen asleep. I'd had so many minutes, so many
hours, to do that on the steamer! The deckchair, the fresh air, and the gulls
hovering along the bank ... and what did I think about? About the screen-
play I had to finish, about how I had to do it but I couldn't, about the
director who'd make the film, about future editors, about upstairs, and
about the ministry who'd try to convince me to do this and not that – even
though I knew that it had to be done just so. But really, I mostly just sat in
the deckchair, and did some reading, looked out from the boat a bit, and
tried not to think about anything. Then I had tried to give those soldiers
a good lesson: "That's how your fathers fought, you won't find that in the
books, and there's less and less of us fathers left ..."

But I didn't manage to get my thoughts in order. Our walk was coming
to an end. We had made it back to the bunker.

And here it is ... I've got to the most complex moment in this whole astonishing story. Maybe everything would have taken a different turn – God
only knows how it would have ended – if Farber hadn't got back to the
bunker and asked the signallers whether HQ had phoned.

"Nah," the signaller, who was clearly half-asleep, lazily answered. "HQ

didn't call. It's not just Fritz taking a break." Then he remembered something and added: "Ah, yes, Lieutenant Kerzhentsev phoned and asked if
you'd be long."

Lieutenant Kerzhentsev? What on earth? Impossible. Stuff and nonsense.
It's one thing to make things up, to alter, to imagine, to add, to move, but
Kerzhentsev and I are one and the same man. Truth be told I wasn't even
sure who they took me for. They didn't use my first or last names, just "engineer," "comrade engineer," or "lieutenant." I wouldn't have been surprised
if they'd called me Yury – except that Yury himself had phoned here and
might have done it again, or he might even have arrived and tried to shake
my hand, at any moment. You've got to admit we'd really have been at a
dead-end then.

I put it to Farber right to his face.

"Who's this Kerzhentsev?"

"What do you mean, who?" Farber said in surprise. "He's the second
battalion commander."

"He's called Yury?"

"That's right."

"And he's from Kiev?"

Farber looked at me uncomprehendingly.

"I don't understand your questions. What do you mean by them?"

"I mean what I mean. Can we be serious for a second?"

Farber kept on looking at me uncomprehendingly.

"Please …"

I'm going to relate the relevant parts of the whole of the subsequent conversation verbatim, even though I didn't write a single word of it down at
the time or afterward. Even today I can hear every last note of Farber's quiet
little voice. I can see his badly shaved face lit up by the dull flicker of the artillery casing lamp, I can see his eyes, his hands, and the dishevelled, long,
uncut hair falling onto his face. I can easily remember the little signaller, as
if he were sitting right in front of me now. At first, he was dozing, his head
in his hands, then he started to listen in, then even to take part in our conversation. His ears stuck out from his perfectly round, shaven head in a
funny way. He had a funny name too: Landrin. I remember a sudden rustling coming from the corner in the middle of the conversation. It was

Farber's sergeant major. He looked at us with sleepy, uncomprehending eyes and said, "What is it she wants from me? What is it? What is she, my wife?" Then he fell asleep again. In a nutshell, I remember everything. Every last minute and every last word.

So. Farber said, "Go ahead."

I gathered every last ounce of sobriety and sense and began.

"I ask that you treat our conversation with the utmost seriousness. A lot – no, likely all – of what I'm going to say is going to seem odd or impossible … maybe downright crazy. I won't be surprised if you think I've lost it, but you'd be wrong. I'm not crazy, despite the crazy situation I've found myself in. I can't deal with it on my own. So I'm turning to you. I have faith in you."

This whole opening tirade was delivered very slowly. I picked out and stressed every word. Farber listened in silence. At the end he nodded his head as if to say, "I'm listening."

I went on: "What would you say, what would you think of me, for instance, if I were to tell you that this very morning I was standing on the deck of the glorious, snow-white turbo cruiser *Russia?* That I leaned on the railing and watched the boat dock at a quay emblazoned with the word 'Volgograd' in enormous letters?"

"Well now," smiled Farber. "First I'd be astonished, then I'd ask you, 'What's Volgograd?'"

"Volgograd is Stalingrad. It was renamed in 1961 after the 22nd Party Congress."

I screwed up my eyes before I fired that phrase out. I had expected something of a reaction: incomprehension, embarrassment, an awkward smile, or a suggestion to report to the medical battalion. But Farber didn't even smile. He simply said: "Right, so what's happening now, what's that called? The Battle of Volgograd?"

"Can you believe that at some point people really do call it that?"

We were silent for a few seconds before I screwed up my eyes again and fired a second shot:

"Out of everything I said, the only thing that struck you was the renaming of Stalingrad? Nothing else?"

"Beg your pardon, but you didn't say anything else."

"No, I told you about the 22nd Congress." Silence again. "There was a 21st and a 20th too. And the cult of personality was exposed. And before that a whole host of other events, including victory over Germany and the defeat of the Germans right here at Stalingrad."

Farber perked up.

"Defeat? Victory? I didn't doubt it for a second. Believe me. Not even a second. But when? When?"

"Here in Stalingrad on 2 February 1943. And the defeat of Germany itself was in 1945, on 9 May ..."

Farber counted it out on his fingers.

"October, November, December, January ... It's still four months. That's quite a while ..."

Landrin, the signaller, piped up. "D'you know how many folks are going to get slaughtered in the next four months? What a terrifying thought." He added, "Especially if they keep sending in the young lads and the old-timers. They can't stop dropping their rifles."

I couldn't hold back: "Listen here, Farber, do you think I'm playing some sort of game with you here?"

"If it's a game then it's a very entertaining one. But I don't think you're playing a game at all."

"Then what do you think?"

"Nothing at all for the time being. I'm waiting."

"For what?"

"For you to explain."

At that point the sergeant major woke up, and a private came in to say that the platoon commander was asking why dinner still hadn't been brought up from the bank. The signaller phoned through and was told that the dinner was on its way. As the private left, Farber looked at me with a smile (at least, it seemed to be a smile), gentled touched my shoulder, and quietly spoke:

"I said that I was waiting for your explanation, but I'm not. I'll accept that there are some things in this world that can't be explained. What, for instance, is ball lightning? Or signal fading? What was the Tunguska meteor? What's telepathy? I, for example, believe in telepathy, I believe that thoughts can be transmitted at a distance. I knew a man who swore he was living a second life. First time around he'd lived into his sixties and was put to death by the *oprichniki*.[66] Everybody thought he was nuts, but I found it fascinat-

ing to talk to him, especially when he'd talk about Prince Kurbsky, whom –
since he had been a Muscovite baron – he'd known well. Perhaps he really
did know him ..."

"You don't really think that I'm ..." I began, but Farber cut me off.

"God forbid. I don't think anything. I just want to make this easier for
you. I want you to understand that I don't believe in your morning – what
was it, *turbo cruiser*? – any less than I believe in the intersection of parallel
lines. They may intersect at infinity, but intersect they do. We're told they
intersect, so what can we do but believe? We believe in infinity, but we can
neither comprehend nor explain it."

"Thank you," I said.

"You don't need to thank me," Farber replied in the same vein. "You need
to thank the Germans, it's them letting us speak so calmly today."

(Incidentally, I must say that the unnatural quiet at the front had me in a
constant state of wonderment the whole day and night. I hadn't touched my
book for many a year, but after all this I rushed to reread it. I noticed that
the Germans actually had given us two days off at the beginning of October.
They must have been giving their equipment a clean. There weren't even any
planes, excepting the Messers.)

"Right then," continued Farber. "We haven't a minute to waste. It's almost
morning. You mentioned the cult of personality. What is that exactly? You
can't be talking about ..." He ground to a halt.

"That's right."

"Unbelievable ..."

Farber turned to Landrin and said: "You'd best be off to bed. I can take
phone duty."

"Getting in the way, am I?"

"When you're told to go to bed, you do it, soldier."

That was the first hint of a commanding tone I'd ever heard in Farber's
voice.

Landrin reluctantly left.

"This is all too much for him. Best he heads off to bed. He's got quite the
mouth on him, too. God knows what he'll yap about to the rest of the regiment." After a short silence, he added, "And were there other changes too?
Or, rather, will there be any?"

"There were. Big ones, too."

I tried to get my thoughts in order, but they were unravelling fast. There
was nobody else in the bunker. It was just me and Farber. This was it. It was
time. I couldn't put it off any longer. I had to tell him everything I knew,
everything that those of us who'd stayed alive had seen and heard. But
Farber didn't let me.

"Hold up. Don't rush. Maybe that's about enough for one night. You can
think what you like, you can think I'm sticking my head in the sand, but I'm
not so sure I ought to know everything. I need to discover it for myself – by
living. But right now we're at war, and that's the be all and end all, right?
We've still got another four months of fighting to get through right here.
Up 'til February, right?"

"Right. Until 2 February. Then you'll freshen yourself up a bit, get some
reinforcements, then you'll be over at Kupyansk in Ukraine until July."

Farber got out a round red tobacco box – we all had the same ones back
then – and put it on the table.

"D'you have a bit of newspaper?"

I dug around in my pockets and, much to my surprise, found a leather
wallet embossed with a picture of a deer I'd bought in Tallinn last year.
There was a letter of credit and a few stamps inside. I'd got them – part of
a stamp issue for the twentieth anniversary of the end of the war – a few
months back on 9 May at the Central Telegraph Office in Moscow.

"Here's some small proof that I really was on the turbo cruiser *Russia*
this morning."

Farber took the stamps from my extended hand. Big and square, with
gold lettering, they had the dates 1945–1965 and famous pictures from the
war on them. Yuon's *Victory Salute* – all Kremlin, Red Square, and sky on
fire – was on the sixteen-kopeck stamp.[67] Farber stared at it for a long time
before he said anything.

"I want to live. Just imagine. I wish I could ..."

I remembered that Smoktunovsky had fought at Stalingrad and before
I knew it I'd blurted out: "You'll live, Kesha. You'll live."

"What did you say?"

"You'll live, I tell you. I know it for a fact."

Farber raised his eyes to look at me.

"What? You and I meet after the war?"

"We do. Right here in Stalingrad."

Farber took off his glasses and stared off into the corner in silence for a few moments.

"Mmm, it's all … rather odd. Odd indeed."

He put his glasses back on and began to inspect another stamp, a reproduction of Fyodor Bogorodsky's *Glory to Fallen Heroes*. A dead sailor is lying, covered in a greatcoat, on what's presumably a stretcher. His mother is bent over him. In the foreground, an officer wearing an elegant cape and a whole array of medals is down on one knee. Two soldiers in capes and helmets sternly hold submachine guns in the background. At the very back hangs an enormous banner. Maple leaves are floating down from somewhere or other. I'm not describing this stamp that had just happened to turn up because I'm some diehard stamp collector. I'm describing it because it was this very stamp that distracted Farber and me from the conversation that each of us was utterly desperate to have, but which terrified us both so much that we were putting it off.

"Know what I wondered when I looked at this splendid stamp?" said Farber after a moment's pause. "I wondered what people will say about us when the war's over. How will they explain things?" I could have answered that question, but I stayed quiet. I wondered what Farber would say next.

"Imagine some time passes. Ten, twenty, thirty, a hundred years. People start visiting this spot where you and I are sitting right now. Schoolchildren, pioneers, tourists. There's a tour guide with them. What's he going to say? What will they see? How much of it will they really understand?"

"It's a bit hard to explain what they'll see." I recalled my first trip back to the Mamaev Kurgan. "But they'll obviously hear about the fighting and the heroism, and all about the steadfast Stalingraders …"

"That's all talk. It's all wrong. I know exactly how to explain it: leave everything – the trenches, the dugouts, the bunkers – leave it all as it is. People could come and see and say: 'So that's how they fought. They sat in their little burrows, beating back the attacks with their three-liners.[68] They grumbled and swore, they smoked one fag between three of them, crawled around face down in the dirt, slept through every bombardment going, and, if I'm getting it right, that's how we won the war.'"

He carefully and accurately tore in two a sheet from the calendar the sugar was on, then proffered one half to me.

"There's more in heaven and earth, Horatio, but it's too soon to talk about that. Let's have a smoke."

"You're a Shakespeare fan," I said.

Farber smiled for just the second time.

"I'll let you in on a secret. Back in the day I auditioned for the theatre school and totally bombed it. But I still adore Shakespeare."

He looked at his watch. "Oho! Almost time to get up. Should we get a snooze in? I'm a bit worried the Hun might try and make up for the quiet day today."

I looked at my watch as well. It was quarter to seven. The smart thing would have been to use the last hour of darkness to go back to the bank or to see Benyash, but I suddenly felt so exhausted after such a big day, after laying the mines, and after the late-night conversation, that I couldn't bring myself to even think of a long trip like that.

"I'll stay here," I said to Farber, "if you won't chuck me out?"

"Of course I won't." He looked off to the side: "Will the sergeant major's bunk do? He's probably had a hundred and forty winks by now!"

The sergeant major coughed as he got up and headed outside. I followed him. It was getting light. The left bank of the Volga was outlined clearly. Our airfields were somewhere over there, way beyond the horizon. The first rays of the sun brought the frenetic buzz of the Ilyushins racing overhead. They'd be back, their chassis riddled with holes and their tales blown off, almost immediately, and we'd be lucky if they didn't crash into us with their undercarriages. Only half, maybe fewer still, would make it back at all. The Messers would be circling over the Volga for a long while yet. Somewhere far off, past Akhtuba, a black mushroom cloud from a burning plane would float upward.

And then the Ju-87s (the Germans called them *Stukas*, but we called them "singers" or "musicians") – red-beaked, web-toed birds ready for the hunt – would show up. They'd dive in at us and drop their bombs, timing the doses for the maximum psychological effect and blaring their horrid sirens all day long from first to last light. The whole of October would carry on like that. The beginning of November too. The last bombing raid was on 13 November. That was Heinkels and Junkers 88s. They made three trips, bombing indiscriminately without even bothering to dive in, before they left for good. And then our counterattack had come on 19 November.

Why didn't I just tell all of that to Farber? Was I afraid? Afraid of what? Did I feel to blame in some way? To blame for what? After all, it's easier to fight when you know you're going to win, and I'd already told Farber about that.

Farber of course knew about all the challenges of our prewar life without my telling him. But we didn't talk about that at all. We didn't mention the friends and fathers who couldn't pick up a rifle to defend the Motherland like we did. We avoided the topic. But now? I could tell you a lot of things that Farber didn't know: about people returning from the camps, about the restoration of honour and dignity to those who, alas, never came back, and about the many things that have changed in our lives since 1953. But how could I explain all of that in the single hour left before the dawn, when one might be called on to rouse the soldiers and send them into the breach? No. Farber was obviously right. You have to discover these things for yourself – by living.

A horn sounded low and weak somewhere down by the foot of the *kurgan*. I shuddered. Then I heard the sound of wheels on rails. The steam engine's rattle rang in my ears for a long while. At long last silence returned, then a cock began to crow. Three bloody times ... Jesus, if I don't go to sleep right now, I'm going to lose my mind ...

But I wasn't fated to sleep that night. As for Farber's bunker, the same bunker I'd just left, where my foot had been bandaged, where I had drunk tea and spoke with Farber? As for that unassuming little bunker with its flickering lamp, snoring sergeant major, and jug-eared Landrin? Well, none of that was there anymore. Just like that it had ceased to exist. No sign of it. Not a trace ...

That said, in front of me, just to the left of the water tanks, something enormous and unfamiliar reared up. From far off it looked like a great craggy rock or a ruined building. From a bit closer, I could make out the gigantic image of a half-clothed figure holding a submachine gun. I was terrified ...

✳ ✳ ✳

Later that day I was leaving my cabin and I bumped right into my soldier lads. They said a polite hello and walked on by, but then one of them – the older one – turned around to me.

"Excuse me, but we'd really like ... You can say no if you want ..."

We couldn't find a table in the restaurant so we had to share with an old man who was working his way sadly through a sturgeon and a half-empty decanter of what looked like port.

"Are we interrupting?," asked the older soldier.

"Not in the slightest. Might as well sit down now you're here."

We raised a toast to the hero-city we'd just departed. Then the younger soldier, hoping to spark a conversation that didn't seem to want to get going, asked, "How did you cut up your arms like that?"

I looked at my arms, which were indeed covered in scratches.

"On the Mamaev Kurgan," I said.

"Were you there?"

"I was."

"Did you see the Shah?"[69]

"No."

"We did."

"What was he like?"

"Nothing special. Decent size. Grey hair. Dark glasses. Born in 1919, apparently. The queen was with him. What black eyes she has …"

"She's an architect by training," our neighbour said glumly.

"That's right, an architect," readily volunteered the younger of the soldiers. "They say she studied in Paris."

We talked about the Shah and his wives, his entourage, his cars, the wreaths, and the guard of honour for a while. Then the conversation started to dry up. I was silent and the soldiers felt awkward. But then our gloomy neighbour, who'd ordered himself another decanter, suddenly livened up a bit:

"When I look at you young 'uns, the defenders of our motherland, know what I think? You paid a visit to the sites of great battles and bloodshed, the places where people gave their lives so that you'd have it easy. They did it for you, not for themselves. And you didn't look at a thing except the Shah and his queen. Well, the Shah came and laid a wreath. Everyone lays a wreath, so what? You just stood there and gawped."

"It was our first time, it was interesting …" the soldiers said timidly.

"What was interesting? Getting a look at a tsar? I fought on that *kurgan* too. I had to. Well, I didn't fight on the *kurgan* itself, but I did go there a few times. It's unrecognizable now. It's not a *kurgan*, it's a symbol of your fathers, of heroes."

That offended the lads. "Don't lecture us," said the older one. "We know what happened here just as well as anybody else."

Our neighbour fell silent and, clearly embarrassed at how sharply he'd spoken, proffered a packet of Kazbeks.

"We don't smoke, grandfather. We quit ages ago. It's been two years already. I don't cough at all in the mornings these days. Don't believe me?" – he looked at me – "You should try it. You're chain-smoking them; there's always one in your mouth. It's no good. No good at all, and you're no spring chicken. You read books and the papers, so you obviously know about the damaging effects of nicotine."

"And of vodka." I looked at my lads. They could barely contain their laughter. "Maybe we'll do the same as yesterday and head to my cabin, eh?"

Off we went to my cabin. But I didn't mention the war again. We just drank a reasonable quantity for three people and then we parted ways. I made a compress from the remaining vodka. My ankle was still swollen and had now turned purple.

※ ※ ※

I could finish this extremely strange story on that idyllic note. But I simply must tell you about another incident that has an important bearing on the story. I bumped into Smoktunovsky about a month and a half, maybe two months, later in Moscow. He wasn't alone. A man who introduced himself as Vasily Grigorevich was with him.

He wasn't young – sixty, I'd say – and was very pale. He had a high forehead and a somewhat ironic look in his eyes. He was dressed simply – you might even say slovenly, like a been-there-done-that, journeyman actor. But what really got me was a ring adorned with a heart-shaped seal on his index finger. He kept twisting it back and forth, almost mechanically, as we talked. I wanted to have a really good look at it, but I was embarrassed to get up close.

After Vasily Grigorevich had gone, Smoktunovsky said to me: "He's an interesting fellow. Used to be an actor. I'm told he wasn't bad. Now he's a prompter. Keeps himself to himself, but he's a decent sort. Well read, but you can tell that, right? But he's got this crazy thing. Did you see that ring?

He claims that no less than Prince Kurbsky himself gave it to him. Spend some time with him and you won't want for the sorts of tales Count Aleksey Konstantinovich Tolstoy would have given his right arm for ..."[70]

But I haven't met Vasily Grigorevich again. Perhaps we'll meet on the off chance someday. Still an interesting tale, mind. But you won't surprise me with interesting encounters like that these days.

ACKNOWLEDGMENTS

Masha and Varya, for love, support, and beautiful evening concerts.

I am especially grateful to the family members of the frontline correspondents who have given advice, support, and permission to include materials here: Leila Koroteeva and Aleksey Koroteev, Ekaterina Simonova and Aleksey Simonov, Elena Ermakova, Aleksandr Nilin, and Viktor Kondyrev. My thanks also to Natalya Dolmatovskaya, who granted permission to use her mother Natalya Bode's extraordinary frontline photographs, and Vera Kavetskaya, Sergey Ivanyuk, Ekaterina Klyukova, and Aleksandr Gaidashev for their help with other illustrations.

Thank you to Ollie Heppenstall and Sean Sykes, my readers and chief military advisers, for their enthusiasm and support.

Others who have provided work in progress, advised on aspects of my research, or generally been there for me: Robert Chandler, Donna Orwin, Svetlana Ishevskaya, Matthew Ford, Hugh and Philip Garner, Susan Grunewald, Allyson Edwards, Iain MacGregor, Nick Budd, Prit Buttar, Dustin Du Cane, Bob Denham, and, of course, my parents.

Full credit to Richard Ratzlaff for his editorial skills and belief in the potential of this oddity of a book. Many thanks to his colleagues at McGill-Queen's University Press who have helped bring the work to publication.

There are many others who've responded to my questions about military history, translation, cultural specificities, and a million more topics. You've all been instrumental in bringing this project to completion. I owe you all a pint (two if you're lucky).

"On the Volga," "In the Gully on the Steppe," "In Stalin's City," "The Battle of Stalingrad," and "Today in Stalingrad," used by permission of the Vasily

NOTES

ARCHIVAL KEY

APRF   *Arkhiv Prezidenta Rossiiskoi Federatsii* (Archive of the President of the Russian Federation)

HPSSS   Harvard Project on the Soviet Social System

MIDV   *Muzei istorii Dal'nego Vostoka imeni V.K. Arseneva* (V.K. Arsenev Historical Museum of the Far East)

RAN   *Arkhivy Rossiiskoi akademii nauk* (Archives of the Russian Academy of Sciences)

RGALI   *Rossiiskii gosudarstvennyi arkhiv literatury i iskusstva* (Russian State Archive of Literature and Art)

RGASPI   *Rossiyskii gosudarstvennyi archiv sotsialno-politicheskoy istorii* (Russian State Archive of Socio-Political History)

TSAMO   *Tsentral'nyi arkhiv Ministerstva oborony* (Central Archive of the Ministry of Defence)

TSDNIVO   *Tsentr dokumentatsii noveishei istorii Volgogradskoi oblasti* (Centre for Documentation of Modern History of Volgograd Province)

NOTES TO PREFACE

1 "Kazhdyi vtoroi zhitel' Kieva pokinul gorod – Klichko," *Gordon UA*, 10 March 2022, https://gordonua.com/news/war/kazhdyy-vtoroy-zhitel-kieva-pokinul-gorod-klichko-1599267.html.
2 Antony Beevor, *A Writer at War: A Soviet Journalist with the Red Army, 1941–1945*, trans. Luba Vinogradova (New York: Vintage books, 2007)

contains some excerpts of Grossman's wartime writing. Jochen Hellbeck, *Stalingrad: The City That Defeated the Third Reich* (New York:
Public Affairs, 2016) includes a translation of Grossman's Stalingrad
story "On the Axis of the Main Attack."

3 K.S. Simonov, "Letter to Comrade Ianin," January 1945, f.1814, op.1, ed.
khr.596, RGALI.

NOTES TO INTRODUCTION

1 A *kurgan* is a hill formed over an ancient burial site. That much of the
worst fighting took place on what was already effectively a cemetery
was symbolically significant.

2 "Putin v Volgograde: Ravniatsia na podvig otstoiavshikh Stalingrad!,"
EurAsia Daily, 2 February 2018,
https://eadaily.com/ru/news/2018/02/02/putin-v-volgograde-ravnyat-
sya-na-podvig-otstoyavshih-stalingrad.

3 "Kazhdyi dom Stalingrada – krepost!," *Izvestiia*, 27 September 1942.

4 "Dokladnaia zapiska zaveduiushchego orginstruktorskim otdelom
Stalingradskogo obkoma TsK VKP (B) Tingaeva v TsK VKP (B) Sham-
bergu o rabote po vosstanovleniiu goroda," July 1943, f.17, op.88, d.226,
RGASPI.

5 A period of whitewashing suggesting that the German soldiers of
Stalingrad were innocent victims took place in postwar Germany. See
Christina Morina, *Legacies of Stalingrad: Remembering the Eastern
Front in Germany Since 1945* (Cambridge: Cambridge University Press,
2011).

6 Katerina Clark, *The Soviet Novel: History as Ritual* (Chicago: University
of Chicago Press, 1981), 194, 199.

7 See Ian Garner, "The Myth of Stalingrad in Soviet Literature, 1942–
1963" (PhD diss., University of Toronto, 2018), 246–8.

8 For example, the untranslated postmodernist musings of Viktor Ero-
feev's *Five Rivers of Life* (*Piat' rek zhizni*; Moscow: Podkova, 1998), the
bizarre satire of Sergey Zverev's *A Bomb for Generalissimus Stalin*
(*Bomba dlia Generalissimusa Stalina*; Moscow: Eksmo, 2006), or the
string of nationalist "sci-fi Stalingrad" works released by publishing
house Eksmo in the 2010s.

9   Konstantin Simonov, *Sto sutok voiny* (Smolensk: Rusich, 1999), 4–7.

10 K.S. Simonov, *Raznye dni voiny* (Moscow: Molodaia gvardiia, 1977), 6–7. On military unpreparedness, see Peter Whitewood, *The Red Army and the Great Terror: Stalin's Purge of the Soviet Military* (Lawrence: University Press of Kansas, 2015).

11 A.Ia. Livshin and I.B. Orlov, *Sovetskaia propaganda v gody Velikoi Otechestvennoi voiny: "kommunikatsiia ubezhdeniia" i mobilizatsionnye mekhanizmy* (Moscow: ROSSPEN, 2007), 100–7.

12 "Molotov Addresses the Soviet People," 22 June 1941, RG-60.0880, US Holocaust Memorial Museum.

13 Peter Kenez, *The Birth of the Propaganda State: Soviet Methods of Mass Mobilization, 1917–1929* (Cambridge: Cambridge University Press, 1985), 8.

14 Louise McReynolds, "Dateline Stalingrad: Newspaper Correspondents at the Front," in *Culture and Entertainment in Wartime Russia*, ed. Richard Stites (Bloomington: Indiana University Press, 1995), 29.

15 A.Yu. Davydov, "Sovetskoe Informbiuro: Organizatsionnaia struktura na nachal'nom etape Velikoi Otechestvennoi voiny," in *SSSR vo Vtoroi Mirovoi voine (1939–1945gg.)*, ed. S.V. Vinogradov and A.V. Venkov (Saint Petersburg: Politekh. universitet, 2020), 124.

16 As qtd in Davydov, "Sovetskoe Informbiuro," 125.

17 David Ortenberg (Oral History), 1997, 19550, Imperial War Museum; "Ukaz Prezidiuma Verkhnogo Soveta," 11 August 1944, f.33, op.686043, ed.khr.103, TSAMO; Matthew E. Lenoe, *Closer to the Masses: Stalinist Culture, Social Revolution, and Soviet Newspapers* (Cambridge, MA: Harvard University Press, 2009), 133.

18 Davydov, "Sovetskoe Informbiuro," 127.

19 D.I. Ortenberg, *Stalin, Shcherbakov, Mekhlis i drugie* (Kodeks: Moscow, 1995), 11.

20 Aileen G. Rambow, "The Siege of Leningrad: Wartime Literature and Ideological Change," in *The People's War: Responses to World War II in the Soviet Union*, ed. Robert W. Thurston and Bernd Bonwetsch (Champaign: University of Illinois Press, 2000), 163.

21 Simonov, *Sto sutok voiny*, 5–7.

22 D.I. Ortenberg, "Letter to A.I. Bezymenskii," 1941, f.129, op.3, ed.khr.126, RGALI.

23 Antony Beevor, *A Writer at War: A Soviet Journalist with the Red Army, 1941–1945*, trans. Luba Vinogradova (New York: Vintage Books, 2007), 4–5.

24 D.I. Ortenberg, "Letter to Stalin," 19 July 1943, f.558, op.11, d.717, ed.khr.101, RGASPI.

25 Ortenberg, *Stalin, Shcherbakov*, 37.

26 Pavel Troyanovsky, qtd in B.S. Burkov and V.A. Miakushkov, eds., *Letopistsy pobedy* (Moscow: Politizdat, 1984), 87.

27 Such was Simonov's fame that, even as the fighting grew more intense at Stalingrad, he was already working with the director Vsevolod Pudovkin on a film version of his play *The Russian People* (Alexander Werth, *The Year of Stalingrad: An Historical Record and a Study of Russian Mentality, Methods, and Policies* [London: Hamish Hamilton, 1946]), 189.

28 Ilya Ehrenburg, *The War Years* (London: MacGibbon and Kee, 1964), 9.

29 Marc Slonim even in the 1940s noted the spontaneous patriotic enthusiasm of wartime Soviet writers. During the Cold War, the idea was not widely believed by either the public or academics (Slonim, "Soviet Prose After the War," *The Annals of the American Academy of Political and Social Science* 263, no. 1 [1949]: 101–13).

30 Slonim, "Soviet Prose After the War," 7.

31 Konstantin Simonov, *Glazami cheloveka moego pokoleniia: razmyshleniia o I.V. Staline* (Moskva: Kniga, 1990), 101.

32 Il'ia Ehrenburg, "Pisatel' na voine," *Literaturnaia gazeta*, May 1943. Writing, argued Ehrenburg, provided "spiritual-military supplies to the front" ("V boevom poriadke," *Znamia* 5 [1943], 235).

33 L. Lazarev, *Voennaia proza Konstantina Simonova* (Moskva: Khudozh. lit., 1974), 4.

34 Simonov received at least one letter harshly criticizing him for supposedly posturing as a *frontovik*. Simonov's reply patiently emphasized the time he had spent at the front under fire (K.S. Simonov, "Letter to Comrade Buturlakin," April 1945, f.1814, op.1, ed.khr.596, RGALI).

35 K.S. Simonov, *Tak nazyvaemaia lichnaia zhizn'* (Moscow: Goslitizdat, 1957).

36 Lars T. Lih, *Lenin Rediscovered: What Is to Be Done? In Context* (Leiden: Brill, 2006).

37 See Lee Baker, *The Second World War on the Eastern Front* (Abingdon: Routledge, 2013), for a summary of the historiography on the war's "unprecedented" nature.

38 Samuel Weber, "Wartime," in *Violence, Identity, and Self-Determination*, ed. Hent de Vries and Samuel Weber (Stanford: Stanford University Press, 1997), 80.

39 John P. Wilson, Zev Harel, and Boaz Kahana, *Human Adaptation to Extreme Stress: From the Holocaust to Vietnam* (New York: Springer Science and Business Media, 2013), 10.

40 Aleksandrov, "Uvazhenie k deistvitel'nosti," *Oktiabr'*, no.10 (1942).

41 For all the criticism of Socialist Realist art, readers' responses were, far from being an afterthought, the genre's immanent project (Alla Efimova, "To Touch on the Raw: The Aesthetic Affections of Socialist Realism," *Art Journal* 56, no. 1 [Spring 1997]).

42 Clark, *The Soviet Novel*, 37–9.

43 Gregory Nagy, "Introduction to the Homeric Iliad and The Odyssey," in *The Iliad*, trans. Robert Fitzgerald (New York: A.A. Knopf, 1992), v–xx; M.M. Bakhtin, *The Dialogic Imagination: Four Essays*, ed. Michael Holquist (Austin: University of Texas Press, 1981), 5.

44 Svetlana Boym, "Paradoxes of Unified Culture," in *Socialist Realism without Shores*, ed. Thomas Lahusen and Evgeny Dobrenko (Durham: Duke University Press, 1997), 197. Boris Groys argues that Socialist Realist artists, like those of the avant-garde, strove to "create an entirely new world" (*The Total Art of Stalinism: Avant-Garde, Aesthetic Dictatorship, and Beyond* [Princeton: Princeton University Press, 1992], 20–1).

45 Groys, *The Total Art of Stalinism*, 22.

46 Angela Brintlinger, *Chapaev and His Comrades: War and the Russian Literary Hero across the Twentieth Century* (Boston: Academic Studies Press, 2012), 31.

47 Bakhtin, *The Dialogic Imagination*, 5.

48 Katerina Clark terms this contradiction a "modal schizophrenia" (*The Soviet Novel*, 37).

49 Raymond Aron, *The Opium of the Intellectuals*, trans. Terence Kilmartin (New York: W.W. Norton, 1962), 66.

50 For a history of the importance of deification in Russian Orthodox culture, see Ruth Coates, *Deification in Russian Religious Thought: Between the Revolutions, 1905–1917* (Oxford: Oxford University Press, 2019).

51 Kenez, *The Birth of the Propaganda State*, 10.

52 D.S. Likhachev, *The Poetics of Early Russian Literature* (Lexington Books, 2014); James Billington, *The Icon and the Axe* (New York: Vintage, 1970), 651.

53 See Gregory Carleton, "Victory in Death: Annihilation Narratives in Russia Today," *History and Memory* 22, no. 1 (April 2010): 135–68.

54 Karen Petrone, "Masculinity and Heroism in Imperial and Soviet Military-Patriotic Cultures," in *Russian Masculinities in History and Culture*, ed. Barbara Evans Clements, Rebecca Friedman, and Dan Healey (London: Palgrave Macmillan, 2002), 173.

55 Andrew Barratt, "Gorky's My Fellow Traveller: Parable and Metaphor," in *The Silver Age in Russian Literature*, ed. John Elsworth (New York: St Martin's Press, 1992), 137.

56 Barratt, "Gorky's My Fellow Traveller," 139.

57 Irina Gutkin, *The Cultural Origins of the Socialist Realist Aesthetic, 1890–1934* (Evanston: Northwestern University Press, 1999), 26.

58 For example, see John McCannon, "Positive Heroes at the Pole: Celebrity Status, Socialist-Realist Ideals, and the Soviet Myth of the Arctic, 1932–39," *Russian Review* 56, no. 3 (1997): 346–65.

59 Likhachev, *The Poetics of Early Russian Literature*, 126.

60 Irina Paperno, *Stories of the Soviet Experience: Memoirs, Diaries, Dreams* (Ithaca: Cornell University Press, 2011), xii, xv, 1, 7.

61 See Livshin and Orlov, *Sovetskaia propaganda*, 107–8.

62 Alexandra Popoff, *Vasily Grossman and the Soviet Century* (New Haven: Yale University Press, 2020), 124.

63 Simonov, *Sto sutok voiny*, 4–5.

64 For discussions of how Ortenberg and Koroteev created the Panfilov legend, see Denis Kozlov, *The Readers of Novyi Mir: Coming to Terms with the Stalinist Past* (Cambridge, MA: Harvard University Press, 2013); and N. Petrov and O. Edelman, "Novoe o sovetskikh geroiakh," *Novyi mir*, no. 6 (1996): 140–51.

65 Livshin and Orlov, *Sovetskaia propaganda*, 289.

66 Wendy Z. Goldman and Donald Filtzer, *Fortress Dark and Stern: The Soviet Home Front during World War II* (Oxford: Oxford University Press, 2021), 342–3.

67 Alexander Werth, *Russia at War, 1941–1945* (London: Barrie and Rock-liff, 1964), 167; Beevor and Vinogradova, *A Writer at War*, xiii.

68 "It was difficult," Ortenberg remembered, "to keep Grossman [safe]. He regularly crossed into the city on barges, on boats, and by walking across the ice" (D.I. Ortenberg, *God 1942: rasskaz-khronika* [Moscow: Politizdat, 1988], 19).

69 S.M. Isachenko, *Gody, otlitye v stroki* (Moscow: Voenizdat, 1973), 64.

70 Ortenberg, *Stalin, Shcherbakov*, 13.

71 Contemporary observers hailed the writers of Stalingrad for their ex-hausting and perilous approach to their work. See, for example, Leonid Kudrevatykh, *Radost' vstrech. Dok. povest', rasskazy, ocherki, vospomin-aniia* (Moscow: Sov. pisatel', 1976).

72 For Grossman's actions during the first year of the war, see Popoff, *Vasily Grossman and the Soviet Century*, 154–60; and Beevor, *A Writer at War*. Neither book accords much space to anyone *except* Grossman during the war, nor do their authors mention the existence of the original wartime newspaper publications I have unearthed.

73 V.S. Grossman, "Letter to Semen Osipovich," 6 March 1942, box 2, folder 33, Garrard Collection, Houghton Library.

74 "Report on Casualties," 27 August 1942, f.58, op.818883, d.649, TSAMO.

75 Livshin and Orlov, *Sovetskaia propaganda*, 338.

76 L. Lazarev, "Russian Literature on the War and Historical Truth," in *World War 2 and the Soviet People*, ed. John and Carol Garrard (New York: St Martin's Press, 1993), 32.

77 Ortenberg, *Stalin, Shcherbakov*, 27.

78 See Ortenberg, "Letter to A.I. Bezymenskii," 1941, f. 129, op. 3, ed.khr. 126, RGALI.

79 Ilya Ehrenburg, *The War Years*, details the writer and his colleagues' extensive contacts with ordinary and elite Soviets and with Western correspondents in Moscow.

80 Livshin and Orlov, *Sovetskaia propaganda*, 155–7.

81 Livshin and Orlov, *Sovetskaia propaganda*, 193.

82 For example, one minor *Pravda* correspondent apologized for a "mis-take" and begged for his job back after submitting an unacceptable ar-ticle in early 1943. There was, however, no hint that anything untoward might happen to him (Livshin and Orlov, *Sovetskaia propaganda*, 213).

83 Simonov, *Sto sutok voiny*, 10–16.

84 Jan Plamper, *The Stalin Cult: A Study in the Alchemy of Power* (New Haven: Yale University Press, 2012), 48–53.

85 Wartime freedoms were new, but not nearly as expansive as some have suggested (Anatoly Pinsky, "The Origins of Post Stalin Individuality: Aleksandr Tvardovskii and the Evolution of 1930s Soviet Romanticism," *Russian Review* 76, no. 3 [2017]: 461).

86 David Brandenberger, *National Bolshevism: Stalinist Mass Culture and the Formation of Modern Russian National Identity, 1931–1956* (Cambridge, MA: Harvard University Press, 2002), 29. Almost any part of the non-Marxist past could be incorporated into art so long as it was "comprehensible to or created by the masses" (Matthew Cullerne Bown, *Socialist Realist Painting* [Yale University Press, 1998], 145).

87 Livshin and Orlov, *Sovetskaia propaganda*, 367–8.

88 As quoted in Edward Acton and Tom Stableford, eds., *The Soviet Union: A Documentary History*, vol. 2 (Exeter: University of Exeter Press, 2007), 105.

89 Richard Wortman, *Scenarios of Power: Myth and Ceremony in Russian Monarchy* (Princeton: Princeton University Press, 1995), 12; Hubertus Jahn, *Patriotic Culture in Russia during World War I* (Ithaca: Cornell University Press, 1995), 6.

90 Nikolay Nekrasov (1821–1878) – no relation to Viktor Nekrasov, the Stalingrad author translated in this volume – was a nineteenth-century Romantic poet. Sergey Aksakov (1791–1859) was an acquaintance of Gogol and a keen Slavophile. (Vasilii Semenovich Grossman, "Zapisnye knizhki," in *Gody voiny* [Moscow: Pravda, 1989], 19; "Letter to Semen Gekht," 1938, box 2, folder 30, Garrard Collection).

91 See Clark, *The Soviet Novel*, 48–9, on the short story in Soviet writing; for material on the interplay between short form and novel, see Gary Morson, *The Long and Short of It: From Aphorism to Novel* (Stanford: Stanford University Press, 2012).

92 Joshua Rubenstein, *Tangled Loyalties: The Life and Times of Ilya Ehrenburg* (Tuscaloosa: University of Alabama Press, 1999), 191.

93 Kevin Williams, *A New History of War Reporting* (Abingdon: Routledge, 2019), Ch. 2.

94 R.F. Christian, *Tolstoy: A Critical Introduction* (Cambridge: Cambridge

University Press, 1969), 58–9; John Newman, *Classical Epic Tradition* (Madison: University of Wisconsin Press, 2003), 478–9.

95 Grossman's *The People Immortal* is available in a new translation by Robert Chandler (New York: NYRB Press, 2022).

96 Vitalii Borisovich Smirnov, *Voeval pod Stalingradom* (Volgograd: Izdatel , 2006).

97 For many soldiers sent into Stalingrad, the experience really did seem infernal: "Soldiers used to say: 'We are entering hell.' And after spending one or two days here, they said: 'No, this isn't hell, this is ten times worse'" (qtd in Beevor and Vinogradova, *A Writer at War*, 151).

98 Margo Kitts, *Sanctified Violence in Homeric Society: Oath-Making Rituals in the Iliad* (Cambridge: Cambridge University Press, 2005), 97.

99 Victor Terras, ed., *Handbook of Russian Literature* (New Haven: Yale University Press, 1985), 70.

100 Babel was as well-known among frontline readers as he was among writers (G. Estraikh, "Jews as Cossacks: A Symbiosis in Literature and Life," in *Soviet Jews in World War II*, ed. H. Murav and G. Estraikh [Boston: Academic Studies Press, 2018], 89). Grossman was a particularly keen admirer both before and during the war (Popoff, *Vasily Grossman and the Soviet Century*, 74–75). For more on Babel's Civil War work, see C.D. Luck, *Figures of War and Fields of Honour: Isaak Babel's Red Cavalry* (Keele: Keele University Press, 1995).

101 Note the masculine emphasis in the choice of heroes. Stalingrad as a textual space was generally closed to women, even though many thousands of female soldiers fought at the front. In the stories I translate, the only significant female character – albeit a highly influential one – is Simonov's nurse, Shchepenya, in September's "Days and Nights."

102 Ortenberg, *Stalin, Shcherbakov*. 159. Even Vasily Grossman, who would later be known as a dissident writer, only complained of cuts to, rather than distortions of, his work. See, for example, letters to his father from 1941 and 12 July 1942 (Garrard Collection).

103 For material on the official fairy tales of the 1930s, see Boym, "Paradoxes of Unified Culture," 133.

104 Werth, *Russia at War, 1941–1945*, 255.

105 K.S. Simonov, "Letter to Comrade Blokhin," April 1945, f.1814, op.1, ed.khr.596, RGALI.

106 Simonov, "Letter to Comrade Blokhin."

107 "'Volgogradskoi Pravde – 100 let' (online exhibition)" (TSDNIVO, 2017), https://cdnivo.ru/volgogradskoy-pravde-100-let.

108 "Frontovoi prikaz," 30 January 1943, f.33, op.682527, ed.khr.22, TSAMO.

109 For discussions of fragmented memories and trauma in literature, see Cathy Caruth, *Trauma: Explorations in Memory* (Baltimore: Johns Hopkins University Press, 1995).

110 Livshin and Orlov, *Sovetskaia propaganda*, 359.

111 Joshua Rubenstein, *The Last Days of Stalin* (New Haven: Yale University Press, 2016), Ch. 6; Alexei Yurchak, *Everything Was Forever, Until It Was No More: The Last Soviet Generation* (Princeton: Princeton University Press, 2006), 47; Leonid Heller, "A World of Prettiness: Socialist Realism and Its Aesthetic Categories," in *Socialist Realism without Shores*, ed. Thomas Lahusen and Evgeny Dobrenko (Durham: Duke University Press, 1997), 69.

112 A.A. Grabel'nikov, ed., *Zhurnalisty XX veka: Liudi i sud'by* (Moscow: OLMA-PRESS, 2003), 160.

113 "Refugee Interview 643," n.d., 643, S.A, vol. 30, HPSSS.

114 Plamper, *The Stalin Cult*, 145.

115 Clark, *The Soviet Novel*, 60–3.

116 The continuity between production novel and wartime story was widely praised in the postwar era. See, for example, V. Pertsov, *Pisatel' i novaia deistvitel'nost'* (Moscow: Sov. pisatel', 1958), 208.

117 For more on Chapaev, see Brintlinger, *Chapaev and His Comrades*.

118 Petrone, "Masculinity and Heroism," 186.

119 Clark, *The Soviet Novel*, 149.

120 Grossman's daughter recalls singing folk songs about the river with her father as a child (Ekaterina Korotkova-Grossman, "Vot umer papa," n.d., box 1, folder 18, Garrard Collection). For more on the Volga's cultural significance in the Soviet Union, see Janet M. Hartley, *The Volga: A History* (Yale University Press, 2021), 229–85.

121 Aleksandr Fursenko and Timothy Naftali, *Khrushchev's Cold War: The Inside Story of an American Adversary* (New York: W.W. Norton, 2010), 25.

122 Jochen Hellbeck, "War and Peace for the Twentieth Century," *Raritan* 26, no. 4 (Spring 2007), 183.

123 Lazarev, *Voennaia proza Konstantina Simonova*, 78.

124 See Rick McPeak and Donna Tussing Orwin, *Tolstoy On War: Narrative Art and Historical Truth in "War and Peace"* (Ithaca: Cornell University Press, 2016).

125 McPeak and Orwin, *Tolstoy On War*.

126 Alexei Tolstoi, "Trends in Soviet Literature," *Science and Society* 7, no. 3 (1943), 233.

127 This is a common perception among participants in war (Catherine McLoughlin, *Authoring War: The Literary Representation of War from the Iliad to Iraq* [Cambridge: Cambridge University Press, 2011], 117; Paul K. Saint-Amour, "On the Partiality of Total War," *Critical Inquiry* 40, no. 2 [Winter 2014]).

128 A German infantryman's diary is quoted in Stephen G. Fritz, *Frontsoldaten: The German Soldier in World War II* (Louisville: University Press of Kentucky, 1995), 44.

129 For more on Pavlov's House, see Iain MacGregor, *The Lighthouse of Stalingrad: The Siege at the Heart of WWII's Greatest Battle* (New York: Scribner, 2022).

130 Many scholars have noted that the pages of the wartime Soviet papers were filled with new voices (Richard Stites, "Soviet Russian Wartime Culture," in *The People's War: Responses to World War II in the Soviet Union*, ed. Robert W. Thurston and Bernd Bonwetsch [Champaign: University of Illinois Press, 2000], 175).

131 O.A. Gomanenko, *Stalingradskaia gruppa voisk. 1943–44. Dokumenty i materialy* (Volgograd: Administratsiia Volgogradskoi oblasti. Tsentry po izucheniiu Stalingradskoi bitvy, 2017); Goldman and Filtzer, *Fortress Dark and Stern*, 82.

132 Goldman and Filtzer, *Fortress Dark and Stern*, 25.

133 Olga Kucherenko, *Soviet Street Children and the Second World War: Welfare and Social Control under Stalin* (London: Bloomsbury, 2016), 1–2.

134 M.S. Shumilov, "Velikoe srazhenie," *Oktiabr'*, no. 2 [1973], 146.

135 Joshua Rubenstein, "Il'ia Ehrenburg and the Holocaust in the Soviet Press," in *Soviet Jews in World War II*, ed. Estraikh and Murav, 36.

136 Viktor Nekrasov, "Novichok," *Novyi mir*, no. 11 (1963): 123–35.

137 Viktor Nekrasov, *V zhizni i pis'makh* (Moscow: Sov. pisatel', 1971), 149.

138 Werth, *The Year of Stalingrad*, 80; see also Simonov, *Dvadtsat' dnei bez*

voiny. Some Soviets rejected the "din" of constant propaganda, but these readers were in a minority (e.g., see "Refugee Interview 163," n.d., S.B, vol. 8, HPSSS.)

139 V.S. Grossman, "Letter to Semen Osipovich," 25 February 1942, box 2, folder 33, Garrard Collection.

140 I.T. Avelichev, "Letter to Avelicheva V.G.," 22 November 1942, MIDV.

141 For example, the saving of cuttings is mentioned in V.F. Zhbanov, "Letter to Korovaiko, R.A.," 7 March 1943, MIDV.

142 D.I. Ortenberg, *Vremia ne vlastno* (Moscow: Sov. pisatel', 1979), 317–18.

143 Jochen Hellbeck, *Revolution on My Mind: Writing a Diary under Stalin* (Cambridge, MA: Harvard University Press, 2009); Igal Halfin, *From Darkness to Light: Class, Consciousness, and Salvation in Revolutionary Russia* (Pittsburgh: University of Pittsburgh Press, 2000); Sheila Fitzpatrick, *Everyday Stalinism: Ordinary Life in Extraordinary Times* (Oxford: Oxford University Press, 2000); Stephen Kotkin, *Magnetic Mountain: Stalinism as Civilization* (Berkeley: University of California Press, 1995).

144 On the expectations of Soviet readers as the "object of reshaping," see Evgeny Dobrenko, *The Making of the State Reader: Social and Aesthetic Contexts of the Reception of Soviet Literature* (Stanford: Stanford University Press, 1997), 2.

145 See Jonathan Brunstedt's new study of entangled Russian and Soviet nationalities and war myths, *The Soviet Myth of World War II: Patriotic Memory and the Russian Question in the USSR* (Cambridge: Cambridge University Press, 2021).

146 Kotkin, *Magnetic Mountain*, 24.

147 Jeffrey W. Jones, *Everyday Life and the "Reconstruction" of Soviet Russia during and after the Great Patriotic War, 1943–1948* (Bloomington: Slavica, 2008), 281.

148 Amir Weiner, "The Making of a Dominant Myth: The Second World War and the Construction of Political Identities within the Soviet Polity," *Russian Review* 55, no. 4 (1996): 640. See also Weiner, *Making Sense of War: The Second World War and the Fate of the Bolshevik Revolution* (Princeton: Princeton University Press, 2001).

149 Oleg Budnitskii, "Jews at War: Diaries from the Front," in Estraikh and Murav, *Soviet Jews in World War II*, 62.

150 Juliane Furst, "In Search of Soviet Salvation: Young People Write to the Stalinist Authorities," *Contemporary European History* 15, no. 3 (August 2006): 334; Sheila Fitzpatrick, "Supplicants and Citizens: Public Letter-Writing in Soviet Russia in the 1930s," *Slavic Review* 55, no. 1 (1996): 80.

151 Hellbeck, *Stalingrad*, 45, 68, 345, 351. David Brandenberger finds more wartime examples: a soldier who in a letter home invoked Napoleon as a national *bête noire*; a visitors' book from a 1943 Moscow exhibition that employs official phraseology to describe inspirational tsarist generals (*National Bolshevism: Stalinist Mass Culture and the Formation of Modern Russian National Identity, 1931–1956* (Cambridge, MA: Harvard University Press, 2002), 154, 165).

152 M. Altshuler, "Jewish Combatants of the Red Army Confront the Holocaust," in *Soviet Jews in World War II*, ed. Estraikh and Murav, 17.

153 K.S. Simonov, *Pis'ma o voine, 1943–1979* (Moscow: Sov. pisatel', 1990), 173. Likewise, the author Mikhail Alekseev defended the "truth" of his Stalingrad work by its resemblance to "possible" stories from Stalingrad ("Seiatel' i khranitel'," *Nash sovremennik*, no. 9 [1972], 100).

154 The cognitive dissonance between lived experience and acceptance of myth was not uniquely Soviet. Many British citizens accepted the co-existence of the myth of the Blitz and their own, often contradictory, recollections (Angus Calder, *The Myth of the Blitz* [London: Jonathan Cape, 1991], 144).

155 The author Mikhail Alekseev describes one such incident of mistaken self-identity in "Seiatel' i khranitel'," 100.

156 Victor Nekrasov, "Tragediia moego pokoleniia," *Literaturnaia gazeta*, 12 September 1990, 15.

157 Werth, *The Year of Stalingrad*, vi.

158 Werth, *The Year of Stalingrad*, 77, 176.

159 See Linda Gerstein, "Review: Culture and Entertainment in Wartime Russia by Richard Stites," *Slavic and East European Journal* 41, no. 1 (Spring 1997), 180–1.

160 Serhy Yekelchyk, *Stalin's Citizens: Everyday Politics in the Wake of Total War* (Oxford: Oxford University Press, 2014), 4.

161 Even though district- and city-based papers provided had high distribution numbers, their editors were guided by the central authorities (Beate Fizeler and Roger Markwick, eds., *Sovetskii tyl 1941-1945: povsed-*

nevnaia zhizn' v gody voiny [Moscow: ROSSPEN, 2019]). Local papers received material from Moscow – as much as 1,200 lines of copy per day (Livshin and Orlov, *Sovetskaia propaganda*, 338) – and reprinted major articles from *Pravda* and *Krasnaya Zvezda.*

162 Wayne Dowler, *Russia in 1913* (Ithaca: Cornell University Press, 2010), viii.

163 Sarah Young's recent work *Writing Resistance: Revolutionary Memoirs of Shlissel'burg Prison, 1884–1906* (London: UCL Press, 2021) dextrously illustrates the possibilities of corpus analysis and distant reading in similar bodies of work. An examination of the *entire* body of Stalingrad literature published until the end of the Soviet Union would benefit from such an approach, but using it in this volume might diminish the aspects of authorial agency that I explore.

164 N.A. Narochnitskaya, *Stalingrad: Velichaishii proval Gitlera. 1942–3. Stalingradskaia bitva glazami amerikanskikh i britanskikh zhurnalistov* (Moscow: Veche, 2013), 19–20.

165 Narochnitskaya, *Stalingrad*, 12.

NOTES TO CHAPTER ONE

1 Alfred Price, *Luftwaffe Handbook, 1939–1945* (London: Ian Allan, 1986).

2 Aleksei Isaev, *Stalingrad. Za Volgoi dlia nas zemli net* (Moscow: Litres, 2020).

3 B.S. Burkov and V.A. Miakushkov, eds., *Letopistsy pobedy* (Moscow: Politizdat, 1984), 52.

4 Rebecca Manley, *To the Tashkent Station: Evacuation and Survival in the Soviet Union at War, 1941–1946* (Ithaca: Cornell University Press), 75. Once evacuation began, however, it became a high priority (Wendy Z. Goldman and Donald Filtzer, *Fortress Dark and Stern: The Soviet Home Front during World War II* [Oxford: Oxford University Press, 2021], 82).

5 "Memorandum I.V. Stalina U. Cherchilliu po voprosu ob otkrytii vtorogo fronta," 13 August 1942, f.558, op.11, d.257, l.13–14, RGASPI; "Pis'mo posla SSHA v Moskve V. Stendli V.M. Molotovu s tekstom lichnogo poslaniia F. Ruzvel'ta I.V. Stalinu o polozhenii na frontakh," 19 August 1942, f.558, op.11, d.364, l.59, RGASPI.

6 For an eyewitness account of the defenders' disarray, see "Nagrady geroev khraniat istoriiu" (Museum of the Battle of Stalingrad, Volgograd, 18 April 2011), https://stalingrad-battle.ru/projects/emploee-writes/2011/4053/?sphrase_id=5876.

7 D.I. Ortenberg, *God 1942: rasskaz-khronika* (Moscow: Politizdat, 1988), 283.

8 Grossman, "Letter to Semen Osipovich," 19 August 1942.

9 Grossman, "Zapisnye knizhki," 176.

10 Grossman, "Zapisnye knizhki," 205.

11 Grossman, "Zapisnye knizhki."

12 Grossman, "Zapisnye knizhki," 341–4.

13 D.I. Ortenberg, *Stalin, Shcherbakov, Mekhlis i drugie* (Kodeks: Moscow, 1995), 163.

14 A.Ia. Livshin and I.B. Orlov, *Sovetskaia propaganda v gody Velikoi Otechestvennoi voiny: "kommunikatsiia ubezhdeniia" i mobilizatsionnye mekhanizmy* (Moscow: ROSSPEN, 2007), 309–10.

15 Ortenberg, *God 1942*, 328.

16 Participants and their families are interviewed in Sergei Torgashin, "Stalingrad. Podvig 33-x. Dokumental'nyi fil'm" (Volgograd 24, 2019).

17 L. Kovalev, "Letter to Kovaleva, L.," 10 September 1942, MIDV.

18 L. Kovalev, "Letter to Parents," 15 September 1942, MIDV.

19 See Kovalev's letters from 17 October and through November at MIDV.

20 David Brandenberger and Mikhail Zelenov, eds., *Stalin's Master Narrative* (New Haven: Yale University Press, 2019), 664.

21 "Frontovoi prikaz."

22 K.S. Simonov, *Raznye dni voiny* (Moscow: Molodaia gvardiia, 1977), vol. 2, Ch. 6.

23 "Frontovoi prikaz 1/n," 29 August 1942, f.33, op.682524, ed.khr.992, TSAMO; K.S. Simonov, "Notebook, Feb-Sep 1942," April 1945, f.1814, op.1, ed.khr.5, RGALI.

24 As quoted in Burkov and Miakushkov, *Letopistsy pobedy*. 64; "Ortenberg and Simonov in Conversation," f.1814, op.10, ed.khr.467, RGALI.

25 The pre-Soviet Russian scout was also a figure whose depiction combined many patriotic and religious elements (Karen Petrone, "Masculinity and Heroism in Imperial and Soviet Military-Patriotic Cultures,"

in *Russian Masculinities in History and Culture*, ed. Barbara Evans Clements, Rebecca Friedman, and Dan Healey [London: Palgrave Macmillan, 2002], 177).

26 "Na mokroi mechetke," in Vasily Koroteev, *The Miracle of Stalingrad* (*Stalingradskoe chudo* [Volgograd: Obl. kn. izdatel'stvo, 1967]), 52.

27 Simonov, *Raznye dni voiny*, vol. 2, 30.

28 "Ortenberg and Simonov in Conversation."

29 Koroteev, "Ya eto videl," in *Stalingradskoe chudo*, 9.

30 "Ortenberg and Simonov in Conversation"; Simonov, *Raznye dni voiny*.

31 Koroteev, "Na Mamaevom kurgane," in *Stalingradskoe chudo*, 42.

32 "Ortenberg and Simonov in Conversation."

33 The editorial appeared on 11 September on the front page of *Krasnaya Zvezda* under the title "Defend Stalingrad!"

34 Burkov and Miakushkov, *Letopistsy pobedy*, 69.

35 Burkov and Miakushkov, *Letopistsy pobedy*, 78.

36 Aleksei Shakhov, "Traktorozavodskii shchit Stalingrada," *Pravda*, December 2012.

37 "Prikaz voiskam Stalingradskogo fronta," 6 November 1942, f.33, op.682525, ed.khr.163, TSAMO. Tkalenko would later also receive the Order of Suvorov for his "wise leadership" of a regiment in Poland in 1944. He ended the war as a Lieutenant Colonel.

38 Tkalenko and Simonov never met again, but they kept up a healthy correspondence throughout the 1960s and even collaborated on materials for Marina Babak's 1975 semi-documentary film *Shel soldat* (*There Went the Soldier*)

39 "Ortenberg and Simonov in Conversation."

40 Ortenberg, *God 1942*, 198. One of Simonov's many medal citations specifically notes his bravery under direct fire ("Frontovoi prikaz 132/n," 30 May 1945, f.33, op.687572, ed.khr.2929, TSAMO).

41 Simonov and Ortenberg crossed in and out of Stalingrad four times. Koroteev was astonished by this risky behaviour (Burkov and Miakushkov, *Letopistsy pobedy*, 89).

42 Ortenberg, *Vremia ne vlastno*, 231.

43 K.S. Simonov, "Letter to Comrade Svinarenko," 1945, f.1814, op.1, ed.khr.596, RGALI. Note the misspelling of Shchepetya's name in the published story, which was a frontline telegraphist's mistake.

44 Burkov and Miakushkov, *Letopistsy pobedy*, 89.

45 See, for example, the masthead, communiqués, and editorials of *Pravda* and *Krasnaya Zvezda* on 24 and 30 September 1942.

46 Vera Inber, "Vpered!," *Pravda*, 30 September 1942.

47 The Russian *vasilek* is a type of thistle with a dainty purple-blue flower.

48 This is an excerpt from the Russian folk tune "Oh, you, my steppe, the steppe, the Mozdok steppe."

49 Stralsund and Schneidemühl are provincial German towns.

50 The Russian "name days" – *imeniny* – are based on the Orthodox calendar and traditionally celebrated something like a birthday.

51 The Russian word *yazyk*, which translates literally as *tongue*, is military slang for an enemy combatant captured for intelligence. The term "squeaker" is occasionally used in British military circles.

52 The *verst* is a Russian measure of length that equates to about a third of a mile.

53 Khristinovka is in Cherkasskaya province, Ukraine.

54 Simonov suggests that Bondarenko resembles a member of the Decembrist uprising. In 1825, military officers had led a failed uprising against the new tsar, Nicholas I. The failure of the revolt led to a harsh conservative backlash.

55 *Berliner Börsen-Zeitung* (*The Berlin Stock Exchange Times*) was a German daily.

56 Aleksey Stakhanov was a miner hailed in propaganda for his apparently extraordinary output in the 1930s.

57 Simonov is referring to Ortenberg. In later versions of the story, Simonov names Ortenberg as "Vadimov," the editor's authorial pseudonym during the war.

58 *Krasnaya Zvezda* had covered the four characters' *podvig* in an anonymously authored article on 12 August's front page.

59 Located just southwest of Moscow, Naro-Fominsk was the site of heavy fighting in December 1941.

60 The Soviets widely used the PPSh-41 submachine gun, with its distinctive stub barrel and drum magazine, during the Second World War.

NOTES TO CHAPTER TWO

1 Leonid Kudrevatykh, *Radost' vstrech. Dok. povest', rasskazy, ocherki, vospominaniia* (Moscow: Sov. pisatel', 1976), 74-6.

2 Grossman briefly left Stalingrad in either late September or early October (V.S. Grossman, "Letter to Jenny Genrikhovna," 5 October 1942, box 2, folder 33, Garrard Collection).

3 "Lichnoe poslanie I.V. Stalina U. Cherchilliu ob ukhudshenii polozheniia sovetskikh voisk pod Stalingradom i pros'boi ob uvelichenii postavok istrebitelei po lend-lizu," 3 October 1942, f.558, op.11, d.257, l.73-76, RGASPI.

4 Viktor Nekrasov, "Stalingrad, Oktiabr' 1942 goda," in *Sochineniia* (Moscow: Knizhnaia palata, 2002).

5 Viktor Nekrasov, "Stalingrad, Noiabr' 1942 goda," in *Sochineniia.*

6 "Refugee Interview 446," n.d., S.B, vol. 17, HPSSS.

7 K.S. Simonov, "Letter to Comrade Rubanovich," July 1945, f.1814, op.1, ed.khr.596, RGALI.

8 "Frontovoi prikaz 114/n," 27 May 1945, f.33, op.687572, ed.khr.2928, TSAMO. See also A.Ia. Livshin and I.B. Orlov, *Sovetskaia propaganda v gody Velikoi Otechestvennoi voiny: "kommunikatsiia ubezhdeniia" i mobilizatsionnye mekhanizmy* (Moscow: ROSSPEN, 2007), 315.

9 Leontev would spend four and a half months in hospital after a grievous injury, yet still made it to Berlin in 1945 and returned home ("Ukaz Prezidiuma Verkhovnogo Soveta SSSR," 6 November 1947, f.33, op.744808, d.700;50, TSAMO).

10 Makarov was decorated several times for his bravery. His citations describe his military *nous* and "excellent" work in language glowing even for a Soviet military record ("Prikaz Kremenchugskoi strelkovoi divizii," 30 October 1943, f.33, op.686044, ed.khr.2570, TSAMO).

11 See "Nagradnoi dokument," 29 April 1944, f.33, op.690155, ed.khr.2132, TSAMO; "Nagradnoi dokument," 30 August 1942, f.33, op.682524, ed.khr.990, TSAMO; "Nagradnoi dokument," 5 November 1942, f.33, op.682524, ed.khr.1006, TSAMO.

12 Svetlana Aleksievich, *U voiny ne zhenskoe litso* (Moscow: Litres, 2020). The Luftwaffe's reaction to the U-2 was similarly dismissive: "As a rule they didn't fire right away when they came across [a U-2]. They'd have

a good laugh at the pilot, circling around him and showing him that death was nigh. Then a single machine gun burst and the plane goes up in flames" (F.A. Iskander, *Stoianka cheloveka* [Moscow: Prospekt, 2007]).

13 "Stenogramm besedy s Chuykovym V.I.," January 1943, f.2, r.III, op.5, d.2a, RAN.

14 "100 let ispolnilos' so dnia rozhdeniia aviakonstruktora Nikolaia Poli-karpova," *Volgogradskaia pravda*, 10 June 2017.

15 David Ortenberg, *Sorok tretii: rasskaz-khronika* (Moscow: Politizdat, 1991), 11.

16 The "hero-city" title would later be officially bestowed upon thirteen towns that had shown "mass heroism and bravery in defence of the Motherland" (A.A. Gruzdeva, A.A. Solov'ev, et al., *Istoriia Rossiia. Veli-kaia Otechestvennaia voina 1941–1945gg.* [Moscow: Kontsep, 2014], 260). Writers at the front were first to suggest the idea of Stalingrad as "hero-city" to David Ortenberg ("Geroicheskii Stalingrad," *Pravda*, 5 October 1942; S. Tiul'panov, "Vrag o boiakh pod Stalingradom," *Krasnaia Zvezda*, 6 October 1942).

17 Ilya Ehrenburg, *The War Years* (London: MacGibbon and Kee, 1964), 11.

18 K.S. Simonov, *Raznye dni voiny* (Moscow: Molodaia gvardiia, 1977), vol. 2, 44; Eduard Grafov, "Na voine ia ponial, chto takoe chelovek," *Izves-tiia*, 14 September 2006.

19 Evgenii Kriger, "V dni voiny," in *Sbornik vospominanii ob I. Il'fe i E. Pet-rove*, ed. G. Munblit and A. Raskin (Moscow: Sov. pisatel', 1963).

20 Kudrevatykh, *Radost' vstrech*.

21 Grafov, "Na voine ia ponial."

22 B.S. Burkov and V.A. Miakushkov, eds., *Letopistsy pobedy* (Moscow: Politizdat, 1984), 63.

23 D.I. Ortenberg, *God 1942: rasskaz-khronika* (Moscow: Politizdat, 1988), 155.

24 "Nagradnoi dokument," 8 February 1943, f.33, op.682525, d.12, TSAMO.

25 Ortenberg, *Sorok tretii*, 11. Grossman wrote to David Ortenberg to com-plain of cuts to the published version that appeared in late October in *Krasnaya Zvezda*. The editor apologized profusely (Ortenberg, *Vremia ne vlastno* [Moscow: Sov. pisatel', 1979], 325).

26 Ortenberg, *God 1942*, 388–92.

27 Marshall Konev, one of the leading Soviet generals, would single Pole-voy out as the ideal *frontovik* writer: "Readers love him ... His corre-spondence is ... in all its seriousness and succinctness utterly persuasive [and] filled with warmth" (I. Konev, "O voine," *Ogonek*, 1945).

28 L. Kovalev, "Letter to Kovaleva, L.," 14 October 1942, MIDV.

29 Livshin and Orlov, *Sovetskaia propaganda*, 395–6.

30 Ortenberg, *Vremia ne vlastno*, 322. See also Simon Markish, *Le cas Grossman* (Paris: Julliard, 1983).

31 L.A. Medvedeva, "Letter to Parents," 17 November 1942, MIDV.

32 L.A. Medvedeva, "Letter to Parents," 22 October 1942, MIDV.

33 The "bat" lamp, so-called after its German name, the *Fledermaus*, was particularly effective in windy conditions and widely used by the Red Army.

34 *Obshchestvo sodeistviya oborone, aviatsionnomu i khimicheskomu stroi-telstvu*, the *Volunteer Society for Cooperation in Defence, Aviation and Chemical Production*, was a volunteer paramilitary defence organiza-tion. The concatenation of the verbose official name into *Osoaviakhim* is typically Soviet.

35 *Hütte's Handbook* was an engineering manual first published in 1857. Regularly updated, it was widely used in the Soviet Union.

36 Lev Ruvimovich Gonor, Director of the Barricades Factory, received numerous civilian awards during a long career. The Hero of Socialist Labour award was one of the Soviet Union's highest honours for those working in industry.

37 Viktor Stepanovich Kholzunov was a renowned pilot who had taken part in Stalin's defence of Tsaritsyn. The bronze statue commemorating Kholzunov towered over part of the city centre. Both Grossman and Koroteev were struck by its survival in the early part of the battle.

38 Grossman is referring to the Mamaev Kurgan.

39 "Sunny," "Red Factory," and "Republican" Streets.

40 Henry King's 1938 dramatization of the Great Chicago Fire of 1871. The film would only be released in the Soviet Union in June 1943, so Kriger either describes a film he has not seen or, equally likely, had used his contacts as a screenwriter to see a private screening.

41 Dmitry Matveevich Pigalev was a local mainstay. He would head many of the committees that oversaw the reconstruction of Stalingrad.

NOTES TO CHAPTER THREE

1 Vasilii Semenovich Grossman, "Zapisnye knizhki," in *Gody voiny* (Moscow: Pravda, 1989).

2 Orlando Figes, *The Whisperers: Private Life in Stalin's Russia* (New York: Picador, 2008), 421.

3 L.A. Medvedeva, "Letter to Parents," 19 November 1942, MIDV.

4 Viktor Nekrasov, "Stalingrad, Oktiabr' 1942 goda," in *Sochineniia* (Moscow: Knizhnaia palata, 2002).

5 Stalin wrote to Churchill and Roosevelt on 20 November to announce that "the operation is not going badly" ("Telegramma V.M. Molotova sovetskim poslam v Londone i Vashingtone," 20 November 1942, f.558, op.11, d.257, l.136, RGASPI).

6 B.S. Burkov and V.A. Miakushkov, eds., *Letopistsy pobedy* (Moscow: Politizdat, 1984).

7 Boris Solov'ev, "Stalingrad," *Izvestiia*, 29 November 1946.

8 "Goroda-geroi," *Krasnaia Zvezda*, 26 November 1942.

9 "62-ia armiia," *Krasnaia Zvezda*, 1 December 1942; P. Doronin, "Sila boevykh traditsii," *Pravda*, 11 December 1942.

10 "Refugee Interview 651," n.d., S.B, vol. 11, HPSSS; "Refugee Interview 488," n.d., 488, S.B, vol. 11, HPSSS; "Refugee Interview 144," n.d., S.B, vol. 10, HPSSS.

11 P.A. Borisov, "Letter to D.A. Borisov," 22 November 1942, MIDV.

12 For the text of Stalin's order, see I.V. Stalin, *Sochineniia*, vol. 15 (Moscow: Pisatel', 1997), 129-131. The phrase is also the title of a Mikhail Svetlov poem published in *Krasnaya Zvezda* on 10 November 1942.

13 D.I: Ortenberg, *Stalin, Shcherbakov, Mekhlis i drugie* (Kodeks: Moscow, 1995), 165; *God 1942*, 410.

14 Serhy Yekelchyk explains that wartime "victory was gradually incorporated into the Stalin cult as another 'gift' to the people from their leader" (*Stalin's Citizens*, 42).

15 Livshin and Orlov, *Sovetskaia propaganda*, 168–69.

16 Ibid., 409–10.

17 Viktor Nekrasov, "Stalingrad, Dekabr' 1942 goda," in *Sochineniia*.

18 John Erickson, *Stalin's War with Germany: The Road to Berlin* (New Haven: Yale University Press, 1999), 24.

19 V.S. Grossman, "Letter to Semen Osipovich," 11 December 1942, Box 2, Folder 33, Garrard Collection.

20 D.I. Ortenberg, *God 1942: rasskaz-khronika* (Moscow: Politizdat, 1988), 438.

21 V.R. Kolomiits, "Letter to N.B. Glebovaia," 29 December 1942, MIDV.

22 "Prikaz ob iskliuchenii iz spiskov," 15 October 1947, f.33, op.563784, d.35, TSAMO.

23 Viktor Nekrasov, "Stalingrad, Dekabr' 1942 goda," in *Sochineniia* (Moscow: Knizhnaia palata, 2002).

24 "Ortenberg and Simonov in Conversation," f.1814, op.10, ed.khr.467, RGALI.

25 An edited version of *Days and Nights* is available in a 1945 English translation by Joseph Barnes.

26 David Ortenberg, *Sorok tretii: rasskaz-khronika* (Moscow: Politizdat, 1991), 1.

27 Pinsk and Slutsk are towns in Belarus that had seen fighting in the Civil War. Pinsk is some two thousand miles from Tsaritsyn/Stalingrad.

28 The Red October Factory had been known as the "French Factory" when it opened in 1897. The area housing the engineers and workers was known as "Little France," while the group of large houses for managers was idiosyncratically called "Big France" ("V Volgograde vspomnili pervye dni zhizni 'Krasnogo,'" *Volgograd onlain*, 10 April 2017, https://v1.ru/text/business/2017/04/10/57293591).

29 Petr Nikolaevich Krasnov was a general who fought against the Bolsheviks in the Civil War, wrote anti-Soviet novels in exile, and collaborated with Germany during the Second World War.

30 Nikolay Rudnev was a Civil War hero who died at Tsaritsyn. Aleksandr Parkhomenko was a Ukrainian Bolshevik commander. He too was killed during the Civil War.

31 The reference is to a letter from Tsaritsyn veterans masterminded by Vasily Koroteev. Boris Polevoy was sent on a wild goose chase to deliver

NOTES TO PAGES 169–87

the letter to Moscow in early November only to discover the text had already arrived.

32 A quote from Stalin's speech marking the twenty-fifth anniversary of the Revolution.

33 *Voentorg*, the Red Army's trade department, ran retail outlets for the troops throughout the war.

34 Tuapse, on the Black Sea coast, had managed to repel German attacks in the last weeks of 1942.

35 Mozdok is an Ossetian city some 600 kilometres from Tuapse.

36 Chongar is in the Crimea and was the scene of heavy fighting in the year before Stalingrad.

37 Shtakhanovsky is referred to as a *chekist*, a member of the Bolshevik's secret police force between 1917 and 1922. Shtakhanovsky's credentials as an old Bolshevik would have been as apparent as they were impeccable to readers of 1943.

38 Aleksandr Kolchak, the Civil War White admiral.

NOTES TO CHAPTER FOUR

1 Viktor Nekrasov, "Stalingrad, Dekabr' 1942 goda," in *Sochineniia* (Moscow: Knizhnaia palata, 2002).

2 "1943 god," *Krasnaia Zvezda*, 1 January 1943.

3 D.I. Ortenberg, *Stalin, Shcherbakov, Mekhlis i drugie* (Kodeks: Moscow, 1995), 149.

4 Viktor Nekrasov, "Stalingrad, Ianvar' 1943 goda," in *Sochineniia*.

5 For detail on Grossman and Ehrenburg in January 1943, see David Ortenberg, *Sorok tretii: rasskaz-khronika* (Moscow: Politizdat, 1991), Ch. 1.

6 Ortenberg, *Sorok tretii*, Ch. 1.

7 B.S. Burkov and V.A. Miakushkov, eds., *Letopistsy pobedy* (Moscow: Politizdat, 1984), 76.

8 Ilya Ehrenburg, *The War Years* (London: MacGibbon and Kee, 1964), 92.

9 Nekrasov, "Stalingrad, Ianvar' 1943 goda."

10 Davydov, "SIB: Organizatsionnaia struktura," 125; Livshin and Orlov, *Sovetskaia propaganda*, 196–97, 208-10.

11 A.Ia. Livshin and I.B. Orlov, *Sovetskaia propaganda v gody Velikoi Ote-chestvennoi voiny: "kommunikatsiia ubezhdeniia" i mobilizatsionnye mekhanizmy* (Moscow: ROSSPEN, 2007), 188.

12 Burkov and Miakushkov, *Letopistsy pobedy*, 76.

13 Ilya Ehrenburg did manage to find some room for sympathy for the Germans. In "The Path," from 10 January's *Krasnaya Zvezda*, a German soldier explains: "This is a real *kotel*. Death awaits us. We are being boiled like sausages in a pot." The trend in January is perhaps best encapsulated in a cartoon from 16 January's *Pravda* that depicts a German soldier as a wizened old man in tattered winter clothing, his neck in the noose of the Don encirclement.

14 Ortenberg, *Sorok tretii*, 23.

15 P.E. Mikhnov, "Letter to Family," 1 February 1943, MIDV.

16 L. Kovalev, "Letter to Lidochka," 26 January 1943, MIDV.

17 Ortenberg, *Sorok tretii*; V.S. Kolesnichenko, *Rodnaia zemlia Volgograds-kaia* (Volgograd: Nizhne-Volzhskoe kn-oe izd., 1983), 173.

18 Viktor Nekrasov, "Stalingrad, Fevral' 1943 goda," in *Sochineniia*.

19 "Otprazdnovali slavnuiu pobedu," *Prihoper*, 31 January 2019.

20 "Refugee Interview 651"; "Refugee Interview 488."

21 Ortenberg, *Sorok tretii*. It is no surprise that "Goodbye, Stalingrad" was reprinted in several anthologies of war stories after 1945.

22 Nekrasov, "Stalingrad, Fevral' 1943 goda."

23 "'Stalingradskii komsomol na vosstanovlenii rodnogo goroda' (Online exhibition)" (TSDNIVO, 2017), https://cdnivo.ru/stalingradskiy-komso mol-na-vosstanovlenii-rodnogo-goroda.

24 L. Kovalev, "Letter to Parents," 15 June 1943, MIDV.

25 L.A. Medvedeva, "Letter to Family," 9 February 1943, MIDV.

26 Qtd in Ortenberg, *Sorok tretii*.

27 The *sazhen* is an archaic length of about seven feet.

28 The English offensive Ehrenburg mentions is the defeat of Rommel's forces at El Alamein. The *galop* is a lively dance, chaotic in comparison to the ordered *quadrille*.

29 *Munich's Latest News*, a German daily that eventually ceased publication in 1945.

30 Ehrenburg refers to atrocities covered in the Soviet papers. Reports of the hanging of eight innocent civilians at Volokolamsk in December

1941, for example, were accompanied with graphic photographs of the dead (For example, see O. Kurganov, "Vosem' Podveshennykh," *Pravda*, 27 December 1941.)

31 The *Ilyushin* or *Il-2* was the most heavily produced, and the most effective, of the Soviet Union's wartime planes.

32 One of the many lurid claims about Hitler made in the Soviet papers was that the German leader was a cannibal. See, for example, G. Aleksandrov, "Bibliya lyudoedov," *Pravda*, 16 July 1941.

33 I have translated the text of Göring's speech based on Ehrenburg's article, which may mistranslate the German. An English version is available in "Göring's Speech of Jan. 30, 1943." *Bulletin of International News* 20, no. 3 (1943): 104–5.

34 Ehrenburg is ridiculing the idea that the Germans defeated at Stalingrad could be compared to characters from the thirteenth-century German epic, the *Nibelungenlied*.

35 The mention of "oak leaves" is a reference to the Knight's Cross with Oak Leaves, a high military honour.

36 Ugo Cavallero, Chief of the Italian Supreme Command, had been fired by Mussolini in January 1943.

37 The Battle on the Ice (1242) and Kulikovo Field (1380), two clashes renowned in pre-revolutionary Russian patriotic lore.

NOTES TO CHAPTER FIVE

1 "Poteri grazhdanskogo naseleniia," Ministerstvo oborony Rossiiskoi Federatsii, 2013, https://function.mil.ru/news_page/country/more. htm?id=10335986@cmsArticle. For more on conditions in cities being reconstructed, see Robert Dale, "Divided We Stand: Cities, Social Unity, and Post-War Reconstruction in Soviet Russia, 1945–1953," *Contemporary European History* 24, no. 4 (November 2015): 493–516; and Karl D. Qualls, *From Ruins to Reconstruction: Urban Identity in Soviet Sevastopol after World War II* (Ithaca: Cornell University Press, 2009).

2 "Postanovleniia Stalingradskogo gorodskogo komiteta oborony, No. 410–449," May 1943, f.17, op.88, d.530, RGASPI.

3 Susan Grunewald, "Applying Digital Methods to Forced Labor History: German POWs During and After the Second World War," in *Rethinking*

the Gulag, ed. Alan Barenberg and Emily D. Johnson (Bloomington: Indiana University Press, 2022), 129; "Dokladnaia zapiska Tingaeva," July 1943, f.17, op.88, d.226, RGASPI.

4 Both films are widely available on YouTube and other video-sharing websites.

5 "Stenogramm besedy s Chuykovym V.I."

6 V.I. Chuykov, *Ot Stalingrada do Berlina* (Moscow: Sov. Rossiia, 1985).

7 A. Leites, "O glavnom i podrobnostiakh," *Literaturnaia gazeta*, 24 December 1944, 3.

8 "Refugee Interview 144"; "Refugee Interview 308," n.d., S.A, vol. 32, HPSSS.

9 For more on Simonov's postwar work, see Orlando Figes, *The Whisperers: Private Life in Stalin's Russia* (New York: Picador, 2008); Ian Garner, "The Myth of Stalingrad in Soviet Literature, 1942–1963" (PhD diss., University of Toronto, 2018); and Polly Jones, *Revolution Rekindled: The Writers and Readers of Late Soviet Biography* (Oxford: Oxford University Press, 2019).

10 M.M. Iunovich, "Letter to Oktiabr'," 1942, f.619, op.1, ed.khr.348, RGALI.

11 "Nagradnoi dokument," 8 February 1943.

12 *For a Just Cause* is published in English translation under the title *Stalingrad* (New York: NYRB Classics, 2019).

13 Grossman, *Stalingrad*, 891.

14 D.I. Ortenberg, *Stalin, Shcherbakov, Mekhlis i drugie* (Kodeks: Moscow, 1995); see also David Shneer, "From Photojournalist to Memory Maker," in *Soviet Jews in World War II*, ed. H. Murav and G. Estraikh (Boston: Academic Studies Press, 2018), 198; and Schneer, *Through Soviet Jewish Eyes: Photography, War, and the Holocaust* (New Brunswick: Rutgers University Press, 2011), 123.

15 D.I. Ortenberg, "Pros'ba D. Ortenberga I.V. Stalinu," 6 May 1949, f.17, op.143, d.118, l.9-12, RGASPI.

16 A.A. Grabel'nikov, ed., *Zhurnalisty XX veka: Liudi i sud'by* (Moscow: OLMA-PRESS, 2003), 190.

17 David Ortenberg, *Sorok tretii: rasskaz-khronika* (Moscow: Politizdat, 1991), 12.

18 "Brigada Zhurnalistov v Stalingrade," 48, 1942, f.13226, op.1, d.62, TSDNIVO. In one group letter, a group of workers seemed to draw

directly on phrases from the narrative of Stalingrad to express their desire to work on the rebuilding effort: "We grew up with the factory … Our hero-city has always resisted, and will always resist, those who try to capture it. Stalingrad will be resurrected with the utmost speed. We burn with desire to begin resurrecting our beloved city and our factory" ("Pis'mo rabochikh i sluzhashchikh g. Stalingrada, zaniatykh na stroitel'stve Magnitogorskogo metallurgicheskogo kombinata," 5 May 1943, F.17, op.21, d.195, l.65, RGASPI).

19 "'Stalingradskii komsomol na vosstanovlenii rodnogo goroda' (Online exhibition)" (TSDNIVO, 2017), https://cdnivo.ru/stalingradskiy-komso mol-na-vosstanovlenii-rodnogo-goroda.

20 K.S. Simonov, "Letter to Comrade Rubanovich," July 1945, f.1814, op.1, ed.khr.596, RGALI.

21 I translate the original version of Nekrasov's text from the journal *Novy mir*. I have used the 1952 version of Koroteev's story from the anthology *Stalingrad Sketches* (*Stalingradskie ocherki* [Moscow: Voenizdat]). A post-Stalinist edit in *The Miracle of Stalingrad* (*Stalingradskoe chudo* [Volgograd, 1967]) eliminates some of the more overwrought references to Stalin found in the first publication from 1952 and renames "Stalingrad" as "the Battle on the Volga."

22 V.I. Koroteev, "Letter to K.S. Simonov," 1944, f.1814, op.9, ed.kh.442, RGALI.

23 I. Pospelsky, *Vozrozhdenie Stalingrada*. Tsentral'naia studiia dokumental'nykh fil'mov, 1944.

24 Svetlana Aleksievich, *U voiny ne zhenskoe litso* (Moscow: Litres, 2020).

25 On lieutenant's prose, see E.A. Zhindeeva, *Istoriia russkoi literatury XX veka* (Moscow: Kontsep, 2014), 94–5.

26 Viktor Nekrasov, *V samykh adskikh kotlakh pobyval* (Moscow: Molodaia gvardiia, 1991), 415. Khrushchev himself criticized Nekrasov's *Two Sides of the Ocean* (*Po obe storony okeana*). For Nekrasov's complaints, see "Letter to Brezhnev," 1965, f.3, op.24, d.495, l.72–6, APRF; "Letter to Brezhnev," 1966, f.3, op.24, d.495, l.86–8, APRF.

27 Il'ia Ehrenburg, *Liudi. Gody. Zhizn'*, vol. 2 (Moscow: Sov. pisatel', 1990), 350.

28 For more on the monumentalizing "cult" of the Great Patriotic War under Brezhnev, see Nina Tumarkin, *The Living and the Dead: The Rise*

and Fall of the Cult of World War II in Russia (New York: Basic Books, 1994).

29 Viktor Nekrasov, "Letter to Literaturnaia Gazeta," 1960, http://nekras-sov-viktor.com/Books/Nekrasov-Kto%20zhe%20spas%20a%20kto%20prisutstvoval.aspx.

30 For example, see Nekrasov, *V samykh adskikh kotlakh pobyval*, 414–18. Nekrasov's correspondence with various veteran acquaintances revolved around remembrance events, pensions, and access to medical care.

31 Robert Dale, *Demobilized Veterans in Late Stalinist Leningrad: Soldiers to Civilians* (London: Bloomsbury, 2017), 5. Female veterans were excluded from an ever more masculine narrative of the war (see Introduction in Erica L. Fraser, *Military Masculinity and Postwar Recovery in the Soviet Union* [Toronto: University of Toronto Press, 2019]).

32 In response to editorial cuts to his novel *In the Trenches of Stalingrad*, Nekrasov revealed that he "was not at all bothered" by many changes to the story, but "aggrieved" at the "nonsensical" changes to events in Stalingrad that altered what he remembered (Viktor Nekrasov, "Letters to K.S. Simonov," 1965, f.1814, op.9, ed.khr.1949, RGALI. See also Viktor Nekrasov, "Letters to K.D. Vorob'ev," c.1964, f.3146, op.1, ed.khr.160, RGALI).

33 The journal of publication, *Novyi mir*, had played a leading role in the de-Stalinization of the Khrushchev years. Under the auspices of its editor, Aleksandr Tvardovsky, it remained a venue for discussion of social and cultural politics.

34 Nekrasov thought the monument an eyesore, referring to it mockingly as "that woman with the sword" (V.P. Nekrasov, "Letters to Slavich S.K.," 1980, 1964, nekrassov-viktor.com/Letters/Nekrasov-Letters-Slavich.aspx).

35 V.P. Nekrasov, *Saperlipopet, ili Esli by da kaby, da vo rtu rosli griby* (London: Overseas Publications Interchange, 1983), 56–7; Nekrasov, *V zhizni i pis'makh*.

36 K.S. Simonov, "Letters to V.P. Nekrasov," 1965, f.1814, op.9, ed.khr.608, RGALI.

37 As above.

38 Vasily Grossman happened to stumble across Benyash's grave just

before New Year's Eve in 1942, writing to his father of his sadness that "there's nobody here to cry over him. No mother, no grandmother" (V.S. Grossman, "Letter to Semen Osipovich," 31 December 1942, box 2, folder 33, Garrard Collection).

39 Il'ia Mar'iasin, "Moi dalekie molodye gody," *Zametki po evreiskoi istorii* 16, no. 88 (October 2007).

40 Evgeny Kriger was also left with a difficult psychological memory of Stalingrad. He long battled the traumatic depression caused by his war-time experiences and was hospitalized in the year that "An Incident on the Mamaev Kurgan" was published. Konstantin Simonov, still a close friend, helped his colleague obtain a place in a leading Moscow psychiatric hospital. Nevertheless, Kriger continued to pen stories about Stalingrad (K.S. Simonov, "Letters to Kriger E.K.," 1965, 1972, 1979, f.1814, op.9, ed.khr.440, RGALI).

41 Nekrasov, *V samykh adskikh kotlakh pobyval*; Nekrasov, "Letters to Slavich S.K."; V.P. Nekrasov, "Letters to Solov'ev Iu.V.," 1959, 1975, http://nekrassov-viktor.com/Letters/Nekrasov-Volegov-Letters-Solov'ev.aspx.

42 "Pis'mo Ministerstva prosveshcheniia SSSR ministram prosveshcheniia soiuznykh respublik, Akademii ped. nauk i dr.," 4 April 1975, f.3418, op.1, ed.khr.397, RGALI.

43 @elinapov. Instagram, 14 October 2021. https://www.instagram.com/p/CVBT5WLIet3/; @shik_shi4ok. Instagram, 9 October 2021. https://www.instagram.com/p/CU0YCLFKieK/; @ira.kochkina. Instagram, 5 May 2021. https://www.instagram.com/p/COgQIu2D5FM/.

44 Sergey Gorokhov had commanded the 149th Rifle Brigade at Stalingrad from September 1942 and throughout the battle. He had become well-known as a Stalingrad hero in the years since the battle.

45 The two construction projects are the Stalingrad Hydroelectric Station, which was once the world's biggest power station, and the Volga-Don Canal, which opened in 1952. For more on these projects, see Boris Erakhtin and Viktor Erakhtin, *Stroitel'stvo gidroelektrostantsii v Rossii* (Moscow: Izdatel'stvo Assotsiatsii stroitel'nykh vuzov, 2007).

46 *Glavstalingradstroi*, a concatenation of *Glavnoe upravlenie po vosstanovleniyu Stalingrada*, the "Stalingrad Reconstruction Directorate," operated from 1945 to 1954.

47 Olga Kuzminichna Kovaleva, a worker at the Red October factory.

Kovaleva joined one of the factory brigades as the Germans advanced on Stalingrad in summer 1942 and perished on 25 August. Kovaleva is commemorated by a plaque at the Stalingrad memorial complex on the Mamaev Kurgan.

48 Many of the ambitious projects Koroteev describes were never completed. After much bickering, the House of the Soviets plan was shelved by Moscow.

49 Koroteev's paragraph mentions various important civil and wartime leaders, including Stalin's deputy Georgy Malenkov and Minister of Defence and wartime general Aleksandr Vasilevsky. Koroteev finds space even ten years later to mention the hero of "The Man from the Volga," his fellow Stalingrader, Ivan Polyakov.

50 Koroteev refers to an unpublished but widely circulated front page of the pro-German Belgian newspaper from 16 September 1942, which hailed the "successful" German storming of Stalingrad ("Counting Chickens," *La Legia*, K3981, Imperial War Museum).

51 The same Nobel Prize–winning Mikhail Sholokhov who wrote the novel *And Quiet Flows the Don*: one of many famous visitors to Stalingrad in the postwar years.

52 Reverend James Endicott, a Canadian peace activist and socialist, received the Stalin Prize in 1953.

53 Bredel, a communist German writer, had fought for the Red Army and was a leading figure in the founding of the East German state. His writing was used as pro-Soviet propaganda against the German forces at Stalingrad.

54 Hewlett Johnson, the "Red Dean of Canterbury," was a Soviet-sympathizing Anglican priest who had visited the Soviet Union in the 1930s and helped organize a fund for rebuilding Stalingrad's main hospital in 1943.

55 Novo-Annenskaya is a village in the Stalingrad region.

56 Vladimir Hill, in central Kyiv, is home to a large monument to St Vladimir, the founder of medieval Rus'. It was also the site of a cathedral destroyed by the Soviet regime in the 1930s.

57 *The Thibaults* is Roger Martin du Gard's novel about families in the First World War.

58 Nekrasov presumably deliberately misstates the date of the bombing of Stalingrad, which actually took place on 23 August.

59 Nekrasov uses the prewar term "dekulakized": Bolshevik looting of purportedly rich peasants' hoarded food supplies.

60 Mikhail Volegov – Valega – had not actually met Nekrasov until after Stalingrad.

61 Nekrasov alludes to the "Fabulous Four," a group of Soviet sailors who had survived being adrift on a barge in 1960 and were subsequently heroized in the press.

62 Nekrasov managed to find and correspond with the real Valega shortly after this story's publication.

63 Innokenty Smoktunovsky (1935-1994), the renowned Russian and Soviet actor, who had indeed been the star of *Soldiers*.

64 Nekrasov introduces Kerzhentsev, his fictional proxy from *In the Trenches of Stalingrad*.

65 This conversation is a verbatim excerpt from *In the Trenches of Stalingrad*.

66 The *oprichniki* were Ivan the Terrible's group of brutal enforcers.

67 Nekrasov refers to a well-known painting by the artist Konstantin Yuon.

68 The "three-liner" is the Soviet Mosin Nagant three-line rifle used during the war.

69 Nekrasov refers to Shah Pahlavi, the last Shah of Iran, who visited Stalingrad in 1956. His narrator's interlocutors could not have seen the shah on their trip in 1965.

70 Kurbsky was a prince who lived during Ivan the Terrible's reign. Aleksey Tolstoy was a nineteenth-century author known for his historical tales.

INDEX